THE FUTURE OF THE PAGE

The most basic unit of the physical bo … d the historical evolution of the book, the typ… communicated, and how readers access that information.

Unique and rewarding in both its scope and approach, *The Future of the Page* is a collection of essays that presents the best of recent critical theory on the history and future of the page and its enormous influence on Western thought and culture. Spanning the centuries between the earliest record of the page and current computerized conceptions of page-like entities, the essays examine the size of the page, its relative dimensions, materials, design, and display of information.

The page is broadly defined, allowing the volume to explore topics ranging from medieval manuscripts to non-European alternatives to the page, Algonquian symbolic literacy, and hypertext. This thought-provoking collection will appeal to literary scholars, book historians, graphic designers, and those interested in the impact of evolving print technologies on intellectual and cultural life.

(Studies in Book and Print Culture)

PETER STOICHEFF is a professor in the Department of English at the University of Saskatchewan.

ANDREW TAYLOR is an associate professor in the Department of English at the University of Ottawa.

STUDIES IN BOOK AND PRINT CULTURE

General editor: Leslie Howsam

Hazel Bell, *Indexes and Indexing in Fact and Fiction*

Heather Murray, *Come, bright Improvement! The Literary Societies of Nineteenth-Century Ontario*

Joseph A. Dane, *The Myth of Print Culture: Essays on Evidence, Textuality, and Bibliographical Method*

Christopher J. Knight, *Uncommon Readers: Denis Donoghue, Frank Kermode, George Steiner, and the Tradition of the Common Reader*

Eva Hemmungs Wirtén, *No Trespassing: Authorship, Intellectual Property Rights, and the Boundaries of Globalization*

William A. Johnson, *Bookrolls and Scribes in Oxyrhynchus*

Siân Echard and Stephen Partridge, eds, *The Book Unbound: Editing and Reading Medieval Manuscripts and Texts*

Peter Stoicheff and Andrew Taylor, eds, *The Future of the Page*

The Future of the Page

Edited by Peter Stoicheff
and Andrew Taylor

UNIVERSITY OF TORONTO PRESS
Toronto Buffalo London

Toronto Buffalo London
Printed in Canada

ISBN 0-8020-8802-3 (cloth)
ISBN 0-8020-8584-9 (paper)

Printed on acid-free paper

Library and Archives Canada Cataloguing in Publication

The future of the page / edited by Peter Stoicheff and Andrew Taylor.

(Studies in book and print culture)
ISBN 0-8020-8802-3 (bound). – ISBN 0-8020-8584-9 (pbk.)

1. Books – Format. 2. Books – Format – History. I. Stoicheff, R. Peter (Richard Peter), 1956– II. Taylor, Andrew III. Series.

Z116.A2F88 2004 002 C2004-904114-2

University of Toronto Press acknowledges the financial assistance to its publishing program of the Canada Council for the Arts and the Ontario Arts Council.

This book has been published with the help of a grant from the Canadian Federation for the Humanities and Social Sciences Federation of Canada, through the Aid to Scholarly Publications Programme, using funds provided by the Social Sciences and Humanities Research Council of Canada.

University of Toronto Press acknowledges the financial support for its publishing activities of the Government of Canada through the Book Publishing Industry Development Program (BPIDP).

Contents

Acknowledgments

The editors would like to thank the University of Saskatchewan Publications Fund and the University of Ottawa Faculty of Arts for their financial support of this volume. They would also like to thank the Social Sciences and Humanities Research Council of Canada, and the University of Saskatchewan's College of Arts and Science and President's Office for their financial support of the original Future of the Page conference that led to this volume, held at the University of Saskatchewan and the Mendel Art Gallery, Saskatoon, in June 2000.

Illustration Credits

Figures 0.1 and 1.1 by permission of the British Library. Figures 2.1, 2.4, 2.6–2.8, 2.11–2.20 by permission of the Biblioteca Nacional, Madrid, with credit to the Laboratorio Fotográfico de la Biblioteca Nacional. Figures 2.3 and 2.5 by permission of the Réunion des Musées Nationaux / Art Resource, New York. Figure 2.9 by permission of the Österreichische Nationnalbibliothek. Figure 2.10 by permission of the Bibliothèque Nationale. Figure 3.1 by permission of the Beinecke Rare Book Library, Yale University. Figures 3.2 and 3.6 by permission of the Huntington Library. Figures 3.3 and 3.5 by permission of the Folger Shakespeare Library. Figure 3.4 by permission of Bruce Peel Special Collections, University of Alberta. Figures 4.1–4.6 by permission of the Houghton Library, Harvard University. Figures 5.1 and 5.3 by permission of the Nova Scotia Museum, Halifax. Figure 5.2 by permission of Fernwood Press, Halifax. Figure 5.4 by permission of Nimbus Publishing, Halifax. Figure 6.2 courtesy of the Collection of Western Americana, Princeton University. Figure 6.3 courtesy of the Massachusetts Historical Society. Figure 6.5 courtesy of the New York State Library, Albany, New York. Figure 6.6 courtesy of the Missouri Historical Society. Figure 6.9 courtesy of the Newberry Library, Chicago. Figure 10.1 by permission of the Gaddis Estate and the

Special Collections in Modern Literature at the University of Washington. Figure 11.1 by permission of Paul Coddington, University of Adelaide. Figure 11.2 is the logo of the National Library of Medicine's Visible Human Project and appears by permission of the National Library of Medicine, Bethesda, Maryland. Figures 11.3 and 11.4 by permission of the Thomas Fisher Rare Book Library, University of Toronto. Figures 12.1, 12.3, and 12.5 by permission of Melinda Mollineaux. Figure 12.2 by permission of Edward Poitras. Figure 12.4 by permission of Lori Blondeau.

THE FUTURE OF THE PAGE

Introduction: Architectures, Ideologies, and Materials of the Page

Peter Stoicheff and Andrew Taylor

The page and its predecessors have existed for at least 3,000 years, and its modern rectangular form is now so familiar that we seldom notice its appearance, shape, layout, or materials. Yet the page has had a profound influence on Western culture and thought. From papyrus roll to manuscript codex to printed book to hypertext, the page has shaped the way people see the world. It has been the most significant site for displaying information, and in the process it has determined what counts as intellectual authority, logical argument, and useful information.

The earliest forms of the page such as stone tablets, the papyrus roll, and parchment, the subsequent emergence of paper, the invention and consequences of the printing press – together these draw a line that leads inevitably toward the conceptual space of the book, which in the late age of print has been perceived as the penultimate technology of writing, superseded only by the computer. Yet the book's enduring power as a complex instrument of communication is due to the obedient collaboration of its pages – the book's most frequently encountered, compressed, turned, torn, punctured, inked, cut, bound, marked, fingered, numbered, burnt, and read component. The book is a library of pages, and it is at the level of the page that the real business of communication proceeds. The book itself is never fully encountered except as an expectation or recollection or closed volume. The page, by contrast, is seen in its entirety, simultaneously. It is the constant presence, directly encountered, in the otherwise insubstantial engagement with the mirage of the book. As if it were infinitely thin, the page is successively encountered and abandoned to permit the book its three-dimensional life. Yet despite its importance, and probably because of its familiarity, the page itself has remained relatively unexamined.

Recent studies of the book's history and impact have increased our understanding of the relationships between the book and political, cultural, literary, and economic power. It seemed likely to the editors of this volume that the page too – the book's fundamental structural and informational unit – has had an undeniable impact on the development of human societies. As we explored this issue of the page's role in the development of communication and of knowledge, we began to recognize that the book's phenomenal impact is itself a product of the page's characteristics, and that Western culture has been in many ways crucially determined by the page's materials of information transfer and organization. For this reason it seemed valuable also to contemplate the ways in which the transformed digital page may be restructuring aspects of contemporary life. Harold Innis, Marshall McLuhan, Elizabeth Eisenstein, Adrian Johns, Christian Vandendorpe, and many others have shown how the consequences of the printing press have been innumerable and pervasive, revolutionizing human communication, scientific discovery, and literature. A most important question now is, 'How do we situate within the long history of the book, of reading, and of relations to the written word, the revolution ... which transforms the book (or the written object) as we know it – with its quires, its leaves, its pages – into an electronic text to be read on a screen?'[1] The advent of the digital page has created a writing space of tremendous flexibility and ease of use, and texts that are readily communicable around the globe. Digital texts can spread into infinite commentary and response, thus inserting 'every text into a web of relations ... for they allow nonsequential reading and thinking.'[2] Now 'text' can be released from the strictly alphabetical to include the pictorial, acoustic, and cinematic. Its components can be readily copied, edited, and modified; its information is easily sent, received, and searched; it can circumvent the rituals of publication and be instantaneously available for wide access. Such preliminary thoughts on the history, transformations, and future of the page inspired us to hold a conference called The Future of the Page at the University of Saskatchewan in June of 2000 to explore them further, of which this volume is the result.

What exactly is the page? Or, more precisely, what are the principles of the page's identity and influence? When we talk about 'the page' do we refer to its present rectangular shape, to a single entity or an open-book display, a randomly or specifically shaped piece of paper, a surface particularly inscribed? Three aspects of the page begin to emerge in response to such inquiry. One is the page's materials, such as papyrus (a mat of crushed Nile reeds), parchment and vellum (sheep, calf, or goat skin), paper, and the digitized screen. Another is its architecture: the underlying arrangement of information on a page or what medieval writers called its *ordinatio*. A third is its ideologies: the ways in which the arrangement of information shapes or reflects cultural systems. These aspects of the page are not mutually exclusive. The architectures of the page, while capable of separate study, are related to the ideologies that otherwise structured the cultures that designed and read them. Cultures with an ideological investment in information hierarchies produced pages whose organization helped consolidate those hierarchies. Page design and its related ideologies are themselves by-products of the materials of the page that have helped determine its shape and size. These categories do not exist in isolation, therefore, but influence and are influenced by each other.

The page's rectangular shape and vertical format, for instance, are so familiar to us that we cease to see them as artificial. Yet a complex combination of material, social, and economic practicalities have over the last 3,000 years led to those configurations. One of the standard explanations of the page's shape and format is that they were determined by the dimensions of sheepskin used to make parchment. The dried skin was artfully trimmed and folded to maximize the surface area available for eventual inscription, a process generating a space similar to that of the modern rectangular page.[3] The vertical (or 'portrait') format of the sheepskin page was determined by a related material necessity, for the stitching had to follow the longer fold line to support the weight of the parchment. If the parchment were folded and stitched on the shorter side it would be weakened by the weight of the wider page and incapable of supporting as many folds (and consequently pages) as would the long-side stitch.

Two aspects of the page's dimensions are involved here. One is the rectangular shape itself, and the other is the vertical orientation of that shape. Both can be partly explained in these ways through the materials of its production at the parchment stage of its history. Yet several components of its history and design remain unexplained by the sheepskin theory. In fact, the theory applies mostly within the larger history of the book and is based on the assumption that the page emerged as an indirect result of the folding procedure that generated an early form of the book – the parchment codex. The reasons behind the rectangular, vertical space of the page probably predate the determining factor of sheepskin, though: Roman wax tablets, some Egyptian and oriental stone tablets, and the units of text on papyrus and parchment scrolls were rectangular and vertical as well.

Other material and psychological necessities may account for the precodex 'page' format and for its lasting influence through at least two millennia. One is the rectangular and vertical space of the human hand that held the text. In fact, the hand's dimensions that might have determined the clay and wax tablets' size and shape might also have organized the vertical reading and writing process of oriental ideogrammic inscription, for the tablet endured longer there than in the Occident where the scroll emerged relatively quickly as a horizontal solution to the problem of how to contain more information within a document. Ancient scrolls contained units of text in lateral sequence that resembled the modern page. Called *paginae*, whence our term derives, they were taller than they were wide, a format that aided the process of reading.[4] Spaces between words would not become commonplace until the medieval period, and the unbroken line of text was more easily read if shorter, from left to right, than longer, allowing information to be absorbed more readily, and to be read aloud more consistently without losing one's place. The width of the *pagina* varied; in the Dead Sea Psalms Scroll, for example, it was between eight and eleven centimetres, approximately the range of text widths found in standard paperbacks today.

Yet the dimensions of the page might have contained and reflected value independent of its material (sheepskin/parchment) and human (hand, eye, and brain) determinants. The width-to-length ratio of the average contemporary page, the medieval parchment page, the ancient stone and wax tablets, and the human hand, is essentially a consistent 5:8 (or 0.61). That ratio is familiar – but usually in different contexts from the history of the page or the book. Commonly known as the Golden Ratio or Golden Section, it can be found in the base-to-height relationship of the Great Pyramid in Giza of 2600 B.C., the exterior dimensions of the 438 B.C. Parthenon, the internal visual structures of da Vinci's 1498 *Last Supper*, and many other architectural and artistic constructions. For the scribes and page designers in medieval scriptoria it became a 'proportional canon' for the width:height ratio of text on the page; those manuscripts would in turn influence Gutenberg's strict formatting of text on the page of his 42-line Bible.[5] The ratio is also replicated in nature: the ratio of sequential skeletal portions of the human arm is 5:8; the chambers of the nautilus shell are arranged in accordance with the ratio on an ever-increasing scale; the patterns visible in the seedheads of various plants replicate it. The 5:8 ratio produces a series of numbers that increasingly approaches 0.61, called the Fibonacci sequence after the Italian mathematician Fibonacci (ca. 1170–ca. 1200) who devised it: 0, 1, 1, 2, 3, 5, 8, 13, 21, 34, 55. In this sequence, the sum of any two consecutive numbers results in the third (i.e., 2+3=5; 3+5=8; 5+8=13, etc.), creating at any point two numbers whose relationship is close to the 0.61 of the Golden Ratio. The ratio is often invoked as a mathematical template for phenomena in nature that just as easily conform to other numerical patterns, yet it remains, if not a universal template, a nevertheless tantalizing pattern in the hidden designs of nature and art.

Conformance to the Fibonacci sequence might be as significant as material and anatomical practicality in determining the page's width:height ratio. Despite millennia of material variation that ratio has remained constant and, evidently, appealing as a circumference for the space upon which information is inscribed and ordered. The geometrically simpler default boundary of the square, not as economical a use of the sheepskin as the rectangle, is also dismissed by nature and by the history of artistic construction as an inappropriate vessel for containing information. The page, participating as it does in the same activity, may be no less determined by such an arithmetic and aesthetic code.

Those relative dimensions, compelled materially, anatomically, or aesthetically, have had consequences for the reading and ordering of its subject. Most noticeably, the page's shape encourages a vertical and hierarchical display of information. *Sacra Pagina* or *Holy Page* – the medieval term for scripture – reminds us that the page is one of the most fundamental intellectual constructs in the Western tradition. Before the page was the roll, the elite format for publishing in classical antiquity. Prosperous Roman citizens would read from, or listen as slaves read from, the parchment or papyrus rolls that preserved serious works of literature, philosophy, and history. But the small and often impoverished Christian communities used a cheaper technology, binding flat sheets between wooden boards producing what is now technically called a codex (from Latin *caudex*, meaning block of wood) but is normally just called a book. As the new religion gained authority, so too did its favoured method for preserving its central texts. While the mechanical advantages of the codex (chief among them that it could use lower quality parchment and permitted easier consultation of specific passages) must have played a significant role in its increased use, it was its association with Christianity that made it respectable. As Yvonne Johannot puts it, 'It was the victory of Christianity in the Empire ... that assured the definitive victory of the codex over the roll.'[6]

From around 400 A.D. on, therefore, the rectangular parchment page bound between two hard covers became the dominant form of textual support in the Western world and the prevailing symbol for any authoritative text. Régis Debray points out, for example, that 'the Pentateuch was surely written on [a] scroll, but the tables of the Law in Christian iconography have taken on retrospectively the aspect of an open book.'[7] In general parlance, a book meant a parchment codex, and continued to mean a parchment codex until the paper revolution of the late Middle Ages. From around 1450 it increasingly meant a paper codex. From 1500 on it increasingly meant a printed codex. The influence of the format has been enormous and is very difficult to assess. The codex, and with it the page, have set the parameters for what in the Western tradition constitutes a text. In this tradition a text is stable, has clear boundaries, and is silent. Yet this is not the inevitable condition of writing, typography, or other means of mechanical reproduction. If 'the idea of the book ... always refers to a natural totality,' as Jacques Derrida argues, this totality is 'profoundly alien to the sense of writing.'[8] One might raise what is probably an unanswerable question, and ask to what extent this sense of totality reflects the salient visual totality of neatly laid-out pages bound between two covers, the books that let us always feel with our right hand where the end is as we read them.

The book is one of the most fundamental symbols in the medieval world. The world was a book written by God, the book of Nature; human fate was written in the *Book of Life* or *Book of Judgment*; human conduct was governed by the book of God's word. All were in reinforcing harmony. As David Jeffrey notes, 'From Augustine forward, the idea that the book of God's word essentially accords with the book of his Works is the keystone of Christian thought and particularly of the doctrine of creation.'[9] The idea is expressed in a famous passage by the twelfth-century Neoplatonist Alain de Lile:

Omnis mundi creatura
quasi liber et pictura
nobis est in speculum:
nostrae vitae, nostrae mortis,
nostri status, nostrae sortis
fidele signaculum.

[All the world's creatures, as a book and a picture, are to us as a mirror; in it our life, our death, our present condition and our passing are faithfully signified.][10]

The idea has a long legacy. In this symbolic world, the page had particular significance as a physical enactment of the central truth that in the beginning was the Word and the Word was made Flesh. Each Bible was a recapitulation of the Incarnation. On the manuscript page the word of God was etched into flesh, etched into the flesh of the sheep, calf, or goat in a writing process of intense physicality, which involved scraping the flesh with a knife and then writing on it with caustic inks. Textual metaphors like 'writing,' 'the page,' or the 'book' retained strong concrete grounding.

Today digitization has opened up endless possibilities for visual and acoustic innovation, but our understanding of what constitutes a text remains rooted in the traditions of the medieval page. The architecture of the page has not changed significantly since then, a result of its tremendous economy and functionality. Technological innovation in transportation contributed the rocket to what used to be only the foot; in communication it contributed the satellite to what used to be only voice and gesture. The physical format of the page, however, has stayed the same despite revolutionary alterations in our technological environments. That resistance to technological adaptation might reflect several things. For one, change has not always been necessary: the page has been, from its beginning, an efficient space for information display requiring little modification. While a scroll demands that the reader work through the entire text, a collection of bound pages facilitates selective reading.[11] The ease of manipulation also frees the hands of the reader, making it easier to add written commentary. For another, it may have so successfully embedded patterns of logic, thought, reading, writing, and information retrieval that possibilities for any shift in its conception have been minimal, and dependent upon larger shifts in cultural habits that have become, if anything, more ingrained and reflexive as a result of the power of the page.

If so, the history of the page becomes a story both of communication (in the page's unsurpassed economy) and of control (in its unchanging determination of intellectual activity). The more recent emergence of a digital environment has not yet changed the page substantially either. The word processing programs we are using now display the traditional features of the page for us to work on, behind which lurk outline templates recalling the medieval *ordinatio* structure with astonishing accuracy. So great is the gravity of the traditional page that web sites conceived, designed, and programmed on the horizontal or 'landscape' orientation of the typical computer screen stubbornly retain a vertical axis.

It might be argued that what we are seeing in much contemporary web design is a failure of imagination, a case of what is sometimes called 'the horseless carriage phenomenon' – the tendency to conceive of a new technology in terms of the old, and therefore to reproduce the features of an old technology even when these features are no longer functional. But the traditional design features of the page are still highly functional because they developed along with our understanding of what constitutes information. Specifically, current page design, for both Web and print, inherits many of its features from high medieval academic texts, and there is a close correlation between the development of academic text design and the development of academic culture. If web sites still tend to reproduce the features of medieval page design, they do so because these features have become fully integrated with our habits of thought and with the structures of academic publishing. This means both that there are many good reasons for doing things the same old way and that it will be exceedingly difficult to do things differently.

Page layout and design, seemingly modern concepts, have in fact always had a significant relationship with the semantics of a text. In an eighth-century Bible, for example, the word of God keeps chaos at bay, driving it back to the margins so that the space becomes a force field and the text is defined by its opposition to its margins (see fig. 0.1). In the twelfth and thirteenth centuries, however, this space began to be coded far more elaborately. This development in book design corresponds closely to the contemporary development of academic institutions and professional academic culture, first in the cathedral schools of the early twelfth century, and then in the universities, such as Bologna, which came into being in the early twelfth century, Montpellier, which was granted papal recognition in 1220, or Paris, formed from various schools in the second half of the twelfth century. The thirteenth century saw further expansion and internal consolidation of the universities, accompanied by the expansion and consolidation of academic publishing, so that regulations governing curricula and regulations governing the copying of

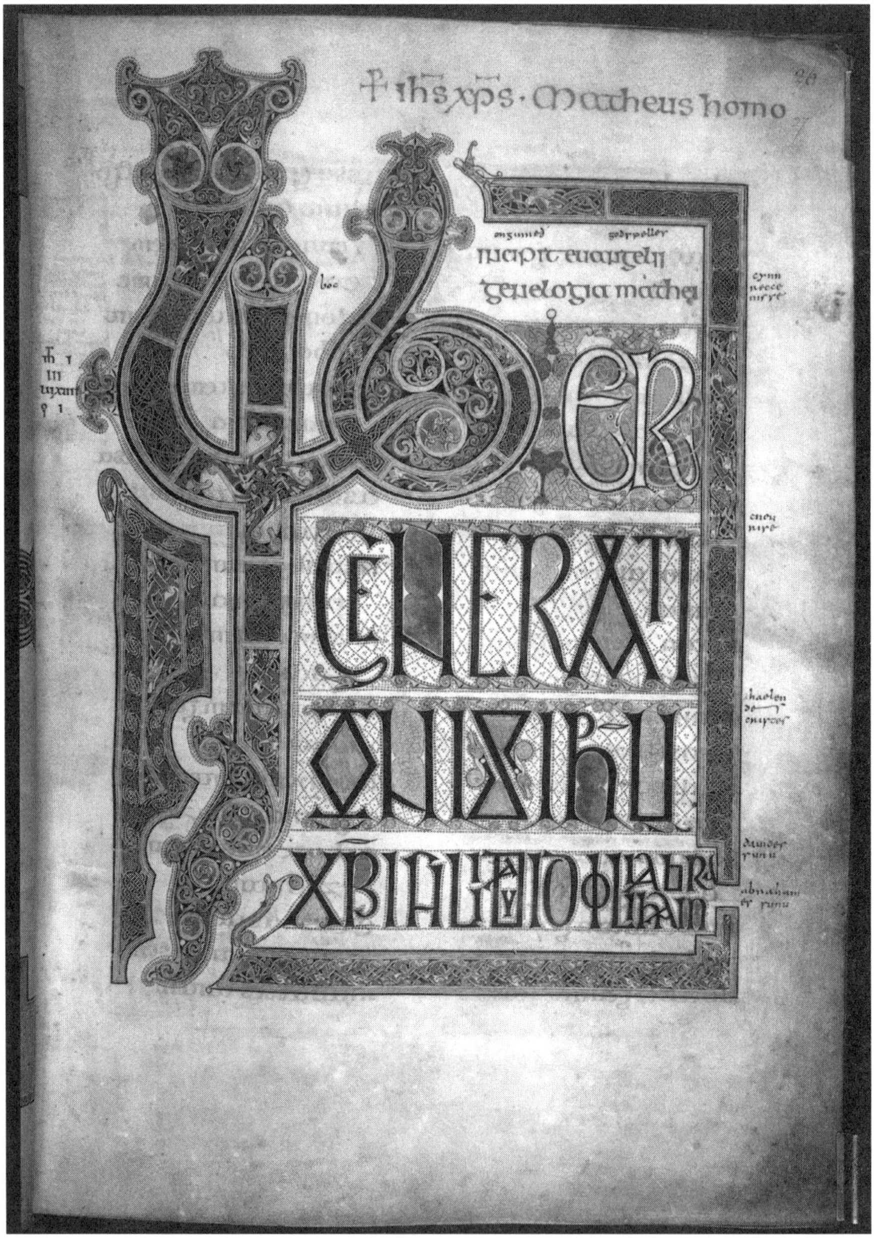

Figure 0.1. 'Liber generationis.' Lindisfarne Gospels, fol. 27r (British Library, MS Cotton Nero D. IV).

textbooks often follow hard upon each other. During the second half of the thirteenth century, for example, the University of Oxford defined its curriculum, took measures to bring all students in the city under the control of official university professors, and fought for its independence from ecclesiastical control.[12]

At roughly the same period in major university centres there developed a professional core devoted to book production, including stationers (who were both book sellers and makers), scribes, parchment sellers, and illuminators, many of them clustered together in the same quarter or even, in the case of Oxford, along a single street. In response, the university took various measures to control publication, most notably the development of the *pecia* system of copying textbooks, in which a licensed stationer kept an approved exemplar (the *pecia*) that he would rent out to students for them to copy.[13] This method depended upon the existence of a well-defined and stable curriculum and of a well-defined and stable corporate body that controlled it and whose licensing rights were supported by civic and ecclesiastical authorities, however much they may have been resented by the stationers.

The socio-economic formation of academia and book production was in turn reflected in the physical make-up of university books. At the most fundamental level there was a profound shift in the way books were read as, from about the year 1000 on, scholastic or analytic reading increasingly replaced the older, slower, subvocalizing rumination of monastic reading, transforming the page 'from a score for pious mumblers into an optically organized text for logical thinkers.'[14] Page layout now became crucial, arranging different levels of information according to clearly delineated hierarchies: text, authoritative gloss, less authoritative gloss, student's personal gloss. All these categories could be arranged and subdivided according to the demands of scholastic logic, so that, as Malcolm Parkes argues, during the twelfth and thirteenth centuries 'the structure of reasoning came to be reflected in the physical appearance of books.'[15] Parkes finds telling parallels between the visual clarity of the thirteenth-century school text, often laid out in two columns, with clear separation between words and an elaborate gradation of textual authority, from major to minor glosses, and the structure of scholastic thought, with its elaborate division and subdivison of an argument.

As Parkes observes, in the glossed biblical commentaries of the twelfth century 'the whole process of indicating text, commentary and sources was incorporated into the design of the page' (116). The rediscovery of Aristotelean logic and its elaborate categories in the thirteenth century, and 'the consequent interest in more rigorous philosophical procedures entailed the adoption of principles which demanded a more precise method of dissecting and defining human knowledge' (119). These in turn led to an even more elaborate and clearly defined *ordinatio*.

The term *ordinatio* is more than just a synonym for layout. It alludes to the combination, or mutual reinforcement, of layout and certain kinds of intellectual structure. The more modest claim, advanced by Malcolm Parkes, is that *ordinatio reflected* the structure of high scholastic reasoning, with its elaborate subdivision of knowledge, a subdivision that can be seen in the schematic outline of one of the most famous scholastic collections, or *summae*, the *Summa theologiae* of Thomas Aquinas.

A more radical claim is that these principles of layout *set* fundamental conceptual parameters that prevail to this day, shaping our conceptions of textual authority. Even such an aggressively presentist notion as 'information,' which reduces knowledge to a kind of electronic liquidity, privileges the visual, and ignores the acoustic in ways that can be traced back to medieval scholastic culture.

The basic social logic of *ordinatio* is very clear in any academic text: an authoritative critical edition is one that has notes. Commentary by a doctor (one who is learned, or *doctus*, and whose learning has been officially recognized, i.e., in most cases a professional academic) is a crucial indicator of a text's status. Unlicensed commentary, such as that offered by interested amateurs, does not count, anymore than do nontextual extrapolations (such as illustrations, readings, or dramatic performances). To publish means to generate fixed texts (and has very little to do with any attempt to make commentary publicly available). In the humanities the medieval legacy is even more marked, for here publishing means essentially to gloss. Nor is this understanding of textual authority limited to academe. In particular, prevailing methods of legal judgment, in Canada and internationally, operate according to similar principles.

It is scarcely surprising, given this close relation between our habits of reasoning and these long-standing ways of presentation, that approaches to page design, especially among academics, remain so similar to those of the thirteenth century. After all, modern academic buildings (with their lecture halls and, for the more privileged, monastic quadrangles), corporate structures (with their largely self-licensing and self-governing professoriate), hierarchies of degrees, and traditions of textual commentary are all based on medieval models.

Just as modern academics continue to work within these medieval structures, we continue to work in the intellectual framework of the medieval page. The present digital hypertext environment, for example, with its elaborate hierarchy of information and privileging of visual over acoustic data, is a continuation of this tradition. 'Hypertext' is a term devised by Theodor Nelson in 1965 to name 'nonsequential writing – text that branches and allows choices to the reader, best read at an interactive screen.'[16] At the time, it represented a politicized vision of reading that swung authority from the writer to the reader. It was a vision (minus the interactive screen) arrived at from a different direction by numerous literary theorists, of that decade and later, who sought to give a reader's interpretive interaction with a text precedence over its author's intention. Nelson's desire, though, was not interpretive so much as mechanical – hypertext would disentangle readers from the sequential physical book and allow them to determine in what order and in what context its information would be accessed. The vision was considered realizable because of the swift and simultaneous evolution of the computer, capable of organizing information in a variety of ways and displaying it on a screen.

Writers such as George P. Landow, Jay David Bolter, Geoffrey Nunberg, Richard Lanham, Christian Vandendorpe, and Espen Aarseth – forerunners in the emerging discipline of hypertext studies – consistently trace the hypertextual activity back to concepts first articulated by the MIT information theorist Vannevar Bush. His work, described in a 1945 *Atlantic Monthly* article entitled 'As We May Think,' involved developing a new system of information retrieval that would escape the *ordinatio*-like system of categorization.[17] In its place he hoped to create a process that allowed the scholar's information search to be 'an enlarged intimate supplement to his memory' (103) that operated by association rather than categorization. As Landow points out, Bush achieved two things in this digital period: he recognized the need to 'append one's own individual, transitory thoughts and reactions to texts' and the need for the 'conception of a virtual, rather than a physical, text.'[18]

Amid these reconceptions of information retrieval and display, the page remained serenely undisturbed. Landow's early hypertext projects such as the *In Memoriam* site, and the early *Story Space* platform that was designed and marketed to realize Bush's 'memex' in a digital environment, alter the dynamics of access to, but not the inscription site of, information display. The ideology of hypertext, formulated by its early proponents and practitioners, is a result of a conditioned return to Bush, the 'memex,' Nelson, and mid-twentieth-century information theory that tends to ignore the material and aesthetic determinants of information display and transfer. Thus, while the dynamic pattern of information retrieval has been altered by the new digital environment and, according to Landow, by the convergence of contemporary critical theory and technology, the page has retained its traditional architecture.

Initially, new media emulate the media that they replace, before creating any new paradigms. As George Bornstein and Theresa Tinkle point out, 'Electronic editions represent another stage in cultural transmission rather than an ultimate stage replacing its antecedents.'[19] There are signs, however, that the digital screen and its evolving design have begun to break from such a strong influence and to begin altering hierarchical notions of the central and the primary, the marginal and the secondary. The digital page now encourages a nonlinear progression through a text, which in turn has begun to reshape how literary texts, written for the digital platform, are conceived and structured. Since the mid-1990s attempts have been made to redraw the architecture of the page to exploit the possibilities of the digital medium. Electronic editions of literary texts have witnessed a good part of the early work in this respect. In 'Rationale of Hypertext' Jerome McGann argues that the examination or representation of a book through another book will yield only predictable results that are determined by the fact that the scales of subject and vehicle are the same:

> We no longer have to use books to analyze and study other books or texts. That simple fact carries immense, even catastrophic, significance. Until now the book or codex form has been one of our most powerful tools for developing, storing, and disseminating information ... Brilliantly conceived, these works are nonetheless infamously difficult to read and use. Their problems arise because they deploy a book form to study another book form ... The problems grow more acute when readers want or need something beyond the semantic content of the primary textual materials – when one wants to hear the performance of a song or ballad, see a play, or look at the physical features of texts.[20]

A growing number of projects have responded to such a challenge in many ways, ranging from regarding the computer as a way of enhancing indexing capabilities through SGML and XML, to visually reengaging the reader with a text's material conditions, to providing an archive of related information of a geographical, historical, or biographical nature. The list, lengthening considerably each year, includes the many at University of Virginia's Institute for Advanced Technology in the Humanities, the British Library Board's *Electronic Beowulf*, De Montfort University's *Canterbury Tales* project, the University of Indiana's *Victorian Women Writers* project, and more. The motivations behind the creation of these digital projects varies. Some, such as The *Walt Whitman Archive* at the University of Virginia, are a response to the fact that Whitman's 'work defies the constraints of the book. [His work] was always being revised, was always in flux, and fixed forms of print do not adequately capture his incessant revisions.'[21] Others, such as the *Rossetti Archive* at the University of Virginia, exploit the visual capabilities of the digital environment: 'All texts deploy a more or less complex series of bibliographical codes, and page design – if not page ornament and graphic illustration – in a rich scene of textual expression. Computerized tools that deploy hypermedia networks and digitization have the means to study visual materials and the visibilities of language in ways that have not been possible before.'[22] The *Canterbury Tales* project has still another mandate. The *Tales* are in a state of textual disarray and present the reader with many questions concerning the composition history and the status of the manuscripts. Peter Robinson describes the project's origins as lying 'in the perception that the advent of computer technology offers new methods, which might help us ask these questions in a new and more fruitful manner.'[23]

Yet as the MIT Media Lab designer David Small noted in 1996, 'the display of information by computers does not often fulfil the promise of the computer as a visual information appliance.' He has explored ways of transcending the two-dimensional, page-inspired tendencies of computerized texts:

> The glowing glass screen of the computer is seen as a flat surface on which are pasted images that resemble sheets of paper. Window-like systems have advanced this emulation only to the extent that they allow for many rectangular planes of infinitely thin virtual paper to be stacked haphazardly around the glass surface of the computer display. The graphic power of computer workstations has now advanced to the point where we can begin to explore new ways of treating text and the computer display. By allowing the computer to do what it can do well, such as compute three-dimensional graphics and display moving images, we can develop a truly new design language for the medium.[24]

Choosing Shakespeare's plays as an example of complex information, he has designed a navigational process that regards the page as a landscape that can be entered, moved behind, and rotated. The result is a three-dimensional text in the shape of a cube that 'escap[es] the confines of the flat sheet of paper' and 'arrange[s] information into meaningful landscapes that exhibit qualities of mystery, continuity, and visual delight.'[25] The three-dimensional environment also enlarges possibilities for supplemental information display. For instance, glosses on the text can appear at right angles to it, so that when the text is read directly in front of the reader the 90-degree gloss disappears. When the cube is slightly rotated the gloss begins to appear, simultaneously keeping the primary text in view. The design has the added advantage of permitting an infinite sense of scale. A panoptic view of all Shakespeare's plays reveals structural patterns at a glance, such as the frequent brevity of the fourth act, and the relative lengths of the texts. Scrolling through incremental stages of proximity draws the reader to single plays, acts, scenes, speeches, lines, and words, with commensurate 90-degree commentaries and glosses. Such experiments defamiliarize the rectangular two-dimensional architecture of the modern page and reinterpret it as an artificial and still highly flexible space that is capable not only of containing more and different information but also of altering how information is accessed and how reading occurs.

'The page disappears in its very function.' So argues Alberto Manguel, introducing the issue of page design, its pleasures, and its restrictions. If we take the most general definition, 'a single spatial unit within which a portion of text is contained,' then the term 'page' would include Sumerian clay tablets, papyrus scrolls, the parchment pages in a handwritten codex, and the scrolling pages on a computer screen. Each of these containers imposes its own restrictions. The rectangular printed paper page is convenient and portable, and has been familiar for centuries. The shape of the page reflects the size and shape of the hand. The flicking of the pages is a mark of our progress through the text and through time. The white space between lettering and the edge of the page offers gaps where readers can exercise their power. The standard modern page is a container to which we are deeply attached and forms part of our pleasure in reading. Yet Manguel provides numerous examples of writers who have resisted, inserting blank pages, carving pages into strips of a single line, urging the reader not to follow the standard order of chapters, or even building their own giant typing machines to produce giant rolls.

John Dagenais's concern is the way the cultural norms or habits of thought associated with print have prevented us from *seeing* the medieval manuscript page, reducing it to typing. For Dagenais, the manuscript page must be understood not as a venerable, impersonal, static icon, and not even as a finished product, but as a human process. Drawing on postcolonial theory, John Dagenais argues that we have 'colonized' the medieval page, transforming it into a simple origin without history, much as European historians did in their depiction of Indigenous peoples. Dagenais shows how common it is for allegedly medieval manuscripts to be overwritten for centuries. While any piece of writing or printing can be overwritten or marked up – a point Dagenais illustrates with a purloined copy of the conference poster – medieval manuscripts were written in the expectation that further commentary would be added. Glossators took liberties with their texts, even going so far as to scrawl their notes across decorative elements. Stressing the manuscript's physical nature and idiosyncratic layout, Dagenais suggests we think of these pages as organisms, each with its own rules. His page is not a two-dimensional space but a three-dimensional skin, whose depth is reinforced by occasional holes that allow us to peer through to the next. The pages he selects have bewildering layouts, are filled with rude personal notes, graffiti, and abandoned efforts at indexing. They are carnal objects, meant to be touched at the blank spaces around the edges.

If Dagenais is concerned that our familiarity with print has prevented us from seeing the visual complexity of manuscripts, William Slights is concerned that we have not yet done justice to the complexity of the early printed page, a far less static or univocal object than is sometimes believed. Unlike modern hypertexts, which generally endeavour to free the reader as much as possible, the early printed page uses a range of typographical devices to control the reader's response. In his 1577 treatise *General and Rare Memorials Pertayning to the Perfect Arte of Navigation*, Queen Elizabeth's court astrologer John Dee makes his case for a standing royal navy, employing a number of sigla, including numbers and pointing hands, to press his case to a select group of influential and busy courtiers. Dee appears to have been in full control of these devices, but in many other cases the author was not. Like the glossed manuscript, the early printed book was often a collaborative effort, carrying the contributions of printers and other members of the book trade on the same page as the author's words. It is not until the eighteenth century that such devices began to seem low, smacking of scholarly drudgery rather than gentlemanly appreciation, and were relegated to the bottom of the page.

How fully a new technology, above all the new technology of print, determines what can be said, written, or thought, is a recurring question raised by the advent of digitization. David Carlson approaches this question through the figure of Nicholas Jenson, the man who advertised himself as the inventor of print and a second Daedalus. Jenson, a French printer working in Venice, dominated the market in legal textbooks by developing effective new designs that allowed him to squeeze more information into a page, thus saving on the printer's single greatest expense, the cost of paper. His commercial success, Carlson argues, was based on his willingness to surrender to the demands of the new machinery, in which letters are not written but carved. Abandoning the manuscript tradition, with its irregular letter sizing and colouring, Jenson drew on stone carving, that is, on Roman tombstones and public inscriptions, to produce his tightly controlled and regularly spaced pages. Printing, in this case, is the descendant not of calligraphy but of epigraphy. While rejecting complete technological determinism, Carlson insists on the degree to which the machines decide what can be communicated.

Manguel, Dagenais, Slights, and Carlson study the significance of the page for the Western cultures in which it has emerged and been transformed. Yet the page has had an enormous impact on cultures whose traditions of communication did not include the page and who conceived of 'writing spaces' in entirely different ways. In fact, the significance of the printed page for Western culture can perhaps best be measured by early Euro-Christian resistance to the nonpaginated inscription by Aboriginal peoples in North America. As Marie Battiste argues, Aboriginal ideographic and symbolic literacy was 'destroyed, transformed, or simply ignored' by Europeans whose written communication was exclusively page-based. Aboriginal peoples' marks on 'nature's irregular "page"' in the form of pictographs, ideographs, and petroglyphs were meaningless to travellers and missionaries whose texts were shaped by the layout of the page. Unlike the European page whose boundaries implied the self-contained logic and linearity of its text, ideographic inscription was symbolic, it interacted with oral traditions in order to be deciphered, and it was 'never precisely defined or fully explained, since their purpose was to stimulate a dialogue rather than resolve the paradoxes of life concretely.' For Battiste the page is part of the 'colonial shadow' that has descended over Aboriginal forms of communication and custom, rendering them invisible through centuries of erasure and misunderstanding. If a postcolonial framework is to be constructed, it cannot be without 'Indigenous peoples renewing and reconstructing the principles underlying their own world view, environment, languages, [and] communication forms,' potentially assisted by new information technologies.

A by-product, and determinant, of European ascendancy in North America, the paper page became the surface upon which Indigenous cultures were compelled to record, communicate, and express. Len Findlay studies how the otherwise unusable stock of financial ledgers was distributed to First Nations prisoners 'to amuse themselves, so that they could "doodle" their way through dispossession on the road to assimilation or extinction,' producing graphic texts both ironically prized by their captors and 'exoticized, infantilized, or eliminated-and-archived in the name of progress.' In other examples of First Nations art of the nineteenth and early twentieth centuries the classroom is depicted as a quasi-military environment in which the page is enlisted as an 'endlessly replicable ... agent of socialization' colonizing and assimilating Indigenous experience. The technology of the page has, as such, inhabited and deformed cultures upon which it was imposed as a location for identity and inscription. If so, how is the emergence of the digital page to be managed and negotiated so as not to repeat the process? Extending the implications of Benedict Anderson's study of the relationships between print-capitalism and nationhood, Findlay sees the need to 'place, or recognize the imposition of, new information technologies in order to understand and perhaps manage the interactions of social text and hypertext,' an activity that is the responsibility of the academic community.

The page might appear to be a two-dimensional surface upon which words are placed. The act of reading draws those words out of that plane, however, into what Jerome McGann terms an 'n-dimensional space' of multiple meanings and rich semiotic interactions. When the two-dimensional page is examined through the identical perceptual filter – the two-dimensional page of the hard copy critical edition, for instance – the resulting analytic power is minimal. The digital space offers a more flexible means of accessing information in and about texts. But, as McGann asks, to what end? Can electronic tools 'help us to see and understand (in a Blakean sense) works of imagination [and] ... advance our learning' of complex literary texts? If the answer to those questions is yes, as McGann argues it is, this is because the act of examining the paginated text from a digital perspective 'consciously deforms' the object of scrutiny, simultaneously revealing formal textual patterns and escaping the tendency to read from within them. The medium through which a text is represented, therefore, reveals in productive ways the many activities of the text, in the process revising critical assumptions about 'the logical and ontological status of the original works.'

McGann's work since 1992 on the digital *Rossetti Archive* has frequently raised issues involved in the translation of paper- and canvas-based texts into computerized versions. The shift to a different medium of textual transmission has also turned the Archive's collaborators back to fundamental questions of literary production: 'what is a literary work, what are its parts, how do they function?' As Michael Groden observes, the page is one of those crucial parts, and once an originally paper-based text is translated to computer screen, page units become 'especially vulnerable and problematic.' As director of the James Joyce's *Ulysses* in Hypermedia project Groden, like McGann, has recognized how digitizing an edition returns one to fundamental questions of textual identity. In the case of *Ulysses* in particular, 'if the pages should be preserved in some way in the digital presentation, how should they be retained, since in all their forms they are bigger than a screen? What would the pages be preserved *as* in a medium lacking the tangibility of printed pages and also lacking anything that corresponds to a printed page's front and back?' Although the medium shift retains a text's linguistic code it nevertheless alters its bibliographic code, and that alteration eventually pervades every dimension of a text's reading. The inclusion of intertextual links, scholarly commentary, images, and audio versions of songs renders the boundaries of the original paper page invisible. The new hypertext environment within which a variety of *Ulysses* versions can appear, depending upon the reader's wishes, acknowledges the uncertainty of the digital 'page.' It also points to the elusive nature of the 'original' page since each edition 'offers different page units and paginations.'

The material page carries with it medieval notions of reading and quantifying information. The electronic writing space, seldom as yet responsible for revolutionizing those notions, nevertheless holds out the possibility for doing so. Such a possibility can only be realized if not just the differences but the similarities between the material page and its electronic counterpart are recognized. As McGann notes, 'the "hyper" media powers of the book ... [still] far outstrip the available resources of digital instruments.' Joseph Tabbi examines this threshold between print and electronic pages to see what truly distinguishes them. Rather than looking yet again at how the hypertext environment literalizes theoretical notions of text from the late 1960s on (as demarked by variable lexias and intertextual activity), Tabbi argues that if the distinctions between the print page and the electronic page are to be discerned, we need instead to 'look at the page itself, its inherent dynamism and changing topography, as a material basis for what is authentically new about the digital text' and not at what occurs on the page semantically. Literature depended upon a 'stable, simplified, largely forgotten page as a material carrier capable of fixing language at the level of the signifier.' The electronic page, however, can be visually three-dimensional, and does 'not so much ... stack texts one on top of another [as] *enfold* various texts into one another.' Constantly in a state of potential mutability, the electronic screen presents us with possible pages whose stability is determined now only by the reader. If so, 'it may no longer be meaningful to speak of a "page" at all.' In the absence of a publisher stabilizing the page for us, for instance, it will become fixed only if we choose to make it so. The page, then, reflects 'only what the author makes of materials that the reader can, in turn, cast into further potentials.' Tabbi sees these dynamics as crucial to understanding the work of various American postmodern fiction writers from William Gaddis to Harry Mathews, and of various contemporary digital text designers whose work appears in online environments.

A media migration to the electronic, virtual page has sparked an intense controversy that extends beyond the boundaries of the page to embrace issues of democracy and cultural decline. As Allison Muri reminds us, the page has a long history of embodiment – the material of the medieval page was literally animal flesh, and the architecture of the page includes a 'body,' a 'header,' a 'footer,' possibly an appendix, a connection to a spine. The advent of the virtual page, therefore, has created a debate haunted by the old philosophical questions of the physical body and its relationship to the spirit, charged by the potential redundancy of the human body and loss of our humanity. Yet it is not only the page that has been historically regarded in terms of the body. Recent developments in medical imaging and genetic research illustrate how the reverse is also true: the human body is conceived of in terms of the page. The Visible Human Project has dissected a body 'not to reveal gross physical units such as a given muscle, organ, or tissue, but rather in cross-section as fine leaves ... [that] now exist in the form of an enormous and readable book.' The Human Genome Project has effectively transcribed the genetic code of the human into a book of life, with a finite number of pages containing alphanumeric text. If 'the metaphor of transcription, the analogy between human life and text, is one that has dominated the rhetoric of human DNA since its discovery,' as Muri points out, who retains the copyright for the text? Any scepticism concerning the tenuous metaphoric relationship between text and body quickly vanishes in the face of this far-reaching and increasingly relevant question.

Of all the contributors, it is Edison del Canto who sees the sharpest break between the evolving digital page and the older forms that it may eventually displace. He argues that the technological evolution will entail a fundamentally new way of reading and challenges us to break with the parameters of the Enlightenment and the mechanical age. The digital page he has in mind is multidimensional and mobile, and will incorporate sound and a wide array of visual images. It will appeal to new modes of sensory/mechanical interaction, for, as del Canto's title suggests, 'our bodies are not final'; our sensorium itself is being modified by the new technologies. The radically new form of page he seeks is best represented by a live multimedia presentation or on a web site (and one version of del Canto's paper has been mounted as a web site). Its reproduction within the structure of print involves a fundamental contradiction of form, which del Canto explores through the concept of file corruption. His printed paper begins as a series of electronic files which are then subjected to various transformations. Like McGann, del Canto is intrigued by the recalcitrance of image files. Since downloading image files into standard word-processing files corrupts some of the data, but never corrupts it in quite the same way twice, each of del Canto's print-outs (including those reproduced in chapter 11) is slightly different. Like a manuscript page, each of his digital pages is unique. But he also draws upon a universal language, HTML, to provide stable descriptions of his text's layout. Once again, as with the medieval scholastic page, layout, or *ordinatio*, is closely linked to specialized professional knowledge. The result is not easily readable, but the process does raise numerous questions about how page design may be evolving. Like many of the other contributors, del Canto draws attention to the materiality of the page, no longer an animal's skin or a piece of paper stamped with cut letter forms, but a collection of electronic files that can be reproduced, transmitted, and modified in a dizzying variety of ways.

Pages that are actually printed, by pressing type on paper, are now, in much of the world, rarer than handwritten pages. The vast majority of what we call 'print' is actually produced by various forms of photographic reproduction of electronic files. The new technology has allowed a vertiginous play of type fonts, seen in works such as Derrida's *Glas* or Avital Ronnel's *The Telephone Book: Technology, Schizophrenia, Electric Speech.* It also permits artists to manipulate page design more easily than ever before. Lynne Bell examines a number of visual artists who have created their own pages, poaching familiar page designs, such as the cover of *Cosmopolitan*, travel brochures, or literary classics, such as *Little Women*, and then adding their own images as a subversive collage. One set of images in particular might be seen as an equivalent in the digital age of the aggressive glossing and scribbling of the medieval manuscripts described by Dagenais. In a 'guerrilla act of memory,' Melinda Mollineaux has crafted a series of pages of alternate history and sewn them into staid heritage guide books. These semitransparent pages tell the largely hidden history of the nineteenth-century Black community of Victoria in British Columbia, and through them the reader – who may have picked up the modified volume unsuspectingly in the public library – can still see the host narratives.

We may soon have electronic screen displays that approach the sharpness of print, if the recent prototypes, such as MIT's E*Ink, Microsoft's ClearType, and the Electronic Paper produced by Gyricon (an offshoot of Xerox), fulfil their promise. Many designers clearly believe that when this happens it will remove the last major obstacle to the wholesale adoption of electronic books.

However, the transition is unlikely to be this simple. Certainly, the exuberance which greeted the advent of large-scale digital publication ventures in 2000 has faded of late, particularly since 4 December 2001 when Times Warner announced the closing of its iPublish eBook division.[26] Even if they become widely popular, the new books may for some time remain horseless carriages, unwittingly reproducing outmoded design features that do not reflect the inherent logic of the new technology, while at the same time losing vital features of the old. The traditional page design has become so familiar that it is difficult to think outside it, and it is scarcely surprising that prototypes for electronic books, such as SoftBook and Rocket Book, are so closely modelled on late print. They offer a series of pages that are identical in layout. Only the letters change – their spacing, the background, and the settings for the margins and text block are constant. This unwitting conservatism might disappoint those, like Slights, who champion the rich variety of early modern print, or those, like del Canto, who call for a radical transformation. More fundamental changes are certainly possible. As Carlson points out, the regularity of spacing seen in early printed works such as Jenson's reflects the machinery of print. There is no mechanical reason that digital texts should follow these constraints; no reason that the pages should be silent; no reason, as Tabbi points out, that they should stand still.[27]

At the same time, older forms of page design engage readers in powerful ways they may not even be aware of, but will nonetheless miss. Dagenais notes that when we read a book we normally see not one page (as we might in an electronic version) but two, so that 'the page is almost always accompanied by a "failed mirror" of itself [and] we are always aware, peripherally, of what is to come and what has come before.' Manguel notes how the pages that flip through our fingers mark not only our progress or location in a volume, but the time of our reading. Instead, the electronic screen is encased in a plastic frame. The blank spaces of the margins are still there, but the reader will no longer touch them to turn the pages. An old intimacy has been lost. So too have certain fundamental aids to textual navigation. Dagenais stresses that the manuscript page is three-dimensional, the cuts and holes in the leather making the page more than just a visual grid. Each page of a manuscript looks, and may even feel, slightly different. This texture is a vital guide to the reader, providing a continual sense of place. In contrast, a genuinely two-dimensional page, which could be stacked in infinite number, evokes for some a disorienting Borgesian nightmare.

Should electronic books aim to reproduce the clarity of late print, or the multiplicity of the manuscript, or the mobility of the web? The layout of the standard printed page facilitates rapid silent reading, which depends on one kind of pattern recognition. Inasmuch as silent reading remains the core of our reading practice this traditional form will continue to serve us well. The old layout also reflects traditional intellectual hierarchies; here too, inasmuch as we remain committed to these hierarchies, the old forms may serve us best. The electronic page may suit other needs. Slights calls for an electronic page that will have clear hierarchies of information, be conspicuously edited, be copiously illustrated, and have an equivalent of the wide margins in which readers could enter their own contributions. He sees this primarily as a teaching aid. McGann and Tabbi, on the other hand, whose *Rossetti Archive* and *Electronic Book Review* (*ebr*), respectively, incorporate some of these features, suggest that the reconceptualization of page design may merge with the reconceptualization of reading practice and of the book as a whole. As McGann notes, large bodies of complex information (which we might conceive of as archives rather than as texts) are not well served by the traditional book. Like the vortices in Rossetti's paintings, which emerge in the course of their electronic manipulation, new patterns and new ways of knowing may emerge with a new design.

NOTES

1 Roger Chartier, *Forms and Meanings: Texts, Performances and Audiences from Codex to Computer* (Philadelphia: University of Pennsylvania Press, 1995), 14.
2 George P. Landow, *Hypertext 2.0*, rev. ed. of *Hypertext: The Convergence of Contemporary Critical Theory and Technology* (Baltimore: Johns Hopkins University Press, 1997), 82.
3 The numerous accounts of this process include D.V. Thompson, 'Medieval Parchment Making,' *The Library*, 4th series, 16 (1936): 113–17, and Jacques Stiennon, *Paléographie du moyen âge* (Paris: Armand Colin, 1973). Stiennon draws attention to the illustration of a parchment maker's atelier in the *Encyclopédie ou dictionnaire raisonné des sciences, des arts et des métiers* (Paris, 1765), 11: 929–31. By far the most detailed account, however, is that of R[onald] Reed in *Ancient Skins, Parchments and Leathers* (London and New York: Seminar Press, 1972), 118–73, and *The Nature and Making of Parchment* (Leeds: Elmete Press, 1975).
4 Christian Vandendorpe, *Du papyrus à l'hypertexte: Essai sur les mutations du texte et de la lecture* (Quebec: Boreal, 1999), 193–5.
5 See Albert Kapr, *Johann Gutenberg: The Man and His Invention*, trans. Douglas Martin (Aldershot: Scolar Press, 1996), 163. Kapr notes that the Golden Ratio became 'a proportional canon applied in monasteries throughout the Middle Ages' (161), and derives this finding from S. Corsten, 'Die Drucklegung der zweiundvierzigzeiligen Bible: Technische und chronologische Probleme,' *Kommentarband zur Faksimile Ausgabe* (Munich, 1979). See also Jan Tschichold, *The Form of the Book: Essays on the Morality of Good Design*, trans. Hajo Hadeler (Washington: Hartley and Marks, 1991), 36–64, for a fascinating examination of what Tschichold calls 'the Golden Canon of book page construction as it was used during late Gothic times by the finest of scribes' (44). He discerns the Golden Ratio as a fundamental determinant of medieval manuscript page and type form and goes on to find others. Common to most scribes' pages is the

principle of text height equaling page width. Tschichold recognizes that 'an integral part of the construction' is the 'use of the diagonal of the double page spread,' as opposed to the single page unit, as a determinant of layout.

6 Yvonne Johannot, *Tourner la page: Livre, rites et symboles* (Paris: Éditions Jérôme Millon, 1988), 29, drawing on the important initial survey of Colin H. Roberts, 'The Codex,' *Proceedings of the British Academy* 40 (1954): 169–204, revised as Colin H. Roberts and T.C. Skeat, *The Birth of the Codex* (London and New York: British Academy and Oxford University Press, 1983).

7 Régis Debray, 'The Book as Symbolic Object,' in *The Future of the Book*, ed. Geoffrey Nunberg (Berkeley and Los Angeles: University of California Press, 1996), 141.

8 Jacques Derrida, *Of Grammatology*, trans. Gayatri Chakravorty Spivak (Baltimore: Johns Hopkins University Press, 1976), 18.

9 David L. Jeffrey, *People of the Book: Christian Identity and Literary Culture* (Cambridge: Institute for Advanced Christian Studies, 1996), 147. The classic introduction to this topic is Ernst Robert Curtius, *European Literature and the Latin Middle Ages*, trans. Willard R. Trask (Princeton, NJ: Princeton University Press, 1953), 319–26.

10 *Psalterium Profanum*, ed. Joseph Eberle (Zurich: Manesse Verlag, 1962), 126, cited in Jeffrey, *People of the Book*, 147.

11 Vandendorpe, *Du papyrus*, 53.

12 We echo here the comments in Andrew Taylor, *Textual Situations: Three Medieval Manuscripts and Their Readers* (Philadelphia: University of Pennsylvania Press, 2002), 149. See also Alexander Murray, *Reason and Society in the Middle Ages* (Oxford: Clarendon, 1985), who traces the formation and self-aggrandizement of medieval university scholars as an intellectual elite, and the essays gathered together in J.I. Catto, ed., *The History of the University of Oxford*, vol. 1, *The Early Oxford Schools* (Oxford: Clarendon, 1984), especially M.B. Hackett, 'The University as a Corporate Body,' and J.M. Fletcher, 'The Faculty of Arts.'

13 Jean Destrez, *La 'Pecia' dans les manuscrits universitaires du XIII et du XIV siècle* (Paris: Éditions Jacques Vautrain, 1935). Destrez's conclusions are summarized by Marcel Thomas, 'Manuscripts,' a prefatory essay in *The Coming of the Book: The Impact of Printing, 1450–1800*, Lucien Febvre and Henri-Jean Martin, trans. David Gerard (London: Verso, 1976), 21, who describes the *pecia* system as one intended to give the university 'intellectual as well as economic control over the use of books.' Mary A. Rouse and Richard H. Rouse provide some useful corrections in 'The Book Trade at the University of Paris, ca. 1250–ca. 1350,' originally published in *La production du livre universitaire au moyen âge: exemplar et pecia*, ed. L.J. Battailon, B.G. Guyot, and R.H. Rouse (Paris: Editions du Centre national de la recherche scientifique, 1988), 41–114, and reprinted in Mary and Richard Rouse, *Authentic Witnesses: Approaches to Medieval Texts and Manuscripts* (Notre Dame, IN: University of Notre Dame Press, 1991), 259–338. See also their recent study *Manuscripts and Their Makers: Commercial Book Producers in Medieval Paris,*

1200–1500 (Turnhout, Belgium: Harvey Miller, 2000). Claire Donovan provides an evocative description of the early Oxford book trade in *The de Brailes Hours: Shaping the Book of Hours in Thirteenth-Century Oxford* (Toronto: University of Toronto Press, 1991), 13–17.

14 Ivan Illich, *In the Vineyard of the Text: A Commentary to Hugh's Didascalicon* (Chicago: University of Chicago Press, 1993), 2. The fullest account of this transition is that of Paul Saenger, *Space between Words: The Origins of Silent Reading* (Stanford, CA: Stanford University Press, 1997), which is particularly valuable for its discussion of eleventh-century Latin manuscripts.

15 M.B. Parkes, 'The Influence of the Concepts of *Ordinatio* and *Compilatio* on the Development of the Book,' in *Medieval Learning and Literature: Essays Presented to Richard William Hunt*, ed. J.J.G. Alexander and M.T. Gibson (Oxford: Clarendon, 1976), 121.

16 Theodor Nelson, *Literary Machines* (Sausalito, California: Mindful Press, 1992), 0/2.

17 Vannevar Bush, 'As We May Think,' *Atlantic Monthly* 176 (July 1945): 101–8.

18 Landow, *Hypertext*, 8.

19 George Bornstein and Theresa Tinkle, eds., *The Iconic Page in Manuscript, Print, and Digital Culture* (Ann Arbor: University of Michigan Press, 1998), 3.

20 Jerome McGann, 'The Rationale of Hypertext,' in *Electronic Text: Investigations in Method and Theory*, ed. Kathryn Sutherland (Oxford: Clarendon, 1997), 20 (online version at http://~jjm2f/rationale.html).

21 Ken Price, Introduction to the *Walt Whitman Archive* (http://www.iath.virginia.edu/whitman/introduction/).

22 Jerome McGann, 'The Rossetti Hypermedia Archive: An Introduction' (http://jefferson.village.virginia.edu/rossetti/introduction.html).

23 Peter Robinson, 'New Methods of Editing, Exploring, and Reading the *Canterbury Tales*' (http://www.cta.dmu.ac.uk/projects/ctp/desc2.html).

24 David Small, 'Navigating Large Bodies of Text,' *IBM Systems Journal* 35. 3, 4 (1996): 515.

25 Ibid., 516.

26 In 'Electronic Paper Turns the Page' (*Technology Review* 104.2 [March 2001]: 42–7) Charles C. Mann reports on the electronic book conference held in New York in November 2000 to discuss the 'forthcoming transformation of the book world by digital technology' (42). Mann gives a good sense of this period of euphoria, noting the comment by one Microsoft executive that 'the last paper edition of the New York Times will appear in 2018' (42).

27 A recent, extreme example of the itinerant 'page' is the short story 'Skin' by Shelley Jackson. 'Each of its 2,095 words [is] tattooed on a different person' (*Globe and Mail*, 18 November 2003: A19) in a 'classic book font.' Each participant tattooed for the story will be considered a 'word.' No other version of the text will exist, and 'the full text will be known only to participants' (http://ineradicablestain.com/skin.html). The result recalls Tabbi's observation that 'it may no longer be meaningful to speak of a "page" at all.'

1 Turning the Page

Alberto Manguel

The page leads an underhand existence. Lost among its brethren within the covers of a book, or singled out to carry, all on its own, a limited piece of scribbling; turned, torn, numbered, dog-eared; lost or recalled, lit up or deleted, skimmed or scrutinized, the page comes into our reader's consciousness only as a frame or container of what we mean to read. Its brittle being, barely corporeal in its two dimensions, is dimly perceived by our eyes as they follow the track of the words. Like a skeleton supporting the skin of a text, the page disappears in its very function, and in that unpreposessing nature lies its very strength. The page is the reader's space; it is also the reader's time. Like the changing numbers of an electronic clock, the pages mark the numbered hours, a doom to which we, the readers, are called to submit. We can slow down or speed up our reading, but whatever we do, as readers, the passing of time will always be clocked by the turning of a page. The page limits, cuts, extends, censors, reshapes, translates, stresses, defuses, bridges, and separates our reading which we arduously attempt to reclaim. In this sense, the act of reading is a power struggle between reader and page over the dominion of the text. Usually, it is the page that wins.

But what exactly is a page?

According to Jorge Luis Borges, the infinite Library of Babel which he imagined containing all the books in the universe (not only all those that have already been written but all those that may or may not be written one day), could be reduced to no more than one book.[1] In a footnote to the story, Borges suggests that the vast library is useless: one single volume would suffice, if that volume were made up of an infinite number of infinitely thin pages. The handling of this volume would, of course, be painfully cumbersome: each apparent page would unfold into other pages, and the inconceivable middle page would have no verso.

Here we have, in one nightmarish moment, the page in all its glory and all its horror: as an object that allows or demands a frame for the text it contains so that we, the readers, can address it piecemeal and enquire into its meaning; and also as an object that restricts the text to fit its frame, cutting it down to size, separating it from its whole, changing or circumscribing its sense. Every page is of this double nature.

If we define page as the single spatial unit within which a portion of text is contained, then the Sumerian clay tablets and large granite slabs of 5000 to 2000 BC count as pages. For practical reasons, the Sumerian page appears to have been considered mainly as a setter of limits.[2] Any given text must fit the space allotted to it: if the text runs on, it must divide itself in units of self-contained sense. The Sumerian tablet doesn't break off in mid-sentence, and continue on another tablet. The space of the tablet and the space of the text coincide.

Both the Sumerian stone slabs and clay tablets were conceived as two-sided. The slabs stood as high as monuments, bearing inscriptions on one or both sides. The tablets, like those used by students, for instance, in order to learn how to write in the scribe schools, carried on the recto the teacher's text, and then, on the verso, the student's attempt at reproducing that text. The learning system required that the student learn literally to bear in mind the teacher's writing until he reached the tablet's other side.

This dual notion ceased almost entirely with the creation of the scroll around the sixth century BC. Most scrolls were written on one side only, on which the fibres ran horizontally, but there were also scrolls written on both sides – such a scroll was known as *opisthograph*, and was fairly uncommon.[3] In the scroll, both the idea of frame and the idea of recto-verso seem to disappear. The sheets of papyrus used to form most scrolls were no larger than fifteen inches high by nine inches wide and did not break the text up into something akin to our individual, separate pages. Though the scrolls had margins and were divided into columns, with no space between words, it was the scroll itself that determined the extension of the text (in Greece they were generally twenty to thirty feet long). An ordinary scroll could contain one book of Thucydides or two or three books of the *Iliad*.[4]

The scroll granted both writer and reader apparent freedom: no truncated lines, except from column to column; no cumulative sense of progression, except as the scroll unfurled and rolled up again; no imposed unit of text, except as the scrolling allowed for only one section to be viewed at a time. Trying to demonstrate the paradoxical quality of this freedom, many centuries later, in 1969, the Spanish writer Juan Benet was to write a novel, *Una meditación*, on a single roll of paper attached to his typewriter, which an elaborate mechanism prevented him from reversing – that is to say, whatever he wrote became the final draft, without the guidance or division of pages.[5]

The appearance of the codex lends a new meaning to the concept of page. It has been suggested that the invention of the codex stemmed from the need to produce a more portable container for the text, and that a folded sheet was obviously more easily transportable than a scroll. Clay was cumbersome, papyrus was brittle, and so parchment and vellum became the preferred materials for codex making in Europe until the first paper mills were installed in Italy in the twelfth century. Other materials had been used in other parts of the world: fanlike wooden books in Korea and Egypt, block-printed books on paper in China, cloth books in other parts of the Asian subcontinent.[6] Whatever the material – vellum, parchment, cloth, paper, or wood – all these pages quietly imposed their limits on the text.

But once the limiting qualities of the page were recognized by readers and writers, those very qualities called for disruption. Whether through shape, interior space, marginalia, or reshuffling, the page's characteristics were to be constantly altered. In the struggle over the supremacy of the text, the writer and the reader decidedly wanted to be in control.

The first shape of the page was perhaps dictated by the measurements of the human hand. The Sumerian clay tablet fit the hand of a child (the student scribe) or the hand of an adult (that first remote accountant to whom we owe the art of writing). The vagaries of social needs and political propaganda blew the amiable tablet to gigantic proportions: a code of laws from Ashur, for instance, from the twelfth century BC, measured 6.7 square feet.[7] But periodically, the page reverted to its manufactured origins: the codex that Julius Caesar is supposed to have created by folding a scroll into pages, to send dispatches to his troops;[8] the medieval books of hours, meant for private devotions; Aldus Manutius's pocket classics; the standard-size books decreed by François I in 1527;[9] the paperbacks of the twentieth century. In our time, the French publisher Hubert Nyssen created the elongated format that distinguishes the Actes Sud publications by measuring vertically the distance between the metacarpal bone and the tip of his index finger, and horizontally, from the root of his thumb to the far edge of his palm.[10]

All these pocket-size pages give the illusion of being contained in the hand, but that illusion does not carry far. On the page, the strings of words are cut off by the blank space of the margins and trail away in order to resurface on the next page, thereby forcing the reader to hold the text's meaning in constant suspense. Widows, hanging lines, irritants to the eye, have caused printers to suggest to the author changes (especially in journalism), so that the text itself is altered to fit the demands of the page's tyranny.

Partly to subvert these special demands, writers and readers created odd-shaped books: round, horizontally elongated 'à l'italienne,' heart-shaped, infolded and accordion-style, which then, in turn, imposed their own individual limitations. In our time, the so-called artists' books routinely interfere with the classic shape: they enlarge the text to cross over the gutter, or reduce it to fit in its entirety a given space, or work the text into shapes that overwhelm the shape of the page itself. The shape of a page seems to cry out for counteraction.

When not changing the format or shape, the writer can change the text the page contains, so that the subversion becomes internalized. Laurence Sterne, publishing his *Tristram Shandy* in 1760, introduced blank pages, pages filled with ellipses, and even a page printed completely in black.[11] Lewis Carroll, in order to provide a limitless map for his Snark-hunters, designed a page that was completely white.[12] And Apollinaire with his *Calligrammes*, poems written in the physical shape of their subject, and concrete poets such as the Brazilian Haroldo de Campos, imposed a new shape to the page from inside, drawing the reader's attention away from the straight margins, into new and startling textual designs.[13]

This interior restructuring is of course quite ancient. Many are the medieval manuscripts that play with acrostics and crossword-puzzlelike grids, multiplying the use of a page many times. As the broadening of restrictions became apparent, the text began to breed its own commentary. The page metamorphosed into a series of concentric spaces, as when scripture, for instance, written in a narrow central panel of the page, was carefully surrounded by a gloss, which was in turn surrounded by further annotations, which then received the reader's scribbles on the margins. These spaces are not in themselves protectionist: the comments of the third space, for example, may annotate either the central text or the gloss; the scribbles may refer to the notes, the gloss, or the central text. To take just one among thousands of possible examples, let me describe a manuscript of Aristotle's *Parva naturalia*, now in the British Library[14] from the second half of the thirteenth century (fig. 1.1). The text itself occupies the centre top right; it is framed by glosses derived from Averroes, and written presumably by a certain Henry de Renham. In turn, there are interlinear commentaries on both Aristotle and Averroes that look a little like our own proofreader's notes and are written in a smaller hand, filling the spaces left by the glosses.[15] In his Letter to Can Grande, Dante proposed four possible levels of reading: literal, allegorical, analogical, and anagogical.[16] These four levels acquire physical reality on Henry de Renham's page, as text, gloss, commentary on text, and commentary on gloss, quadruplicate the space allotted by the page to the text.

Sometimes the tyranny of the page is subverted on one level only, but in a way that is powerfully intimate and personal. Montaigne, whose scribbling habits amounted to a conversation, would continue the dialogue at the back of the book he was reading, including the date on which he had finished it in order to better recall the circumstances of the event. Though Montaigne's books were in various languages, his marginal notes were always in French ('no matter what language is spoken by my books,' he tells us, 'I speak to them in my own') and in French he extended the text and its notes through his own critical comments.[17] For Montaigne, this reading method was necessary for what he called his 'quest for truth': not the story as given by the words within the confines of the page, but the reflection of that story, mused

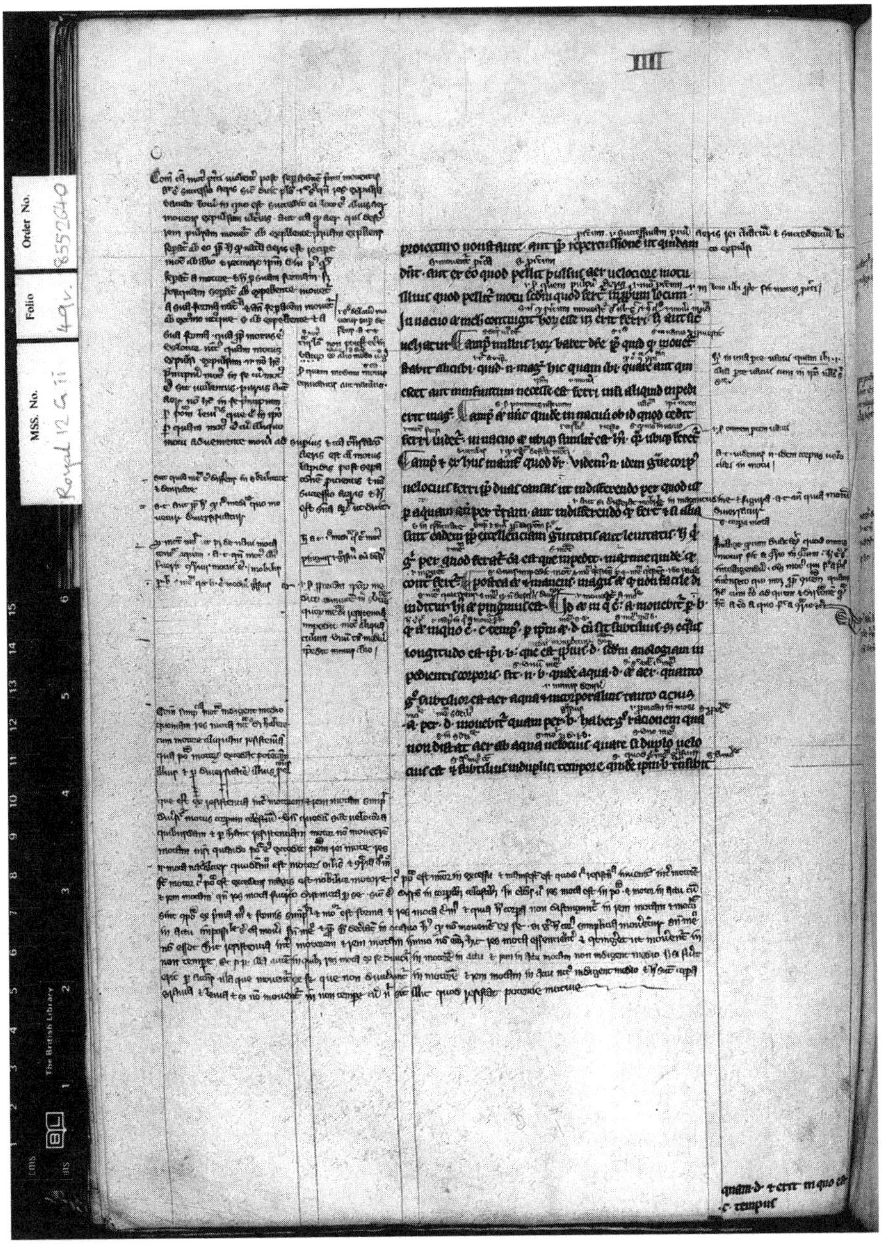

Figure 1.1. Aristotle, *Parva naturalia*. British Library, MS Royal 12 G. ii, fol. 49v.

upon and retold by the reader Montaigne in spaces reclaimed, there where the page left itself vulnerable to encroachment.

These blank spaces, left after the writer has crossed the page to vanquish what Mallarmé, once and for all defined as 'le vide papier que la blancheur défend' (the agony of the white page), are the very spaces in which the readers can exercise their power, in those gaps that were for Roland Barthes the very essence of the erotic thrill, the interstices in the text (but we can apply this to the physical text on the page as well) which he described as there '*where the garments gape*.'[18] In those openings between the edge of the paper and the edge of the ink, the reader (let us stretch this image as far as it will go) can cause a quiet revolution and establish a new society in which the creative tension is established no longer between page and text but between text and reader.

This is the distinction made by Jewish medieval scholars regarding the Torah. According to the Midrash, the Torah God gave Moses on Mount Sinai was both a written text and an oral commentary. During the day, when it was light, Moses read the text God had written, and in the darkness of the night he studied the commentary God had spoken.[19] The first action submits the reader to the authority of the page; the second forgoes the page and submits the text to the authority of the reader.

Conscious of the danger of the page's supremacy, the great eighteenth-century Hasidic master Rabbi Levi Yitzhak of Berdithev attempted to explain why the first page of each of the treatises of the Babylonian Talmud was missing, obliging the reader to begin on page 2. 'However much a man may learn, he should always remember that he has not even gotten to the first page.'[20] That is to say, the commentary of the Word of God has no foreseeable beginning, neither on paper nor in the reader's mind. By eliminating the first page, no page can be said to force the Word of God into an explanation.

Since the page defines the text it contains by marking its beginning, middle, and end, eliminating the first page can be seen as an act of defiance. The nineteenth-century moralist Joseph Joubert went further. According to Chateaubriand, Joubert's library contained only the texts that Joubert was truly fond of. 'When he read,' says Chateaubriand, 'he would tear out of his books the pages he didn't like, thereby achieving a library entirely to his taste, composed of hollowed-out books bound inside covers that were too large for them.'[21]

Joubert did not in fact destroy the sequence of pages; he merely interrupted it with moments of silence. In our time, the French novelist Raymond Queneau tried to destroy the order imposed by the numbered pages by dividing each page into dozens of strips, each carrying a line of text. In this way, readers could construct their own pages by composing (as in the child's game-book of mix-and-match) a near infinity of new texts. Queneau called his book *A Hundred Thousand Billion Poems*.[22] The Argentinian Julio Cortázar, in a better-known example, proposed a book, the novel *Hopscotch,* that had the appearance of submitting to the given sequence of pages, but then destroyed that semblance of order by suggesting first that the reader should follow a sequence of chapters other than the one set out in the table of contents, and then that the reader allow either chance or personal choice to dictate the order in which the chapters were to be read.[23] Here the reader claims supremacy over both the space and time of the reading.

Flaubert, as he was writing *Madame Bovary,* read certain sections of the novel to his friend Bouilhet, but confessed that in doing so the narrative time of those pages (114 pages, from page 139 to page 251) was not his own but that it was dictated by the flicking of the pages itself. 'This afternoon,' he wrote to Louise Colet, 'I ended up abandoning my corrections; I no longer understood anything; immersed in my work, it became overwhelming; what seemed now like a mistake, five minutes later no longer seemed like one; it's all a series of corrections and corrections of corrections that are endless.'[24] And earlier he had written: 'The middle pages of all long books are always awful.'[25]

Is our lot, in this electronic age, at all different? Electronic reading alters certain parameters. Reading on the screen precludes (up to a point) the time-restricting quality of reading on paper. The scrolling text (like that of the Roman or Greek scrolls) unfurls at a pace that is not dictated by the dimensions of the page and its margins. In fact, on the screen, each page shifts shape endlessly, remaining the same in size but altering its content, since the first and last line keep changing as we scroll, always within the fixed frame of the screen. Though reading a long text on the screen is thoroughly inconvenient (for physiological reasons that may, no doubt, change as we evolve), it does free us (if we want to be freed) from the very temporal realization of progress illustrated by the thickening bulk of pages held in the left hand and the diminishing bulk of pages held in the right.

In fact, Borges's imaginary book finds its incarnation in the not-quite-infinite pages of an e-book. The e-book page exceeds the nightmarish quality of Borges's book, since none of its pages has a verso. Since text can always be added to the 'volume,' the e-book has no middle. The e-book page is the frame applied by the reader to what is essentially Borges's borderless text. Like every other literary creation, the e-book was foreseen in Borges's Library.

For the common reader, the notion of page becomes confused with the notion of leaf or folio; the dictionary defines 'page' as both 'the leaf of a book' and 'one side of it.' In this sense, a short poem by Goethe, on the infolded leaf of the ginkgo tree, perhaps best describes the dual nature of the page. The gingko tree is called a living fossil, since it is the only modern representative of a species long vanished, and, like the page of a book, does not exist in the wild. Each of its leathery leaves, though born from a single stem, seems double, and this ambiguity led Goethe to write his poem.[26] This is my English translation.

Gingko Biloba

This small leaf that travelled eastwards
And now in my garden lies,
Offers rich and secret meanings
That bear wisdom to the wise.

Is it one green living creature
Split in two and yet left whole?
Are they two that fused together
To become a single soul?

The right answer to these questions
Can be found by everyone.
Can't you tell from my own verses
That I'm also two and one?

NOTES

1 Jorge Luis Borges, 'La biblioteca de Babel,' in *El jardin de senderos que se bifurcan* (Buenos Aires: Sur, 1941); and *Ficciones*, ed. and trans. Anthony Kerrigan (New York: Grove, 1962).
2 Béatrice André-Salvini, 'Les tablettes du monde cunéiforme,' in *Les tablettes à écrire de l'antiquité à l'époque moderne*, ed. Elisabeth Lalou, *Bibliologia* 12 (Turnhout: Brepols, 1992), 15–34.
3 David Diringer, *The Book before Printing: Ancient, Medieval and Oriental* (New York: Dover, 1982), 138.
4 Ibid., 130–4.
5 Juan Benet, *Una meditación* (Barcelona: Seix-Barral, 1970); *A Meditation*, trans. Gregory Rabassa (New York: Persea, 1982). Benet himself describes the whole procedure in an interview with Antonio Nuñez, 'Encuentro con Juan Benet,' *Insula: Revista de Letras y Ciencias Humanas* 269 (April 1969): 4.
6 M.R. Guignard, 'Le précédent chinois,' in *L'apparition du livre*, Lucien Febvre and Henri-Jean Martin (Paris: Albin Michel, 1958), 97–105; trans. David Gerard, *The Coming of the Book: The Impact of Printing, 1450–1800* (London: NLB, 1976), 71–6.
7 Diringer, *The Book before Printing*, 109.
8 Suetonius, *Lives of the Caesars*, ed. J.C. Rolfe (Cambridge, MA.: Harvard University Press, 1970), 79.
9 François I, *Lettres de François Ier au pape* (Paris, 1527).
10 Hubert Nyssen, private conversation. See also his *Du texte au livre: les avatars du sens* (Paris: Nathan, 1993), 70.

11 Laurence Sterne, *The Life and Opinions of Tristram Shandy, Gentleman*, ed. Ian Campbell (Oxford: Clarendon, 1983), 181, 377, 499, 512, 513.

12 Lewis Carroll, 'The Hunting of the Snark,' in *The Illustrated Lewis Carroll*, ed. Roy Gasson (London: Jupiter, 1978), 230.

13 Guillaume Apollinaire, *Calligrammes: Poèmes de la paix et de la guerre (1913–1916); Calligrammes: Poems of Peace and War (1913–1916)*, trans. Anne Hyde Greet (Berkeley and Los Angeles: University of California Press, 1980); Haroldo de Campos, *Os melhores poemas de Haroldo de Campos*, ed. Inês Oseki Dépré (São Paulo: Global, 1992).

14 London, British Library, MS Royal 12 G. ii, fol. 49 verso.

15 George Warner and Julius P. Gilson, *Catalogue of the Western Manuscripts in the Old Royal and King's Collections in the British Museum*, 2 vols (London: Longmans, 1921), 2: 68–9, and A.B. Emden, *A Biographical Register of the University of Oxford to A.D. 1500*, 3 vols (Oxford: Clarendon, 1959), 3: 1565.

16 Dante, Letter to Can Grande della Scala, in *Le opere di Dante*, Testo critico della Società Dantesaca Italiana, *Epistole*, ed. Ermenegildo Pistelli (Florence: Società Dantesca Italiana, 1921), Epistola 13: 438.

17 Montaigne, 'Au lecteur,' in *Essais*, ed. André Tournon, 3 vols (Paris: Imprimerie nationale, 1998), 1: 45; trans. Jacob Zeitlin, *The Essays of Michel de Montaigne* (New York: Alfred A. Knopf, 1934), 1: 1.

18 Roland Barthes, *Le plaisir du texte* (Paris: Éditions du Seuil, 1973), 19; trans. Richard Miller, *The Pleasure of the Text* (New York: Farar, Straus, and Giroux 1975), 9, italics in original.

19 Louis Ginzberg, *The Legends of the Jews* (Baltimore: Johns Hopkins University Press, 1998), 3, 116. See also *Yemenite Midrash: Philosophical Commentaries on the Torah*, trans. Yitzhak Tzvi Langerman (San Francisco: HarperCollins, 1996), 219.

20 Martin Buber, *Tales of the Hasidim*, trans. Olga Marx, 2 vols (New York: Schocken, 1947), 1: 232.

21 François-René de Chateaubriand, *Mémoires d'Outre-Tombe*, ed. Maurice Levaillant and Georges Moulinier, 2 vols (Paris: Gallimard, 1951), 1: 450.

22 Raymond Queneau, *Cent mille millard de poèmes* (Paris: Gaillimard, 1982).

23 Julio Cortázar, *Rayuela* (Buenos Aires: Sudamerica, 1963), Tablero de dirección; trans. Gregory Rabassa, *Hopscotch* (New York: Random House, 1966).

24 Gustave Flaubert, Lettre à Louise Colet, 2 July 1853, in *Correspondance*, ed. Jean Bruneau, 4 vols (Paris: Gallimard, 1973), 2: 372–3.

25 Gustave Flaubert, Lettre à Louise Colet, 29 January 1853, in *Correspondance*, ed. Bruneau, 2: 243.

26 Johann Wolfgang von Goethe, 'Gingo Biloba,' in *West-östlicher Divan, Berliner Ausgabe*, vol 3, *Goethe Poetische Werke: Gedichte und Singspiele* (Berlin: Aufbau-Verlag, 1968).

2 Decolonizing the Medieval Page

John Dagenais

Medieval manuscripts are counted among the greatest glories of Western civilization. With their gold and painted decoration and their charming miniatures, they have always had immense appeal, and images from them can be seen everywhere – from greeting cards and wrapping paper to expensive facsimiles.
– Note on inside flap of dust jacket, Christopher de Hamel, *A History of Illuminated Manuscripts*, 2nd ed.

You and me, Baby, ain't nothin' but mammals ...
– From 'Bad Touch,' The Bloodhound Gang

The following remarks arise from a growing concern for the future of the medieval page. This concern involves both of the broad constituencies implicit in the symposium The Future of the Page and in the related web site *Architectures, Ideologies, and Materials of the Page.*[1] On the one hand, we have those who believe that new technologies will finally allow us to transcend the medieval page once and for all, to move beyond it to new forms of organizing information and, therefore, to new ways of thinking about that information. On the other hand, there are those who believe that the page, as it evolved in the codex-form manuscripts of medieval Europe, has become so basic to our modes of thought that it will continue to dominate our attempts to represent that thought for the foreseeable future. In other words, it will take a major cognitive shift, whether spurred by new technologies or not, in order for us to be able to think beyond the margins of the medieval page.

My concern, as a medievalist, involves both these constituencies. I see a danger, in the first instance, that we may bid farewell forever to the medieval page without ever having known it in all its variety, thus effectively erasing numerous potentially innovative models for the representation of thought. A far greater danger, however, comes from the second group whose very enthusiasm for 'the medieval page' may have the effect of instituting certain familiar and privileged forms of medieval pages as *the* medieval page, in a sense condemning thousands of nonconformist medieval pages to the flames.

We stand before the medieval page (and medieval civilizations in general) much as European colonialists stood before the new cultures they conquered.[2] We view the medieval page as a traditional society, one which has no history, or whose history has stopped with our arrival to observe it. It is a society without a future of its own. As a result, we may appropriate and even enshrine certain stereotypical images of native inhabitants, allowing these images to stand, nostalgically, for the entire range of native peoples and their cultures (the Plains feathered war bonnet, often sported by Boy Scouts, comes to mind). The effect, of course, is to level genuine variety and difference among native inhabitants and their cultures in favour of selected artefacts from these cultures which can be displayed as museum-like trophies to our own cultural superiority.[3]

With this background in mind, we need to examine more closely the specific forces at work in the colonization of the medieval page. The primary colonizer of the medieval page is, of course, the *printed* page. Most, if not all, of the ideas we bring to our appreciation of the medieval page are shaped, almost unavoidably, by our prior familiarity with the printed page. And so, as with much else having to do with the so-called Middle Ages, the announced chronology is, in fact, reversed: the printed page comes *before* the manuscript page for us. We inevitably see the medieval page as a set of deviations from and similarities with the printed page.[4] It is far too easy, I myself have discovered in the course of preparing this study, to say 'this looks like *calligrammes*' or 'this reminds us of a web page,' eliding some of the unique and distinctive features of these pages in favour of some easy recognition.

The colonization of the medieval page is most evident, and most deleterious, in our implicit notion of that page as a fixed and finished product. The underlying analogy seems to be: as the printed page is the product of the technology of printing, so the medieval page is the *product* of the varying technologies of the handmade book and of various concepts of *ordinatio* that go into its design. We think we can take a medieval page and let it stand as evidence for the *result* of these technologies, and forget that the medieval page as we have it is almost always only a representative of one stage in a *process*. We think we can put medieval pages on greeting cards or wrapping paper or in expensive facsimiles (or on web sites) and that this static representation captures, legitimately 'a medieval page.' The medieval page was (and still is) 'open,' subject to modification, to 'supplementation' and to an infinite *différance* of sense.[5] It was/is always in movement and it is our challenge to learn to perceive that motion in all its glacial slowness – not just to see it, but to see it as an essential rather than an accidental quality of that page.[6]

The medieval page served all the purposes we associate with the printed page *and* most of those we associate today with the handwritten page. The gist of my argument here is that when we construct our mental image of the medieval page, we must be sure to build into it the post-it note and the brainstorm scrawled on a fast food restaurant napkin along with our images from the Book of Kells.

A second source of our colonization of the medieval page is the modern academic disciplines most engaged in studying it: namely, literary and related text-based studies (history of philosophy, science, or law, for example), art history, and codicology. Art historians are condemned to look at pages bearing 'art.'[7] This already excludes the great majority of medieval pages. Students of *texts* have to look at pages bearing something that fits our categories of text – it has a certain length, or maybe an author, or at least a recognizable genre. We are largely blind to the hundreds of thousands of fragmentary written elements that occupy the margins, flyleaves, and textual and interlinear spaces of the medieval page. Codicologists have to work with objects that can be described using the hieratic descriptive language of codicology, impenetrable to most reasonable men and women. Like the printed page itself, the academic disciplines under which we study the medieval page already predict what we will look at and, as a result, what we will find to be the medieval page.[8]

I want to encourage people to make a special effort here, at what is either the apocalypse or the apotheosis of the physical codex-form page, to be sure we have really looked at the medieval page in all its lively and enduring variety. As should be obvious by now, I think it is most important to see these pages as in process, as in motion, now. It will help if we can see them as organic and therefore as situated, as are we, in time and space. I think it can be extremely useful to think of each individual, concrete manuscript page as an organism of its own, a culture possessing its own mores, interrelations, power structures, discourses, margins. Or as a body with its own anatomy of sacred and profane locations, public and private parts. Our traditional view of the medieval page sees it as a prepared laboratory cross-section, sprayed with fixative and placed on a glass slide for scrutiny under the microscope. The medieval manuscript page and its culture are more like an open petri dish, a living, growing thing, placed within a fertile, organic medium.

Like any organism, its system responds not only internally but is in contact with the world outside it. The act of touching is significant here, for one can feel a real movement in the medieval page from the text which is 'central' to the edges of the leaves where the written word comes, quite strikingly at times, into contact with the physical world of the reader. We should never forget that the broad margins of the medieval page were prepared for the touch of the hand as well as the eye.

The organic nature of the medieval page is not just a metaphor. In the case of parchment pages in particular, we are constantly reminded that the space in and on which the medieval page happens was once all that stood between the sun and the wind and the rain and a living, breathing mammal like us. There are places, such as in this student miscellany, where the manuscript leaf can look positively Frankensteinian (fig. 2.1).[9]

Before we take a look at some examples of the medieval page as process, however, I would like to examine one more recent page which happens to illustrate rather handily most of the points I will make about the medieval page: the official poster for the symposium The Future of the Page (fig. 2.2), by Edison del Canto. I shall be referring here to my own copy of the poster, which I removed surreptitiously from the walls of an underground tunnel joining several buildings on the University of Saskatchewan campus. Habent sua fata cartelli.

One of the first things we notice is that del Canto has left in the crop marks and other marks along the left margin that are part of the technical process of preparing the poster. This is a characteristic of the medieval page as well: we can see in the rulings, often impressed in the parchment page with a dry point, the actual delineations of the spaces, both textual and marginal which go into the creation of the page. As with this poster, the medieval page often dramatizes its own production, keeps us mindful of the processes which brought the written word to the page.

We can note that, like the vast majority of medieval pages, this poster, too, seems to place at its centre, in the authoritative 'textual' (as opposed to 'glossatory') space, an absolutist or universalizing ideology, here Marxism, for the West European medieval page, Roman Catholicism. But as in the vast majority of medieval pages, here, too, we find marginal material coming from the edge and penetrating the textual space. And this marginal material often stands in a far from simple relation to the text it invades. Are the University of Saskatchewan and the Mendel Art Gallery there as *exempla* illustrating the 'text,' supporting its authority? Or are they there in opposition to it? Can the relation between a gloss and its text be, as one suspects here, profoundly ironic?

In the same way, a message taped to the bottom of my copy of this poster (but not evident in fig. 2.2) raises issues of authority:

> FREE FOR U of S STUDENTS
> Register with Conference and Catering in Athabaska Hall, or on the morning.
> Presentations Friday Arts 134, Saturday Mendel Art Gallery, from 9:00 a.m.

Was this a part of the original design of the poster and thus a partner in the authority that went into that design? Is it purely informational, a supplement to other data on the conference, a gloss, a clarification added later, but still within the intent of the original poster design? Can it be, as one might imagine, that, with this taped-on 'afterthought,' the designer is making a

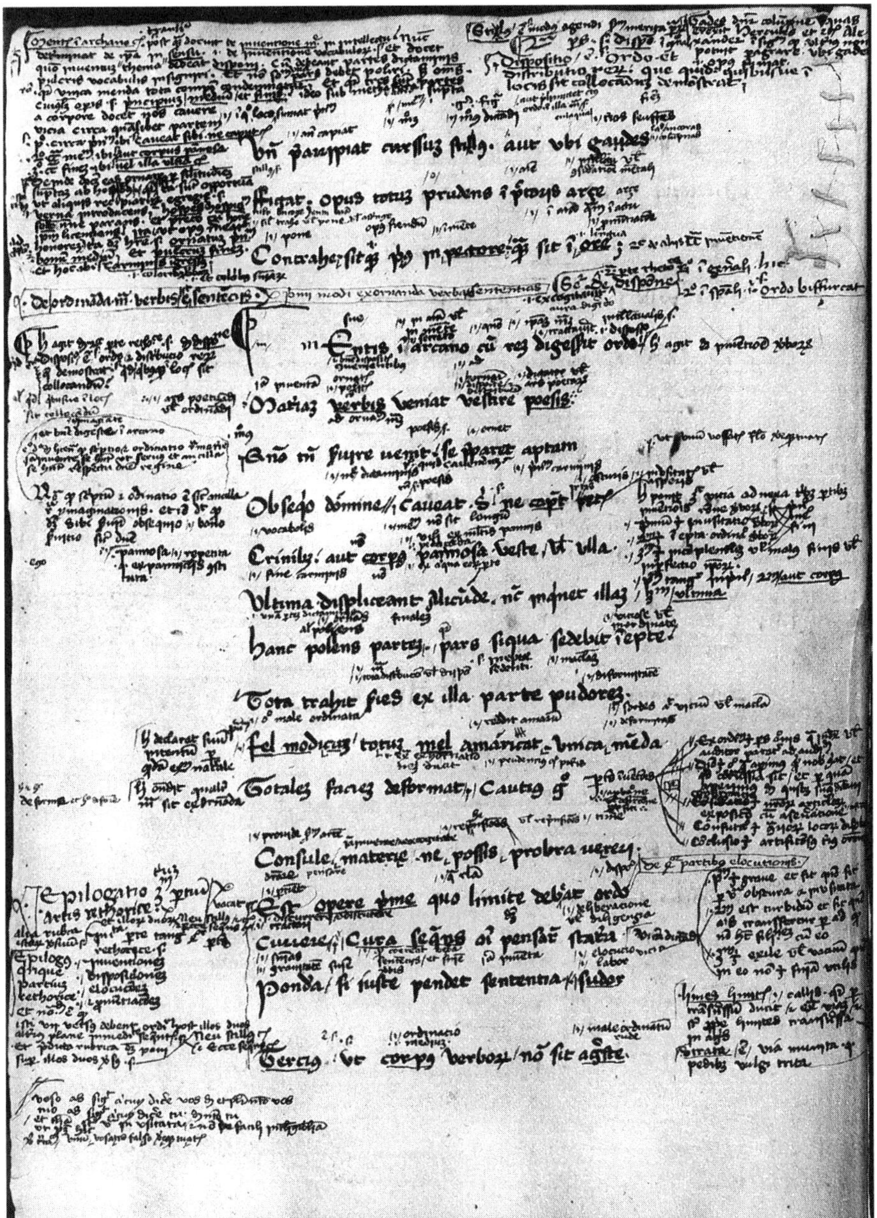

Figure 2.1. 15th-century student miscellany. Madrid, Biblioteca Nacional, Ms. 9589, fol. 2v.

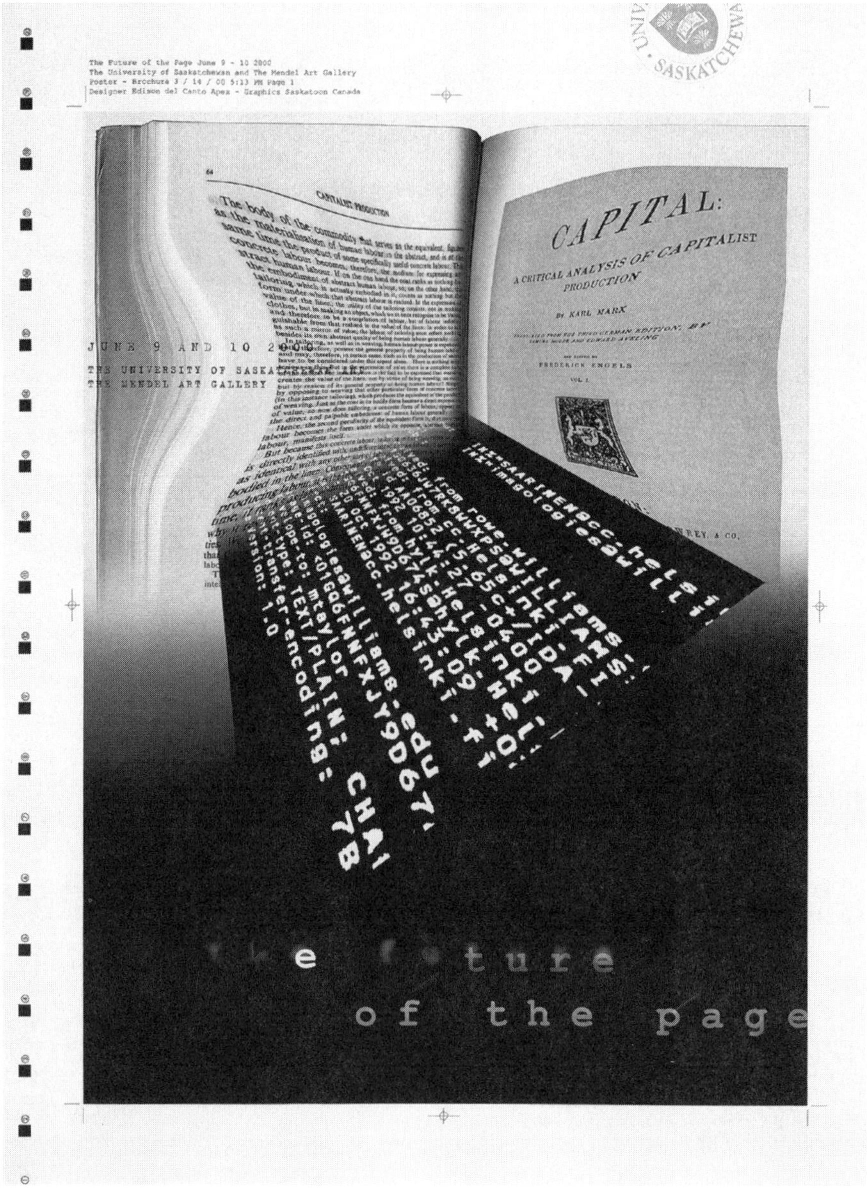
The Future of the Page June 9 - 10 2000
The University of Saskatchewan and The Mendel Art Gallery
Poster - Brochure 3 / 14 / 00 5:13 PM Page 1
Designer Edison del Canto Apex - Graphics Saskatoon Canada
JUNE 9 AND 10 2000
THE UNIVERSITY OF SASKATCHEWAN AND
THE MENDEL ART GALLERY
CAPITAL:
A CRITICAL ANALYSIS OF CAPITALIST PRODUCTION
By KARL MARX
FREDERICK ENGELS
VOL. I.
the future
of the page

Figure 2.2. Edison del Canto, 'Future of the Page' poster.

wry comment on the marginality, the contingency of students in the North American university? Or is it the later work of clever students intent on coopting the authority inherent in such posters and obtaining free admission to the august gathering announced in the poster? It seems clear, then, that the principles of movement and change I have stressed are at work here: the taped-on message must come after the 'text' of the poster, but it is not easy to know by whom and with what intent the addition was made.

The upper margin of the poster bears, as do so many medieval manuscripts, an ownership stamp of sorts: a seal of the Univ[ersity of] Saskatchewa[n] (my best guess at a reconstruction of the ruthlessly guillotined text). In this particular case, however, the ownership stamp is a part of the original design of the poster; in most medieval manuscripts, such stamps and seals are more likely to be affixed as the manuscript enters, usually as spoils of conquest, the massive museum of nationalist annexations that is the national library.

In the upper right of the poster is another stamp, however, which I will assume is not a part of the original design of the poster. It reads:

REMOVE THIS
POSTER ON

JUN 28 2000

U.S.S.U

This poster carries with it, now, a sort of self-awareness of its existence in time and space. The message itself is a sort of an anathema, the opposite of the anathemata found in numerous medieval manuscripts, which enjoined unknown individuals from removing the manuscript from where it was, from stealing it, on pain of death, excommunication, eternal torment, and so on (many such anathemata may be found in manuscripts now housed in national libraries).[10] In contrast, this poster bears the delightfully ironic injunction *to* remove the poster from its location on or after a specific date.

My own copy of this poster has several unique features which arise, for the most part, from the manner in which I obtained it. The upper left corner is missing because, in my haste to tear it free from the wall before a campus policeman happened down the tunnel, I was careless in separating it from another notice which been taped beside it:

Ride needed to Vancouver

Will Share Gas and Expenses

Like the medieval page, this poster has come into contact with other pages, although in this case its impact on the meaning of our poster is minimal (one could see a theme developing on the eternal poverty of students). But what is important here is that our page is in contact with a world. Though the designer may have dramatized the physical processes which went into producing the basic form of the page, his page continues to evolve, without him, beyond his control, in the real world it inhabits. Most striking here is that it is subject to physical damage, but my central point is that this page came into contact with another page of rather different content and purpose and that its meaning, as well as its physical form, was changed by that contact in some way.

The conference poster by del Canto can serve now as a *precis* for the remarks which follow. Figure 2.3, a page from the well-known, fifteenth-century manuscript, Les Très Riches Heures du Duc de Berry, will stand here for what we might think of as a typical medieval manuscript page. Medievalists have every right to take pride in pages like this one. They are objects of remarkable beauty and I think it is fair to suppose that when the general public thinks at all of 'the medieval page,' they no doubt have a mental picture of illustrated pages like this one. This is the kind of medieval page that finds its way onto wrapping paper, men's ties, and into facsimiles. It is, indeed, beautiful, captivating. At the same time it serves to reinforce for us the very idea of an older, static culture that we, perhaps unconsciously, extend from our view of the Middle Ages to our view of the medieval page. Here nobles take a leisurely ride through the fields of August, while dark and lowly peasants skinny-dip in a nearby stream. Even the stars are in their proper, cyclical, alignment. God's in his heaven, all's right with the world.

For every manuscript leaf like this, however, there are dozens where something seems to have gone seriously awry (see fig. 2.4). On the opening flyleaves of this collection of annals and chronicles on the Trojan War, the forgotten bits of history, the measurements of the churches of Rome, and papal bulls fight for space midst worm holes, tears, and stains.[11] The dark blotches which seem to be coterminous with some of the textual spaces are the after-effects of reagents applied by nineteenth-century scholars in a desperate attempt to recover even this fragmented historical knowledge for the national museum of culture. Even as the illumination from Les Très Riches Heures captures in a page a static and cyclical moment in time, an August afternoon with even the stars in their proper place, the flyleaves of Madrid, MS 10046 speak to us about another sort of time, one that has not been successfully captured in the pages of history: of fragmentation, loss and attempted recovery.

Figure 2.5, from the Hours of François and Charles de Guise, shows another 'typical' medieval page. There is a clear intent here to fill every space on the page, to control it, define it. Nothing can be added or taken away without affecting the entire page. We are struck, perhaps, first by how unlike this page is from that shown in fig. 2.6, from a student's notes on John of Wales's

Figure 2.3. 15th-century, 'Les Très Riches Heures du Duc de Berry,' 'August,' Chantilly, Musée Condé, 8v.

Figure 2.4. 13th- and 14th-century, historical miscellany on the Trojan War, BNM, Ms. 10046, av–br (opening flyleaves).

Figure 2.5. 14th-century, Hours of François and Charles de Guise, Chantilly, Musée Condé, Ms. 64/1671, fol. 185v.

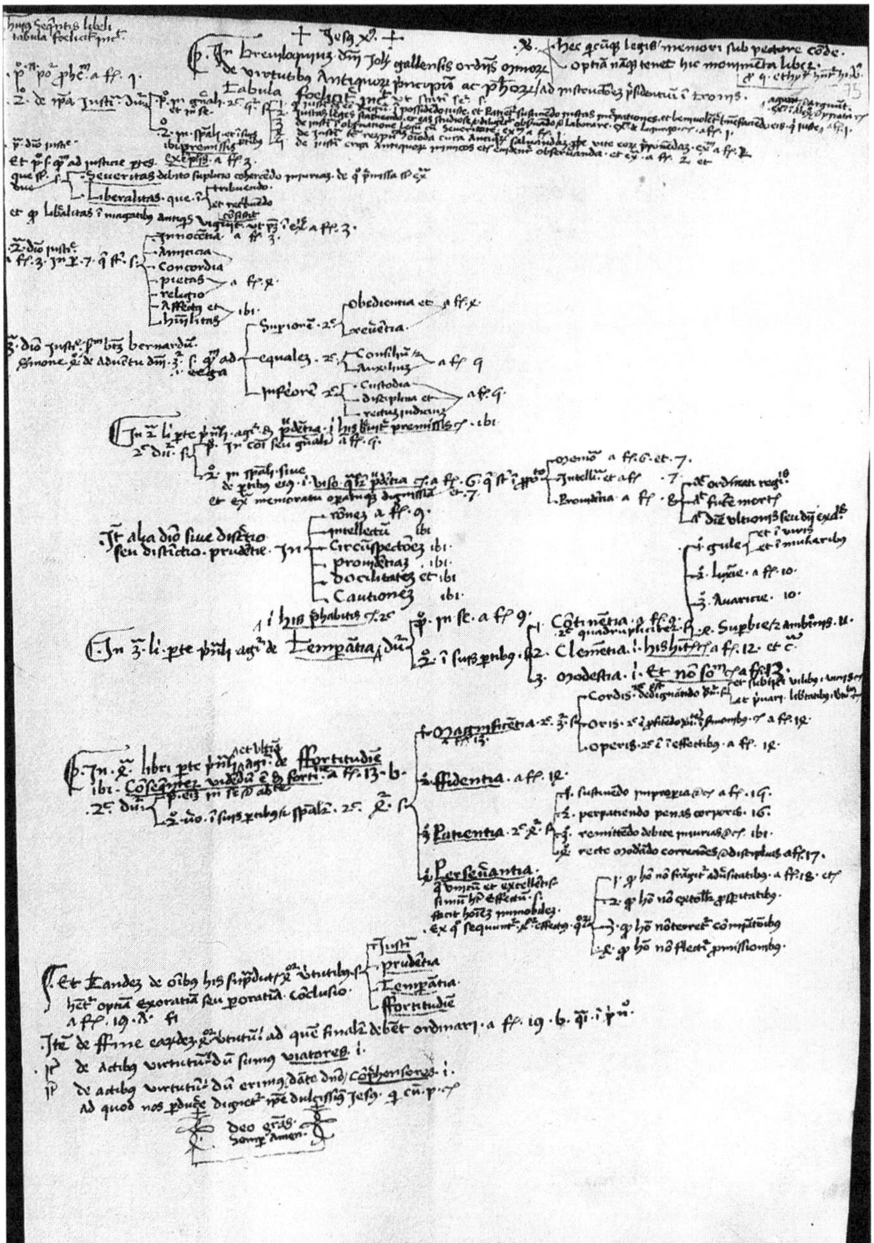

Figure 2.6. BNM, Ms. 9589, fol. 68r.

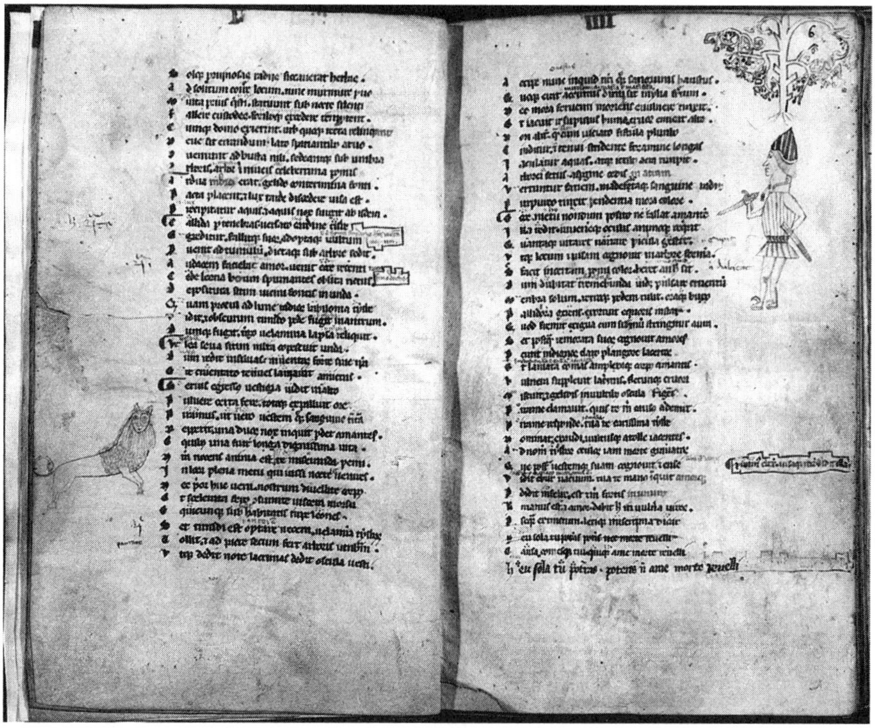

Figure 2.7. 13th-century, Ovid's *Metamorphoses*, BNM, Ms. 603, fols. 5v–6r.

Breviloquium. Although the overall aspect of the page has a certain graphical quality, the focus is on text, with an unusual amount of writing concentrated near the top margin. The resulting imbalance of text and blank space is clearly not a concern of the person or persons who created this page. And yet, the same branching that is a decorative motif in the first image (fig. 2.5) is, in the second, a mode of organizing knowledge into ever more precise units. And the juxtaposition of these two pages suggests that the branching of knowledge was itself understood as organic, natural, whereas for us, such outlines appear artificial and mechanical. Note, too, that on the student page (in the upper third), though not on the decorated page, some of the branches rejoin one another, grow together again, suggesting a principle of extreme interest for those of us who live in excessively analytic times such as the Middle Ages or our own.

The illuminated pages (figs. 2.3 and 2.5) are certainly remarkable, and they do indeed represent one significant variant of the medieval page. But they are by no means the norm. For every illustrated page like these, there are no doubt hundreds, perhaps thousands, with far cruder, ad hoc illustrations that function as readers' glosses rather than as a part of an original page design.

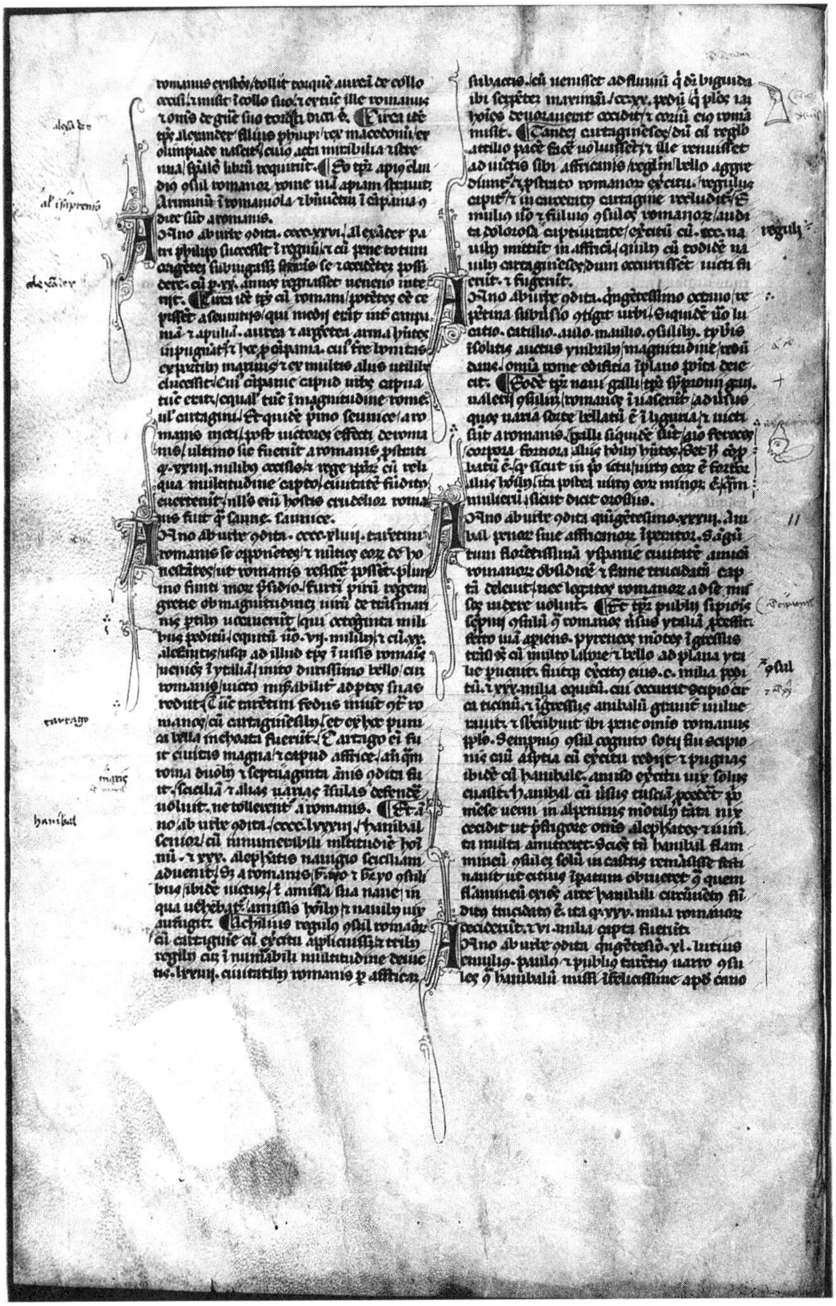

Figure 2.8. BNM, Ms. 10046, fol. 21v.

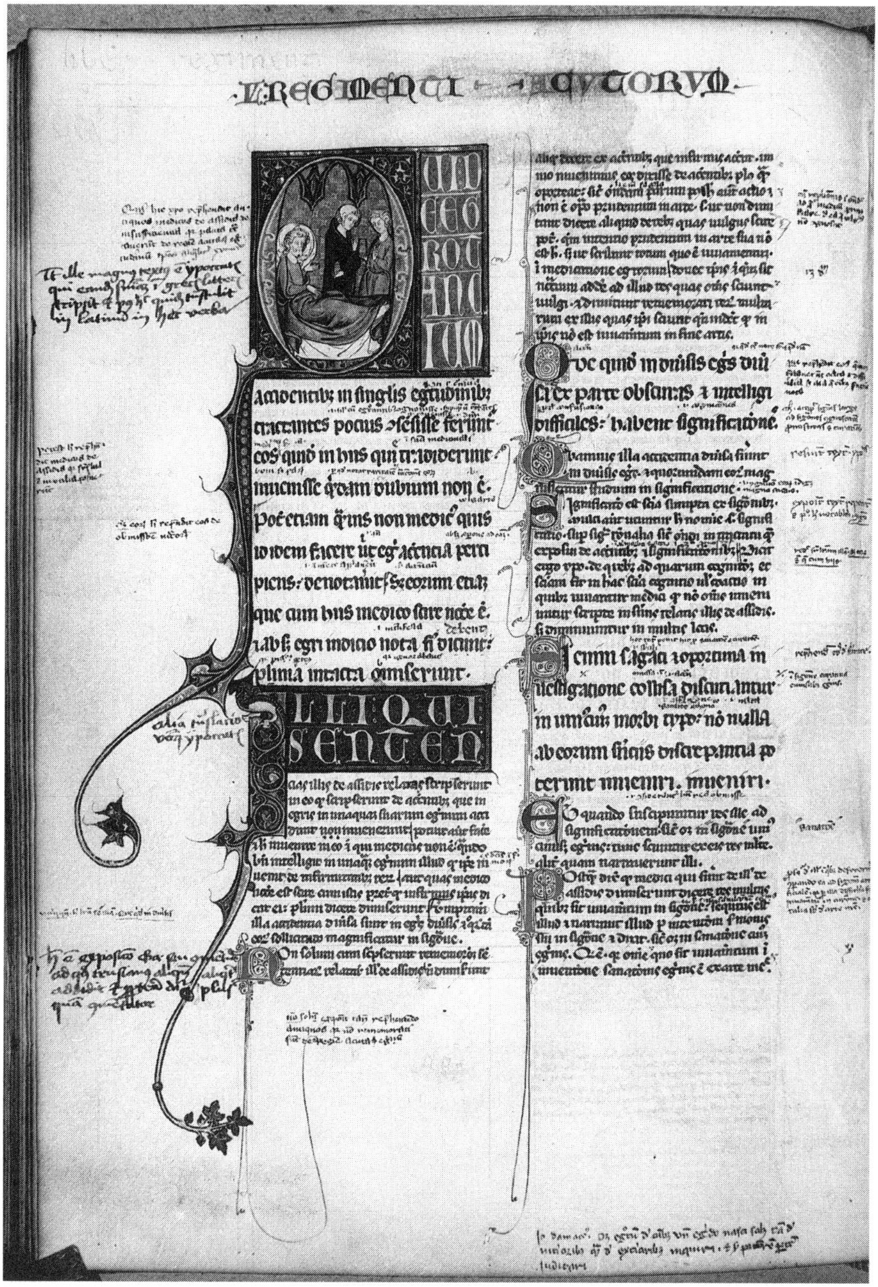

Figure 2.9. 13th-century, medical collection, Vienna, Österreichische Nationalbibliothek, Cod. 2315, fol. 100v. Bildarchiv, ÖNB Wien.

As we might expect, some of these visual glosses show a degree of artistic skill (see fig. 2.7). Others are simply doodles like those any of us might make (fig. 2.8).[12] We will not be able to say that we know the medieval page until we have done a thorough study, not just of manuscript illumination, but of the medieval sketch and doodle.

At the same time, we should realize that distinctions we might make between 'artistic pages' where the aesthetic beauty of the page dominates and 'text pages' where text and gloss dominate is not a clear cut one in many cases. Even pages where we might wish to go on about the aesthetic beauty of the page design are filled in later according to the need perceived at the moment of reading. Often readers seem to us to be oblivious to or even to destroy wantonly the aesthetic beauty of a page's design (fig. 2.9). In this page from a medical collection, in addition to the numerous marginal and interlinear glosses that, to our eye at least, disrupt the elegant balance of the underlying page design, one reader has written his gloss right across one of the decorative elements (lower left). Similar manuscripts may have been laid out with the specific intent of inviting subsequent glosses into their design, as when especially wide margins are left and spaces are ruled for glosses as part of manuscript production, seen in this Artistotle manuscript (fig. 2.10). Even these measures, however, do not protect the page from unruly readers whose annotations (bottom) run at an obviously unaesthetic angle to the other writing on the page.

Text as well as illustration can be used to control the spaces of the medieval page. In a manuscript of the first-century Valerius Maximus's *Factorum et dictorum memorabilium libri IX,* the gloss is shaped and modelled to keep pace with the text, at the same time defining shaped blank spaces (fig. 2.11). Together these elements seem almost to innoculate the page against readerly intervention, making this particular combination authoritative. At the opposite extreme, however, we find many medieval pages with nothing or nearly nothing on them. Figure 2.12 shows one of the front pages of the student miscellany we examined above. Here a student's ambitious plans to index the *sententiae* found in the manuscript seem to end with only a handful of entries recorded, leaving pages that are largely empty.[13] In fact, only one phrase (with one partial variant) appears: 'Lege relege nam poterit mora quod nequit hora' (Read and read again, for delay can accomplish what haste cannot). This is recorded once under 'L' for 'Lege' and again under 'M' for 'mora.' In the 'M' section 'hora' is also underlined, suggesting that there may have to be an entry under 'H' as well. Where does it end? Perhaps this index collapsed under the sheer complexity of the cross-referencing system the user had thought to implement.

Sometimes, however, it is not just an overly ambitious indexing plan that goes awry. Occasionally the plan of textual copying itself seems to crumble. These pages from the *De excidio Troiae* are mostly blank (fig. 2.13). The verso page begins: 'lena menelay uxor cu*m*.' The adjoining recto page begins in the

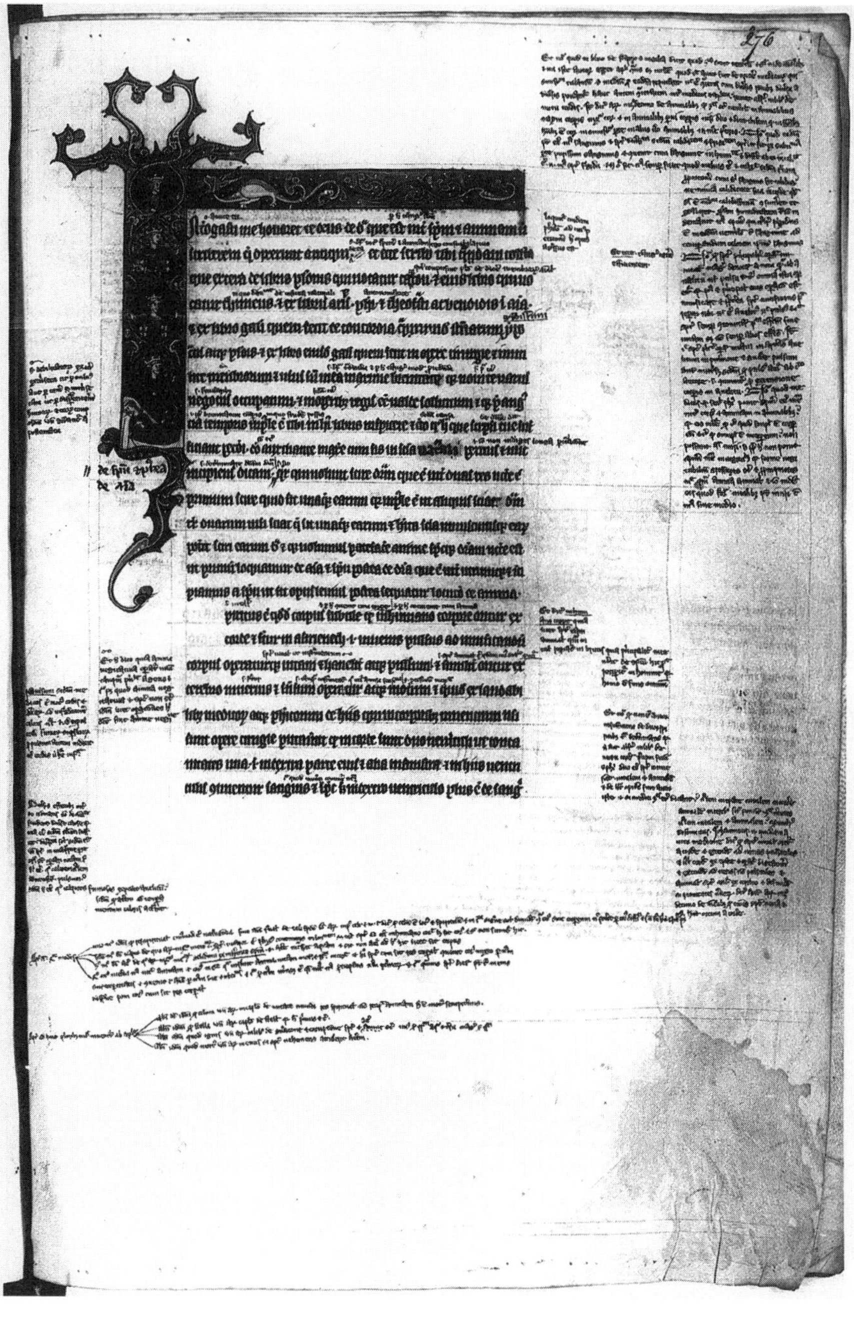

Figure 2.10. 13th-century, spurious and genuine works of Aristotle, Paris, Bibliothèque Nationale, Ms. lat. 12953, fol. 276r.

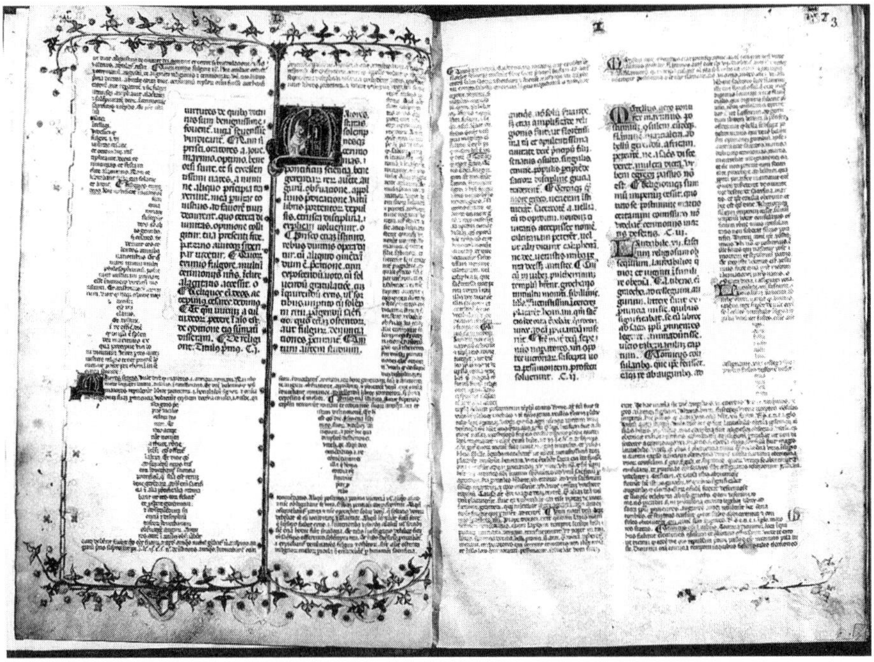

Figure 2.11. Valerius Maximus's *Factorum et dictorum memorabilium libri IX, BNM,* Ms. 7540, fols 2v–3r.

same way and apparently in the same hand. *Both* pages continue the preceding recto side (fol. 16r), which ends with the first two letters of Helen's name: 'At uero he ...' It is difficult to come up with a reason for this stutter step that leaves two pages almost blank, or for the fact that the fuller paragraph ends after a few lines with the message: 'nocte classem soluent de phano helenam eripiant. secum.' Even more mysterious is the single isolated letter 'm' on the verso side a third of the way down. One can imagine an ever less important 'menelaus,' perhaps, abandoned there alone.

In these blank pages we can perceive, perhaps more readily than in those more full of writing, the potential for movement, the essential incompleteness of the medieval page. In the give and take between text and gloss this perpetual supplementation becomes still more apparent, however. There are, in fact, a variety of negotiations going on within the manuscript page, systems of dialogue: blank space and text, text and gloss, scribe and reader, reader and later reader, centre and edge, inside and outside. Some of these systems appeal to us immediately, as in the manuscript of Valerius Maximus, in which the text was surrounded by a gloss (fig. 2.11). In this case, the gloss is

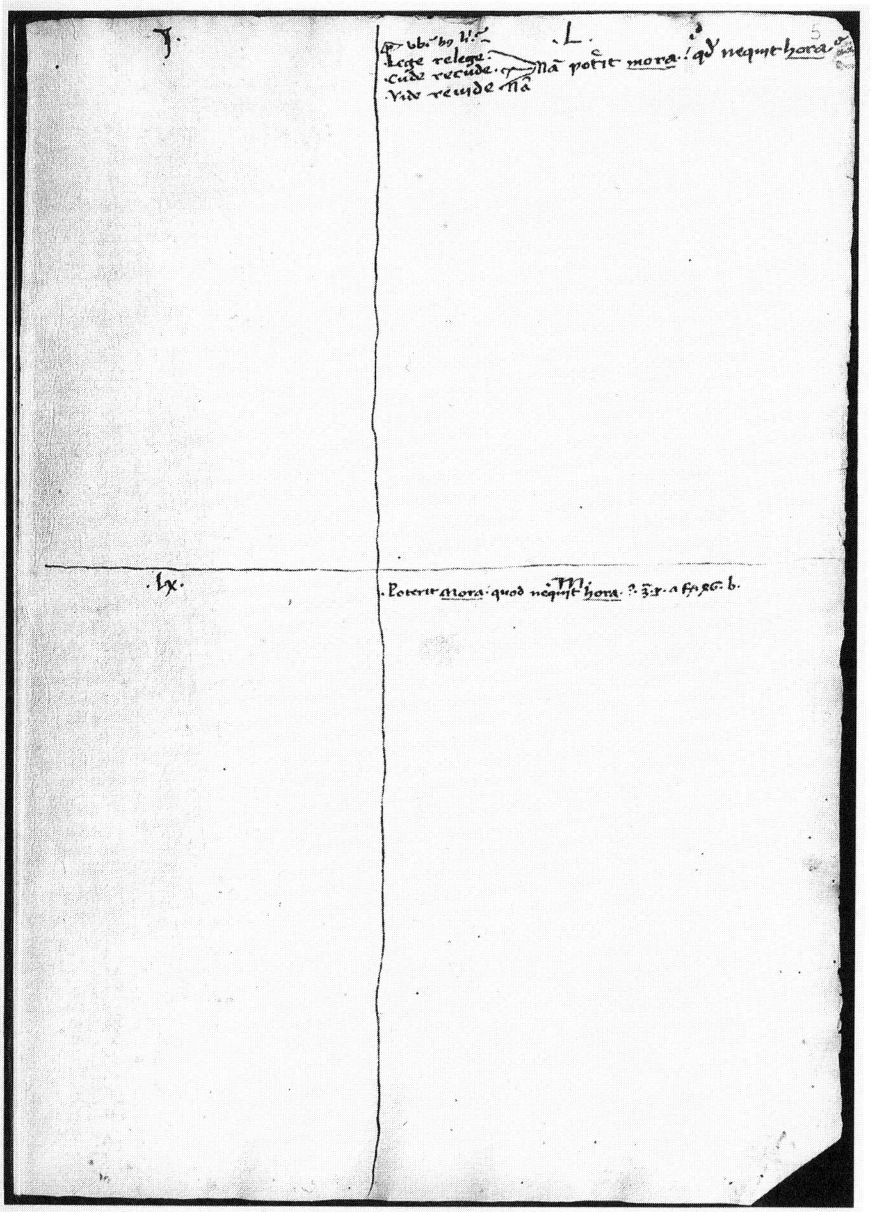

Figure 2.12. BNM, Ms. 9589, fol. [e]r.

Figure 2.13. *De excidio Troiae*, BNM, Ms. 10046, fol. 16v–17r.

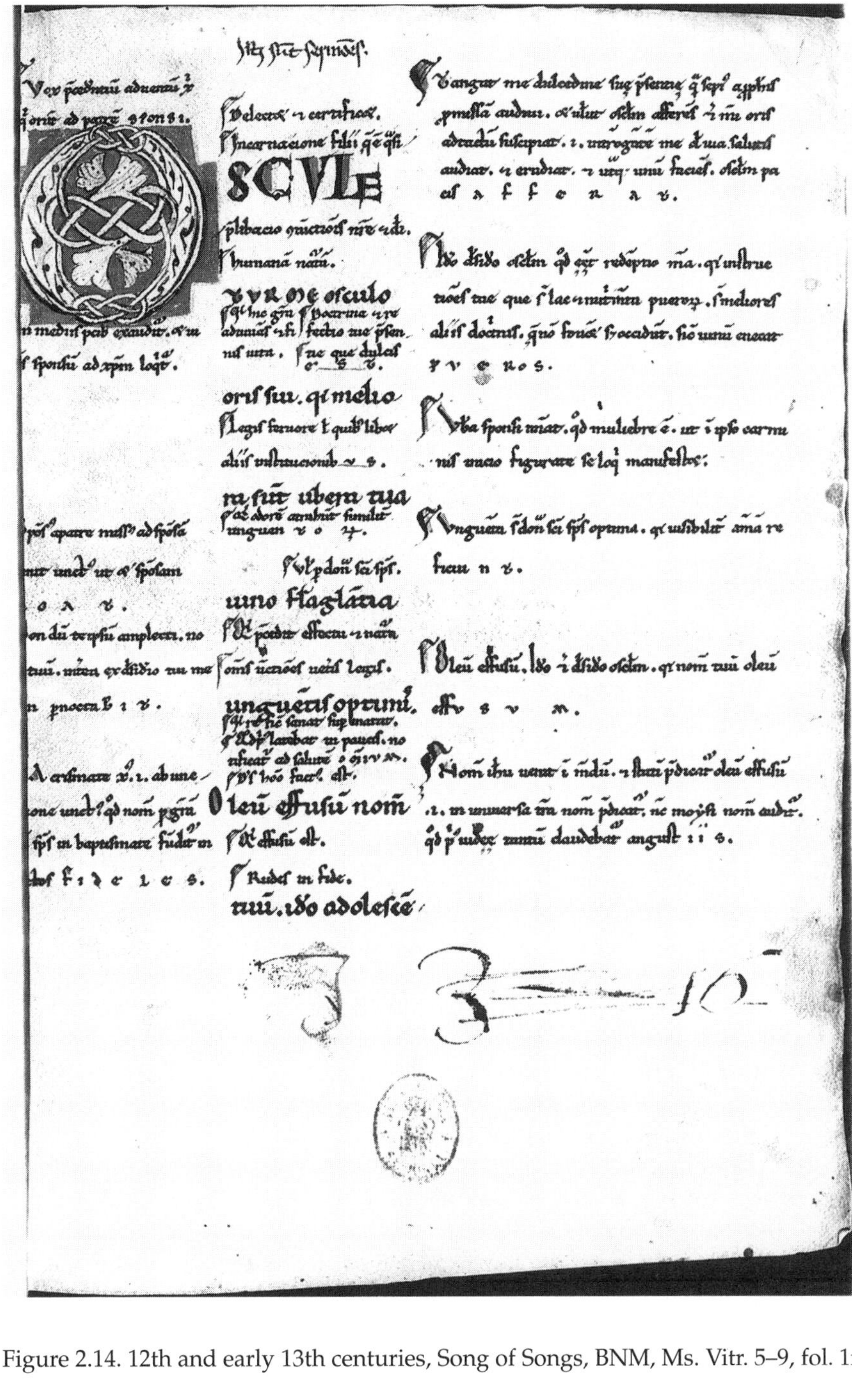

Figure 2.14. 12th and early 13th centuries, Song of Songs, BNM, Ms. Vitr. 5–9, fol. 1r.

so stylized, so ritualistic, that we might feel that the form of the interaction is more important than its content. All effort seems to be devoted to balancing the space of the text with that of the commentary, but at the same time, the text is clearly dominant: the commentary is laid out to keep pace with it, not vice versa. This is obviously a manuscript that took time and money to produce, not to mention a certain visual inventiveness on the part of the manuscript's designers.

Figure 2.14 shows a far more common interaction between text and gloss. In this elaborately laid-out copy of the Song of Songs, commentary dominates the conversation. The large letters of the biblical text and spacious layout appear to afford the text a good deal of respect, but the fact is that commentary is running the show: the spacing of the text serves the commentary, not vice versa. The text is there to explain the gloss. Earlier I referred to the centrifugal movement, from parchment to text to gloss to edge to world. In this page, we begin to see a compensatory centripetal movement, just as common, in which marginalia invade and often take over the central textual space itself.

Other dialogues are taking place here, however. At the very top, a later annotation changes the very genre of the biblical text: 'Isti su*n*t sermo*n*es.' This is rather puzzling: it is obvious that this complex textual layout could not possibly be delivered as an oral sermon in any coherent way. Perhaps the placement of this description over the centre column, which contains the biblical text is, in fact, a return to the centre, a way of extracting the core text, once again, from the glosses that surround it, a way to reemphasize its originary state as text and even as speech.[14]

This is the place to note, too, the numbers scrawled across the bottom of the page and then scratched out: 'J 3 – 16' (also fig. 2.14). This is apparently a call number (eighteenth or nineteenth century?) that was superseded, perhaps when the manuscript moved from the cathedral library in Toledo to the Biblioteca Nacional in Madrid. The page now also bears the institutional stamp of the Biblioteca Nacional. So we can trace here some fascinating, but by no means atypical, movements within the medieval page, from text to gloss and back again, from speech to text (and back), from sacred text to textbook, from sacred text to an object classified for display in the museum: 'Vitr. 5–9' indicates that this manuscript is displayed in a 'vitrina' or showcase, as a monument to the 'national' theatre of 'Spain.'[15]

In the previous two examples, the relation between text and gloss was more or less formal, a part of the manuscript design. Figure 2.15, from a thirteenth-century copy of Ovid's *Metamorphoses*, shows a different case, a far more common one: here the text itself was given the focus during the manuscript's production; the gloss is all added later, in and around the text, by a succession of readers, nearly overwhelming the text in the process.

To this point, I have been discussing 'the medieval page' as if it were a

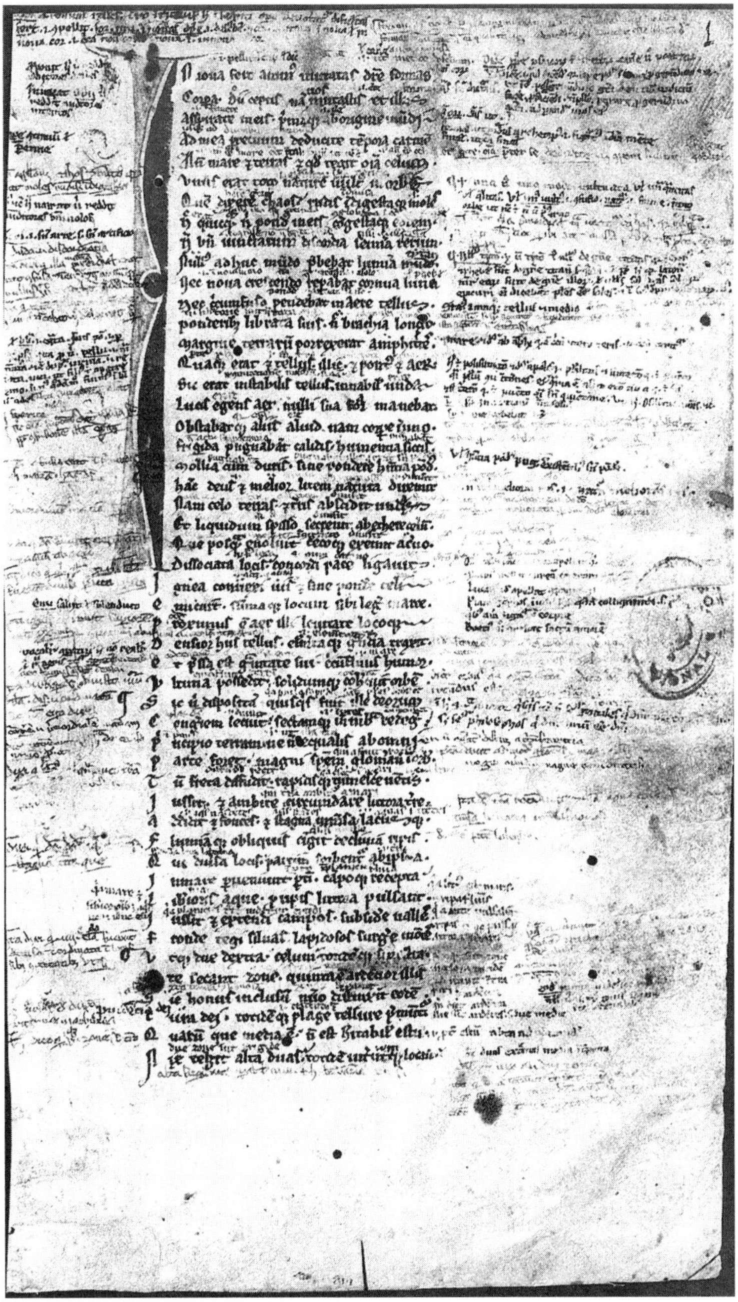

Figure 2.15. 13th century, Ovid's *Metamorphoses*, BNM, Ms. 3767, fol. 1r.

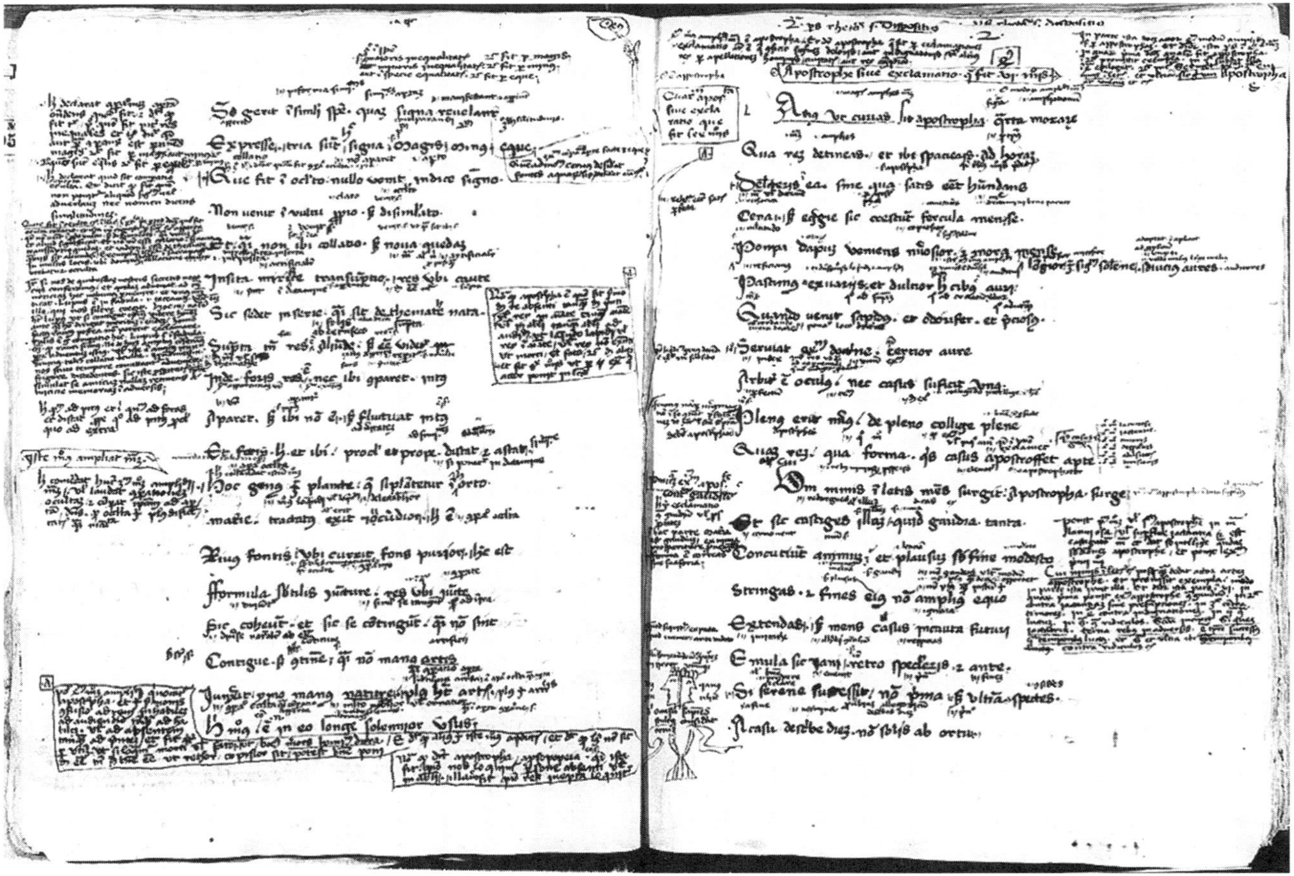

Figure 2.16. BNM, Ms. 9589, fols 7v–8r.

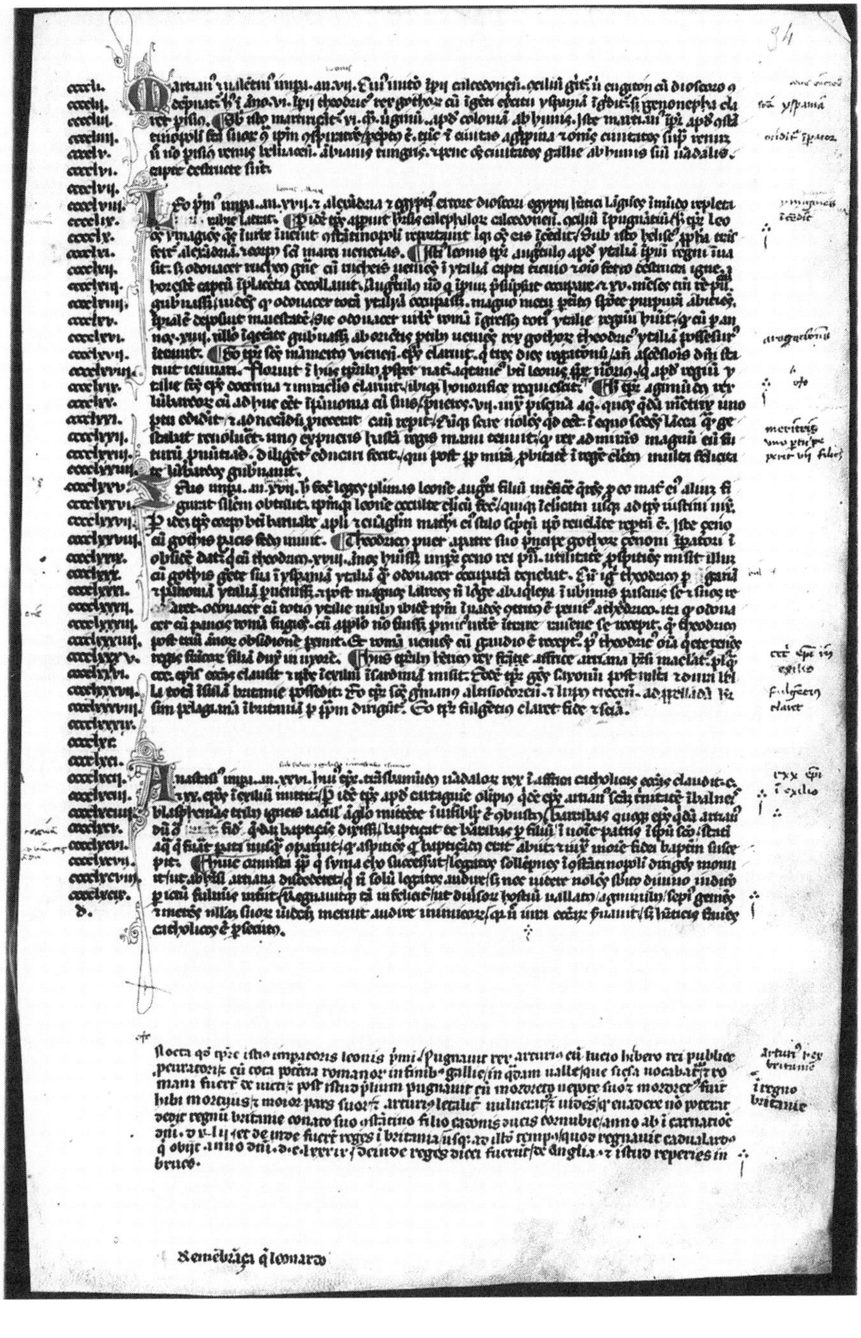

Figure 2.17. BNM, Ms. 10046, fol. 34r.

single two-dimensional entity that exists in contact with the world of the reader, but is mysteriously isolated from other pages. The neat proportions of 'the page' as we have been looking at it so far simply vanish when we turn over that first recto page. As we think of the future of the page, we need to recognize that, in practice, the overwhelming majority of pages, probably more than 99 per cent of them, in both handmade and printed books, are, in fact, *two* pages: a verso page on the left and a recto on the right. (This may be one of the chief differences between the new form of the page based on the computer screen and older forms: for the most part the web page or PDA-based reader allow you to see only one page at a time.) I do not think we can afford to ignore this fact as we seek to understand 'the page.' Even in isolation, the verso and recto pages have a different feel to them, permit different spatial arrangements. In the real world 'the page' is almost always accompanied by a failed mirror image of itself, a lost twin. In the codex form book, we are always aware, peripherally, of what is to come and what has come before, of the past and future of reading.

In another place, I have shown how our tendency to think in terms of 'works of literature' and to privilege the recto page, the page of beginnings (and to relegate to second place the sinister verso leaf) has led students of an important early Iberian poem, 'Razón de amor,' to ignore completely significant clues to the poem's meaning and context that appear on the verso page across from the recto opening of the poem.[16] Our own tendency to reproduce medieval pages in isolation can blind us to the fact that medieval readers operated under no such limitations. As we see in fig. 2.16, annotations could traverse the gutter between pages with no fear of falling off the edge of the world. An annotation on one page refers to text on the next, and vice versa. These pages can only be understood together and, together, they dramatize much of what is going on in the medieval world-page. At the very top, centre of the opening, a hand points to the word 'de*us*,' who seems to reign over this page. Near the bottom, as a sort of counterbalance the pagan figure of Janus appears, sitting, appropriately enough, near the gutter between the two pages. Janus, however, is now thoroughly secularized as a figure for discourse itself: 'Emula sic Jani retro speculeris et ante.' The Janus figure is a handy symbol for the issues I am discussing here: the medieval page does not just look at itself, is not self-contained. Rather, like the open pages here, the page looks both forward and backward, toward the preceding page and the following, toward the front of the codex and the back, toward past discourse and future discourse, toward the past and future of the page, even as it sits firmly in the present.

I want to focus for a bit now on the edge of the page, on the place where the paginal world's encounter with the world of the reader is often recorded. Figure 2.17 presents a rather interesting case where the 'textual' space is already fragmented. The majority of the text occupies the designated space in

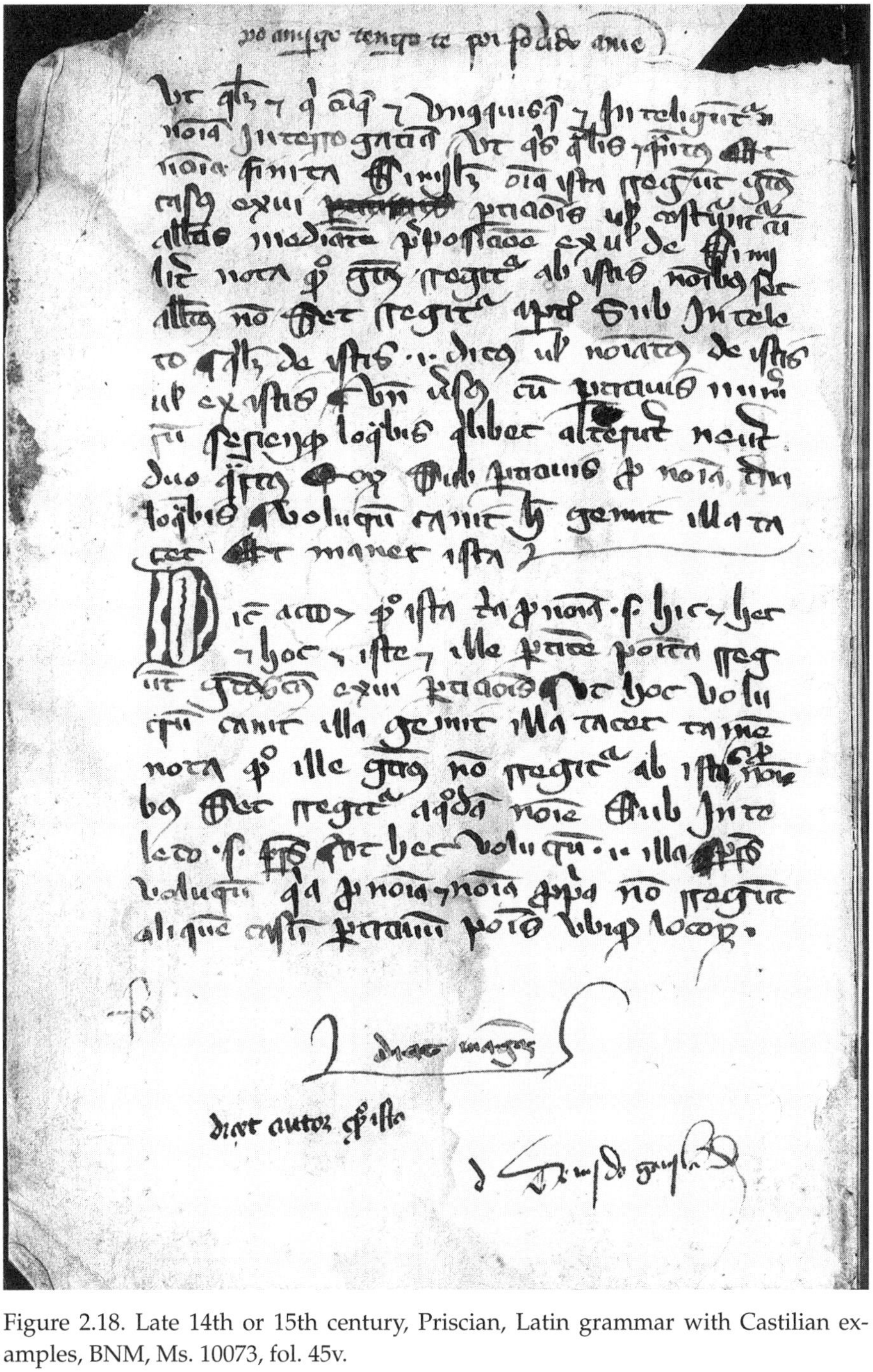

Figure 2.18. Late 14th or 15th century, Priscian, Latin grammar with Castilian examples, BNM, Ms. 10073, fol. 45v.

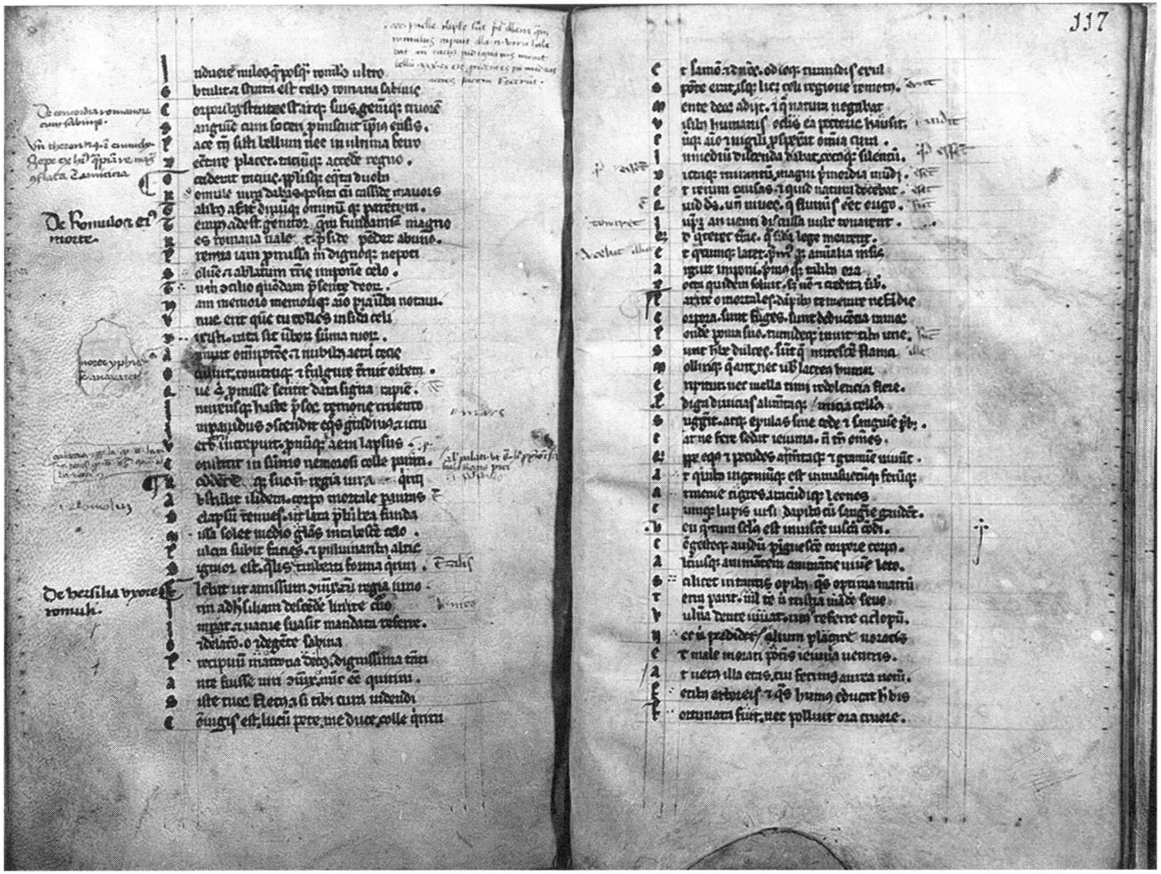

Figure 2.19. BNM, Ms. 603, fols 116v–117r.

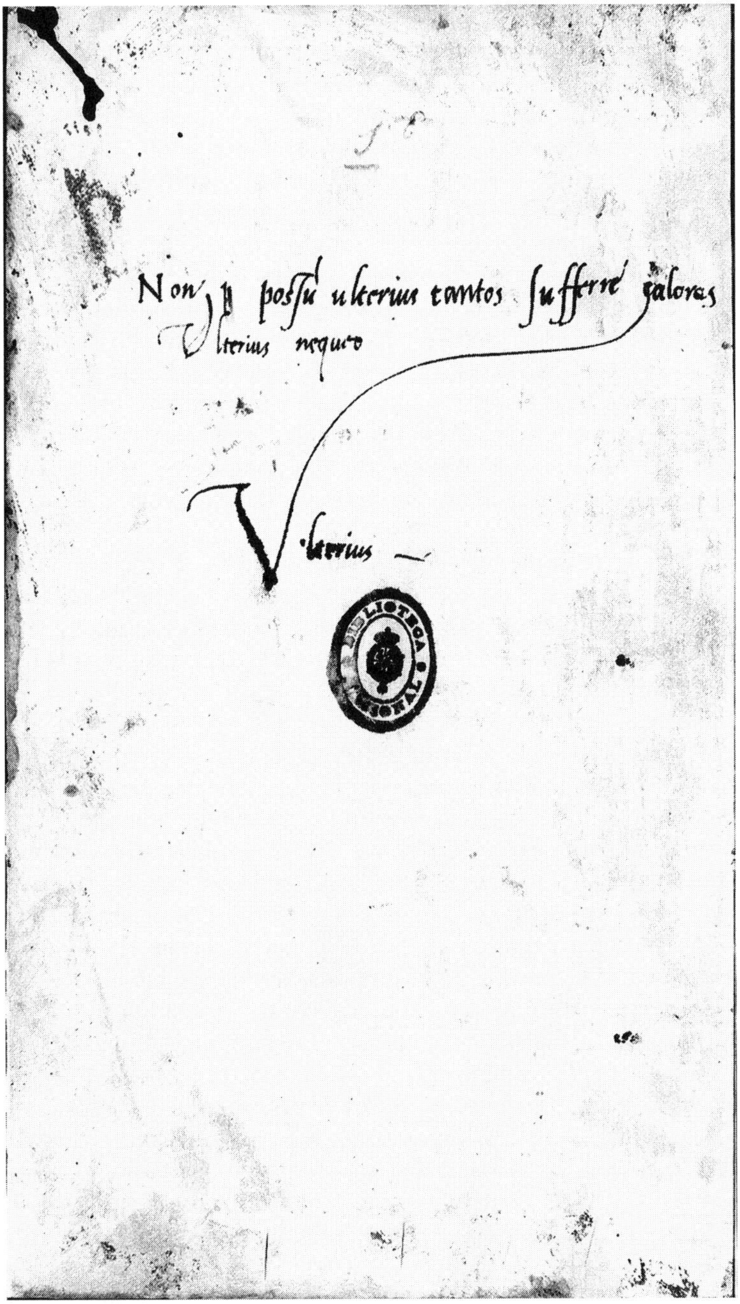

Figure 2.20. 13th and 15th centuries, works of Horace and excerpts from other authors, BNM, Ms. 10036, fol. 63v.

the centre of the page but, apparently because a portion of text was skipped in the copying, a second textual space is created below the main one, linked by a sign that refers to the spot at which the new text should be integrated (in the second paragraph above). Interestingly enough, this large island off the main continent of text refers to 'arturius rex britanie' (as another isle of gloss informs us). Still further at sea, near the edge of the world, is a note, not in the Latin of the text but in the vernacular: 'Reme*m*bra*n*ça q*ue* leonardo.' This seems to be an attempt by a reader (or perhaps the scribe himself) to record a personal memory of some sort. The memory of some thing that 'Leonardo' did (or is supposed to do?). It is a reader's or scribe's memory and life experience that is being 'glossed' here at the edges of this 'history.' Two worlds join at the edge. The act that sets out to record a memory, records, instead, an act of forgetting. And by placing this already broken memory here, the writer almost seems to be positioning it to assure that it will be more fully forgotten, for it is here at the very edge that words most easily disappear, through the rubbing of fingers, through the exposure to the elements, through trimming.

A different sort of 'remembrança' is recorded in fig. 2.18, a Latin grammar with Castilian examples. In the upper margin of the page, someone has written: 'yo amigo tengo te por fodido amen' (I, friend, consider you to be fucked up. Amen). This endearing sentiment is placed in a position not quite as precarious as the 'memory that Leonardo.' It is difficult to determine just who the object of this graffito is: a friend who will also be using this grammar text? If so, it is perhaps an indication that adolescent boys have not changed much in the past 600 years. The faint letters 'fo' which appear in the bottom margin suggest that the scribbler was moved to reiterate the most important part of the sentiment expressed above. But one may also wonder if this evaluation might not be aimed at the Latin grammar text itself. Most of us may well have entertained such thoughts concerning our own Latin lessons. Or perhaps the 'amigo' was the author responsible for this grammar.

In an anticipation, perhaps, of postmodern architecture the page shown in fig. 2.19 exposes its own structural elements: the prickings and rulings are quite reminiscent of the poster by del Canto. Here, probably as the result of overzealous scraping during the preparation of the parchment, the page once again lays bare the processes of its own production. But this page also dramatizes another way in which the so-called material support and manuscript text come together to defy the apparent two-dimensional, sequential, nature of the medium. Here the organic nature of the writing medium is brought home to us: a hole in the parchment allows us to peer through at the past of reading (even as it had previously, when the hole was on the recto side, allowed us to peek ahead). The medieval 'page,' then, challenges by its very nature the conventions, such as two-dimensionality, we might assume are givens of the page.

Our tendency is to see these objects as timeless, as situated in an abstract or static time in which the text is eternal and the page exists at once as venerated object and expendable textual 'support.' We forget too easily that pages live, like us, in a number of moments: moments of distraction when the scraping knife cuts too deep, moments when a given mark is made, perhaps by accident, moments when ink spills on the page, a leaf tears, a worm makes it all the way through. Some of the most interesting moments are moments of reading, moments in which we glimpse not just the scribe's or the reader's inner thoughts but also his physical surroundings. A scribal colophon reads: 'Scriptum per me Leonardum Montalduno Ianuensem a.d. 1462 die 8 decemb. mensis cum calor me multum ymo intense infestaret et pene calamum in manibus tenere poteram.'[17]

The flyleaf, designed to seal the text off from the elements, is in fact one of the prime places in which text meets world. On the flyleaf shown in fig. 2.20 we find a rather similar comment: 'Non p possu*m* ulterius tantos sufferre calores / Vlterius nequeo / Vlterius' (I can go no further because of the heat / I can no further / further). This is no doubt a reader's note rather than a scribal one, and it is difficult to know if this is simply a *probatio pennae,* a citation from one of the works included in this manuscript, a bit of grammar practice (*non possum* vs. *nequeo*), or a genuine observation on the state of weather and body by the reader. Perhaps it is all of these, and that is really the point: the medieval page occupies simultaneously a physical role (flyleaf), a textual role, and personal and temporal roles, necessarily separated at times by decades or centuries, but nonetheless quite concrete (the experiences of the individual scribes or readers).

I would like to close by renouncing the very banner under which I have been sailing thus far: the banner of 'the medieval page.' There are, in fact, no medieval pages. Whatever medieval pages there may have been were all destroyed in the Middle Ages. The pages discussed here are, in fact, twenty-first-century pages. There is absolutely nothing to keep me from writing on one of these pages, from adding my own gloss, nothing beyond a disinclination to experience life in a Spanish jail. Our reasons for using the term 'medieval page,' of course, are that these objects were *produced* in the Middle Ages, *originate* in the Middle Ages, and are therefore 'medieval.' We have chosen to privilege 'origins' over their very real 'presence' to us. We have marked them with their origins and then used these marks to keep them within the institutionalized spaces of the library and of academic discourse. In a move typical of all colonizations, we have denied the coevalness of the manuscript page.[18]

What unquestioned assumptions permit us to deny presence and to consider the evidence of the page's passage through time – trimmings, rebindings, water damage, fire damage, neglect, deliberate mutilation, postmedieval annotations, and so on – as accidents that have befallen an *essentially* medieval object, as erasures *of* the object, as impediments, in short, to our own work as medievalists? Our very work within the discipline of medieval studies imposes on us the need to view our object as synchronic, rather than diachronic, or, in the best of cases, as diachronic across a narrow range of decades or centuries within the boundaries of the Middle Ages, but as somehow intellectually inert thereafter. There are plenty of sixteenth-, seventeenth-, and eighteenth-century notes in medieval manuscripts that are unlikely ever to be seen by anyone simply because medievalists do not look at postmedieval notes in manuscripts and students of later centuries do not look at medieval manuscripts. What would happen if we ceased to deny the coevalness of the page originating in the Middle Ages and removed from it that anthropological gaze which always sees it in another, more primitive time? It comes back to the very question implicit in this book: how do we grant a future to the page?

NOTES

1 http://www.usask.ca/english/architectures/intro.html.

2 For a background to these assertions, see my 'Decolonizing the Middle Ages,' *Journal of Medieval and Early Modern Studies* 30. 3 (2000): 431–8.

3 On the theme of the 'museum,' see Eugenio Donato, 'The Museum's Furnace: Notes Toward a Contextual Reading of *Bouvard and Pécuchet*,' in *Textual Strategies: Perspectives in Post-Structuralist Criticism*, ed. Josue V. Harari (Ithaca: Cornell University Press, 1979), 213-38.

4 Such a perspective haunts the erudite and important book by Paul Saenger, *Space Between Words* (Stanford, CA: Stanford University Press, 1997). Saenger is to be congratulated for exposing yet one more area in which scholars, in their haste to turn manuscripts into typing, have looked through manuscripts rather than at manuscripts. But Saenger often seems far too eager to array the supposed evolution from oral to silent reading along the grid of the master narrative of the 'progress' of Western civilization; for example, the last sentence in the book states: 'This enhanced privacy [afforded by silent reading] represented the consummation of the development of separated writing and constituted a crucial aspect of the modern world' (276).

5 Jacques Derrida, *Of Grammatology*, trans. Gayatri Chakravorty Spivak (Baltimore: Johns Hopkins University Press, 1976), especially Parts I and II, 'Writing before the Letter' and 'Nature, Culture, Writing.' For an exploration of some challenges posed by manuscript culture to Derrida's concept of the supplement, see my 'That Bothersome Residue: Toward a Theory of the Physical Text,' in *Vox Intexta: Orality and Textuality in the Middle Ages*, ed. A.N. Doane and Carol Braun Pasternak (Madison: University of Wisconsin Press, 1991), 246–59.

6 This is most obviously illustrated by the unfinished nature of many familiar

manuscripts: the plan of the production of the manuscript has not been completed. Illuminations or rubrics or musical notation may have been allowed for in the design of the manuscript but were never filled in. It is often instructive to turn through the pages of a manuscript from the end to the beginning. In this order, using the manuscript as a sort of flip book, we can see the manuscript under construction, as the text is first laid down, then the gilded bosses are applied, and finally the illuminations are filled in as we proceed from back to front. This is a fairly typical situation: text tends to be the portion of a manuscript design most likely to be completed, then glosses, then the various procedures of decoration and illumination. In the case of music manuscripts, staves may or may not appear in all indicated places and notation may or may not appear where there are staves. The successive procedures used to produce the manuscript and the various factors which may prevent all of them from being carried out in their entirety leave us, rather frequently, a manuscript which is still 'under construction.' We need to generalize this idea of manuscript pages still in process, however, to *all* medieval pages, to realize by the very nature of the process and the cultures involved that they are all unfinished.

7 Along with art historians goes the entire cultural apparatus devoted to the commercial exploitation of historical artefacts: art auction houses, museums (which generally prefer pages bearing illuminations), small dealers who set up at academic conferences to sell illuminated initials sliced from manuscript pages.

8 One other avenue of colonization can be mentioned only in passing: our tendency to mistake the Western European medieval/modern page for *the* page. Leaving aside the question of whether scrolls, too, can have pages, we are still faced with a host of pages from non-Western cultures, which violate most of the rules we might wish to think of as fundamental to the page. In Southeast Asia, for example, the use of the palm leaf as a support for writing leads to pages which are quite narrow and elongated and which have rounded edges. These pages clearly violate the Fibonacci progression often invoked to explain the elegance of the rectangular and vertical orientation of the Western page. The Southeast Asian palm-leaf, or *pothi,* page form for Buddhist texts becomes naturalized and is extended to other materials. An awareness of these differences allows us to see how closely the shape of the page may be linked to belief systems, as when the use of cow skin may be rejected for religious reasons. 'Old' is another quality we may unconsciously assign to handwritten pages, especially those found in codexes. Because of the use of such fragile material as palm leaves and due to humid conditions, very few, if any, Southeast Asian manuscripts survive from, say, the thirteenth and fourteenth centuries of the Christian era. Manuscripts in this region continue to be made, and remade, until quite recently. See Richard Salomon, *Ancient Buddhist Scrolls from Gandhâra: The British Library Kharosthî Fragments* (Seattle: University of Washington Press, 1999), 8–9 and 101–2. See also now the important collection edited by Judith T. Zeitlin and

Lydia H. Liu, *Writing and Materiality in China: Essays in Honor of Patrick Hanan* (Cambridge, MA: Harvard University Press, 2003).

9 Charles B. Faulhaber, The Date of Stanzas 553 and 1450 of the *Libro de buen amor* in MS 9589 of the Biblioteca Nacional, Madrid," *Romance Philology* 28 (1974): 31–4.

10 Assuming that such anathemata are reasonably familiar to readers, I do not provide medieval examples below. An amusing introduction to anathemata is Marc Drogin, *Anathema!: Medieval Scribes and the History of Book Curses* (Totowa, NJ: Schram, 1983).

11 For a partial description of these leaves, see *BETA: Bibliografía Española de Textos Antiguos,* comp. Charles B. Faulhaber et al., http//sunsite.berkeley.edu/Philobiblon/phhmbe.html, Vol. 2003, n. 2 (April 2003), manid 1184 (http//sunsite.berkeley.edu/Philobiblon/BETA/1184.html), notes following list of previous owners.

12 For an explanation of the relationship of this doodle to the text, see my *The Ethics of Reading in Manuscript Culture: Glossing the 'Libro de buen amor'* (Princeton, NJ: Princeton University Press, 1994), 40.

13 On the beginnings of medieval indexing schemes, see Richard H. Rouse and Mary A. Rouse, 'La naissance des index,' in *Histoire de l'édition française,* ed. H.J. Martin and R. Chartier (Paris: Promodis, 1982), 1:77-85.

14 It is also possible that the text-gloss combination was being pointed out as a *source* for sermons, as many commentaries were, in fact, destined to aid preachers in creating sermons. See the comments concerning the use of Psalter commentaries from around the same date as this manuscript for sermon making: A.J. Minnis, *The Medieval Theory of Authorship* (London: Scolar Press, 1984), 73n6.

15 The manuscript bears near the end the 'Auto de los Reyes Magos,' the earliest surviving work of theatre in a language that resembles Castilian, the language which, in the eighteenth century, became the sole official language of the Spanish state (until some other Peninsular languages – Catalan, Galician, Basque – were granted coofficial status in the late 1970s). For a sensible analysis of the linguistic issues, see Roger Wright, *A Sociophilological Study of Late Latin* (Utrecht: Brepols, 2003). For the place of this vernacular work in the physical context of this manuscript see my *Ethics of Reading*, 43–7.

16 Dagenais, *Ethics*, 47–50. This poem is the subject of a book project in progress.

17 Benedictine Abbey, Saint-Benoît de Port-Valais (Bouveret, Switzerland), *Colophons de manuscrits occidentaux des origines au XVIe siècle,* 6 vols (Fribourg: Editions Universitaires, 1965–82), no. 12483.

18 The locus classicus on this is, of course, Johannes Fabian, *Time and the Other: How Anthropology Makes its Object* (New York: Columbia University Press,1983). Fabian defines denial of coevalness as '*a persistent and systematic tendency to place the referent(s) of anthropology in a Time other than the present of the producer of anthropological discourse*' (31; italics are author's). Substituting 'codicology/-gical' for 'anthropology/-gical' provides a quick take on my point here.

3 Back to the Future – Littorally: Annotating the Historical Page

William W.E. Slights

For years I have been fascinated by the marginal notes printed along the edges of old books, pithy and punchy remarks like 'Here an excellent simile,' 'K. Richard in vtter despaire,' and 'No, no, no not on pain of eternal damnation.' There is no ignoring these in-your-face annotations that dot the littoral boundary of early modern texts. They are the work of authors and printers hell-bent on *managing* readers – telling us what to believe, what to remember, what else to read. The only way to rid ourselves of these meddling marginalists is to reedit the texts, demoting their interventions to the bottom of the page or the end of the book, or else banishing them altogether. But is this wise? By suppressing these marginal voices, as most modern editions do, do we not eradicate the most distinctive feature of the early page and wilfully ignore the fullest stage directions we have for the performance of reading in the first two centuries of mass-produced texts? Moreover, we may be able to project more accurately the shape of future pages by analysing past ones, not in order to imitate them slavishly but to redirect their shaping principles into the creation of electronic as well as print pages with multiple centres and much more elastic littoral regions.

The body of marginal material in the early modern period is enormous. At a conservative estimate, more than half of the books printed in English between 1525 and 1675 carry marginalia of some kind, and I am speaking only of printed sidenotes, not of handwritten marks.[1] There was nothing particularly new about marginating texts, a habit that had its roots in ancient writing cultures and reached its apogee in the monasteries and secular scriptoria of Western Europe and England between the twelfth and fourteenth centuries. During this period, marginalia lent authority to texts, but that authority eventually came under scrutiny in the case of both secular and sacred texts. Writers of the sixteenth and seventeenth centuries refined their theories of the annotated margin in epistles to the reader, in printers' manuals, and even in sermons. One indicator of the energy that went into conceptualizing the margins is the array of metaphors used to describe their contents. Sidenotes were spoken of as lamps to illuminate the text, as blemishes on the skin of the text, as crutches to support its faltering arguments, as lumbering ships that smash into its docking points, and as maps that could be used to navigate its terrain and to patrol its boundaries. The notion of a textual environment marked at its boundaries by a kind of territorial urination emphasizes gestures of production and exclusion. Other prevalent metaphors such as the text-as-edifice likewise stress textual production rather than textual consumption. In a 1625 sermon John Donne defines 'context' as 'the situation, the prospect, how it [the text] stands, how it is butted, how it is bounded; to what it relates, with what it is connected.'[2] Although there are possibilities in this architectural model for intertextual prospects, it is basically constricted by the butting and bounding, the edging and hedging functions of such textual apparatus as marginalia. These are closer to the protocols of authorship than of reading. Donne's is not a paradigm of the reader's freedom in creating meaning at the borders of the text. It is really not until the late twentieth century that freeing readers to exercise their options as joint makers of the text was clearly articulated as a desirable goal.[3] Moving along a continuum of liberationist rhetoric brings us eventually to Gérard Genette's notion of 'paratext' (the extratextual surround that includes marginal annotations, running titles, epilogues, and so forth), which Genette calls 'the thresholds of textuality.'[4] Readers can enter or leave the textual edifice at will across these thresholds. Finally, we come to the more extravagant claims being made today for a digital technology that, we are told, will free us all from the prison of the page to roam in the byways of hypertext.[5] Jacques Derrida threw us a huge curve when he declared that text is margin, and margin is text. With a single stroke, he erased the boundaries that authors (whoever *they* may have been) and printers had been patrolling for centuries. The move seemed to launch us into a margin-less, unbounded future, one hastened along by the development of electro-text environments. Before investigating these 'progressive' and futuristic claims for the power of the page, though, we will do well to consider what the marginators of past pages actually attempted and achieved.

A Short History of Annotation: From Manuscript to Print, From Shoulder Note to Footnote

From the earliest manuscript traditions right through the print productions of the early modern period, marginalia brought the quality of permeability to the page. Whereas decorative borders and pristine white space defined the outer limits of a text, illustrations and annotations created leakage, both into and out of the centred text. Consider a page from a fourteenth-century English Cluniac Psalter (fig. 3.1). The image in the historiated capital 'C'

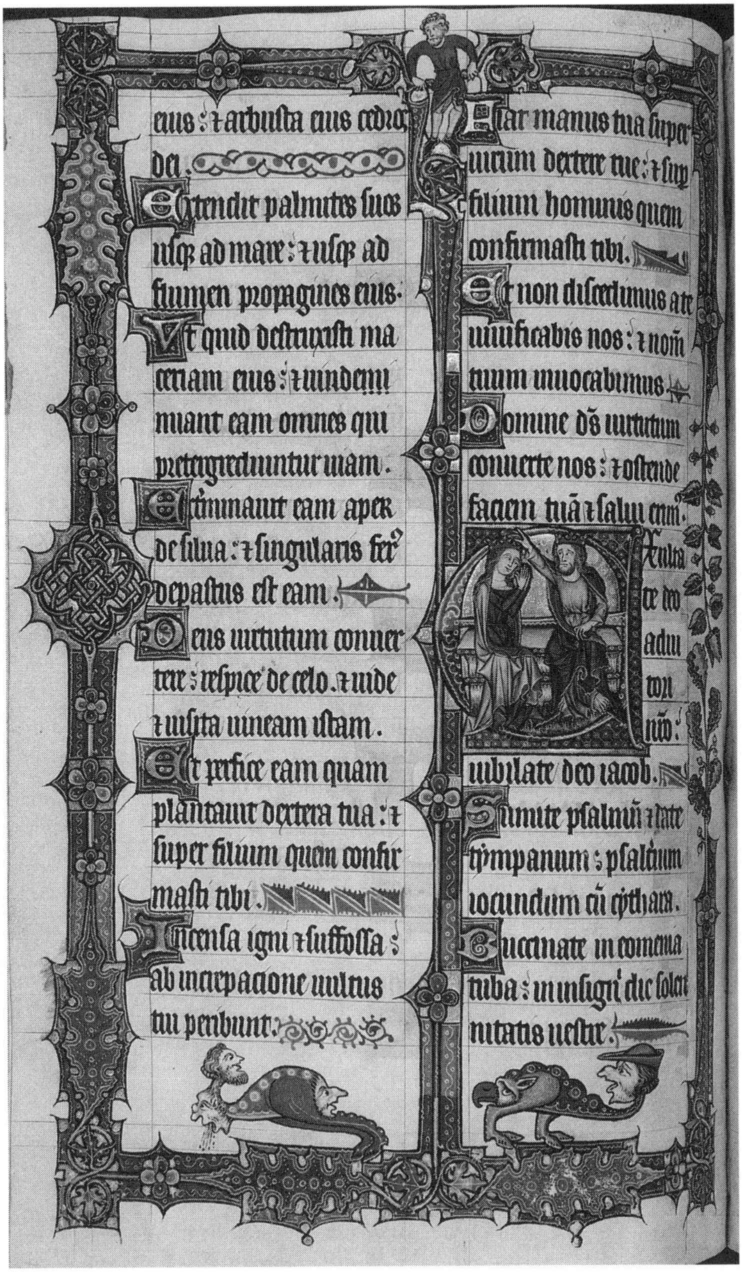

Figure 3.1. English Cluniac Psalter (Thetford Priory?). 14th century.

depicts the coronation of the Virgin. It adds wonderfully to the visual pleasures of the text and provides an attractive finding device. More than that, it imports into a psalm about joyful singing – this is the beginning of Psalm 80 – a specific occasion for song, a divine act of queen making. While the figures at the bottom of each column of text serve to fill a blank space, they also carry the joyous psalm out into the world of festival entertainers and off into the reader's most bizarre fantasies. At the left, a sort of acrobatic, back-bending jester sports two other faces on the tip of his cap, the lower one, having overindulged in the festivities, vomiting. At the right, the handsomely capped, pointy-chinned, bird-beaked figure is mocked by his horizontal avian body, cloven hooves, and prominently beaked nether head. As Andrew Taylor has argued in connection with the roughly contemporary Smithfield Decretals, such illustrations help to bridge the gap between earnestly glossed sacred texts and the Bakhtinian world of carnival.[6] Far from fixing readers' perceptions of text, the management schemes of scribes and, later, printers – their illustrations, marginations, rubrications, and the like – made texts portable into the fluid world beyond the page.

My point about the permeability of textual boundaries becomes more compelling, I think, when we include supplementary marginal text as well as images, as in the case of an annotated page from John Dee's 1577 treatise called *General and Rare Memorials Pertayning to the Perfect Arte of Navigation* (fig. 3.2). Dee's marginalia serve to star (*), to number (2.), to point out (☞), and otherwise to highlight important turns ('A Maister Key') in his argument for the creation of a 'Pety-Navy-Royal'; they cite proverbial sources ('*Principium* ...'); they trumpet forth stirring sentiments ('The marueilous Priuledge of the Brytish Impire'); they fend off inadequate alternatives ('Fisherboates onely, could neuer bring to pas ...'); and they urge Queen Elizabeth's political counsellors to take immediate action ('Presently') on his coastal protection scheme. We know a good deal about the production and distribution of this particular annotated book.[7] Dee, who had been intimately connected with England's most influential navigators and explorers in the mid-1570s, wrote his 'plat politicall' urging the creation of a large coastguard force, hired the master printer John Daye to produce a few copies – perhaps as few as fifty – and asked his friend Sir Christopher Hatton to distribute them to the decision makers closest to the queen. These men required a clear executive summary that would lift Dee's proposal off the printed page and place it immediately into the political arena. This was the function of his subtly crafted marginalia.

Though less precisely targeted at a small reading audience, the marginalia in the pseudo-Chaucerian *Plough-mans Tale* (1606) offer the reader alternative but still doctrinally coercive readings of the text (fig. 3.3). The Antichrist alluded to in the third stanza of the poem's second part, we are informed, could be either Christ's adversary ('against Christ') or his substitute ('insteed of Christ'). In either event, the ultra-Protestant glossator has made his iden-

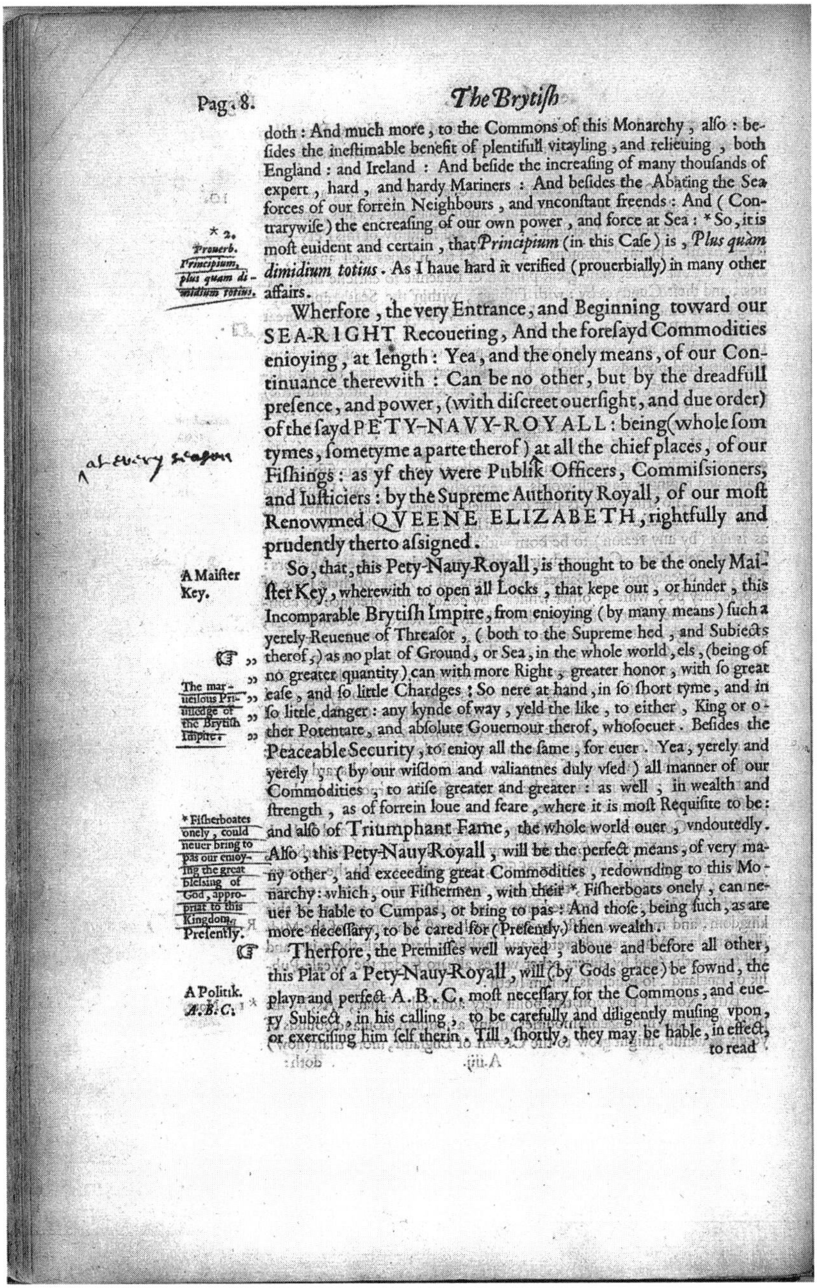

Pag. 8. *The Brytish*

doth : And much more, to the Commons of this Monarchy, alſo : beſides the ineſtimable benefit of plentifull vitayling, and relieuing, both England : and Ireland : And beſide the increaſing of many thouſands of expert, hard, and hardy Mariners : And beſides the Abating the Sea forces of our forrein Neighbours, and vnconſtant freends : And (Contrarywiſe) the encreaſing of our own power, and force at Sea : * So, it is moſt euident and certain, that *Principium* (in this Caſe) is, *Plus quàm dimidium totius*. As I haue hard it verified (prouerbially) in many other affairs.

** 2. Prouerb. Principium, plus quam dimidium totius.*

Wherfore, the very Entrance, and Beginning toward our SEA-RIGHT Recouering, And the foreſayd Commodities enioying, at length : Yea, and the onely means, of our Continuance therewith : Can be no other, but by the dreadfull preſence, and power, (with diſcreet ouerſight, and due order) of the ſayd PETY-NAVY-ROYALL : being (whole ſom tymes, ſometyme a parte therof) at all the chief places, of our Fiſhings : as yf they were Publik Officers, Commiſsioners, and Iuſticiers : by the Supreme Authority Royall, of our moſt Renowmed QVEENE ELIZABETH, rightfully and prudently therto aſsigned.

A Maiſter Key.

So, that, this Pety-Nauy-Royall, is thought to be the onely Maiſter Key, wherewith to open all Locks, that kepe out, or hinder, this Incomparable Brytiſh Impire, from enioying (by many means) ſuch a yerely Reuenue of Threaſor, (both to the Supreme hed, and Subiects therof,) as no plat of Ground, or Sea, in the whole world, els, (being of no greater quantity) can with more Right, greater honor, with ſo great eaſe, and ſo little Chardges ; So nere at hand, in ſo ſhort tyme, and in ſo little danger : any kynde of way, yeld the like, to either, King or other Potentate, and abſolute Gouernour therof, whoſoeuer. Beſides the Peaceable Security, to enioy all the ſame, for euer. Yea, yerely and yerely, (by our wiſdom and valiantnes duly vſed) all manner of our Commodities, to ariſe greater and greater : as well, in wealth and ſtrength, as of forrein loue and feare, where it is moſt Requiſite to be : and alſo of Triumphant Fame, the whole world ouer, vndoutedly.

The marueilous Priuilege of the Brytiſh Impire.

Alſo, this Pety-Nauy-Royall, will be the perfect means, of very many other, and exceeding great Commodities, redownding to this Monarchy : which, our Fiſhermen, with their * Fiſherboats onely, can neuer be hable to Cumpas, or bring to pas : And thoſe, being ſuch, as are more neceſſary, to be cared for (Preſently.) then wealth.

* Fiſherboates onely, could neuer bring to pas our enioying the great bleſsing of God, appropriat to this Kingdom, Preſently.

Therfore, the Premiſſes well wayed, aboue and before all other, this Plat of a Pety-Nauy-Royall, will (by Gods grace) be fownd, the playn and perfect A. B. C. moſt neceſſary for the Commons, and euery Subiect, in his calling, to be carefully and diligently muſing vpon, or exerciſing him ſelf therin, Till, ſhortly, they may be hable, in effect, to read

A Politik. *A. B. C.*

Figure 3.2. John Dee, *General and Rare Memorials* (London: John Daye, 1577), 8. RB 82497, Huntington Library, San Marino, CA.

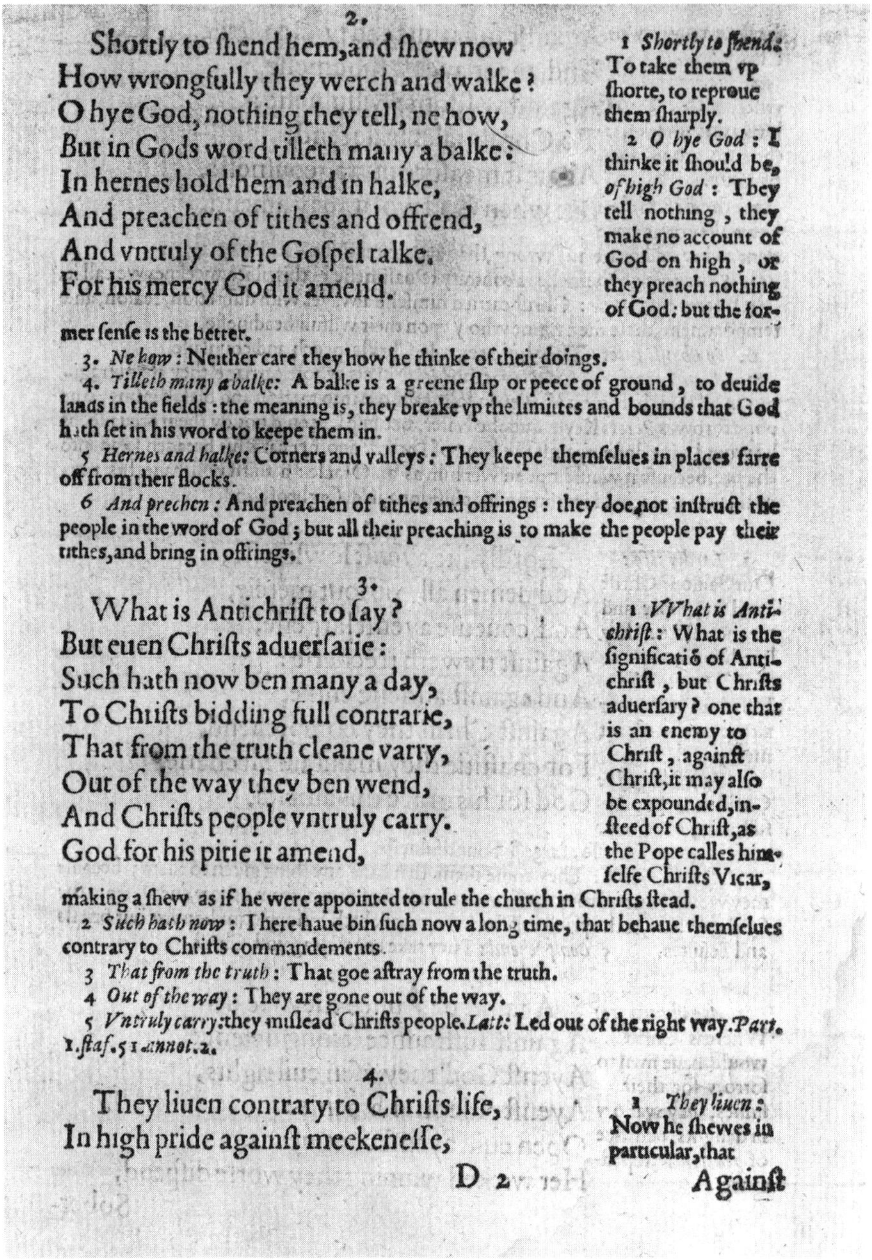

2.

Shortly to shend hem, and shew now
How wrongfully they werch and walke?
O hye God, nothing they tell, ne how,
But in Gods word tilleth many a balke:
In hernes hold hem and in halke,
And preachen of tithes and offrend,
And vntruly of the Gospel talke.
For his mercy God it amend.

1 *Shortly to shend*: To take them vp shorte, to reproue them sharply.

2 *O hye God*: I thinke it should be, *of high God*: They tell nothing, they make no account of God on high, or they preach nothing of God: but the former sense is the better.

3. *Ne how*: Neither care they how he thinke of their doings.

4. *Tilleth many a balke*: A balke is a greene slip or peece of ground, to deuide lands in the fields: the meaning is, they breake vp the limittes and bounds that God hath set in his word to keepe them in.

5 *Hernes and halke*: Corners and valleys: They keepe themselues in places farre off from their flocks.

6 *And prechen*: And preachen of tithes and offrings: they doe not instruct the people in the word of God; but all their preaching is to make the people pay their tithes, and bring in offrings.

3.

What is Antichrist to say?
But euen Christs aduersarie:
Such hath now ben many a day,
To Christs bidding full contrarie,
That from the truth cleane varry,
Out of the way they ben wend,
And Christs people vntruly carry.
God for his pitie it amend,

1 *VVhat is Antichrist*: What is the significatiō of Antichrist, but Christs aduersary? one that is an enemy to Christ, against Christ, it may also be expounded, insteed of Christ, as the Pope calles himselfe Christs Vicar, making a shew as if he were appointed to rule the church in Christs stead.

2 *Such hath now*: There haue bin such now a long time, that behaue themselues contrary to Christs commandements.

3 *That from the truth*: That goe astray from the truth.

4 *Out of the way*: They are gone out of the way.

5 *Vntruly carry*: they mislead Christs people. *Latt*: Led out of the right way. *Part*. 1. *staf*. 51 *annot*. 2.

4.

They liuen contrary to Christs life,
In high pride against meekenesse,

1 *They liuen*: Now he shewes in particular, that

D 2 Against

Figure 3.3. Geffrey Chaucer [pseud.], *The Plough-mans Tale* (London: G.E. for Samuell Macham and Mathew Cooke, 1606), sig. D2r.

tification perfectly clear: the pope is Antichrist. While most poetry of the English Renaissance was not annotated (with such notable exceptions as Spenser's *Faerie Queene* and Sylvester's translation of Du Bartas's *Deuine Weekes and Works*), polemical works like this one consistently were. The commerce of such texts with the world was clearly thought to benefit from the mediating voice of the marginalist. Breaking into and out of the world of discourse could best be managed by an allied but not thoroughly assimilated voice. The intrusive force of such voices as John Bunyan creates in the margins of his allegory *The Holy War* (1682) could be sharp and disconcerting (fig. 3.4). In the allegory, when Diabolus tempts the inhabitants of the town of Mansoul to renew their '*old acquaintance and friendship*' (305), Bunyan cries from the margin, 'No, no, no not upon pain of eternal damnation.' Each reader's soul has been placed in jeopardy. When the warning gets shouted out, two self-contained fictional worlds are shattered: first, the fictional world of the allegory, and second, the silent world of the individual reader. The intrusion is stunning.

By the early eighteenth century readers had begun to object to such intrusions from the margins, not so much on spiritual grounds (though the furore over annotating Holy Scripture had raged for centuries)[8] as on aesthetic and class snobbery ones. Notes placed prominently at the shoulder of a text were thought to detract from its rhetorical elegance and to smack of distinctly unaristocratic, scholarly *work*.[9] In the course of the eighteenth century, annotations were removed from their place beside the text and demoted to the bottom of the page. The architecture of a page from a history book, for example, was no longer that of the duplex or semidetached house, with explanatory notes paralleling the centred account of historical events on the same level, as they had done in the great Tudor chronicles. The ground plan became that of the multistorey house, with a more or less continuous historical narrative happening on the upper floors while the sweaty contention of conflicting authorities was carried out in the understorey of footnotes.[10]

Although the page achieved a certain clean, uncluttered look, much was lost with the change. For example, it can be argued that the marginal summaries and interpretations offered in the margins of the massive English chronicles of Edward Halle and Raphael Holinshed provided precisely the cues that Shakespeare required to recast English history into the dramatic form that dominated the stage in the final decade of the sixteenth century. Those same sidenotes also contributed to the disassembling of the comprehensive chronicles by generating the stripped-down outlines that formed the backbone of abbreviated summaries of English history and by revealing the fault lines along which the larger works would be split up during the next century into 'politic histories' of individual monarchs.[11] To be sure, other factors such as the popularity of smaller book formats contributed to this shift in the way English history was packaged and marketed, but printed marginalia provided a considerable impetus.

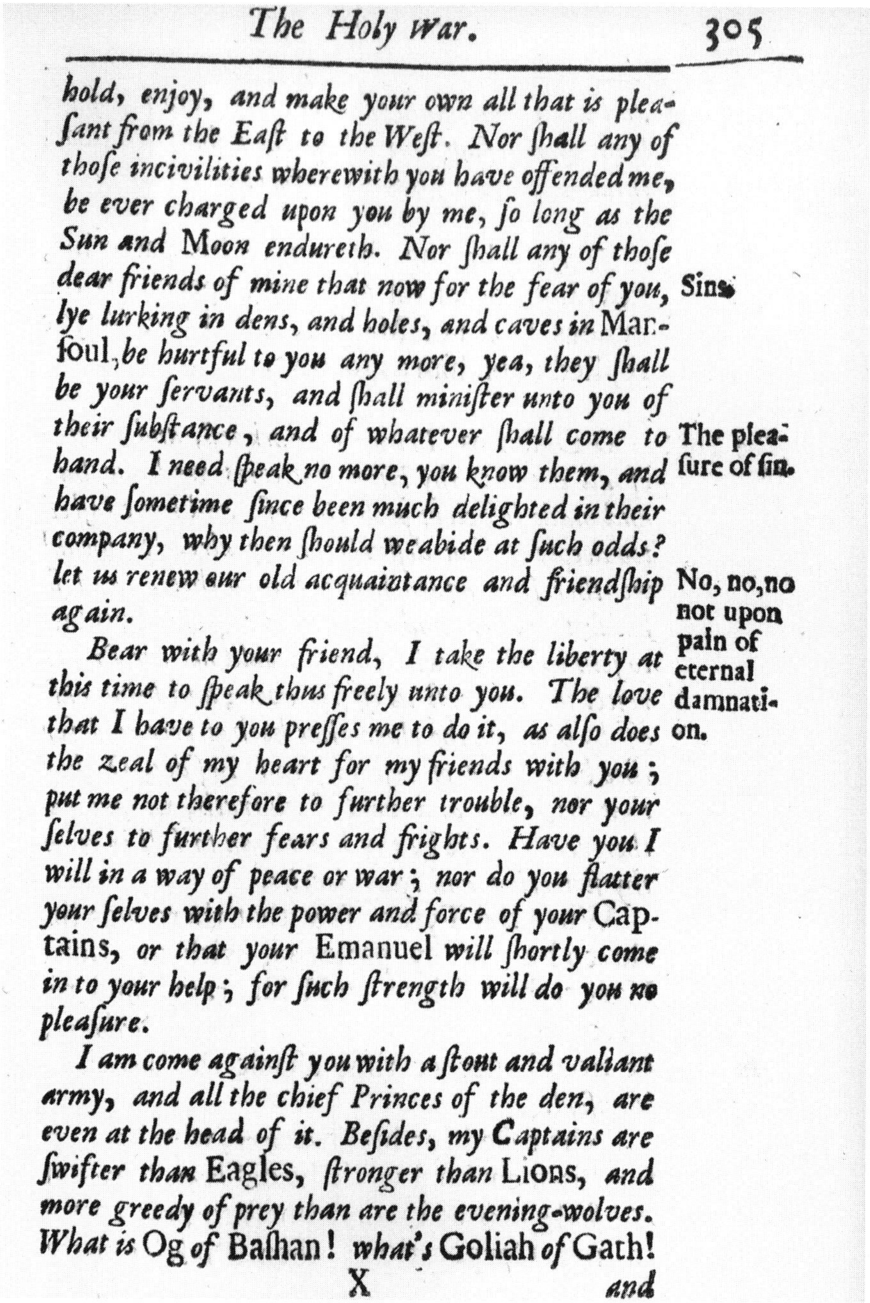
The Holy war. 305

hold, enjoy, and make your own all that is pleaſant from the Eaſt to the Weſt. Nor ſhall any of thoſe incivilities wherewith you have offended me, be ever charged upon you by me, ſo long as the Sun and Moon endureth. Nor ſhall any of thoſe dear friends of mine that now for the fear of you, lye lurking in dens, and holes, and caves in Marſoul, be hurtful to you any more, yea, they ſhall be your ſervants, and ſhall miniſter unto you of their ſubſtance, and of whatever ſhall come to hand. I need ſpeak no more, you know them, and have ſometime ſince been much delighted in their company, why then ſhould we abide at ſuch odds? let us renew our old acquaintance and friendſhip again.

Sins.

The pleaſure of ſin.

Bear with your friend, I take the liberty at this time to ſpeak thus freely unto you. The love that I have to you preſſes me to do it, as alſo does the zeal of my heart for my friends with you; put me not therefore to further trouble, nor your ſelves to further fears and frights. Have you I will in a way of peace or war; nor do you flatter your ſelves with the power and force of your Captains, or that your Emanuel will ſhortly come in to your help; for ſuch ſtrength will do you no pleaſure.

No, no, no not upon pain of eternal damnation.

I am come againſt you with a ſtout and valiant army, and all the chief Princes of the den, are even at the head of it. Beſides, my Captains are ſwifter than Eagles, ſtronger than Lions, and more greedy of prey than are the evening-wolves. What is Og of Baſhan! what's Goliah of Gath!

X and

Figure 3.4. John Bunyan, *The Holy War* (London: Dorman Newman; Benjamin Alsop, 1682), 305. Bruce Peel Special Collections, University of Alberta.

Production, Collaboration, Contestation, and Disruption at the Margins

The work performed by the sidenote in the print culture of the English Renaissance is often, but by no means always, disruptive and deconstructive. Indeed, this distinctive feature of the early modern page can provide a healthy corrective to our mistaken notions of how texts were produced, transmitted, and consumed in the period. Twentieth-century ideas about single authorship, for instance, largely ignored the array of marginal voices I have been describing. Collaborators, printing house personnel, literary executors, and other 'secondary' authors regularly left their marks in the form of printed marginalia, though they were seldom identified as authors. What they added was not an incidental supplement but often a shaping perspective that directed readers to make specific interventions into the centred discourse. What Derrida has argued about reversing centre and margin and about the integral nature of supplementarity using postmodern examples certainly applies equally well to sixteenth- and seventeenth-century marginated books.[12]

The margins of these books constitute an important site of textual disruption and provide an instructive history for experiments with the page in the twenty-first century. It is at the margins of the text that narrative and syntactic continuities were most thoroughly broken down. Verbal signals were drastically reduced by abbreviation. The biblical reference Exod. 3:2 represents a verbal locus without actually reproducing the scriptural text, though the minds of some readers would doubtless have been triggered to recall the passage about Moses and the burning bush. Such acts of recollection are traces of a culture of oral recitation that had not been displaced by written communication.

It is not surprising that what I have called 'marginal voices' at the edges of the text should be implicated in the debate concerning orality and literacy. For example, Tobin Nellhaus, following Paul Saenger and Brian Stock, has argued that the forms of literacy that developed from the twelfth century onward promoted linear thought, complex linguistic subordination, and the recording of information for subsequent rereadings. Orality, on the other hand, depended on concrete materiality, repetitive verbal formulas, and other techniques designed to render recalled events immediately present to the listening audience.[13] If this is true, then printed marginalia are as much a testimony to the survival of orality as to the ascendancy of literacy. Directness of expression and simplicity of syntax are tokens of oral presentation that are also prized in marginalia. Complicated periodic sentence structures from the text are reduced in the margins to catalogues of *topoi*, lists of dates, and abbreviated comments. Such headings – or sidings – also serve as visual reference points. This indexing function is specifically part of the iconology of the page rather than of oral/aural transmission, though marginalia served at times as notes for oral disquisitions upon the material contained on the page. Like modern professors, medieval and Renaissance scholars frequently marked up manuscript and print texts in their margins as they prepared for lectures. And so, the margins served both the silent lector and the voluble lecturer, thus further collapsing any rigid distinction among oral, manuscript, and print transmission.

Such verbal contraction into symbolic marginal keys as I have described promoted a degree of nonlinear expression in early modern annotated books. A kind of intermediate example of literally and litorally nonlinear text is the dedication to Abraham Darcie's English version of Willliam Camden's *Annales of the True and Royal History of Elizabeth* (1625). Through the technology of photo-facsimile reproduction, we see in fig. 3.5 recto and verso of the dedication leaf side by side. By beginning his verbal border, the address 'TO THE TRVE MIRROR ... CHARLES PRINCE OF GREAT BRITANNE' at the right side of the recto page, printing vertically, and making the reader either turn the book or else read upside-down (before going on to the verso to repeat the process), the printer obviously violates the normal left-to-right protocols of reading text, but he also creates an effective image of the monarch-to-be surrounding and embracing the translator's words.

Long before the great twentieth-century age of advertising, text makers knew that they were image makers – and salesmen – and they deployed their images with considerable effect. The image at the front of Bunyan's *The Holy War*, for example, lays out his allegorical narrative of the struggle for the eternal soul of mankind in eye-catching detail (see fig. 3.6) In the centre stands the 'The Towne of Mansoul' and its chief inhabitant of the same name. At the left is the dragon Dioabolus with all his little devils, assaulting the anatomically depicted 'Eare gate'; on the right, echoing the physical appearance of Mansoul and defending 'Eye gate,' is 'Emanuell' with the Army of Shaddai. Below is the globe of the world; above, a louring sky that betokens the action of Bunyan's psychomachia. Figures like the dragon-devil might easily have inhabited the margins of a medieval illuminated manuscript, but the transparency of Mansoul's body that allows us to see 'Heart Castle' through his breast suggests a more complex conception of visual space, one that we associate more readily with the manipulable images of the digital page than with the technologies of fourteenth-century manuscripts or seventeenth-century books.

The relationship between text and image always makes for tricky reading. The hermeneutic situation is made still more difficult when we consider that 'the iconic page' is itself an image with all the attendant complications of symbolism, notation, and referentiality that accompany any image, whether art or non-art.[14] The construction of the early modern page, with its running titles, marginal notes, catch words, and signature designations, is a complex though relatively stable visual icon. It organizes information in ways that move the reading eye around in the centred text and connect it both internally and externally. Like paintings, some print pages are gorgeous and memorable, others grubby and eminently forgettable. I have tried to introduce here some of the more attractive models of early modern English page making.[15]

Futures for the Annotated Page

Not being clairvoyant, I am unwilling to say what a page of an edition of an early modern work will look like twenty or fifty years hence, but only what I tentatively think it *should* look like. What I am after may be something very like those good old wide-margined, heavily annotated, information-packed, large-print texts of yore – only much improved by electronically intercut images, examples, and intertexts. In particular, future pages should be

- multicentred
- conspicuously edited
- loose margined
- copiously illustrated.

These bald specifications require some explanation.

With the term 'multicentred' I intend to call for an information-rich textual presentation that distinguishes scrupulously among various readers' potential uses. However much readers resent being managed, they still need help in studying complex texts. They may choose not to be directed, but the directions must be there nonetheless for the benefit of readers who do not want to be bothered organizing their reading experience. To encourage informed reader-participation requires that the primary text along with its expositions, contexts, and various kinds of illustrative materials be displayed in a relatively simple and clear hierarchy. In this, the makers of the future page have a great deal to learn from the best models of early modern annotated pages. In the hypertext medium, the time-honoured annotational principle of adjacency can readily be achieved with split screens that do the printed page one better by being so expandable. But expansiveness can be overdone, overwhelming and cancelling out the beneficial effects of adjacency. When the text being annotated is scrolled off the screen, for example, an important anchor in the multicentred (not *un*centred) reading experience is lost.

Readers read for wildly different reasons, and the editor of a text can never anticipate all of them. Still, it should be possible, for example, for a bibliographer, a cultural critic, and a theologian approaching Donne's treatise on

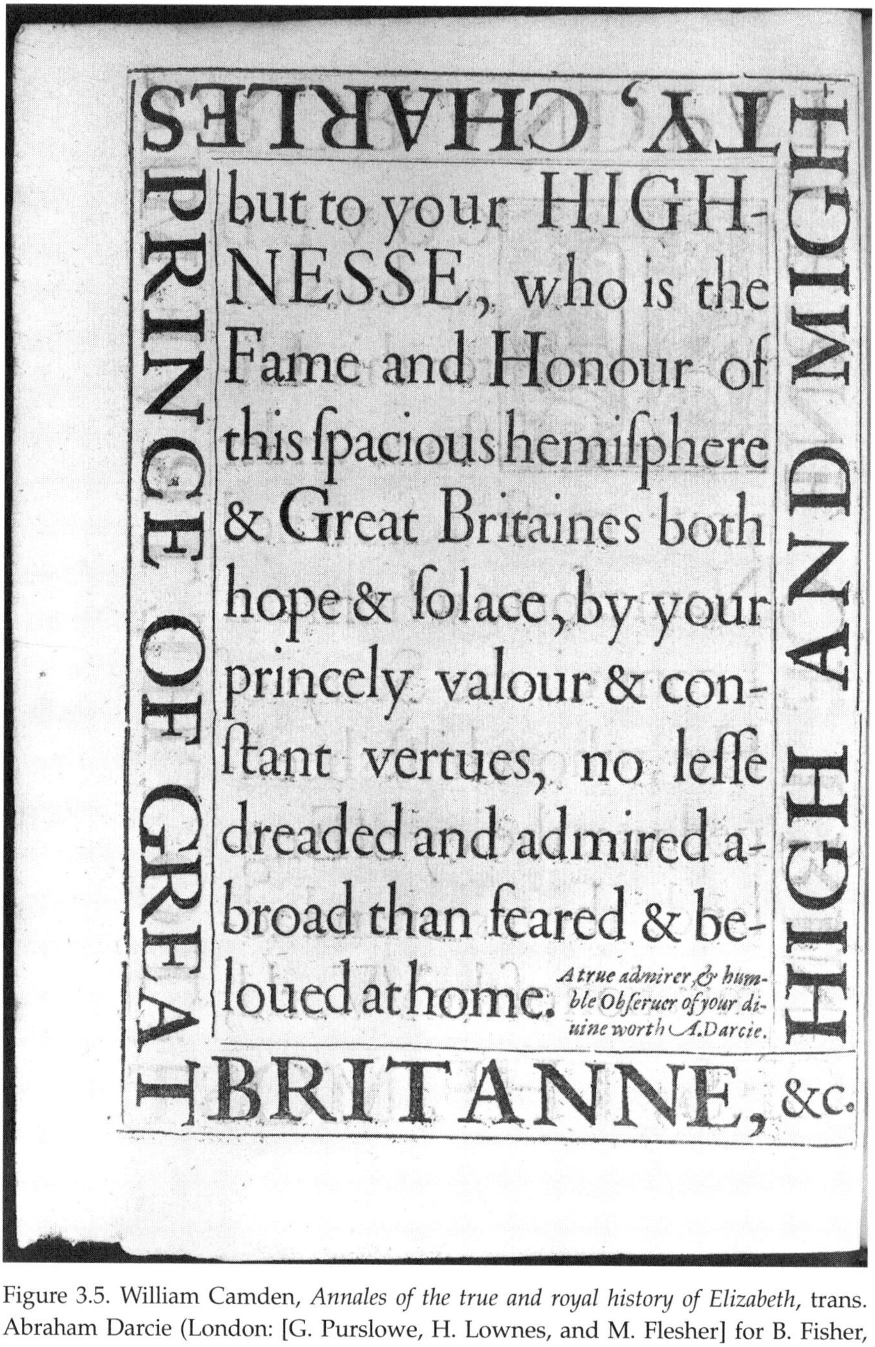
HIGH AND MIGHTY, CHARLES PRINCE OF GREAT BRITANNE, &c.

but to your HIGH-
NESSE, who is the
Fame and Honour of
this ſpacious hemiſphere
& Great Britaines both
hope & ſolace, by your
princely valour & con-
ſtant vertues, no leſſe
dreaded and admired a-
broad than feared & be-
loued at home.

A true admirer, & hum-
ble Obſeruer of your di-
uine worth A. Darcie.

Figure 3.5. William Camden, *Annales of the true and royal history of Elizabeth*, trans. Abraham Darcie (London: [G. Purslowe, H. Lownes, and M. Flesher] for B. Fisher, 1625), Dedication.

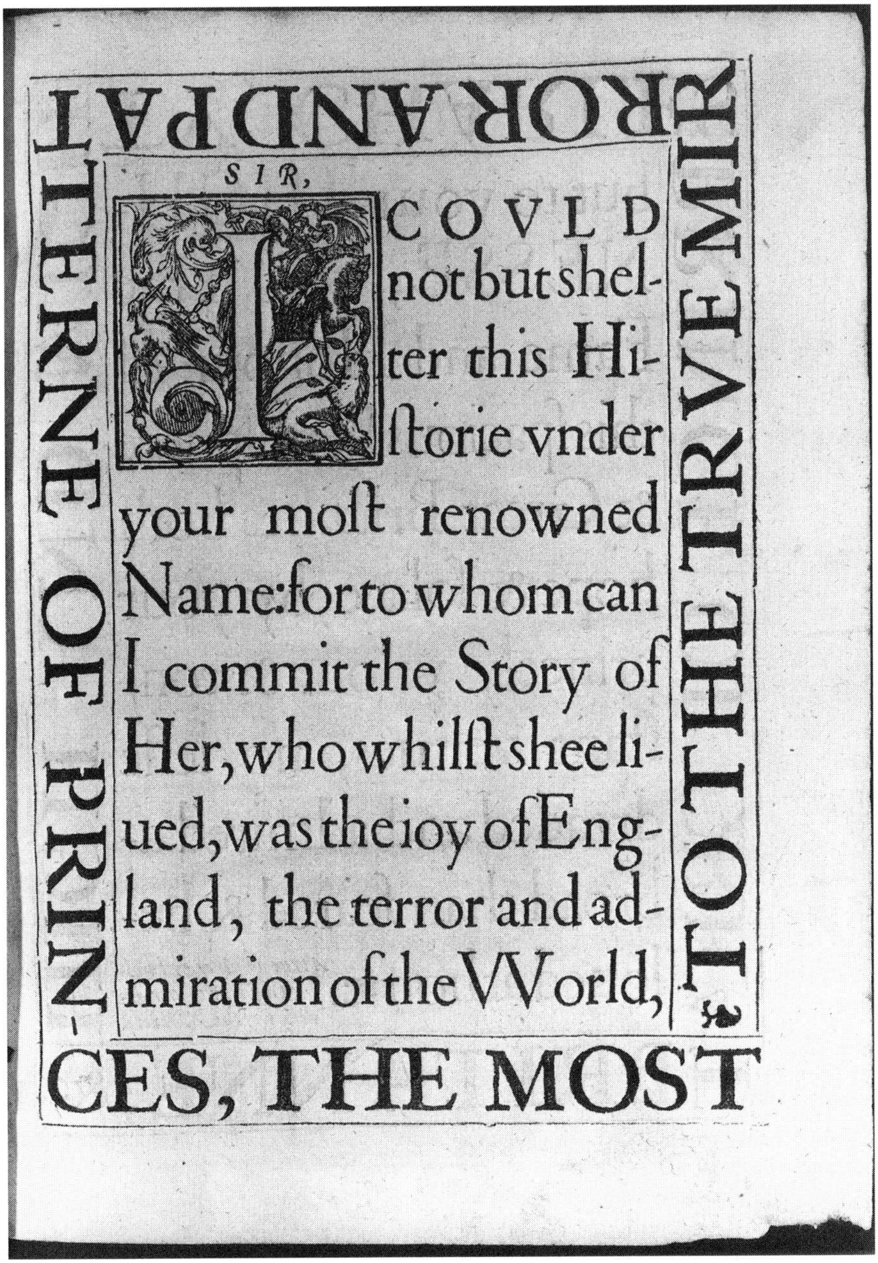

TO THE TRVE MIR-
ROR AND PAT-
TERNE OF PRIN-
CES, THE MOST

SIR,

I COVLD
not but ſhel-
ter this Hi-
ſtorie vnder
your moſt renowned
Name: for to whom can
I commit the Story of
Her, who whilſt ſhee li-
ued, was the ioy of Eng-
land, the terror and ad-
miration of the VVorld,

The Towne of Mansoul.
Emanuell
a Sling.
Shaddai's Army.
London Printed for Dorman Newman at the Kings Armes. and Benj: Alsop at the Angell and Bible in the Poultrey ..

Figure 3.6. John Bunyan, *The Holy War* (London: Dorman Newman; Benjamin Alsop, 1682), front illustration. RB 54203, Huntington Library, San Marino, CA.

suicide, *Biathanatos* (composed ca. 1607–9, revised <1629, printed 1648), to select a cluster of textual supplements that suits his or her interests. Knowing about the provenance of manuscript M may hold little interest or relevance for the student of Donne's indebtedness to Augustinian thought or to the student of seventeenth-century attitudes about taking one's own life. While Donne's text remains central in such a scheme, various constellations of annotation allow for targeted and uncluttered access to explanatory and contextual materials.

By promoting the twin ideas of centrality and marginal *copia*, I am urging that we maintain Renaissance theories of writing and reading, and I am challenging the decentred page-sense of the currently reigning guru of the margins, Jacques Derrida. I hasten to add that I have learned a great deal from Derrida's accounts of marginal supplementarity and *dé-bordement*. As he insists, textual supplements are themselves texts requiring interpretation, and the flanks of the text must be used to assault as well as to defend. But without an editorial compass of some sort, readers can all too easily get lost in the wilderness of *hors-texte* and yet more text. In advocating for thoroughly, hierarchically edited early modern texts, I am challenging some but not all of the recent arguments for 'unediting' the Renaissance. While I agree with such textual critics as Leah Marcus and Jeffrey Masten that readers must be made aware of the choices and interventions that remain hidden in most editorial traditions, I do not agree that this requires even 'a temporary abandonment of modern editions in favour of Renaissance editions.'[16] Even in hypertext editions – appearances to the contrary – the editor's shaping hand is always present.[17] The point is not to try to disguise this salient fact. In electronic formats, we can retain useful material from previous editions so long as we label it prominently. We can identify the assumptions underlying these earlier editions and highlight their emendations of early versions. Rather than stripping away the layers of these wonderfully palimpsestic texts, we should be displaying the layers of cultural accretion for anyone who is curious about the process of textual transmission to see.

Such a flexible and inclusive procedure contributes to what I have called a 'loose-margined' text, one that permits willing, engaged readers to move further into the text through explication or outward from it through hypertext links, all without unduly cluttering the on-screen text. Part of the loosening of the marginal boundaries, the creation of thresholds rather than barriers at the edge of the text, involves a substantial enrichment of the reading experience in the form of images. Printed books generally do not handle images well. In early modern books, with few exceptions, images are monochrome, fairly crude, and infrequent. Life in the electronic environment changes all that. Indeed, some recent print books such as those by Edward Tufte and James Elkins have not only helped to theorize print images but have also presented examples in an array that makes the un- or under-illustrated book feel positively puritanical.[18] Hence, the last of my four recommendations for the future of the page: copious illustration. Here too, though, a caveat is in order.

Images embedded in text have a way of taking over from the words on the page. When I was invited recently to contribute a piece on margins to the web site called *Architectures, Ideologies, and Materials of the Page* that was being constructed by Jon Bath, Allison Muri, Peter Stoicheff, and Andrew Taylor, I wrote a few paragraphs on the subject and added a handful of illustrations to show what I was saying about the width of early printed margins, their placement on the page, their incursions into centred text, and so forth. It soon became clear to me, however, that these were not illustrations of the information I was documenting; they *were* the information. So I added more images of early modern pages and began genuinely to think of the page as a spatial concept, one that needs to be reproduced, not just described. These images still must be 'read,' that is, supplemented with mental or textual commentary, but they cannot be entirely replaced by ekphrastic prose.

In Which the Editor Mounts Up and Rides Off in All Directions

So now we are ready to mount, from the digital platform, our fully annotated text of an early modern text, let us say, Shakespeare's sonnets. The strategically placed keys along its 'loose' margins can instantly take the autobiographical detective to a cluster of notes on Shakespeare's secret life (complete with identifications and images of the Dark Lady and the Rival Poet); the earnest explicator can get to Stephen Booth's wonderful close readings of Shakespeare's syntax; the textual critic can consult a facsimile of the 1609 quarto in order to see precisely where subsequent editorial interventions have occurred; the practitioner of gay studies can access portraits of a variety of eligible earls and a scary list of Elizabethan statutes against sodomy. And what have we got when we have laboured to produce this megakilobyte-sized mouse? What does all this sound and fury signify for the would-be reader of those enchanting sonnets?

What we have created, like it or not, amounts to little more than a very fancy teaching aid, a kind of deluxe-edition Coles Notes. Basically, we are right back with those medieval pedagogues interlining and glossing the grammar, traditional wisdom, and rhetorical skill, this time of Shakespeare's sonnets. Has the reader's experience been facilitated or greatly enhanced by the electronic overlay? I seriously doubt it, and I doubt it because the technology of the *book* is the best one we have for the practice of silent reading, a practice that has been developed to fit into the library, the subway car, and the house full of people, many of them listening to recorded music, cranked. I am not arguing that the computer has no place in the serious study of books, only that it will not replace them.[19] Indeed, the computer is fast coming to be the tool of choice for analysing texts of all kinds, especially ones related to large archives.[20] For this work, skilled editors and site constructors are essential. As the compilers and annotators of Holinshed's massive *Chronicles* knew very well, a serious page of text requires scrupulous editorial selection and arrangement. Hypertext editors can append supplementary text and images till the cows come home, but there is little assurance that without thoughtful guidance any reader will connect the dots into a meaningful pattern. The scattergun approach to presenting information simply is not very effective. As anyone knows who has test-fired a shotgun (scattergun) to check its pattern, unless you know the basic principles of what size circle of evenly distributed shot a given gauge and choke is supposed to throw at a given distance, the resulting page of tiny holes will make little sense. Rifle fire carries further and has far greater integrity, though in this age of increased controls, I hesitate to press the analogy between curling up with a good book and with a warm gun.

We can learn a good deal about annotating texts from the printing and reading habits of the early modern period. We can tweak and refine these habits to make the reading experience a bit more memorable and more inviting than many young readers find it at the start of the twenty-first century. We will not, however, revolutionize the writing and reading industry, no matter what the messianic liberationists and techno-fetishists say. And maybe that is all right.

NOTES

1 The percentage is higher for large-paper books. About 80 per cent of the 800 early modern folios I have surveyed in the Huntington Library were marginated, whereas the figure was about half that for another 1200 quartos, octavos, and duodecimos consulted. On the evidence of handwritten marginalia see Anthony Grafton and Michael Camille, *Image on the Edge: The Margins of Medieval Art* (Cambridge, MA: Harvard University Press, 1992); H.J. Jackson, *Marginalia: Readers Writing in Books* (New Haven and London: Yale University Press, 2001); Anthony Grafton and Lisa Jardine, '"Studied for Action": How Gabriel Harvey Read His Livy.' *Past and Present* 129 (1990): 30–78; and William H. Sherman, *What Did Renaissance Readers Write in their Books?* (Philadelphia: University of Pennsylvania Press, 2002).
2 John Donne, *The Sermons of John Donne*, ed. George R. Potter and Evelyn M. Simpson, 10 vols (Berkeley and Los Angeles: University of California Press, 1953–62), 6: 224.
3 In a paper titled 'From Codex to Computer: Or, Shakespeare Bytes,' delivered at the Shakespeare Association's annual meeting, Montreal 2000, David Scott Kastan recalled a piece of late-1960s graffiti in the Columbia University library that proclaimed, '*FREE THE BOUND PERIODICALS*.' Freedom, whether virtual or political, cannot, however, mean complete freedom from the effects of the past.
4 Gérard Genette, *Paratext: The Thresholds of Textuality*, trans. Jane E. Lewin (Cambridge: Cambridge University Press, 1997).
5 I am thinking here of, for instance, George P. Landow's *Hypertext 2.0: The Convergence of Contemporary Critical Theory and Technology* (Baltimore: Johns Hopkins University Press, 1997) and Jakob Nielsen's *Multimedia and Hypertext* (Baltimore: Johns Hopkins University Press, 1992).
6 Andrew Taylor, 'Playing on the Margins: Bakhtin and the Smithfield Decretals,' in *Bakhtin and Medieval Voices*, ed. Thomas J. Farrell (Gainesville: University Press of Florida, 1995), 17–37.
7 I have looked more closely at Dee's marginalia in my essay 'The Cosmopolitics of Reading: Navigating the Margins of John Dee's *General and Rare Memorials*,' in *The Margins of the Text*, ed. D.C. Greetham (Ann Arbor: University of Michigan Press, 1997). Also see the fine analysis of Dee as recorder of English maritime aspirations in William H. Sherman's essay 'John Dee's Role in Martin

Frobisher's Northwest Enterprise,' in *Meta Incognita: A Discourse of Discovery, Martin Frobisher's Arctic Expeditions 1576–1578*, ed. Thomas H.B. Symons et al. (Ottawa: Canadian Museum of Civilization, 1999) 283–98, and also the comments on Dee as maker of manuscript and print pages in Sherman's *John Dee: The Politics of Reading and Writing in the English Renaissance* (Amherst: University of Massachusetts Press, 1995).

8 On the debate over annotating Holy Scripture, see C.F.R. de Hamel, *Glossed Books of the Bible and the Origins of the Paris Booktrade* (Bury St Edmunds: D.S. Brewer, 1984); Deborah Kuller Shuger, *The Renaissance Bible: Scholarship, Sacrifice, and Subjectivity* (Berkeley and Los Angeles: University of California Press, 1994); William W.E. Slights, '"Marginal Notes that spoile the Text": Scriptural Annotation in the English Renaissance,' *Huntington Library Quarterly* 55 (1992): 255–78; and *The Bible as a Book: The First Printed Editions*, ed. Kimberly Van Kampen and Paul Saenger (New Castle, DE: Oak Knoll Press, and London: The British Library, 1999).

9 Evelyn Tribble has traced this development persuasively in her essay '"Like a Looking-Glas in the Frame": From the Marginal Note to the Footnote,' in *The Margins of the Text*, ed. Greetham, 229–44.

10 This is the thesis argued by Anthony Grafton in *The Footnote: A Curious History* (Cambridge, MA: Harvard University Press, 1998).

11 See my *Managing Readers: Printed Marginalia in English Renaissance Books* (Ann Arbor: University of Michigan Press, 2001), and Daniel Woolf, *The Idea of History in Early Stuart England* (Toronto: University of Toronto Press, 1990).

12 Some of Derrida's most provocative thoughts on the margins are contained in his essays 'Living On: *Border Lines*,' reproduced in *Deconstruction and Criticism*, ed. Harold Bloom (New York: Seabury Press, 1979), 75–176, and 'This Is Not an Oral Footnote,' in *Annotation and Its Texts*, ed. Stephen A. Barney (Oxford: Oxford University Press, 1990), 192–205.

13 Tobin Nellhaus, 'Mementos of Things to Come: Orality, Literacy, and Typology in the *Biblia pauperum*,' in *Printing the Written Word: The Social History of the Book, circa 1450–1520*, ed. Sandra Hindman (Ithaca: Cornell University Press, 1991), 292–321.

14 *The Iconic Page in Manuscript, Print, and Digital Culture*, ed. George Bornstein and Theresa Tinkle (Ann Arbor: University of Michigan Press,1998). See also Mieke Bal, *Reading 'Rembrandt': Beyond the Word-Image Opposition* (Cambridge: Cambridge University Press, 1991).

15 In his essay 'Decolonizing the Medieval Page' in the present volume, John Dagenais makes the case, however, that there may be more to be learned about medieval culture and the transmission of texts from the smudgy, clumsily repaired, and unprofessionally annotated manuscripts of the period than from, say, the pristine Book of Kells.

16 Leah Marcus in *Unediting the Renaissance: Shakespeare, Marlowe, Milton* (London: Routledge, 1996) emphasizes the pernicious, silent intrusion of editors over

centuries and wishes to strip away the layers of ideology that encrust the texts of canonical writers such as the three she chose for her study. I quote from Jeffrey Masten, *Textual Intercourse: Collaboration, Authorship, and Sexualities in Renaissance Drama* (Cambridge: Cambridge University Press, 1997), 5. Masten argues persuasively for the need to highlight the various kinds of authorship in the period, almost none of which is 'individual' in the modern sense.

17 See Jon Bath, Cory Owen, and Peter Stoicheff, 'The Editor in the Machine: Theoretical and Editorial Issues Raised by the Design of an HTML Literary Hypertext,' http://www.usask.ca/english/prufrock.

18 See Edward Tufte's elegant volumes *Envisioning Information* (Cheshire, CT: Graphics Press, 1990) and *Visual Explanations: Images and Qualities, Evidence and Narrative* (Cheshire, CT: Graphics Press, 1997), and also James Elkins's *The Domain of Images* (Ithaca: Cornell University Press,1999).

19 During the closing panel discussion at the Future of the Page conference, Michael Groden, general editor of the *Ulysses* hypertext project, alluded to E. Annie Proulx's now-infamous claim that no one will ever choose to read a novel on 'a twitchy little screen.' The equivocating word here, the one that flattens out a host of interactions between people and pages, is 'read.' 'Reading' for imaginative involvement in a fictional world is not very much like studying the orthographic variants in a Shakespeare text or looking up a telephone number. Only people who need to get out much more 'read' the phone book. Our vocabulary for print consumption needs to be refined, then, though the verb 'read' has not been displaced by the advent of the digitized text any more than has the noun 'page' (as in the Pg Up/Pg Dn keys).

20 See Jerome McGann's assessment of the achievement of the Rossetti electronic archives in this volume.

4 Nicholas Jenson and the Form of the Renaissance Printed Page

David R. Carlson

In the *Minima Moralia* comes a section in which Adorno reflects on being given a series of books as a boy. The books were in a language of which little Theodor was ignorant at the time; nonetheless, the objects still spoke to him, eloquently. In fact, he suggests that out of them – the bibliographical forms of them, purely, apart from any verbal content – a whole culture could be read:

> In my childhood, some elderly English ladies with whom my parents kept up relations often gave me books as presents: richly illustrated works for the young, also a small green bible bound in morocco leather. All were in the language of the donors: whether I could read it none of them paused to reflect. The peculiar inaccessibility of the books, with their glaring pictures, titles and vignettes, and their indecipherable text, filled me with the belief that in general objects of this kind were not books at all, but advertisements, perhaps for machines like those my uncle produced in his London factory.

Form speaks, by itself, is one of the points: in book forms only are evident whole social formations, material and cultural process both, different book forms speaking differently. In the forms of books, Adorno concludes, 'culture displays its character as advertising,' book forms being a means by which culturally specific truths – the Barthesean 'myths' – are propagated.[1]

The Renaissance printed page, as represented, for example, in the work of Nicholas Jenson at Venice beginning in 1470, does this job of proselytizing. The cultural truth that the form of the printed page advertises is the dominance of the machine.

On the inside, printed books are formally different from their manuscript predecessors. Generally speaking, printed pages are smaller, plainer, simpler, and more regular, using fewer varieties and sizes of lettering, fewer columns and blocks, less ornament, and less colour: black and white, regularly spaced and justified lines, a rectangular block – a tombstone, basically. This characteristic, canonical form of the printed page did not emerge immediately into pre-eminence, however, with the invention of printing in the mid-fifteenth century. Until the early or mid-sixteenth century, competing models of page design remained current, among them varieties that sought to rival manuscript pages in formal complexity, and in various particulars, the form of the printed book might well have come out differently. Patterns of commercial exchange, traditions of manuscript manufacture and use, and current cultural activity – especially the humanist movement – provided the local, social context for early printing, and the impact of these transient, overdetermining circumstances is still legible in the form of the printed page.

Still, in the final analysis, the form of the printed page was determined by the nature of the materials and technology with which the early printers worked: wet paper that hardened as it dried, presses, furniture, spacing, and type made of sculpted metal. That the printed page is the way it is is a product of this technology used for fabricating printed books – the technology mediating intention or superseding it. From this perspective, the form of the printed page bespeaks the technology's dominance – the result of introducing complex, costly machinery into the social process of information storage and retrieval.

Of all the early printers, the most accomplished at making the machines and the materials do what he wanted, rather than vice versa, was Nicholas Jenson, a French national who printed at Venice between 1470 and 1480. Even a printer as masterful as Jenson, however, was still subject to the machine, and what follows is an analysis of these two aspects of his work. First, Jenson's technical mastery will be discussed, along with its most remarkable products: a group of law books that he printed at the end of his career, proving his ability to do anything he wanted with type. Jenson's chief legacy has been something else, however: the result of his willingness to submit to the machinery, in effect, rather than struggling against it. This paper ends with a discussion of the books that Jenson printed first. It is a paradox of his career that it was at the beginning of it that he did his most perfect work. The perfection of Jenson's early work is only the result of his willingness to go along with the machines and materials, doing what came most naturally to them.

The Daedalus of Printing

The credit for inventing printing has been widely claimed – appropriately, for an art more cooperative and collaborative than any before the movies – and among the other names put forward for the credit was that of Nicholas Jenson. In 1471 a humanist Italian scholar and schoolmaster named Ognibene da Lonigo wrote: 'Jenson, the Frenchman, is a second Daedalus, if truth be told. He is the inventor of a wonderful book-art: it was he first of all who showed, ingeniously indeed, that books need not be written out with a pen, but could be imprinted, as if in stone, with a seal or stamp of some sort.'[2]

The claim is mistaken, at best. Rather than inventing printing, Jenson stole it. The biographical tradition – a good one, dating from the sixteenth century, but impossible to deny or confirm – is that Jenson, French by birth, was a fine metals worker from a family of goldsmiths; that he worked in a French royal mint, at Tours or Paris, as a die-cutter or mint-master; and that, in about 1458, he was sent into Germany as an industrial spy on behalf of the French monarchy, to find out the secret of printing with movable types and bring it back. As a printer, however, Jenson was active only in Venice, so far as is known, working there with German engineering and venture capital, and with Italian artisans and merchants, only in the decade between 1470 and his death in 1480, that is to say, fifteen to twenty years after the earliest printed books came to market.[3]

The claim that Nicholas Jenson was the inventor of printing was probably a falsehood, rather than a simple mistake, however, for the person responsible for forwarding the claim would have done so knowing it was wrong. The person was Jenson himself. The statement imputed to Ognibene appeared in the preface of a book that Jenson printed: an edition of the *Institutiones oratoriae* of Quintilian, dated 21 May 1471 in a colophon that concludes: 'imprinted, with astonishing skill, for the good of this and future generations, by Nicholas Jenson.'[4] Jenson knowingly put about misinformation, in other words, when he published the claim that he was printing's inventor.

This was not vanity, nor compulsion. It was business. Jenson's interest was not in saying he was the inventor of printing when he knew he was not, nor in being lionized as the inventor of printing, among contemporaries or by posterity. His interest was in gathering up immediately what profits might accrue to him from the credulity of others, from their belief that he had been first among printers and by virtue of his priority remained best. Jenson's claim to precedence was a form of advertising. 'Jenson was remarkable on two counts only,' as Martin Lowry has put this same point: 'his technical expertise, and his adroit sense of public relations.'[5]

The claim that Jenson invented printing was not repeated. However, the claim that he was the Daedalus of printing was to recur again and again. It appeared first in one of the editions of 1470, made during the first few months of Jenson's operation, which notes 'the genius and Daedalean skill' (*ingenio Daedalicaque manu*) with which Jenson worked. Regularly thereafter the colophons and liminary letters, by Jenson and others, that he printed in his books repeated related claims about the 'wonders' of Jenson's technical skill. 'Thank the artificer, reader,' enjoins one book, for 'the artificer's ingenious skill imparts immortality.' ' I, Jenson, printed this,' says another: 'who would deny that the work is a wonder of art?' 'Jenson is easily a great deal better than anyone else working in this medium.'[6]

That Jenson should have mounted a campaign of advertising, using colophons and prefatory matter, is in itself noteworthy, and instructive. More so is his choice to mount the sort of campaign he did, focused on technical skill and using the figure of Daedalus: the legendary Athenian inventor of architectural marvels like the labyrinth as well as cunning, though unpredictable and sometimes harmful machines. According to Plato, these included sculptures that would not stay long in one place except tied down.[7] The advertising campaign bespeaks Jenson's commercial acumen; the choice of Daedalus as an image – not Aphrodite nor Athena nor Asclepius, but Daedalus – bespeaks a perception on Jenson's part that what mattered in a printer, and what he had, was technical mastery. As Jenson presented himself, the printer did not have to be learned, or divinely inspired, nor driven by civic mindedness or something; in addition to having business sense, a printer had to be good, technically, with materials and machines.

Jenson's Law Books

The technical mastery that justifies Jenson's claim to have been the Daedalus of printing is most evident in a series of books of his that are now somewhat difficult to admire: his law books – big, complicated, rebarbative things. Jenson started to print law in 1474, with an edition of the *Decretum* of Gratian; thenceforth, law books came to comprise an increasingly large portion of his production, until 1477 or so, after which time, except for scholastic theology, he was printing nothing but law.[8]

The legal market was a printer's dream: it was captive – lawyers had to have books – it was big, and it kept renewing itself, with each new class of law graduates, statutory augmentation, and developing case law, year after year. The legal market was such a good thing for printers that the problem of working it was not market creation or market exhaustion but competition amongst printers – too many printers chasing after the same book buyers. Because of the way the legal market worked, it was inevitable that a commercially astute printer like Jenson would want to try it; to succeed at exploiting it, however, a printer like Jenson would have to beat out rivals by offering a preferable product. Jenson was able to offer a preferable product, preferable in two ways: his law books were cheaper, because he made them shorter – printed on fewer sheets of paper – and his law books were better designed – though they were more crowded with matter they were still clear and functional.[9]

The pages of Jenson's law books are big, and lots fits on them; but, to a sensibility habituated to other kinds of printed pages, they are repulsive, basically. On the other hand, a less bigoted attention discovers that each page of the law books represents Jenson's solutions to a series of varying technical problems – profound problems, solved so well that the result tends to be dismissed. In fact, extensive resources and great technical artistry were invested in the fabrication of these pages.

By the time he printed his edition of the *Institutiones* of Justinian (fig. 4.1), ca. 1478–80 (probably earlier rather than later during this date range), Jenson was making law books of extraordinary complexity.[10] Like most of them, this one too was printed in two colours, black and red, each at separate pulls. Each side of each sheet passed under the press twice, in other words, once for the red and once for the black. The page uses three types, though others use as many as four at once, selected from among the six different fonts of gothic type that Jenson eventually kept at his disposal for legal printing. Some of the late law books use an extra-large gothic display font (150G) – about a half again as large as his standard text type – this display font appearing predominantly in headlines.[11]

Two of Jenson's other gothic fonts do the bulk of the work: the one for inset primary text (93Gb), the other for circumambient commentary (93Ga). Though these two types are visually distinct, in fact they have the same size body, measuring 93mm for twenty lines. The type used for the commentary, surrounding the columns of primary text, looks smaller than the type used for the inset, because in some dimensions it is smaller: it is lighter, narrower or more compressed along its horizontal axis, and the x-height is less – the face is also somewhat more compressed along its vertical axis, too, in other words. The matching body-heights make it possible to stack the two types up levelly next to one another, simplifying the process of laying out the whole page and regularizing the product, while still keeping a distinction visually between text and commentary.

The greatest of Jenson's typographical achievements in his law books, however, may be the least thing on the page, involving a technique he developed for printing superior figures, in the form of small reference letters appearing above lines printed in his ordinary larger-faced text type (fig. 4.2).[12] Within the inset blocks of text, there occur tiny superlinear letters, in a gothic font that would measure somewhat less than 50mm for twenty lines, possibly as little as a third of the size of the text type. These tiny letters occur in alphabetic order, keying portions of the text to appropriate sections of commentary in the surrounding columns, where a matching alphabetic sequence of letters occurs, extruded by reverse indentation into the margins next to the appropriate sections of the commentary.

The tiny types used for the superior figures appear to have been designed to be set above specially prepared vowel sorts of the (93Gb) text font, the shoulders of which would have been cut away above the face, to make space for setting the guide letters there. All words have vowels, of course, so there was no need for a complete alphabet of trimmed-down sorts. Moreover, and probably more to the point, vowels have no ascenders, except the awkward ascender-like dot of *i*, so the upper portion of the type-bodies on vowels,

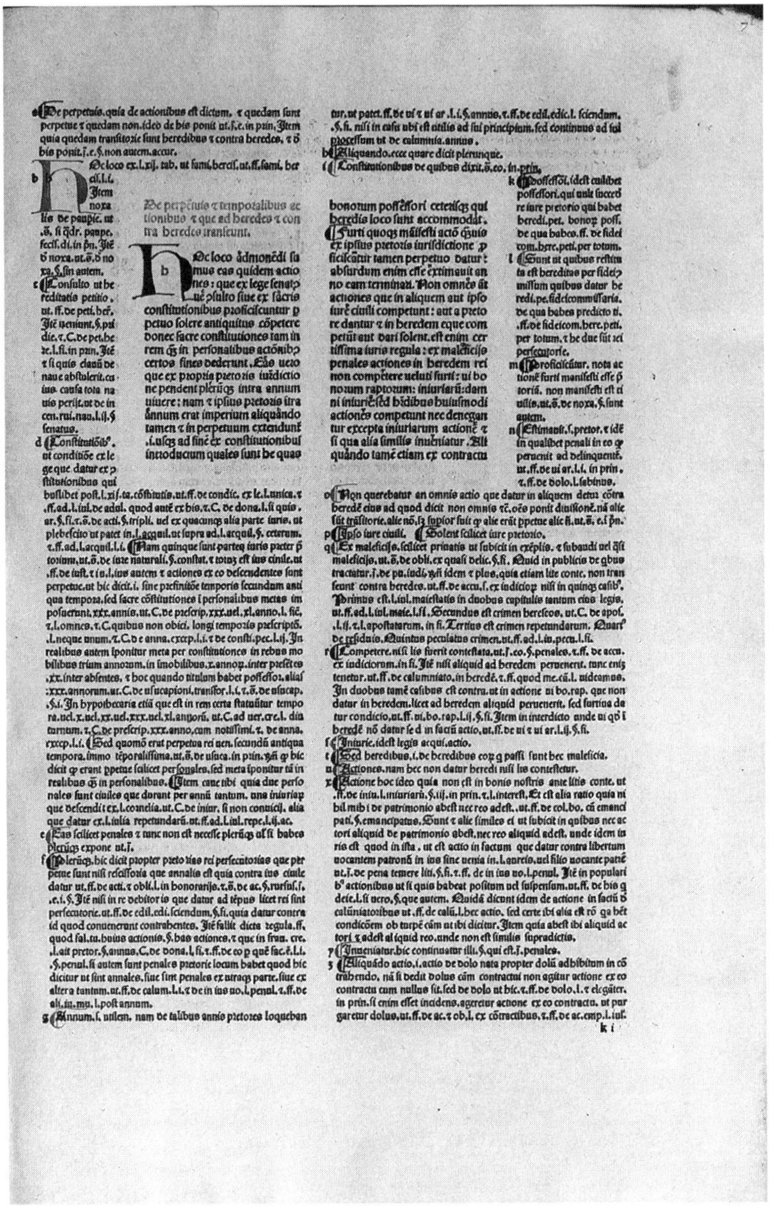

Figure 4.1. Justinian, *Institutiones* (Venice: Jenson n.d. [c. 1478–1480] [GW 7595]), sig. k1r. Copy: Cambridge, MA, Harvard University, Houghton Library, shelf-mark Inc. 4130.5. Page: 431 × 283mm. Type page: 323 × 208mm, for 70 lines of commentary, the inset text in Jenson's 93Gb font, and the surrounding commentary in his 93Ga.

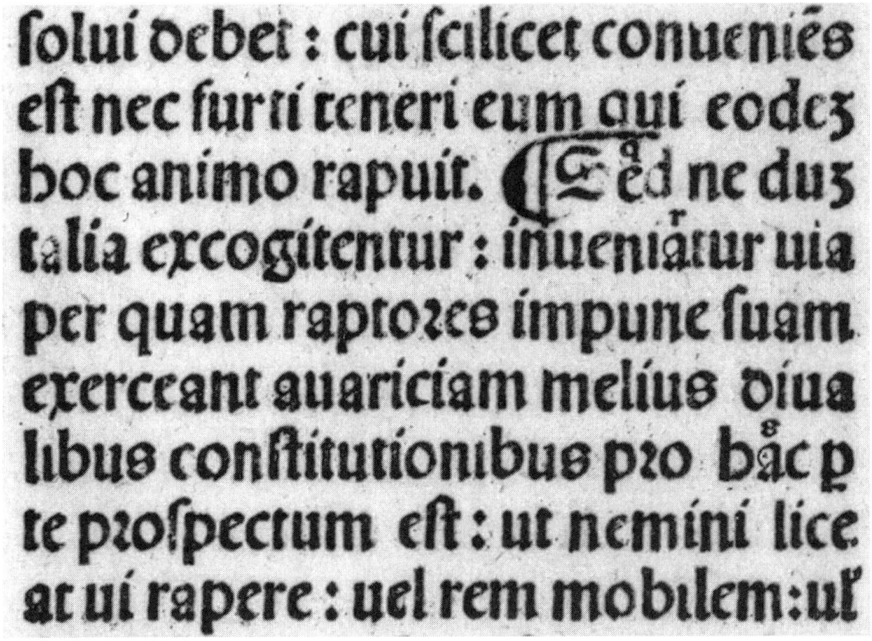
solui debet : cui scilicet conuenies
est nec furti teneri eum qui eodez
hoc animo rapuit. ¶ Sed ne duz
talia excogitentur : inueniatur uia
per quam raptores impune suam
exerceant auariciam melius diua
libus constitutionibus pro hac p
te prospectum est : ut nemini lice
at ui rapere : uel rem mobilem : uel

Figure 4.2. Justinian, *Institutiones* (Venice: Jenson n.d. [c. 1478–1480] [GW 7595]), sig. h3v. From the same copy as fig. 1, with the same dimensions and types.

serving only to prop up the adjacent bodies in a line of type set solid, can be removed without scarring the face and without causing types to lean or lines to collapse, as long as something else fills the space vacated by the trimming. Jenson's tiny reference letters were sized to fit spaces created to hold them, above such specially prepared vowel sorts.

In the earliest example, the *Institutiones*, Jenson's superior figures occur above *a* and *e* only. When the lemmatized term requiring the reference was 'constitutionibus,' for example, or some other term without either *a* or *e* in it, the typesetter had to resort to other expedients, most often postponing the superior figure until a term with an *a* or an *e* in it turned up (in the illustrated example, the typesetter had to wait for the third word, the text reading 'constitutionibus pro hac'). In a later example of Jenson's legal printing, he obviated the need for resort to such expedients. The superior figures occur above *a*, *e*, *o*, and *u*. Evidently, supplies of trimmed down vowel sorts had been procured of all the vowels except *i*, doubling the quantity of special vowel sorts required, though making it possible thereby to manage the otherwise awkward lemmata.[13]

The visually distinct though commensurate types, for distinguishing inset text and surrounding commentary, the one keyed to the other by the system of hung letters and indentations in the commentary and the superior figures in the text, with a display type too sometimes occurring – the extensive typographical resources that Jenson deployed make these pages work. The matter of arranging the blocks of these differing types, with appropriate spacing and furniture, to lay out the pages of these law books, was also a task of some complication, which Jenson also accomplished with characteristic technical flair.

One refinement of Jenson's work here is the fact that though the two inset text columns on the pages of his law books are the same width, the inner columns of commentary – the column nearer the gutter by the spine of the book, be these inner columns on recto or verso pages – are always somewhat narrower than the outer columns. In the illustrated example, figs 4.1–4.2, the inner column is 93mm or 27mm (next to the inset text) wide, while the outer column measures 105mm or 37mm. When the books are laid or held open, and a pair of pages is viewed at once, the columnar asymmetries increase the perspective-like illusion of recession into depth about the pages, heightening an illusion created in the first place already by the frame-and-picture effect of the basic inset with surround layout with which Jenson was working. The books are deep. Their pages move, even when sitting still and flat.

Such subtleties aside, the greater problem for Jenson was that the pages of the law books could not be designed or laid out once and for all. Because of peculiarities of relations between text and commentary – some passages require more comment than others – every page differs from every other. For beginnings and endings and major internal divisions, adjustments always had to be made. Sometimes the commentary can grow so extensive that it all but buries the text; elsewhere the text expands in proportion to the commentary. One solution for the problem of sparse comment was to leave the surrounding columns open, at top or bottom or both; the last resort was to leave only patches of comment at the four corners of the page (that the platen might yet impress evenly at its descent). There are almost as many variant layouts in Jenson's law books as there are pages, and this is the point: not only does the basic layout Jenson used for his law books make great demands on typographic resources and the labour of page layout but these same demands were repeated, over and over, page after page, throughout these books. And the law books are as long as they are complex: Jenson's edition of the *Codex* of Justinian has over seven hundred differently laid out pages.[14]

The successes of Jenson's *Institutiones* and his other law books of the same period came only at the end of a series of experiments on the part of Jenson and his predecessors. The early efforts look primitive by comparison. An example is the edition of the *Decretales* printed at Rome in 1472 in partnership by Ulrich Han and Simon Chardella (fig. 4.3 and detail): in it, a more or less

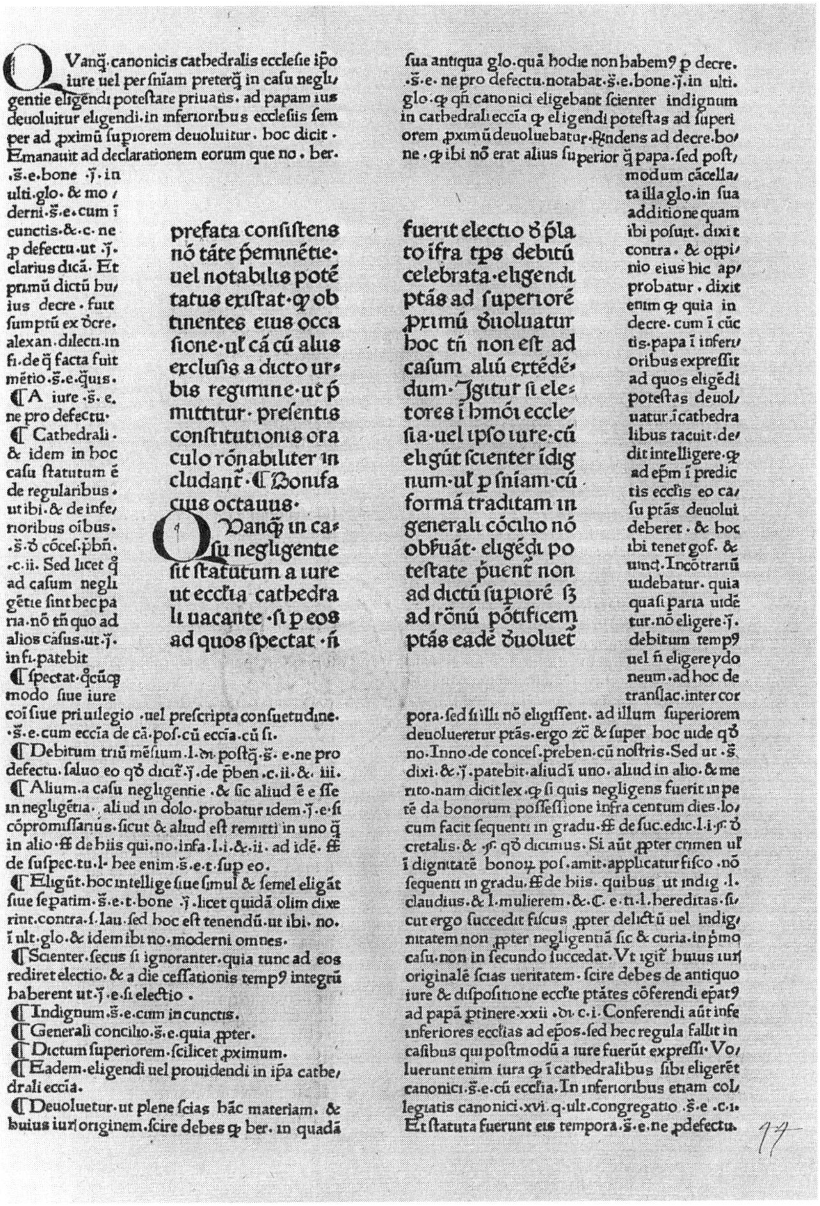
Q Vanq̃. canonicis cathedralis ecclesie ipo iure uel per sñiam preterq̃ in casu negligentie eligendi potestate priuatis. ad papam ius deuoluitur eligendi. in inferioribus ecclesiis sem per ad ꝓximũ sup̄iorem deuoluitur. hoc dicit. Emanauit ad declarationem eorum que no. ber. .s̃.e.bone .ỹ. in ulti.glo. & mo derni.s̃.e.cum ĩ cunctis.&.c. ne ꝓ defectu.ut .ỹ. clarius dicã. Et primũ dictũ huius decre. fuit sumptũ ex decre. alexan. dilecti.in fi. de q̃ facta fuit mẽtio.s̃.e.q̃uis. ¶A iure .s̃. e. ne pro defectu. ¶ Cathedrali. & idem in hoc casu statutum ẽ de regularibus. ut ibi. & de inferioribus oĩbus. .s̃. d cõces.pbñ. .c. ii. Sed licet q̃ ad casum negligẽtie sint hec pa ria. nõ tñ quo ad alios casus.ut.ỹ. in fi.patebit ¶ spectat. q̃cũq̃ modo siue iure coĩ siue priuilegio .uel prescripta consuetudine. .s̃.e.cum eccĩa de cã.pos.cũ eccĩa.cũ si. ¶Debitum triũ mẽsium.l.di.postq̃.s̃. e.ne pro defectu. saluo eo q d dicit̃.ỹ.de pben.c.ii.&. iii. ¶Alium.a casu negligentie .& sic aliud ẽ e sse in negligẽtia. aliud in dolo.probatur idem.ỹ.e.si cõpromissariũs.sicut & aliud est remitti in uno q̃ in alio.ff de hiis qui.no.infa.l.i.&.ii. ad idẽ. ff de suspec.tu.l. hee enim.s̃.e.t.sup eo. ¶Eligũt.hoc intellige siue simul & semel eligãt siue sepatim.s̃.e.t.bone .ỹ.licet quidã olim dixe rint.contra.s.lau.sed hoc est tenendũ.ut ibi. no. ĩ ult.glo.& idem ibi no.moderni omnes. ¶Scienter.secus si ignoranter.quia tunc ad eos rediret electio. & a die cessationis temp9 integrũ haberent ut.ỹ.e.si electio. ¶Indignum.s̃.e.cum in cunctis. ¶Generali concilio.s̃.e.quia ꝓpter. ¶Dictum superiorem.scilicet ꝓximum. ¶Eadem.eligendi uel prouidendi in ipa cathedrali eccĩa. ¶Deuoluetur.ut plene scias hãc materiam. & huius iuris originem.scire debes ꝙ ber. in quadã sua antiqua glo.quã hodie non habem9 ꝑ decre. .s̃.e. ne pro defectu.notabat.s̃.e.bone.ỹ.in ulti. glo.ꝙ qñ canonici eligebant scienter indignum in cathedrali eccĩa ꝙ eligendi potestas ad superiorem ꝓximũ deuoluebatur.ꝛ̃ndens ad decre.bone.ꝙ ibi nõ erat alius superior q̃ papa.sed postmodum cãcellaria illa glo.in sua additione quam ibi posuit. dixit contra. & oppinio eius hic approbatur. dixit enim ꝙ quia in decre. cum ĩ cũctis.papa ĩ inferioribus expressit ad quos eligẽdi potestas deuoluatur.ĩ cathedralibus tacuit.dedit intelligere.ꝙ ad epm ĩ predictis eccĩis eo casu ptãs deuolui deberet. & hoc ibi tenet gof. & uinc̃.Incõtrariũ uidebatur. quia quasi paria uidẽtur.nõ eligere.ỹ. debitum temp9 uel ñ eligere ydoneum.ad hoc de transiac.inter corpora.sed si illi nõ eligissent. ad illum superiorem deuolueretur ptãs.ergo zc̃ & super hoc uide q d no.Inno.de conces.preben.cũ nostris.Sed ut .s̃. dixi.&.ỹ.patebit.aliudĩ uno. aliud in alio.& merito.nam dicit lex.ꝙ si quis negligens fuerit in petẽ da bonorum possessione infra centum dies.locum facit sequenti in gradu.ff de suc.edic.l.i.ꝟ. d cretalis.& ꝟ. q d dicimus. Si aũt ꝓpter crimen uel ĩ dignitatẽ bonoꝝ pos.amit.applicatur fisco .nõ sequenti in gradu.ff de hiis. quibus ut indig .l. claudius.& l.mulierem.&.C. e.ti.l.hereditas.sicut ergo succedit fiscus ꝓpter delictũ uel indignitatem non ꝓpter negligentiã sic & curia.in pmo casu.non in secundo succedat. Vt igit̃ huius iuris originalẽ scias ueritatem. scire debes de antiquo iure & dispositione eccĩe ptãtes cõferendi epat9 ad papã ptinere.xxii .di. c.i. Conferendi aũt infe inferiores eccĩas ad epos.sed hec regula fallit in casibus qui postmodũ a iure fuerũt expressi. Voluerunt enim iura ꝙ ĩ cathedralibus sibi eligerẽt canonici.s̃.e.cũ eccĩa. In inferioribus etiam collegiatis canonici.xvi. q.ult.congregatio .s̃.e .c.i. Et statuta fuerunt eis tempora.s̃.e.ne ꝓdefectu.

prefata consistens nõ tãte ꝑeminẽtie uel notabilis potẽ tatus existat.ꝙ ob tinentes eius occa sione.uel cã cũ aliis exclusis a dicto urbis regimine.ut ꝑ mittitur. presentis constitutionis ora culo rõnabiliter in cludant̃. ¶Bonifa cius octauus. Q Vanq̃ in casu negligentie sit statutum a iure ut eccĩa cathedrali uacante.si p eos ad quos spectat .si fuerit electio d pla to ĩfra tps debitũ celebrata.eligendi ptãs ad superiorẽ ꝓximũ d uoluatur hoc tñ non est ad casum aliũ extẽdẽdum. Igitur si electores ĩ hmõi ecclesia.uel ipso iure.cũ eligũt scienter ĩdignum.uel p sñiam.cũ formã traditam in generali cõcilio nõ obseruãt. eligẽdi potestate puent̃ non ad dictũ supiorẽ s3 ad rõnũ põtificem ptãs eadẽ d uoluet̃

77

Figure 4.3. Boniface VIII, *Liber sextus decretalium* (Rome: Han and Chardella 1472 [GW 4851]), fol. 44r. Copy: Cambridge, MA, Harvard University, Law Library, shelf-mark Aa/ C363p5/ 472/ H3588. Page: 407 × 290mm. Type page: 298 × 204mm, for 58 lines of commentary, the inset text in 125G, and the surrounding commentary in 103R.

roman type (103R) is used for the comments around the text, which is printed in a larger, more or less gothic font (125G).[15] There is nothing subtle or sinuous about their page: symmetrical blocks, plainly put. The chief awkwardness, though, is that the types are incommensurate. The ratio of lines of commentary to lines of text is irrational.

Jenson had his own troubles with this sort of thing early on.[16] His and others' failed experiments confirm that the early printers were slow to arrive at something as successful and sophisticated as the *Institutiones*. The work was technically demanding. Different sizes or styles of letter, variations of layout, not to mention colour or decoration – these are easy in manuscript but hard to do with a press. The market compelled printers to try; the technology was recalcitrant and the resulting books were mostly miserable compromises. In the short term, the story is one of failed printers, who could not make the tools do what would be marketable or who could not find or create markets for what the tools were capable of doing.[17] In the long term, though the press continued to answer to a degree to traditional wants, determined by manuscript traditions, the market learned to want what was technically most feasible for the press to do. In the meantime, what Jenson succeeded at finally was making a manuscript-like page by typographic means – doing with type, an unyielding tool, what had been possible to do before only by a warm, supple means – pen in hand.

In terms of page design, Jenson's law books were throwbacks, representing a step backwards into the old world of preprint manuscript culture. In technical terms, however, the law books represent a great leap forward: technically, Jenson was so good by this point that he could make his presses do the unnatural: he was printing manuscripts.

The Epigraphic Model

With the law books, Jenson made good his claim to be the Daedalus of printing, making type and spacing do things they are not by nature suited to do. What these materials are suited for doing, on the other hand, is what Jenson tried doing with them in 1470, at the very beginning of his career: print – classics and classics-fed early church fathers like Eusebius, as it happens – using fonts and layouts based not on manuscript models but on epigraphic ones.

Jenson has been most admired – properly so – for the perfection of the earliest books he produced, even during his first eighteen to twenty-five months of work: his editions of the *Praeparatio evangelica* of Eusebius, Cicero's letters, Justin's *Epitome*, the *Rhetorica ad Herennium*, the *Vitae imperatorum* of Cornelius Nepos, and so on. The perfection of Jenson's earliest products is easily exaggerated, however, and for two reasons at least: first, others had prepared the way; and, second, there are deliberate imperfections about

Jenson's early books – things deliberately left unfinished – bespeaking a persistent obligation to the manuscript model. There is a third reason: the perfection of Jenson's earliest books, such as it is, is above all a matter of submission, rather than assertion, of his willingness to surrender to the machines: the books' successes are the result of Jenson's trying in them to do no more than was easiest for the machines.

The crucial preparatory work was that of Konrad Sweynheym and Arnold Pannartz – the prototypographers of Italy, 'two Germans of obscure monastic affiliation,' who began printing at Subiaco in 1465 at the Benedictine monastery there, and then moved shop a few kilometers down the road to Rome proper in 1468, where they remained at work only until 1473.[18] Sweynheim and Pannartz invented Roman type – a markedly different style of letterface by comparison with what they could have seen and worked with during a German apprenticeship. In using this innovative face for printing books, Sweynheim and Pannartz laid it out in simple, single blocks of letterpress, the same simple layout over and over again, on otherwise simple, plain pages – pages issuing from the press in plain black and white, making use only of the simple, stark contrast between the one colour of ink and the colour of paper. This is the combination of elements – Roman type, single-block layout, and only the contrast between black and white – that Jenson took up when he started printing in 1470 and did so well by. Sweynheym and Pannartz were there first, so to speak; Jenson, like others, was able to teach himself by their example.

The pages of Jenson's early books were often patently incomplete, however, as they came from the presses. A page from Jenson's 1470 edition of the letters of Cicero (see fig. 4.4), for example, leaves space (in the seventh line up) for a phrase of Greek that Cicero had used as part of his Latin sentence but that Jenson would not have been able to print in Greek until he obtained his first Greek font in late 1471.[19] The blanks left for Greek passages and phrases in all of Jenson's books printed before that time would have had to be filled in by hand. The same page leaves space too for an initial capital at the beginning of an epistle (here it should be a *P*); and it puts space between the end of one epistle and the beginning of another, where salutation formulas or other titlelike matter belongs.

The copy illustrated has been cleaned up, probably, so that only Jenson's typographical work is seen, in a pristine state. More commonly, these books survive in copies in which handfinishing remains, and there is considerable evidence to indicate that much of the handfinishing in such copies would have been done prior to the books' sale, in some cases by in-house manual confectioners in Jenson's employ, confirming an awareness on the printer's part that the products issued immediately from the press were not yet complete books.[20] The typographic design is the same, basically, handfinishing or no: space for Greek (where Greek was requisite); spaces for initial capitals,

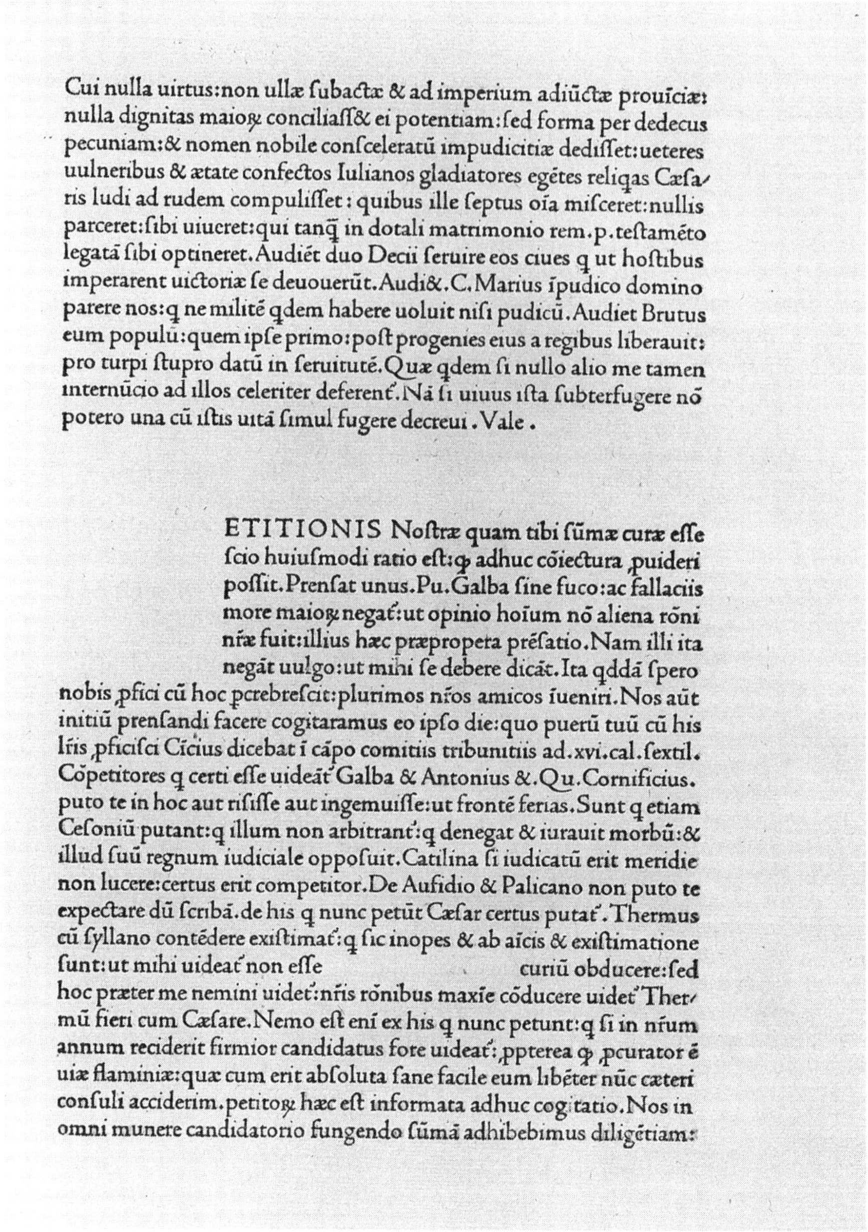

Cui nulla uirtus:non ullæ ſubactæ & ad imperium adiūctæ prouīciæ:
nulla dignitas maioꝝ conciliaſſ& ei potentiam:ſed forma per dedecus
pecuniam:& nomen nobile conſceleratū impudicitiæ dediſſet:ueteres
uulneribus & ætate confectos Iulianos gladiatores egētes reliqas Cæſa/
ris ludi ad rudem compuliſſet: quibus ille ſeptus oīa miſceret:nullis
parceret:ſibi uiueret:qui tanq̄ in dotali matrimonio rem.p.teſtamēto
legatā ſibi optineret. Audiēt duo Decii ſeruire eos ciues q ut hoſtibus
imperarent uictoriæ ſe deuouerūt. Audi&.C. Marius īpudico domino
parere nos:q ne militē qdem habere uoluit niſi pudicū. Audiet Brutus
eum populū:quem ipſe primo:poſt progenies eius a regibus liberauit:
pro turpi ſtupro datū in ſeruitutē. Quæ qdem ſi nullo alio me tamen
internūcio ad illos celeriter deferent. Nā ſi uiuus iſta ſubterfugere nō
potero una cū iſtis uitā ſimul fugere decreui. Vale.

ETITIONIS Noſtræ quam tibi ſūmæ curæ eſſe
ſcio huiuſmodi ratio eſt:ꝙ adhuc cōiectura ꝓuideri
poſſit. Prenſat unus. Pu. Galba ſine fuco:ac fallaciis
more maioꝝ negat:ut opinio hoīum nō aliena rōni
nr̄æ fuit:illius hæc præpropera prēſatio. Nam illi ita
negāt uulgo:ut mihi ſe debere dicāt. Ita qddā ſpero
nobis ꝓfici cū hoc ꝑcrebreſcit:plurimos nr̄os amicos īueniri. Nos aūt
initiū prenſandi facere cogitaramus eo ipſo die:quo puerū tuū cū his
lr̄is ꝓficiſci Cīcius dicebat ī cāpo comitiis tribunitiis ad.xvi.cal.ſextil.
Cōpetitores q certi eſſe uideāt Galba & Antonius &. Qu. Cornificius.
puto te in hoc aut riſiſſe aut ingemuiſſe:ut frontē ferias. Sunt q etiam
Ceſoniū putant:q illum non arbitrant:q denegat & iurauit morbū:&
illud ſuū regnum iudiciale oppoſuit. Catilina ſi iudicatū erit meridie
non lucere:certus erit competitor. De Aufidio & Palicano non puto te
expectare dū ſcribā. de his q nunc petūt Cæſar certus putat. Thermus
cū ſyllano contēdere exiſtimat:q ſic inopes & ab aīcis & exiſtimatione
ſunt:ut mihi uideat non eſſe curiū obducere:ſed
hoc præter me nemini uidet:nr̄is rōnibus maxīe cōducere uidet Ther/
mū fieri cum Cæſare. Nemo eſt enī ex his q nunc petunt:q ſi in nr̄um
annum reciderit firmior candidatus fore uideat:ꝓpterea ꝙ ꝓcurator ē
uiæ flaminiæ:quæ cum erit abſoluta ſane facile eum libēter nūc cæteri
conſuli acciderim. petitoꝝ hæc eſt informata adhuc cogitatio. Nos in
omni munere candidatorio fungendo ſūmā adhibebimus diligētiam:

Figure 4.4. Cicero, *Epistolae* (Venice: Jenson 1470 [Lowry no. 2]), sig. D3r. Copy: Cambridge, MA, Harvard University, Houghton Library, shelf-mark Inc. 4064. Page: 297 × 227mm. Type page: 222 × 136mm, for 39 lines, in 115R.

big ones at bookheads and little ones at chapterheads; and space for titles between sections.

Among the early printers, two approaches to these imperfections, other than handfinishing, were tried – ways to escape the unsettling amalgams that resulted from the handfinishing of machine-made products. First, printers worked out mechanical means for doing what had been done by hand before – further variations of the kind of thing that Jenson was to do later with superior figures in his law books. The early printers' different techniques for red-printing are an example: by means of red-printing, rubrication could be done in print, by means of the press alone, without recourse to manual finishers. More curious is the development of printable approximations of hand-painted initials. Erhard Ratdolt and his partners in Venice, during the period 1476–86, were the first to develop the use of decorative woodcuts to take the place of manual work, including woodcut borders as well as the woodcut initials that occur more commonly.[21] Of course, these print in one colour only, however. Halfway between printed initials and hand-painted ones are hand-stamped initials: Jenson had an alphabet's worth of hand tools, metal hand-held die-stamps cut with patterns that could be inked and stamped into books by hand after the books had been printed (fig. 4.5).[22] The stamped pattern on the page could be coloured in by hand afterwards, though, as the illustrated example shows, colouring was not strictly requisite for completing the page and was not always done. Stylistically, these hand-stamped initials sorted well with Jenson's Roman types. Those who used them were as prone to error as anyone, however, and they were more difficult to correct once the initials had been stamped in place (in the illustrated example, the *E* should be a *V*); in any case, the labour involved was excessive.

The second approach, though technically less curious than woodcuts or hand-stamped capitals, was more efficient and has been more significant historically: instead of evolving ways to make typographic likenesses of manuscript matter, printers also simply substituted typographic matter that did the same job by different graphic means. With hand-stamped and then woodcut capitals, red-printing, and so on, printers perpetuated manuscript traditions of design beyond their natural material limits; with this second approach, printers abandoned manuscript traditions to work out another graphic vocabulary, appropriate to the medium of printing, for doing the same jobs.

Jenson's 1471 edition of the *Vitae imperatorum* (like other editions of the same period) shows the way in which so much was accomplished, by simple means (fig. 4.6). Though in the illustrated example the initial capital is hand painted – a simple, well-conceived, well-drawn Roman 'P' – the title ('Phocionis vita') is printed. It is in black, all capitals, centred in the column, with a slight pull toward the book's spine, line space above and line space below, the contrast of black and white: a comparatively simple, lapidary, but

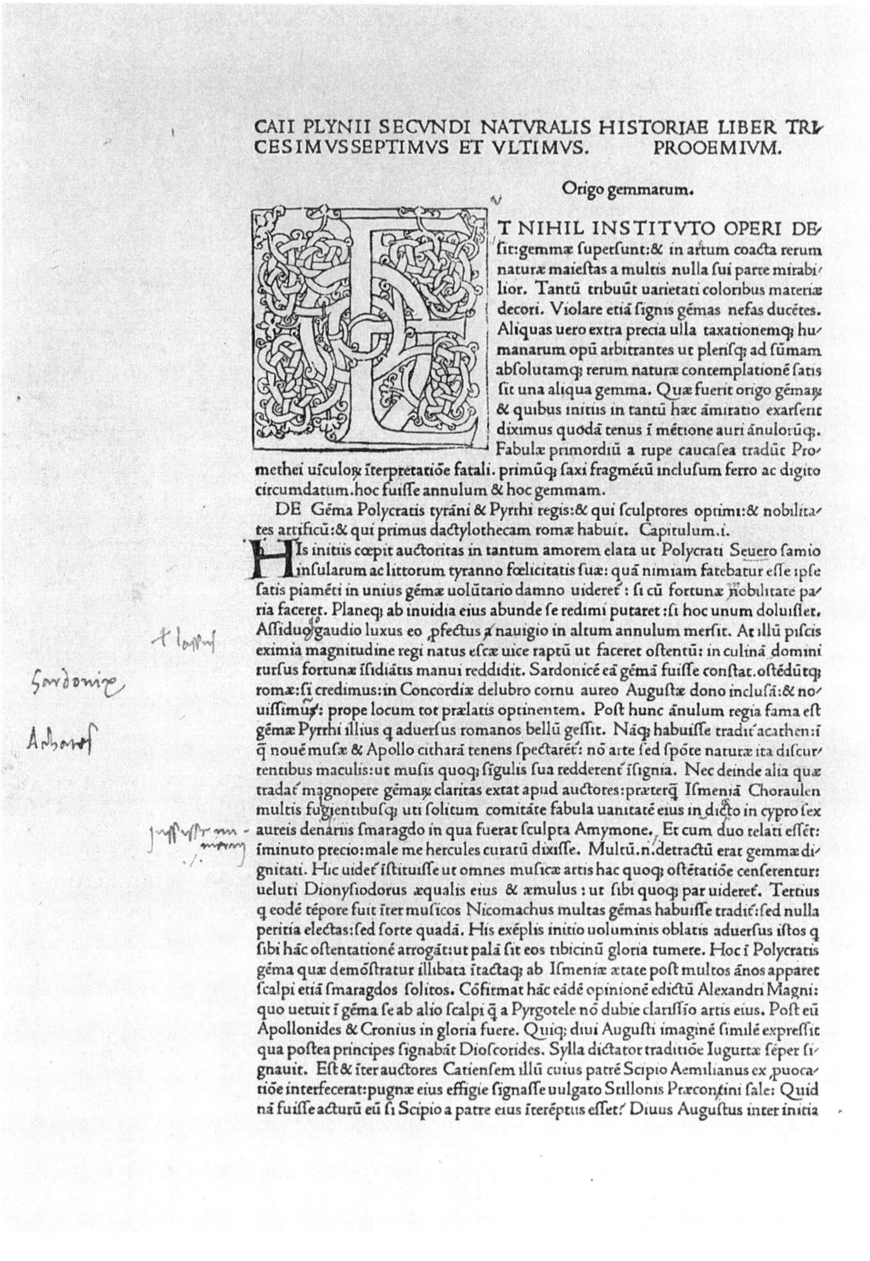

CAII PLYNII SECVNDI NATVRALIS HISTORIAE LIBER TRI-
CESIMVSSEPTIMVS ET VLTIMVS. PROOEMIVM.

Origo gemmarum.

ET NIHIL INSTITVTO OPERI DE-
ſit:gemmæ ſuperſunt:& in artum coacta rerum
naturæ maieſtas a multis nulla ſui parte mirabi-
lior. Tantũ tribuũt uarietati coloribus materiæ
decori. Violare etiã ſignis gẽmas nefas ducẽtes.
Aliquas uero extra precia ulla taxationemq; hu-
manarum opũ arbitrantes ut pleriſq; ad ſũmam
abſolutamq; rerum naturæ contemplationẽ ſatis
ſit una aliqua gemma. Quæ fuerit origo gẽmaꝝ
& quibus initiis in tantũ hæc ãmiratio exarſerit
diximus quodã tenus ĩ mẽtione auri ãnulorũq;.
Fabulæ primordiũ a rupe caucaſea tradũt Pro-
methei uĩculoꝝ ĩterpretatiõe fatali. primũq; ſaxi fragmẽtũ incluſum ferro ac digito
circumdatum.hoc fuiſſe annulum & hoc gemmam.

DE Gẽma Polycratis tyrãni & Pyrrhi regis:& qui ſculptores optimi:& nobilita-
tes artificũ:& qui primus dactylothecam romæ habuit. Capitulum.i.

HIs initiis cœpit auctoritas in tantum amorem elata ut Polycrati Seuero ſamio
inſularum ac littorum tyranno fœlicitatis ſuæ: quã nimiam fatebatur eſſe ipſe
ſatis piamẽti in unius gẽmæ uolũtario damno uideret : ſi cũ fortunæ nobilitate paria faceret. Planeq; ab inuidia eius abunde ſe redimi putaret :ſi hoc unum doluiſſet.
Aſſiduo gaudio luxus eo ꝓfectus a nauigio in altum annulum merſit. At illũ piſcis
eximia magnitudine regi natus eſcæ uice raptũ ut faceret oſtentũ: in culinã domini
rurſus fortunæ ĩſidiãtis manui reddidit. Sardonicẽ eã gẽmã fuiſſe conſtat.oſtẽdũtq;
romæ:ſi credimus:in Concordiæ delubro cornu aureo Auguſtæ dono incluſã:& no-
uiſſimus: prope locum tot prælatis optinentem. Poſt hunc ãnulum regia fama eſt
gẽmæ Pyrrhi illius q aduerſus romanos bellũ geſſit. Nãq; habuiſſe tradit acathen:ĩ
q̃ nouẽ muſæ & Apollo citharã tenens ſpectarẽt: nõ arte ſed ſpõte naturæ ita diſcur-
rentibus maculis:ut muſis quoq; ſigulis ſua redderent ĩſignia. Nec deinde alia quæ
tradat magnopere gẽmaꝝ claritas extat apud auctores:præterq̃ Iſmeniã Choraulen
multis fugientibuſq; uti ſolitum comitãte fabula uanitatẽ eius in dicto in cypro ſex
aureis denariis ſmaragdo in qua fuerat ſculpta Amymone. Et cum duo relati eſſẽt:
ĩminuto precio:male me hercules curatũ dixiſſe. Multũ.n.detractũ erat gemmæ di-
gnitati. Hic uidet ĩſtituiſſe ut omnes muſicæ artis hac quoq; oſtẽtatiõe cenſerentur:
ueluti Dionyſiodorus æqualis eius & æmulus : ut ſibi quoq; par uideret. Tertius
q eodẽ tẽpore fuit ĩter muſicos Nicomachus multas gẽmas habuiſſe tradit:ſed nulla
peritia electas:ſed ſorte quadã. His exẽplis initio uoluminis oblatis aduerſus iſtos q
ſibi hãc oſtentationẽ arrogãt:ut palã ſit eos tibicinũ gloria tumere. Hoc ĩ Polycratis
gẽma quæ demõſtratur illibata ĩtactaq; ab Iſmeniæ ætate poſt multos ãnos apparet
ſcalpi etiã ſmaragdos ſolitos. Cõfirmat hãc eãdẽ opinionẽ edictũ Alexandri Magni:
quo uetuit ĩ gẽma ſe ab alio ſcalpi q̃ a Pyrgotele nõ dubie clariſſĩo artis eius. Poſt eũ
Apollonides & Cronius in gloria fuere. Quiq; diui Auguſti imaginẽ ſimilẽ expreſſit
qua poſtea principes ſignabãt Dioſcorides. Sylla dictator traditiõe Iugurtæ ſẽper ſi-
gnauit. Eſt & ĩter auctores Catienſem illũ cuius patrẽ Scipio Aemilianus ex ꝓuoca-
tiõe interfecerat:pugnæ eius effigie ſignaſſe uulgato Stillonis Præcontini ſale: Quid
nã fuiſſe acturũ eũ ſi Scipio a patre eius ĩterẽptus eſſet: Diuus Auguſtus inter initia

Figure 4.5. Pliny, *Historia naturalis* (Venice: Jenson 1472 [Lowry no. 29]), fol. 344v. Copy: Cambridge, MA, Harvard University, Houghton Library, shelf-mark Typ. Inc. 4087. Page: 411 × 285mm. Type page: 284 × 161mm, for 50 lines, in 115R.

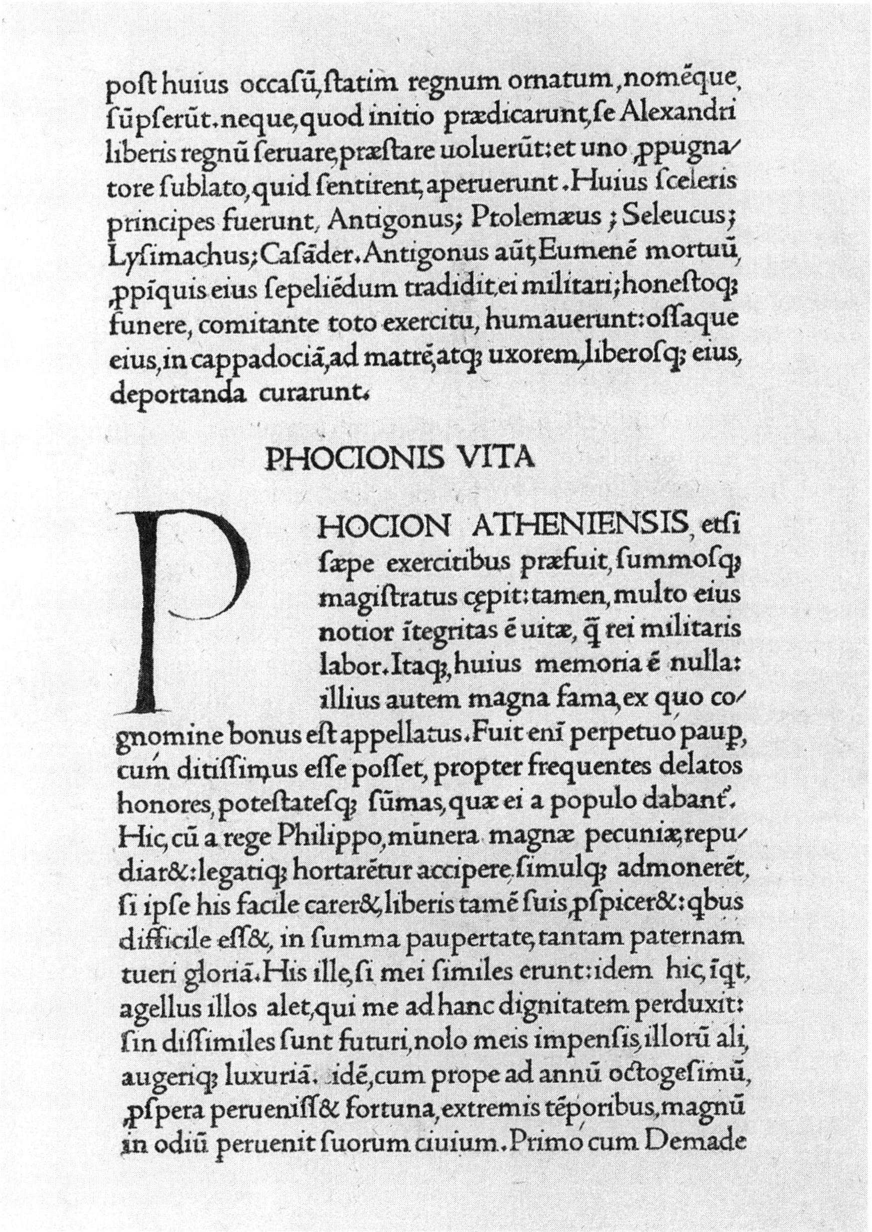

post huius occasũ,statim regnum ornatum,nomẽque,
sũpserũt.neque,quod initio prædicarunt,se Alexandri
liberis regnũ seruare,præstare uoluerũt:et uno ꝓpugna-
tore sublato,quid sentirent,aperuerunt.Huius sceleris
principes fuerunt, Antigonus; Ptolemæus ; Seleucus;
Lysimachus;Casãder.Antigonus aũt,Eumenẽ mortuũ,
ꝓpĩquis eius sepeliẽdum tradidit,ei militari;honestoq;
funere, comitante toto exercitu, humauerunt:ossaque
eius,in cappadociã,ad matrẽ,atq; uxorem,liberosq; eius,
deportanda curarunt.

PHOCIONIS VITA

PHOCION ATHENIENSIS, etsi
sæpe exercitibus præfuit,summosq;
magistratus cępit:tamen,multo eius
notior ĩtegritas ẽ uitæ, q̃ rei militaris
labor.Itaq;,huius memoria ẽ nulla:
illius autem magna fama,ex quo co-
gnomine bonus est appellatus.Fuit enĩ perpetuo paup,
cum ditissimus esse posset, propter frequentes delatos
honores,potestatesq; sũmas,quæ ei a populo dabant.
Hic,cũ a rege Philippo,munera magnæ pecuniæ,repu-
diar&:legatiq; hortarẽtur accipere,simulq; admonerẽt,
si ipse his facile carer&,liberis tamẽ suis,ꝓspicer&:qbus
difficile ess&, in summa paupertate,tantam paternam
tueri gloriã.His ille,si mei similes erunt:idem hic,ĩqt,
agellus illos alet,qui me ad hanc dignitatem perduxit:
sin dissimiles sunt futuri,nolo meis impensis,illorũ ali,
augeriq; luxuriã. idẽ,cum prope ad annũ octogesimũ,
ꝓspera peruenisſ& fortuna,extremis tẽporibus,magnũ
in odiũ peruenit suorum ciuium.Primo cum Demade

Figure 4.6. Cornelius Nepos, *Vitae imperatorum* (Venice: Jenson 1471 March 8 [Lowry no. 5]), sig. e8r. Copy: Cambridge, MA, Harvard University, Houghton Library, shelfmark Inc. 4068. Page: 256 × 181mm. Type page: 183 × 105mm, for 32 lines, in 115R.

effective and purely typographic way to mark a division that before would have been done in colour, in a different script, by hand.

The history of the efforts of early printers to make good the kinds of imperfections that occur on Jenson's early pages is this story of growing independence for print: abandoning the manuscript tradition in favour of purely, distinctively printerly ways of doing things. The imperfections about Jenson's early pages are more immediately instructive, however, for making clear what he could do and what he could not, what was proper for printing and what was not. What Jenson could not do with his presses before 1474 or so were things he need not have troubled over, as it turned out: features of traditional manuscript books, natural or comparatively easy to do in that medium, that were harder or impossible to do with a printing press, and so eventually had to be abandoned; rubrication and illumination and oddities of size and space – things involving irregularity and colour. In the short term, Jenson and others came up with ways to mask their incapacity; in the long term, these traditional features of manuscript books were replaced with typographic equivalents or substitutes – typographic means, stylistically independent, for fulfilling the same graphic functions. Development of a distinctively typographic vocabulary is already apparent in Jenson's work.

What Jenson could do already in 1470 was imitate, in effect, not manuscript, but stone-cut models. In doing so, he and other printers were only doing what was natural and appropriate to their medium. The search for Jenson's particular typographic models has proved fruitless, and no particular epigraphic model for his work is proposed here. There is no evidence to suggest, nor does it seem plausible to suppose, that Jenson studied particular stones, or that he was enthralled by the advice of some individual antiquary, though there was currently much interest in ancient epigraphy.[24]

The nearest analogues for Jenson's pages – like those of Sweynheym and Pannartz before him, only better done – are altars and tombstones: the area covered with lettering tends to be similarly proportioned, as it is not in the better-known public monuments like Trajan's Column, and the stone cutters dealt similarly with problems of big and little letters, centring, proportional spacing, and line justification. These kinds of objects are common in Italy. They did not have to be searched out or studied particularly.

Be that as it may, more consequential is the essential material kinship between printing and this kind of stone cutting, evoked already in the characterization of Jenson's work as akin to the process of forcing impressions 'into stone, with a seal or stamp of some sort.' The long-standing disciplinary distinctions between epigraphy and calligraphy, and between sculpture and painting, reflect real material differences – between the superficial activity, of laying matter over surfaces, on the one hand, and the deep work, of cutting into surfaces, on the other. Manuscript making belongs with painting and calligraphy. Printing belongs with sculpture and epigraphy. That Jenson, like

Sweynheym and Pannartz before him, should have drawn on the tradition of Roman epigraphy is more or less accidental, the result of the local epigraphic traditions of the Western sectors of the former Roman Empire and the current humanist vogue for old stones. It is easy enough to imagine a printing derived from some other epigraphic tradition. What is not so easy to imagine is a printing that would have remained obligated to a calligraphic tradition – materially, it does not make sense.

The Machines Decide

To insist on this determinative force ('in the last instance') of the technology of printing ought not to entail forgetting the overdeterminations contributed from local and international commercial and cultural systems, or even individual agency.[25] 'The moment of any new technology is a moment of choice,' as Raymond Williams has said, addressing the problem of technological determinism directly:

> All technical study and experiment are undertaken within already existing social relations and cultural forms, typically for purposes that are already in general foreseen. Moreover, a technical invention as such has comparatively little social significance. It is only when it is selected for investment towards production, and when it is consciously developed for particular social uses – that is, when it moves from being a technical invention to what can properly be called an available *technology* – that the general significance begins. These processes of selection, investment and development are obviously of a general social and economic kind, within existing social and economic relations, and in a specific social order are designed for particular uses and advantages.[26]

Moreover, it eventually proved possible for a person so skilled as Jenson, the Daedalus of the new machines, to make manuscript-like printed books, mastering the recalcitrance of the materials. Demonstrably, however, it was not easy for him to do so, nor were his efforts of much historical consequence. He tried printing manuscript-like books only late, and only after admitting his incapacity with the blank spaces appearing on his earliest pages.

What Jenson could do from the start, what he did best, and what has been his (and his generation's) enduring legacy, was to submit to the materials, making pages that looked like monuments inscribed in stone. Of course, this monumentalizing of the page that came with printing has had general cultural ramifications and consequences. By the lapidary, funerary properties of the form –once and for always, finally, authoritatively – written matter was rendered dead, inert, represented as the implacable weight of authority (and *de mortuis nihil nisi bonum*). Culture's relation to written matter was altered fundamentally and pervasively, in ways that remain to be undone, and may in fact be undone, as the technology of printing itself obsolesces and dies, to be killed finally by the resolution of the present contradiction between (old) relations of book production and (new) forces of production for the circulation of information. Meanwhile, whatever the ramifications of the form of the printed page, it was the nature of the technology itself – materials and processes – that determined the form. With printing, the machines decided.

NOTES

1 Theodor Adorno, *Minima Moralia*, trans. E.F.N. Jephcott (London: NLB, 1974), 47. The additional allusion is to the 'Myth Today' section of Roland Barthes's *Mythologies*, trans. Annette Lavers (New York: Hill and Wang, 1972), esp. 121–59.

2 'Magistri Nicolai Ienson Gallici alterius (ut vere dicam) Daedali, qui librariae artis mirabilis inventor, non ut scribantur calamo libri, sed veluti gemma imprimantur ac prope sigillo, primus omnium ingeniose monstravit:' in Quintilian, *Institutiones oratoriae* (Venice: Jenson, 21 May 1471 [Lowry no. 13]), sig. a1v. References to Lowry numbers in all such citations herein are to the 'Short Bibliography of Jenson Editions' in Martin Lowry, *Nicholas Jenson and the Rise of Venetian Publishing in Renaissance Europe* (Oxford: Blackwell, 1991), 219–54, where references to fuller descriptions are supplied. For items not listed in Lowry, references to the descriptions in the *Gesamtkatalog der Wiegendrucke*, 2nd ed., vols. 1– (Stuttgart: Hiersmann, 1968–), abbreviated *GW*, are supplied.

3 See Lowry, *Nicholas Jenson*, 48–52.

4 'M. Nicolaus Ienson Gallicus viventibus posterisque miro impressit artificio:' in Quintilian, *Institutiones oratoriae*, sig. x9v.

5 Lowry, *Nicholas Jenson*, 99.

6 'Gallicus hoc Ienson Nicolaus muneris orbi / Attulit ingenio Daedalicaque manu:' in Cicero, *Epistolae* (Venice: Jenson, 1470 [Lowry no. 2]), sig. s5v; 'Artifici grates, optime lector, habe:' in Leonardo Bruni, *De bello gothico* (Venice: Jenson, 1471 [Lowry no. 14]), sig. f12r; 'Quid magis artificem peteret, dux, Christus, et auctor? / Tres facit aeternos ingeniosa manus:' in Eusebius, *Praeparatio evangelica* (Venice: Jenson, 1470 [Lowry no. 1]), sig.o10r; 'Hoc ego Nicoleos Gallus cognomine Ienson / Impressi: mirae quis neget artis opus?' in Suetonius, *Vitae Caesarum* (Venice: Jenson, 1471 [Lowry no. 18]), sig. p10r; 'emendatum illustri insignique Nicolai Jenson Galici, qui huius rei alios opifices facile antecellit:' in Justinian, *Digestum vetus* (Venice: Jenson, n.d. [ca. 1478–80] [*GW* 7658]), sig. y9r.

7 Plato, *Meno* 97d–e. The social and cultural unpredictability of printing at the point of its adoption is discussed, for the English context, in David R. Carlson, 'Chaucer, Humanism, and Printing,' *University of Toronto Quarterly* 64 (1995): 280.

8 On Jenson's legal printing generally, see Lowry, *Nicholas Jenson*, 137–52 and 156–68.

9 Instances of the compression of matter in the law books are detailed in Lowry, *Nicholas Jenson*, 151, 158, and 160.

10 The example discussed and illustrated is Justinian, *Institutiones* (Venice: Jenson, n.d. [ca. 1478–80] [*GW* 7595]).

11 Jenson's types are listed and illustrated with samples in the *Catalogue of Books Printed in the XVth Century Now in the British Museum*, 10 vols (London: British Museum, 1908–70), 5: 165–6. The 150G display font appears first in the part of the *Summa theologica* of Antoninus that Jenson printed in 1477 (Lowry no. 50) and in other books of the same year.

12 The history of this development is discussed in greater detail in David R. Carlson, 'Printed Superior Figures in Nicholas Jenson's Lawbooks, 1478–1480,' *Papers of the Bibliographical Society of America* 96 (2002): 4–22. For explaining to me the way in which Jenson's solution must have worked, I am grateful to Randall McLeod.

13 The book with superior figures over *a* and *e* only is the Justinian, *Institutiones* (Venice: Jenson, n.d. [ca. 1478–80] [*GW* 7595]); the book disposing the four-vowel system is the (again undated) Justinian, *Codex* (Venice: Jenson, n.d. [ca. 1479] [*GW* 7726]). Neither book, nor the cognate *Digestum vetus* (Venice: Jenson, n.d. [*GW* 7658]), is included in Lowry's 'Short Bibliography of Jenson Editions,' 239–54.

14 Justinian, *Codex* (Venice: Jenson, n.d. [ca. 1479] [*GW* 7726]).

15 Boniface VIII, *Liber sextus decretalium* (Rome: Han and Chardella, 1472 [*GW* 4851]).

16 Jenson tried similarly awkward combinations of his 106G and 84G fonts, for text and commentary respectively, in editions of Gratian, *Decretum* (Venice: Jenson, 28 June 1474 [Lowry no. 34]) and of Gregory IX, *Decretales* (Venice: Jenson, 1 March 1475 [Lowry no. 36]). And he first used his second commentary type, the 93Ga, in combination with his 106G text font, in his edition of Boniface VIII, *Liber sextus decretalium* (Venice: Jenson, 1476 [Lowry no. 43]), also with curious results.

17 The career of Caxton's early partner Colard Mansion is instructive: see esp. Paul Saenger, 'Colard Mansion and the Evolution of the Printed Book,' *Library Quarterly* 45 (1975): 405–18.

18 On their work, see esp. Maury Feld, 'Constructed Letters and Illuminated Texts: Regiomontanus, Leon Battista Alberti, and the Origins of Roman Type,' *Harvard Library Bulletin* 28 (1980): 357–79, 'Sweynheym and Pannartz, Cardinal Bessarion, Neoplatonism: Renaissance Humanism and Two Early Printers' Choice of Texts,' *Harvard Library Bulletin* 30 (1982): 282–335 (the quotation is from 283 of this paper), and 'The Sibyls of Subiaco: Sweynheym and Pannartz and the *Editio Princeps* of Lactantius,' in *Renaissance Studies in Honor of Craig Hugh Smyth* (Florence: Giunti Barbèra, 1985), 1: 301–16.

19 Cicero, *Epistolae* (Venice: Jenson, 1470 [Lowry no. 2]). For Greek types, including Jenson's, see now Nicolas Barker, *Aldus Manutius and the Development of Greek*

Script and Type in the Fifteenth Century, 2nd ed. (New York: Fordham University Press, 1992).

20 Cf. Lillian Armstrong, 'The Impact of Printing on Miniaturists in Venice after 1469,' in *Printing the Written Word*, ed. Sandra L. Hindman (Ithaca: Cornell University Press, 1991), 174–202.

21 Cf. Arthur M. Hind, *An Introduction to a History of Woodcut* (1935; rpt. New York: Dover, 1963), 2: 458–62.

22 Pliny, *Historia naturalis* (Venice: Jenson, 1472 [Lowry no. 29]), in the copy Cambridge, MA, Harvard University, Houghton Library, shelf-mark Typ. Inc. 4087.

23 8 March 1471.

24 Cf. Lowry, *Nicholas Jenson*, 76–81.

25 Especially pertinent are the qualifications offered by Louis Althusser, 'Contradiction and Overdetermination,' in *For Marx*, trans. Ben Brewster (1969; rpt. London: NLB, 1996), 87–128 (e.g., 113: 'the lonely hour of the "last instance" never comes'), including his exegeses, 111–14 and 117–28, of the crucial Engels letter to Joseph Bloch, 21 September 1890, in which Engels disavows an economic-determinist intention in his collaborative work with Marx. The fundamental revaluations of the subjective, immaterial pole of Marxist dialectic have been the papers of Georg Lukàcs, collected as *History and Class Consciousness*, trans. Rodney Livingstone (Cambridge, MA: MIT Press, 1971), esp. 'Reification and the Consciousness of the Proletariat,' 83–222, and 'Class Consciousness,' 46–82.

26 Raymond Williams, 'Culture and Technology,' in *Towards 2000* (Harmondsworth: Penguin, 1985), 146 and 129–30; cf. Williams's 'Base and Superstructure in Marxist Cultural Theory,' *New Left Review* 82 (1973): 3–16. The fundamental analysis rejecting technological determinism remains that of Georg Lukàcs, again, 'Technology and Social Relations' (1921), rpt. *in Marxism and Human Liberation*, ed. E. San Juan, Jr (New York: Delta, 1973), 49–60.

5 Print Culture and Decolonizing the University: Indigenizing the Page: Part 1

Marie Battiste

Indigenous peoples throughout the world have used a wide array of forms and systems of communicating or writing or remembering that have shown similarity in strands of symbolic designs, meaning, and function.[1] Early Indigenous literacy in America was largely symbolic and ideographic, reflecting a unified vision of knowledge and thought from one continent to another. A wide diversity of forms exists from the Tupi-Guarani's *Ayvu Rapyta* or Origin of Human Speech,[2] to the Yucatac-Mayan paper screenfolds,[3] to the Algonquian *Walam Olum* or Red Score,[4] Midewiwin or Grand Medicine scrolls,[5] and Mi'kmaw hieroglyphics;[6] these mutually intelligible ideological systems comprised a tribal encyclopedia capable of providing the true knowledge, heritage, and history of early America.[7] Modern social science researchers have tended to denigrate this knowledge or classified these systems as art, religion, or material culture, but not as literature, science, or knowledge. However, Indigenous peoples themselves are beginning to reconstruct their histories and knowledge and to find decolonizing strategies that reclaim and restore their knowledge and symbolic systems. As their efforts emerge in many forms, they offer new scholarship to educational institutions that may begin to dissipate the historic and continuing cognitive imperialism in modern education. The following pages seek to assist this process.

Early Euro-Christian travellers and missionaries destroyed, transformed, or simply ignored most Aboriginal literacies of America or created myths that supported their own ascendancy, holding to their Eurocentric biases favouring paged writing. Some of these myths are reflected in their ethnocentric belief that Indians were not capable of writing. In 1580 Montaigne spoke of the Tupi-Guarani of Brazil as 'so new and infantile, that he is yet to learn his A.B.C.'[8] When Europeans did encounter undeniable evidence of a literacy equivalent to their own, such as Toltec and Mayan paper books, they did their best to eradicate it as a threat to the teachings of the scriptures they brought with them. European scriptures were silent about the American continent and its peoples, a fact immensely distressing to many thinkers of the sixteenth and seventeenth centuries. This Scriptural vacuum and source of moral doubt was filled with the myth that the Native Americans were illiterate savages who 'only' possessed an oral tradition, a myth clearly designed to preserve the moral ascendancy and economic objectives of European knowledge. This mythic projection justified forcing natives to communicate through European languages and literacy. Today, English is the leading killer language, having amassed the greatest structural power and material resources that its number of speakers can be made to justify, at the expense of other languages.[9] Accordingly, only three of the seventy Aboriginal languages in Canada are predicted to survive the century, along with only 100 of the world's languages.

Ideographic and symbolic literacy has been an important foundation for Indigenous peoples. It is a system that interacts with and depends upon oral tradition. The Europeans' inability to understand ideographic symbolic literature and their belief in their own superiority were the sources for developing the myth of the illiterate savage. The importance of this myth was critical to the Europeans' own empire building and to their own interests. It dramatized the Christian world vision and justified the confiscation of tribal wealth. That the myth ignored centuries of Aboriginal literacies and denied human dignity and rights to the natives was unimportant compared to Canada's mythogenesis and colonial destiny.

The living and all-inclusive tradition of Algonkian symbolic literacy was barely noticed in European writing. Early travellers' reports emphasized the 'bestial' nature of natives and only grudgingly admitted them into the ranks of humanity. A few examples of recorded aboriginal literacy in North America nevertheless survive. In 1497, for example, John Cabot was intrigued by 'fallen trees bearing marks.'[10] In 1652 Father Gabriel Druilletes reported Algonkian Indians using coal for pen, bark for paper, and writing with new and peculiar characters. In 1653 Father Bressani reported Indians of New France using 'little sticks instead of books, which they sometimes mark with certain signs ... By the aid of these they can repeat the names of a hundred or more presents, the decisions adopted in councils and a thousand other particulars.'[11]

Yet despite such examples, the myth of the illiterate savage continued to dominate Europeans' assessment of Indian character. One missionary, Father Pierre Biard, offered the following account of the Mi'kmaw mind in 1616, illustrating the inherent contradictions of the myth:

> [The Indians] have rather a happy disposition, and a fair capacity for judging and valuing material and common things, deducing their reasons with great nicety, and always seasoning them with some pretty comparison. They have a

> very good memory for material things, such as having seen you before, or the peculiarities of a place where they may have been, of what took place in their presence twenty or thirty years before, etc.; but to learn anything by heart – there's the rock: there is no way of getting a consecutive arrangement of words into their pates. [Y]ou will see these poor barbarians, notwithstanding their great lack of government, power, letters, art and riches, yet holding their head so high they greatly underrate us, regarding themselves as our superior.[12]

Oblivious to other forms of literacy and ways of knowing, Father Biard and other missionaries imposed their valuation of European literacies on conceptions of knowledge and knowing, a form of superiority underlying cognitive imperialism that continues to reverberate in modern forms. Rather than the sequential grapheme-phoneme relationship of roman alphabets, Aboriginal peoples had developed another form of knowing and cataloguing their knowledge that only recently has been more fully understood. This knowing and knowledge builds rather upon a holistic and implicit world of symbolic literacy and collective dialogue and communication with creation.

Aboriginal Literacy

To understand Aboriginal forms of literacy and their usage, it is important to consider the spiritual, practical, and public functions of symbolic literary traditions of the Aboriginal peoples: their pictographs, petroglyphs, notched sticks, ideographs, and wampum. Algonquian epistemology was derived from the immediate ecology, their experiences, perceptions, thoughts, and memory, including experiences shared with others, and from the spiritual world discovered in dreams, visions, and signs interpreted with the guidance of healers or elders. A holistic ideographic system is partial knowledge meant to interact with the oral traditions, invoking the memory, creativity, and logic of the people. Their most significant meanings quickly passed from family to family, and to succeeding generations through dialogue and appropriate rituals and legends. Through analogies or style, they model the harmony among humans and the environment. Knowledge is derived from the immediate environment through personal and tribal experience, and secondly from one's interaction with the spiritual world. Aboriginal ideographs thus catalogue essential knowledge of the two worlds in holistic, meaningful ideas or visions, and through the oral tradition and appropriate rituals succeeding generations transmitted the collective knowledge and heritage.

A Mi'kmaw story is illustrated in the petroglyph shown in fig. 5.1 with representations of Star Husband, Star Wife, and Crane. Two women wish to marry stars, and upon awakening, they find two star men beside them whom they take as their husbands. Soon the women discover they are in the sky. They are told they can return to earth but must obey certain instructions if

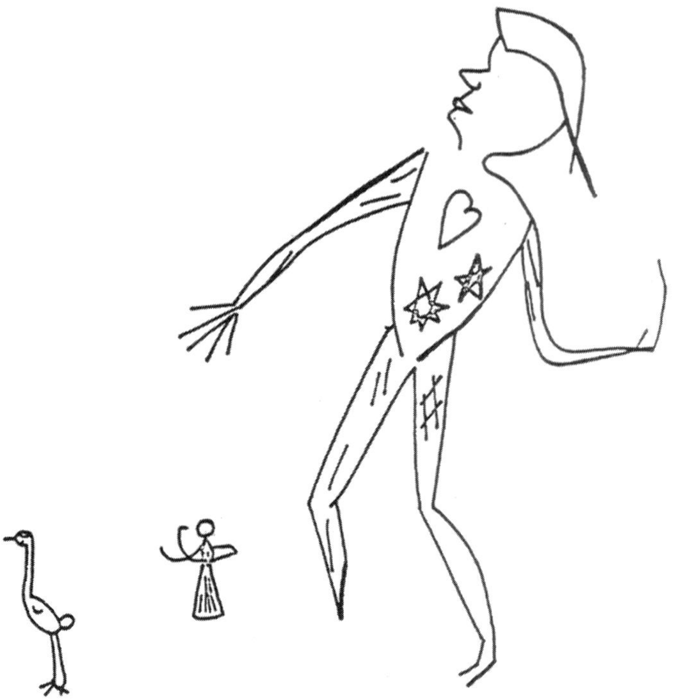

Figure 5.1. A Mi'kmaw story is illustrated in this petroglyph with representations of Star Husband, Star Wife, and Crane, from Robertson, *Rock Drawings*, fig. 3.

they are to reach earth safely. Unfortunately, they disobey and find themselves stuck in the branches of a tall pine tree. The Badger helps them out of the tree and the Crane helps them cross the river.[13]

These ideographic systems maintained a basic cognitive unity and balance, allowing Indigenous peoples to explore universal ideals that lay beyond the grasp of their empirical environment. Some symbols were practical representations of ideals, events, and time. Most symbols were never precisely defined or fully explained, since their purpose was to stimulate a dialogue rather than resolve the paradoxes of life concretely. They represented ideals that were infinite, dialectical (or relational), and indivisible so that any one person or generation could not adequately understand their significance.

The most common Algonkian ideographic text, recorded in patterned forms of wampum, appears to have served both public and private functions, not unlike the written text in European literate cultures. The word 'wampum' is both Mi'kmaq and Wabanaki in origin, derived from the word *wamponpeag*, which means 'white string of shell beads.'[14] However, variations of the word

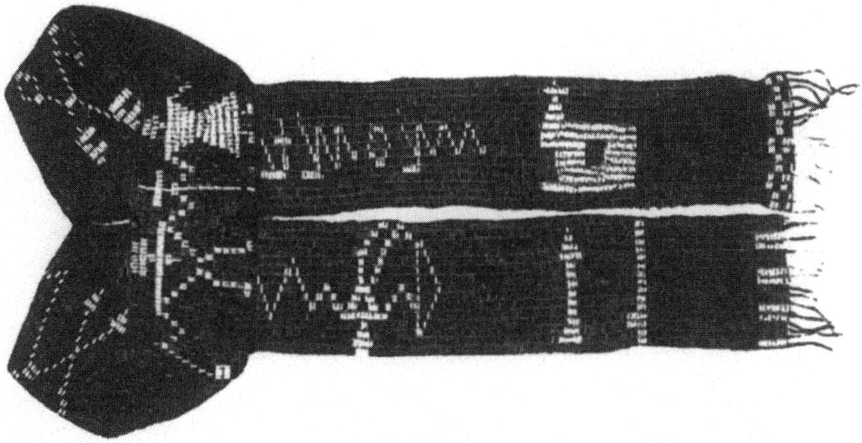

Figure 5.2. Wampum belt recording a 1610 agreement with the Mi'kmaq made in present-day Nova Scotia, from Henderson, *Mi'kmaw Concordat*, 81.

exist among other tribes, but among the Wabanaki Confederacy, patterned wampum was figuratively called *gelusewa'ngan*, meaning 'speech.'[15] Patterned wampum was woven coloured beads made from coastal quahog shells that conveyed shared meaning, knowledge, and heritage, a weaving that converges intriguingly with the roots of *text* in *texere*. Patterned wampum strings and ideographic symbols on belts of tubular shells were the media for history and public records, maintained by a wampum keeper or tribal historian. Among the Mi'kmaq this person was called the 'putus.' The putus's role was to recall past events and announce new ones, including treaties, agreements, and compacts. The arrangement and colours of purple and white beads then conveyed intent or attitude: all white was joyous or ceremonial, while all purple signalled death or war. The wampum belt in fig. 5.2 was reported to have been kept by the Collegio di Propaganda Fide in Rome, recording a 1610 agreement with the Mi'kmaq made in present-day Nova Scotia.[16]

The ideographic symbols used on the wampum belts are characteristically derived from older pictographs and petroglyphs. Petroglyphic writings have been found throughout North America, attesting to their universal usage and similarities in design among Aboriginal nations. Petroglyphic writings have been found on bark records and trees as well as on the rocks that give them their name.[17] The drawings illustrate a period from ancient times up through European contact. The function of pictographs, whether on rocks, birch bark, skins, or other natural materials, has only been superficially studied with writers suggesting themes or possible connections in legends or historical events. What is clear, however, is that the pictographic or symbolic representations were an interactive communication that served purposes similar to contemporary writing.

The interpretation of pictographs and petroglyphs requires an understanding of how Indians created ideas and meaning in their 'verb-based' language systems. The petroglyphs interacted with the oral traditions, which were a nexus of knowledge. A mark on a rock in nature's irregular 'page' not only represented an image but also was part of a lesson or a story or a ceremonial event. Without the oral teachings, most glyphs could not be deciphered as meaningful records. The glyphs did not fully stand for or suppress the oral but called it into being and/or were rendered meaningful by it. Current knowledge of cultural symbols and legendary events, processes, and figures has helped to interpret the focus of petroglyph drawings in which the action and story was implied by various marks around and on the character.[18]

The pictographs represent ecological knowledge, spirituality, geographic and cognitive maps, ideas, and events. Mi'kmaq portrayed the seasons of the year pictorially, differentiating the seasons by the natural changes they observed. Spring had come when buds on the trees appeared, when wild geese appeared, when the calves of moose had grown to a certain size in their mothers' bellies, and when the seals gave birth. Summer had come when the salmon were running up the river and when the wild geese shed their feathers. Autumn was observed by the waterfowls' 'return from the north to the south.' Winter was marked by the harsh cold and abundant snows, and the bears retiring until spring.[19] Another example of ecological knowledge is represented in a fan-shaped design that is said to represent the northern lights, called *wae-g-a-disk*,[20] a term that speaks to changing designs of light.

Mi'kmaq were particularly adept in making pictographic maps that portrayed their knowledge of the land and sea. Making maps and charting courses of travel with birch bark scrolls was a function of pictographic writing.[21] These drawings on bark charted travel routes and described family and common hunting territories; often they were left at places where the hunter turned off the path.[22] Ideographs pictorially express abstract ideas, and 'embody the representation of ideas by aid of certain analogies that the mind sees between the symbol and the idea attached to it.'[23] For example, the symbol of friendship among tribes was represented by hands clasped or by two hands with open palms approaching each other.

Pictographs also represented spiritual knowledge and traditions. Reading of the various signs and symbols was known to those who practised the rituals. Repetition and association served as the primary means of learning Aboriginal knowledge and heritage. But especially, the rituals associated with the figurative signs of Algonquian pictographs, petroglyphs, and notched sticks served more diversified uses. Like the Mesoamerican screenfolds, most described spiritual ideas and concrete experiences.[24] The designs explained

Figure 5.3. This ideographic symbol represents the seven districts of the Mi'kma'ki linked together in the circle with the cross being a significant feature of their relationships with one another, from Robertson, *Rock Drawings*, fig. 4.

cosmogony and were used to communicate with the spirit world and to recall individual visions and experiences among the spirits. As spiritual intermediaries, medicine people helped their people achieve personal communion with the spirits. Prayer and revelation were analogous to the traditional vision quest.

In 1610 this traditional symbolic tradition was incorporated ceremoniously into the agreement or concordat with the Holy See, an event that included both a ceremonial exchange of sacred wampum and a Catholic ritual of initiation (the baptism) of the Grand Chief and his immediate family.[25] The Concordat established Mi'kmaw Catholicism within Mi'kma'ki, their national territory, and consistent with traditional respect accorded grandmothers in Mi'kmaw society and at the request of the Grand Council, the Holy Grandmother, St Anne, became the patron saint of the Mi'kmaq in 1630 (fig. 5.3).

From that time to 1762, Catholic priests lived and worked among Mi'kmaq, learning their language and forms of literacy. Around the middle of the seventeenth century, the elders and Father Christian Le Clerq transliterated the Catholic liturgy, rituals, and prayers into the Mi'kmaw symbolic 'formulary.'[26] Le Clerq was initially very surprised with Mi'kmaw facility in tenaciously grasping 'any association of word, fact, or simple idea with a written arbitrary symbol'(24). He wrote that Mi'kmaq have 'much readiness in understanding this kind of writing and that they learn in a single day what they would never have been able to grasp in an entire week without the aid of these leaflets' (126). Once Catholic rituals had been transcribed as symbolic literature, using analogies with existing symbols, they diffused rapidly throughout the nation within the traditional social contexts. Father taught son, mother taught daughter, and children reinforced the skills among each other. Prayers were recorded in proper Catholic ritualistic order as charcoal designs on birch-bark books, which each family preserved in birch-bark boxes decorated with wampum and porcupine quill designs.[27]

In 1735 Father Pierre Antoine Maillard began a twenty-seven-year mission among Mi'kmaq, during which he expanded hieroglyphic literacy and contributed to the transition from ideographic literacy to roman script.[28] When Maillard became fluent in both the spoken Mi'kmaq and symbolic literacies, he recognized the power of holding the Mi'kmaq to ideographs and not introducing them to alphabetic literacy. After all, this was the eighteenth century and the printed page would prove in many respects revolutionary. If Mi'kmaq became literate in the roman script, this new-found literacy might otherwise strengthen their doubts about French motives, including the new religion in which they might discover further ideological inconsistencies.[29] Despite the fact that Maillard had developed a roman phonetic script for the Mi'kmaw language, which he used for his own linguistic studies, he chose to withhold any knowledge of it from the Mi'kmaq. In the traditions of the medicine people's specialized knowledge of reading and writing sacred symbols, Maillard encouraged catechists among elders and youth to learn the symbols, chants, and rituals, and the nature of the spirit world (fig. 5.4).

The spiritual foundation of Mi'kmaw literacy also paralleled Catholic doctrines. Both systems addressed universal concepts. Catholic teachings of a universal God and his lessons to man affirmed Aboriginal ideals. Thus Mi'kmaw spiritual culture was broadened, not altered, by Catholic theology. The Catholic teaching that humans were destined to eternal damnation unless they practised a Christian life involving faith, ritual, and sacrifice was analogous to tribal beliefs in which the necessity of living up to the great ideals of Mi'kmaw life through self-control was emphasized. Catholic doctrines of love of God and one's fellow man, and prayers for the dead to help them enter the spiritual world, and sacred symbols were all analogous to tribal beliefs and symbols. Mi'kmaw society embraced the two spiritual worlds as one, adding to rituals but not changing the ideological foundation.

Modern sequential literacy was derived from symbols. The early picture writing (pictograms), symbols, and ideograms first represented general and abstract ideas. At some point in European history, the Phoenician traders created an alphabet of symbols that represented individual sounds of speech, rather than ideas. Out of this notion grew the European alphabets and scripts. The Mi'kmaw literacy system and consciousness remain in ideographs and

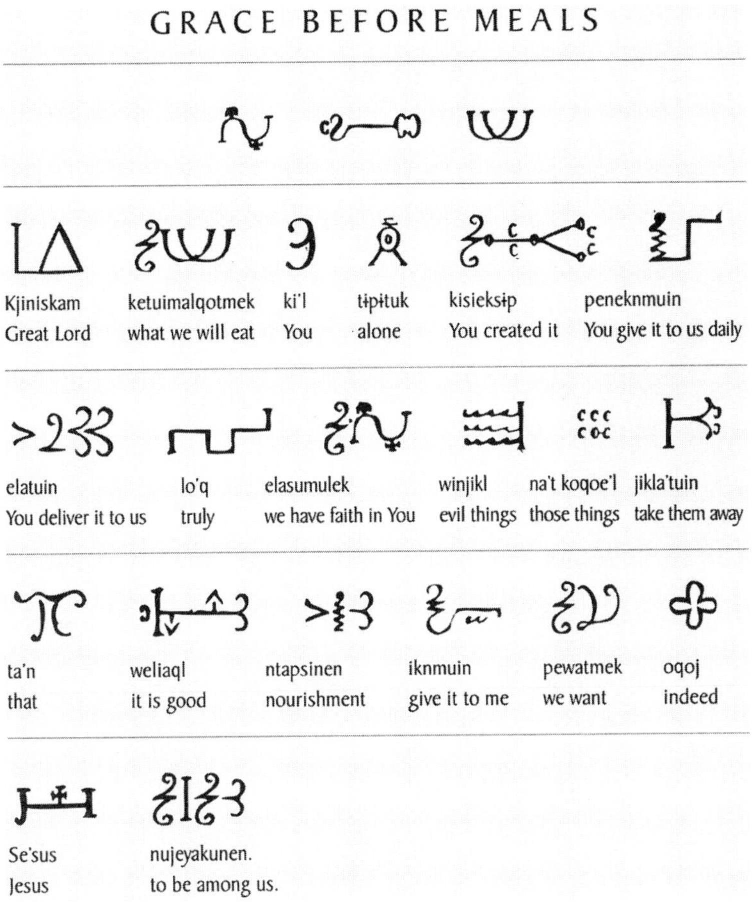
GRACE BEFORE MEALS
Kjiniskam
Great Lord
ketuimalqotmek
what we will eat
ki'l
You
tɨpɨtuk
alone
kisieksɨp
You created it
peneknmuin
You give it to us daily
elatuin
You deliver it to us
lo'q
truly
elasumulek
we have faith in You
winjikl
evil things
na't koqoe'l
those things
jikla'tuin
take them away
ta'n
that
weliaql
it is good
ntapsinen
nourishment
iknmuin
give it to me
pewatmek
we want
oqoj
indeed
Se'sus
Jesus
nujeyakunen.
to be among us.

Figure 5.4. Mi'kmaw hieroglyphics, from Schmidt and Marshall, *Mi'kmaq Hieroglyphic Prayers*, 55.

not by default either. The modern sequential literacies of alphabetic systems imposed on the Mi'kmaq have supplemented their aboriginal world view, but their ideographic literacy continues to shape and define Mi'kmaw consciousness as do European-based linear scripts the consciousness of modern humanity. Modern literacy research has reconfigured presumptuous Eurocentric thinking about the dichotomization of language into the oral and written forms.[30] Furthermore, modern research has invalidated the dichotomized forms, finding that the two modes are superimposed and intertwined.[31] The difference between oral and written culture represents a difference in approach to knowledge and thought.[32] In oral cultures knowledge is embodied in a collective repository of received wisdom, acquired through shared experiences and interpersonal relationships. In written cultures knowledge is seen as a depersonalized and analytic compilation of facts and insights of decontextualized thoughts.[33]

The differing conceptions also imply different modes of transmission[34] and different modes of human consciousness.[35] These understandings reject the older illiterate and literate dichotomization of language skills. Nevertheless, the Canadian educational system continues the process of cognitive imperialism under the illiterate savage myth and the banking concept of education in which educational capacity development is merely the assimilation of Eurocentric knowledge and skills.[36] Despite good intentions and textbook reforms, the seemingly innocuous textbooks continue the mythical portrait of Mi'kmaq and their society, when they mention them at all. Stripped of their wealth and power in eastern Canada, Mi'kmaq maintain their knowledge and heritage through symbolic literacies and language, as they are also becoming increasingly bilingual. They are restoring their knowledge and heritage by taking over the education of the youth, and healing the harmful psychological and economic damage of colonialism.[37]

The resiliency of early Algonquian literacy processes in Mi'kmaw consciousness has demonstrated that any system can function as long as the people value it and have use for it. The aboriginal forms of literacy served a function for Algonquian societies: universal symbols represented concepts and ideas, not sounds of language, and their legitimacy for contemporary tribal society has not been replaced or displaced by print culture and new technologies of the page. Yet missionary and governmental education continues to assimilate Mi'kmaq to transmission of and adaptation to Euro-Canadian society. A contemporary assessment of Mi'kmaw education urges both curricular reform in provincial schools and the need for the continued development of traditional and contemporary functions of literacy and knowledge systems.[38]

Much of the dialogue and discourse among educated Aboriginal educators and scholars in the last twenty-five years has focused attention on colonialism and oppression of peoples worldwide. It has been both a systemic and personalized process through education. We have been seeking an uncensored history that enables us to have a clear sense of our socio-historic reality from which we can heal.[39] Our journeys have led us to multiple ways to express ourselves and to give voice and imagery to our pain and anguish, our hopes and dreams, our strategies and alternatives, and our resistance and resilience. Many of us have come to realize that we do not have to be perceived through a Western lens to be legitimated. Yet we are all too aware that what is defined as knowledge for schools and curricula is not yet sufficiently comparable with Indigenous conceptualizations of knowledge, and that educational practice must continue to find ways to value the participation of Aboriginal peoples in educational discourse, policy, and practice, and in particular to identify and shape what is considered for school texts as knowledge for those schools. Indigenous peoples must be actively part of the transformation of knowledge. As Elizabeth Minnick notes, it is not just knowledge and thought that need to be changed but also 'preconscious cultural assumptions and habits that are fraught with emotion and reflect not only the ignorance but the systemically created and reinforced prejudices of the dominant culture.'[40]

As scholars, both Indigenous and non-Indigenous, unravel those prejudices, Indigenous peoples can begin to see that within their own traditions, within their own knowledge bases lies a store of knowledge from which they can rebuild, heal, and recover and restore healthy and connective relationships. They must acknowledge the colonial shadow through a thorough awareness of the socio-historic reality that has created the current context, accepting that a great collective soul wound has damaged their nations as a whole.[41] Once accepting of this fact, we can move beyond the personal dimension of blaming ourselves and seek to heal the nation with each significant step we take.

What is becoming clear to Indigenous educators is that any attempt to decolonize ourselves and actively resist colonial paradigms is a complex and daunting task. We cannot continue to allow Indigenous students to be given a fragmented existence in a curriculum that offers them only a distorted or shattered mirror; nor should they be denied an understanding of the historical context that has created that fragmentation. A postcolonial framework cannot be constructed without Indigenous peoples renewing and reconstructing the principles underlying their own world view, environment, languages, communication forms, and how these construct their humanity. That framework will no doubt resemble the page and use its traditional powers and protocols. But at the same time, the framework will be reconnected to Aboriginal oral, glyphic, artefactual modes, and conceptualizations of communication and it will be articulated with new information technologies. Finally, the fragmenting tendencies and universalizing pretensions of those technologies need to be effectively countered by renewed investment in holistic and sustainable ways of thinking, communicating, and acting together.

NOTES

1 Gregory Cajete, *Look to the Mountain: An Ecology of Indigenous Education* (Durango, CO: Kivaki Press, 1995).

2 Yves d'Evreux, *Voyage dans le nord du Brésil fait durant les années 1613–14* (Leipzig and Paris: A. Franck, 1864).

3 R.L. Roys, *The Book of Chilam Balam of Chumayel* (Washington, DC: Carnegie Institution of Washington, 1933).

4 D.G. Brinton, *The Lenape and Their Legends with the Complete Text and Symbols of the Walam Olum* (1884; reprint, New York: AMS, 1969).
5 J. Tanner, *Narrative of the Captivity and Adventures of John Tanner* (New York, 1830).
6 D.L. Schmidt and M. Marshall, ed. and trans., *Mi'kmaq Hieroglyphic Prayers: Rereading in North America's First Indigenous Script* (Halifax: Nimbus, 1995).
7 C. Lévi-Strauss, *Mythologiques*, 4 vols (Paris: Plon, 1964–71).
8 Michel de Montaigne, *Essais*, vol. 3, trans. John Florio (London: J.M. Dent, 1910), 141.
9 T. Skutnabb-Kangas, *Linguistic Genocide in Education or Worldwide Diversity and Human Rights?* (Mahwah, NJ: Lawrence Erlbaum, 1999).
10 Maine Historical Society, *Collections and Proceedings*, second series, 8 (Portland, ME: Maine Historical Society, 1897), 347.
11 W. Ganong, introduction to *New Relation of Gaspesia*, by C. Le Clerq, trans. and ed. W. Ganong (Toronto: The Champlain Society, 1910), 23.
12 R.G. Thwaites, ed., *The Jesuit Relations and Allied Documents*, vol. 3 (Cleveland: Burrows, 1897), 73–4.
13 M. Robertson, *Rock Drawings of the Micmac Indians* (Halifax: Nova Scotia Museum, 1973), figs 3, 4.
14 G. Snyderman, 'The Function of Wampum,' *Proceedings of the American Philosophical Society* 98.6 (1954): 469.
15 F. Speck, 'The Eastern Wabanaki Confederacy,' *American Anthropologist* 17.3 (1915): 507.
16 D.J. Bushnell, 'Native Cemeteries and Forms of Burial,' *Bureau of American Ethnology Bulletin*, no. 71 (1920). As cited in J.Y. Henderson, *The Mi'kmaw Concordat* (Halifax: Fernwood Press, 1997), 81.
17 Robertson, *Rock Drawings*.
18 S.T. Rand, *Legends of Micmacs* (1894; reprint, New York: Longmans, Green, 1971).
19 C. Le Clerq, *New Relation of Gaspesia*, trans. and ed. W. Ganong (Toronto: The Champlain Society, 1910), 137.
20 George MacLaren, 'The Arts of the Micmac of Nova Scotia,' *Nova Scotia Historical Quarterly* 4.2 (1974): 169.
21 S.T. Rand, *A Short Statement of the Facts Relating to the History, Manners, Customs, Language, and Literature of the Micmac Tribe of Indians in Nova Scotia and Prince Edward Island* (Halifax, 1850), 25. Also, see Le Clerq, *New Relation of Gaspesia*.
22 F. Speck, *Beothuk and Micmac* (New York: Museum of American Indians, Heye Foundation, 1922), 96–8.
23 W.J. Hoffman, *The Beginnings of Writing* (New York: D. Appleton, 1895), 555.
24 Robertson, *Rock Drawings*.
25 J.Y. Henderson, *Mi'kmaw Concordat*.
26 Le Clerq, *New Relation of Gaspesia*, 131.
27 F. Speck, 'The Double Curve Motive in Northeastern Algonkian Art,' *Memoir 42* (Ottawa: Government Printing Office, 1914); *Beothuk and Micmac*; and 'Symbol-

ism in Penobscot Art,' *American Anthropological Papers. American Museum of National History* 29.2 (1927): 126.

28 Abbé P. Maillard, 'Lettre de M. l'Abbé Maillard sur les missions de l'Acadie et particulièrement sur les missions Micmaques,' *Soirées Canadiennes* 3 (1863): 355.

29 Ibid.

30 J. Goody and I. Watt, 'The Consequence of Literacy,' *Comparative Studies in History and Society* 5.3 (1963): 304–45.

31 D. Tannen, 'The Myth of Orality and Literacy,' in *Linguistics and Literacy*, ed. W. Frawley (New York: Plenus Press, 1982), 3.

32 Ibid., 1.

33 J. Goody, 'Alternative Paths to Knowledge: Oral and Literate Cultures,' in *Spoken and Written Language*, ed. Deborah Tannen (Norwood, NJ: Ablex, 1981), 1.

34 J. Goody, *The Domestication of the Savage Mind* (Cambridge: Cambridge University Press, 1977), 37.

35 R.E. Ornstein, *The Psychology of Consciousness* (Harmondsworth: Penguin, 1972), 51.

36 Marie Battiste, 'Micmac Literacy and Cognitive Assimilation,' in *Indian Education in Canada: The Legacy*, ed. Jean Barman, Yvonne Hébert, and Don McCaskill (Vancouver: University of British Columbia Press, 1986), 37.

37 Marie Battiste, 'Maintaining Aboriginal Identity, Language and Culture in Modern Society,' in *Reclaiming Indigenous Voice and Vision*, ed. Marie Battiste (Vancouver: University of British Columbia Press, 2000), 207.

38 Ibid., 192–208.

39 E. Duran and B. Duran, *Native American Postcolonial Psychology* (New York: State University of New York Press, 1995).

40 E. Minnick, *Transforming Knowledge* (Philadelphia, PA: Temple University Press, 1990), 93.

41 Duran and Duran, *Native American*.

6 Print Culture and Decolonizing the University: Indigenizing the Page: Part 2

L.M. Findlay

Marie Battiste has written about the cognitive imperialism of the Westernized classroom where the promotion of literacy and paginated culture has had a very powerful, though not always negative or irresistible, impact on Indigenous literacies and cultural self-determination. She has also pointed out parts of the history of symbolic literacy that have been casually or deliberately ignored or devalued in the course of monumentalizing the European page. I will begin my section of this joint project with images deriving from two historical conjunctures: one dealing with Aboriginal adaptation and resistance, the other with political liberation; one dealing with the page as surface for drawing, the other with the page as a site for the production of revolutionary literacy. I will then use a major recent argument about print culture and print capitalism to offer an ideological critique of the page as part of the larger project of decolonizing at least *parts* of at least *some* universities and exposing *some* of the defining features of North American colonization of the continent's First Nations.

The Page as Stockade

Let us examine two discrete sets of images which in their different ways show how to decolonize the page. First we have examples of ledger drawings or ledger art produced by First Nations men as their customary share of the gendered production of images by their peoples in the later nineteenth century. These images were often produced in prison but always with a mix of pathos and resistance, a weave of broadly available and narrowly esoteric meanings. These images are drawn mostly on the pages of Indian agent ledgers or account books deemed surplus stock in that actuarial winning of the West impelled by greed, marked by genocide, and ever dependent on the keeping of sound financial records.[1] Or, these ledgers might have been deemed usable stock but nonetheless given out of condescension or fear to First

Nations prisoners to amuse themselves, so that they could 'doodle' their way through dispossession on the road to assimilation or extinction. Ironically, the soldiers sent to subdue them often prized highly the drawings that their prisoners made, opening fissures in the cultural confidence of the United States Government.[2] The resort to paper as a medium for Indigenous image making also bears witness to the increasing scarcity of the buffalo hide (and its four-footed source) as the traditional 'page' for such designs.[3] For the ideological tabula [quasi] rasa, the adapted or the pseudopristine page's blankness was already an expression of dominant values, refuting Joyce Szabo's claim that 'the actual name of the paper is not important.' [4] To the decoration of such pages each Indigenous prisoner – whether in a stockade or reservation – brought distinctive oral, textual, graphic, gestural, and musical competencies that had to be exoticized, infantilized, or eliminated and archived in the name of progress. Only thus could the manifest cultural competencies of the artists be subordinated to or obliterated in favour of the colonial story of savages in need of civilization. How, then, are we to read these pages on which the grid of bookkeeping suggests something of capital's determination of the art of book making as such, while both constraining and enabling Indigenous culturalism and critique of oppression? How are we to read the claims of individually assigned and itemized property against these unsigned images sharing space with other unsigned images sometimes by other hands?

Figure 6.1, a list of property belonging to the Cheyenne Indians lost or destroyed at Sand Creek, Colorado, by Colonel Chivington on 14 October 1865, has more to tell us than might at first appear to be the case with a 'mere' inventory. The image offers a sample of the type of ledger book that gives ledger drawings their name, an act of generic classification which defers to the materiality of the medium but also to the material and political objectives of the book's first owners.[5] This layout promises to the dominant culture accurate and retrievable information. It hence seems a far cry from oral culture, and signals also the reduction of mnemonic oral formulae to make way for the cautious convention of the double entry or the annual X marking the spot of dependency. This page seems to have been adapted by a caring and meticulous military bureaucracy to the project of economic restitution. However, it continues to allow for the assertion of cultural differences regarding the nature of property and its valuation.

Figure 6.2 reminds us that account ledgers form, of course, only one armature of colonial transformation. Here is another, with the photographic, albumen page giving us before and after images of Tom Torlino, Navajo from Arizona, on arrival at the Indian Training School, Carlisle, Pennsylvania, in 1885. Here we see another technology of surveillance and subjection unashamedly at work in the transformation of identity by the 'resident' school photographer, John Choate.[6] The transformation of this Navajo man

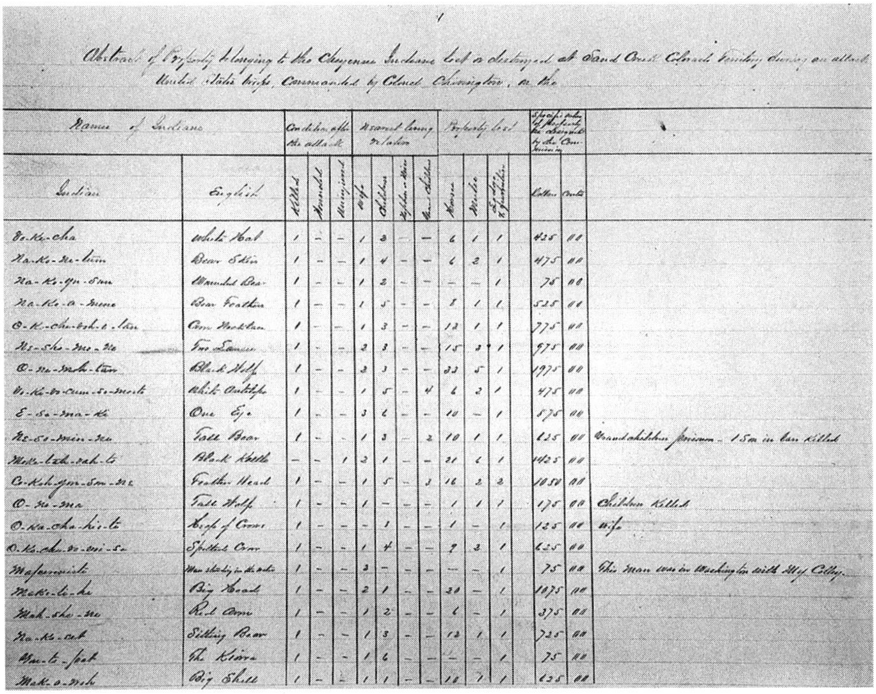

Abstract of Property belonging to the Cheyenne Indians lost or destroyed at Sand Creek Colorado Territory during an attack United States troops, Commanded by Colonel Chivington, on the

Name of Indians		Condition after the attack			Nearest living relation				Property lost			Specific value of property as assessed by the Commission		
Indian	English	Killed	Wounded	Uninjured	Wife	Children	Father or Mother	Grand Children	Horses	Mules	Lodges & furniture	Dollars	Cents	
O-ko-cha	White Hat	1	–	–	1	3	–	–	6	1	1	425	00	
Ha-ko-ne-tun	Bear Skin	1	–	–	1	4	–	–	6	2	1	475	00	
Na-ko-yu-sun	Wounded Bear	1	–	–	1	2	–	–	–	–	1	75	00	
Na-ko-a-mene	Bear Feather	1	–	–	1	5	–	–	8	1	1	525	00	
O-ko-cha-tok-e-tun	Crow Necklace	1	–	–	1	3	–	–	12	1	1	775	00	
Ne-sko-me-na	Two Lances	1	–	–	2	3	–	–	15	3	1	975	00	
O-ne-mok-tun	Black Wolf	1	–	–	2	3	–	–	33	5	1	1975	00	
Vo-ke-vo-cum-e-mocte	White Antelope	1	–	–	1	5	–	4	6	2	1	475	00	
E-so-ma-ke	One Eye	1	–	–	3	6	–	–	10	–	1	575	00	
Ne-so-min-na	Tall Bear	1	–	–	1	3	–	2	10	1	1	625	00	Grandchildren prisoners – 1 son in law killed
Moke-tah-vah-to	Black Kettle	–	–	1	2	1	–	–	21	6	1	1425	00	
O-kah-yon-son-ne	Feather Head	1	–	–	1	5	–	3	16	2	2	1050	00	
O-ne-ma	Tall Wolf	1	–	–	1	–	–	–	1	1	1	175	00	Children killed
O-ka-cha-hi-to	Chief of Crows	1	–	–	–	1	–	–	1	–	1	125	00	Wife
O-ko-cha-vo-mi-se	Spotted Crow	1	–	–	1	4	–	–	9	3	1	625	00	
Mapaneniste	Man standing in the water	1	–	–	3	–	–	–	–	–	1	75	00	This man was in Washington with Maj Colley.
Make-li-ke	Big Head	1	–	–	2	1	–	–	20	–	1	1075	00	
Mah-sho-ne	Red Arm	1	–	–	1	2	–	–	6	–	1	375	00	
Na-ko-vet	Sitting Bear	1	–	–	1	3	–	–	12	1	1	725	00	
Ma-to-fat	The Kiowa	1	–	–	1	6	–	–	–	–	1	75	00	
Mah-o-mih	Big Shell	1	–	–	1	1	–	–	11	7	1	625	00	

Figure 6.1. Abstract of property belonging to the Cheyenne Indians lost or destroyed at Sand Creek, Colorado, by Colonel Chivington on 14 October 1865. Berlo fig. 1.

via literacy and industrial training will produce skills useful to Pennsylvania employers (most notably the ability to make hats and shoes) but worse than useless to those who alienate themselves from their culture and lose their independence in acquiring and exercising such skills. The page can be predominantly or entirely an image but still works with paper of a standard size (5 $^{1}/_{8}$ × 8 $^{3}/_{8}$ inches) in order to record and permit ongoing access to details of the civilizing mission underway. The lighting of a particular shot, like the massaging of a particular prose account, or the cooking of a particular set of books, may exaggerate a process of assimilation that can then be further legitimated and accelerated by reproducing and disseminating sets of text, images, or numbers.

Figure 6.3 shifts us toward Indigenous agency within the contexts of exchange and surveillance sketched above. Bear's Heart, a Cheyenne artist, depicts troops amassed against a Cheyenne village, 1876–7. In this drawing collectivities are contrasted. Colour, social formation, and page division all underscore, after the fact and amidst the fallout, the clash of values and practices, the juxtaposition of a green and grounded, circular and linear

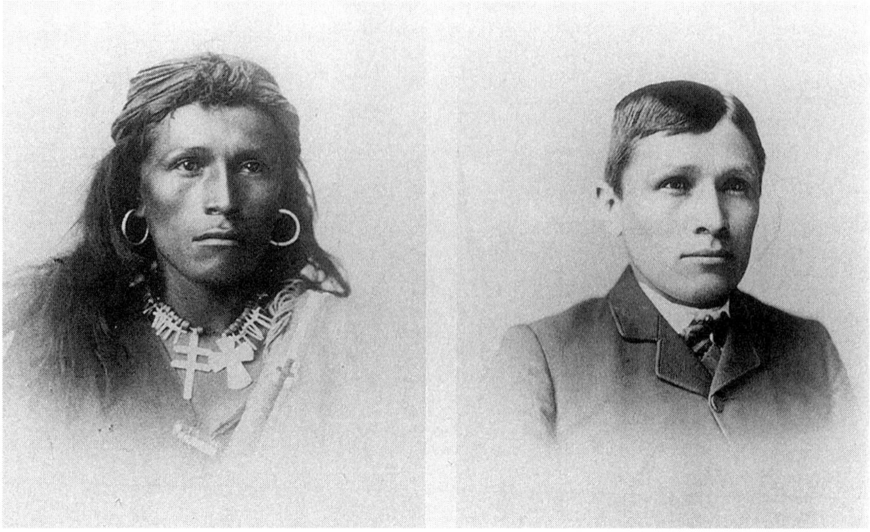

Figure 6.2. Before and after images of Tom Torlino, Navajo from Arizona, on arrival at the Indian Training School, Carlisle, Pennsylvania in 1885. Berlo fig. 3.

encampment and the apparently endless, linear regiments advancing from the West on the quasi-blank ground of ledger paper. This diptych reconstructs military defeat in the elegiac commemoration of a way of life increasingly imperilled and unavailable to the person doing the drawing here – except on these visually documentary pages and the secret rituals and 'opaque' conversations of Indigenous inmates. One kind of column of figures takes over from another to seal the fate of the dispossessed whose casualties are already accumulating. Uniformity under a single flag is captured only too accurately, before military discipline achieves an outcome that educational disciplines will endeavour to consolidate, legitimate, and complete in the name of progress. Yet the artist knows this already to be the case and his drawing is an earnest of resistance based on understanding. There is nothing naive about this drawing at all. A keeping of detailed financial accounts could be no more hard-headed than this visual practice.

Of course not all clashes were explicitly military. After conquest come negotiation, administration, legislation, and hegemony, as in fig. 6.4, Howling Wolf and Soaring Eagle at Fort Marion in St Augustine, Florida, home of a well-heeled, 'white,' market for native Americana. This drawing is a kind of pictorial accounting. It commemorates a formal gathering for the distribution of annuity or treaty goods, where commodities are not represented by numbers and words but are centrally displayed in an overdetermined and internally conflicted process of exchange. Once again, though, there is vul-

Figure 6.3. Bear's Heart, Troops Amassed against a Cheyenne Village, 1876–7. Berlo plate 1.

nerability as well as pride in the physical disposition and diversity of the First Nations figures within the page frame where the Stars and Stripes now flies over everyone and does its symbolic work without the visible presence of uniformed troops. The page, in the very rectangularity it shares with the flag, functions as a kind of cultural or semiotic stockade, having the very shape that Chief Joe Mathias would later have in mind when, after the collapse of the fourth Canadian Conference on Aboriginal Self-Government, he told his people that they would never 'be contained within the four corners of a history book.'[7]

The fifth of the images I have selected complicates matters further. It is an example of the work of Howling Wolf of the Southern Cheyenne in Fort Marion, Florida (fig. 6.5). Here the tendency to formalize and control space in a quasi-military or industrial way is evident in the scene of instruction. The classroom demands ominous uniformity of its Indigenous students; the page is prominent and endlessly replicable as an agent of socialization, in situations where the instructor from the dominant culture is now – and usually is in these drawings – female rather than male. Note the pathos and historically determinate ambiguity of these versions of the stylus, doubling as lance and spear, each infantilizing backview of a pupil offering an analogy to the transformation of the young Navajo, Tom Torlino.

Note also the ominous fidelity with which the picture of Christ and his disciples is reproduced, and the new pupil being directed with his chair to an

Figure 6.4. Howling Wolf & Soaring Eagle at Fort Marion in St Augustine, Florida. Szabo plate 25.

appropriate spot in the classroom. The scribal gesture of the teacher is reproduced by the pupils, while the non-Indigenous male figure who maintains written records in wooden pigeonholes and spatial order in the classroom employs an equally directive gesture echoed in the religious painting on the wall. The blackboard next to the painting represents a reusable page employed in tandem with the Christian image, script, and scripture, the one replete with meaning even though for the moment rasa and the other glorifying teaching but also conveying the pathos of an outdoor scene within a confined and thoroughly regimented space. Such classrooms are not always rendered so sombrely (the whole schoolroom is even smiling, with the matching adults and attentive pupils apparently ratifying the civilizing mission in Wohaw, Kiowa, Fort Marion [fig. 6.6]), but neither humour nor apparent acceptance can quell the sense of indoctrination and the residual power of Indigenous tradition. In the Kiowa image, the adults are in reality more rivals than collaborators, the detached and spectral Indigenous figure a symbol of self-containment contrasting powerfully with the didactic gestures of the teacher and the legitimating instruments she holds in her hands, the pointer

Figure 6.5. Howling Wolf, 26 Sept 1876 in Fort Marion, Florida. Szabo plate 12.

and the page. The traditional figure appears to be behind the seated students as an active ally as well as an adjacent memory. As Anna Blume astutely notes, 'This enigmatic Native figure ... looms like the image of an inner eye, faint yet present, present in the drawing as evidence of a split and troubled consciousness.'[8]

Of course the future of the colonizing and assimilating page was to affect almost every aspect of Indigenous life, including the one captured in fig. 6.7, a drawing by an unknown Cheyenne artist that forms the frontispiece to the Evans Ledger. A well-dressed couple share a log together and exchange a parasol. Other drawings by males use the ledger page to remember courtship rituals that might otherwise be painted on teepee linings or clothing. Some things are better said than written, even though their certification will soon require official stationery and the witnessing of signatures to be legal. Courtship scenes and oral exchange mark the capacity of and necessity for a people to reproduce themselves, but the pictorial reproductions of such scenes are framed and shadowed by the colonial realities into which Indigenous children will now be born and the ways in which Indigenous sexuality, especially female sexuality, will be brutalized and exploited by white society.

Figure 6.6. Wohaw, Kiowa, Fort Marion. Berlo plate 3.

The signs of hybridization come early and fast as markers of profound cognitive shifts and the process of internalizing categories and conventions on which hegemony depends. Keeping track of time calendrically did not stop when there were no more buffalo to keep track of and upon.[9] The tribal historian had to turn to paper from hide, and therefore to a degree had to accept if not accentuate his people's colonization, and the cholera and smallpox epidemics that punctuated it (see fig. 6.8). The knowledge needed to negotiate with the dominant society meant a choice between dependencies, each of which presumed defeat and marginality: depending on the colonizer's interpreter of choice, or on learning to use the colonial master's tools and hence forego if not yet forsake traditional knowledge and authorities.

Facing pages like these two in fig. 6.9 by an unknown Cheyenne artist are devoted to separate incidents, with the number '48' floating as if disconnected entirely from a scene irreducibly hybrid but interpreted in a later annotation as a change in artistic intention. This change is said to entail updating the white enemies to Indigenous ones within the colonizing project of divide and rule. However, unless the interpretation of marks on the ledger page begins with the purpose and distribution history of the page itself, all attempts to read the page aesthetically are doomed to distortion and irresponsibility. Attending seriously to such material, cultural, and economic history is in effect a refusal to depoliticize interpretation and a refusal also of such staggeringly glib accounting for change as that offered even by informed and sympathetic commentators like Mari Sandoz, when she observes: 'The horse was the first readily negotiable property of universal value that the Sioux possessed, and made an Indian on the Plains not only a

Figure 6.7. Unknown Cheyenne artist, frontispiece to the Evans Ledger. Berlo plate 24.

mobile warrior and hunter but a capitalist, changing much of his largely communal society.'[10] By this token, Indigenous people should have rapidly become the commercial competitors of the colonizers, using the ledger books like good capitalists did (and do), for numeric tracking of the movement of goods and money, and certainly not for doodling.

Paginating Revolution

Resistance can sometimes grow into revolutionary transformation, and this is certainly the case with the literacy movement in Cuba during and after the overthrow of Batista's dictatorship in 1959.[11] The following set of two images gives a sense of the interior of a small house, next to Batista's former mansion, which is now itself a school; the surrounding military barracks have also been turned into additional schools whose pupils visit in due course the collections held in the modest building, namely, visual and textual records of the literacy campaign. This small house is now a Literacy Institute run by a wonderfully informative director, aided mainly by women volunteers from the close to 100,000 young men and women, armed with copies of *Alfabeticemos* and *Venceremos,* who participated in the literacy campaign and who still revere its martyrs and its accomplishments. One of its most memorable images (fig. 6.10) is a variation on the ambiguous stylus (of fig. 6.5) with young women carrying huge missile-pencils over their shoulders during that infamous missile crisis. When Bulwer-Lytton famously declared that 'the pen

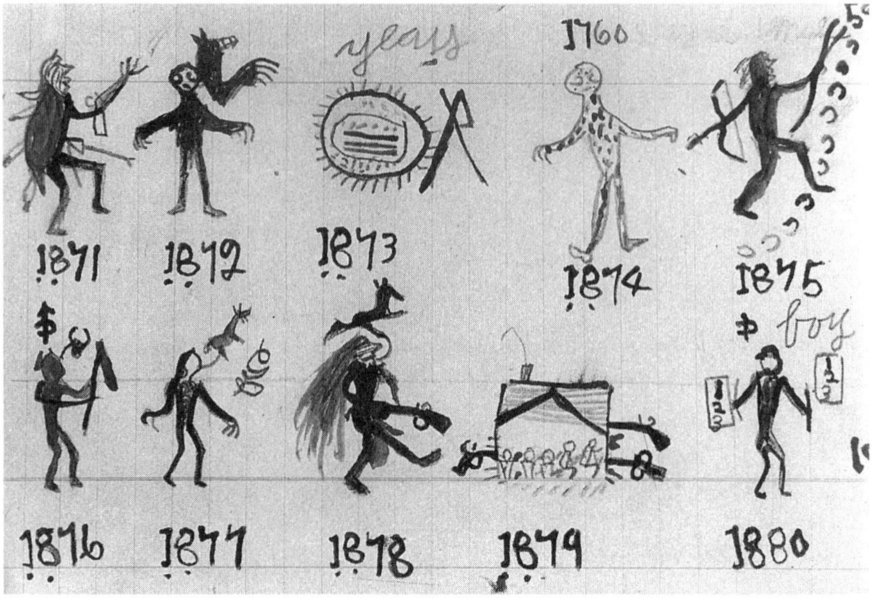
years
1760
1871
1872
1873
1874
1875
boy
1876
1877
1878
1879
1880

Figure 6.8. Battiste Good, Brown Hat, Brule Sioux. Winter Count, kept by the artist. Szabo figure 3.

is mightier than the sword,' he first stipulated that that was true only 'beneath the rule of men entirely great.'[12] This proposition is given a freshly revolutionary inflection in such demonstrations of militant literacy as the one illustrated here, but also in transformative personal encounters with the pages of ledgers as captured in the following passage from an interview with a Cuban woman:

> The new government was running all sorts of on-the-job training programs but you had to take a course that was given in political education before you could be elected by your colleagues to apply for one of those training programs. It was a good course – it really made me think. When I talk now to Chileans and people from Angola and even you [MacDonald], I think how lucky I am to be a Cuban living in this revolution.
>
> You know, when you think about it, everything is politics – everything. We treat each other the way our society structures us to, and society structures us according to certain objective laws. It is hard to explain. You really do see it in ledger work. *A ledger is full of the lives of working people*. Every hour recorded is an hour of productivity which has made a difference to someone else. *It is all relationships between people, and between people and the means of production.*[13]

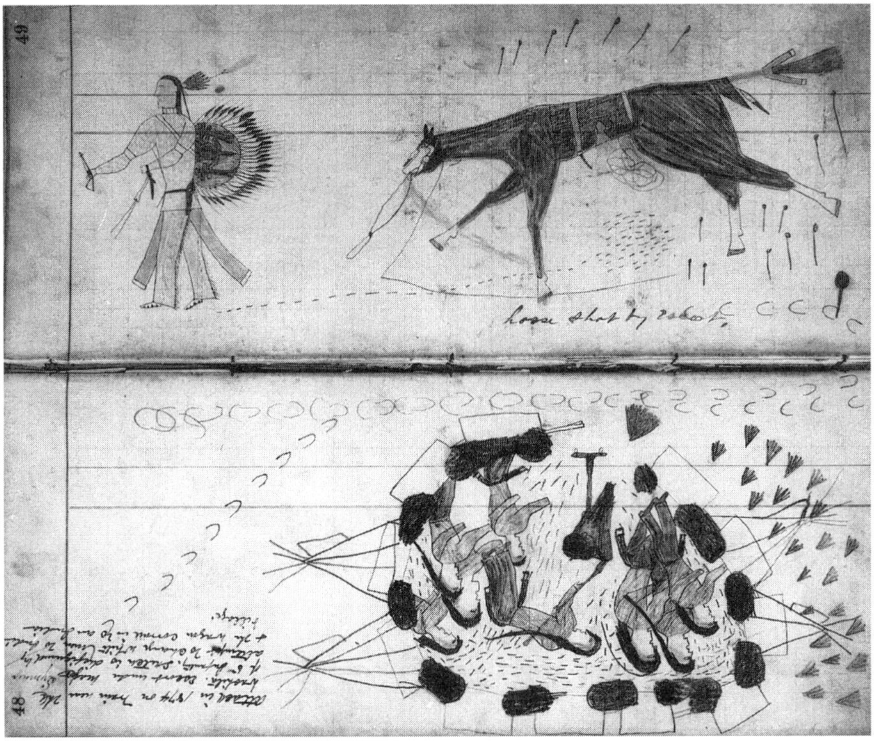

Figure 6.9. Unknown Cheyenne artist. Berlo figs 2, 3.

This woman interviewee, Yolanda Perez, now a financial analyst in the Department of Trade and Commerce, had started life before the Cuban Revolution with 'her two brothers, half-sister, father and two aunts ... in a tumble-down shed divided into two rooms at one end of a golf course behind one of Havana's leading hotels' (84). Her understanding of the ledger page is shaped by this experience, her exposure to revolutionary literacy, and a politicizing of education some would see as brainwashing and bribery, though such perception is itself too often born of illusions of objectivity and freedom.[14]

The second of these Cuban images (fig. 6.11) depicts the foyer of the Institute where the literacy martyrs murdered in the countryside by CIA-sponsored operatives are honoured, while below them Fidel is depicted at the United Nations in New York in 1960, making the promise about universal literacy that was fulfilled to an amazing degree and remains astonishing to this day. There are forty universities now in Cuba serving a population of approximately 11,000,000. During the literacy campaign students from grade

Figure 6.10. Young women carrying missile-pencils over their shoulders during Cuban Missile Crisis.

10 through early university went out into rural Cuba to teach the more than a million adults who needed teaching. The director of the Institute showed me one of the several hundred bound volumes containing letters written by the newly literate of all ages to Commandante Castro. The handwriting is as various as the kind and condition of the paper on which these people write. The content is no more arresting, so far as I could tell, than the fact of its existence and preservation in such a locale, so that the children who visit here know something of the history that underwrites their every encounter with the printed, manuscript, and electronic page, in and out of the classroom. Indoctrination? Arguably. Education? Certainly!

Paginated print culture, in the cases of Aboriginal resistance, memory, and mourning, is strongly but not exclusively or irrevocably linked to print capitalism, even as these images move from bound page to disbound page, to be used and eventually mounted, framed, curated, exhibited, aestheticized, and reproduced and rebound in illustrated books of cultural analysis and art history. This cycle or contingent sequence is marked by value change but never shakes off the primacy of its economic determinations. In the Cuban

MÁRTIRES DE LA ALFABETIZACIÓN
Y SEGUIRAN
SIENDO
MAESTROS
FIDEL

Figure 6.11. Foyer honouring literacy martyrs.

examples, print culture mobilizes itself as print dissidence and scribal anti-capitalism in which pages emanating from all over the country and bearing all kinds of signs of Batista's regime and American imperialism are consolidated, collected, monumentalized as a mass epistolary tribute to charismatic leadership, the fulfilment of a revolutionary promise of entitlement and transformation. What then are the implications of these examples for the celebrated argument about print capitalism made by Benedict Anderson in *Imagined Communities*?[15] What are the implications for the multimediated future of the page?

Revisiting Benedict Anderson

Anderson, you may recall, is interested in 'large cultural systems' (12) and their role in establishing and sustaining 'the basic morphology of the modern nation' (46), including its 'literate bourgeoisie' (77) and intellectual entrepreneurs. Drawing on but going beyond important work on the history of the book by scholars like Elizabeth Eisenstein, Lucien Fèbvre, and Henri-Jean Martin, Anderson argues for the book as the first industrial commodity and links print culture firmly to print capitalism whose three principal concomitants are 'unified fields of exchange and communication below Latin and above the spoken vernaculars ... a new fixity to language, which in the long run helped to build that image of antiquity so central to the subjective idea of the nation ... and languages-of-power of a kind different from the older administrative vernaculars' (44–5). Chronologically considered, these three were 'largely unselfconscious processes resulting from the explosive interaction between capitalism, technology and human linguistic diversity. But as with so much else in the history of nationalism, once "there," they could become formal models to be imitated, and, where expedient, consciously exploited in a Macchiavellian spirit' (45). This sequence in time, however, does not tell the whole story of a shift from latent to manifest and manipulable process. Anderson therefore goes to Walter Benjamin in order to theorize new forms of social simultaneity enjoyed by consumers of print and the imagined connections and collective identities they sustain in the empty, homogeneous time of the now (Benjaminian *Jetztzeit*).

The audacious hyphenation through which Anderson produced print-capitalism provoked opposition and criticism of which he takes explicit account in the preface to the revised edition of his book, which appeared twelve years after the first. Here he confesses how 'startled' he was to find that 'in many notices of *Imagined Communities* Eurocentric provincialism remained quite undisturbed, and that the crucial chapter on the originating Americas was largely ignored' (xiii). Anderson's response is to play up the notion of 'Creole pioneers' (47) and the role of the 'printer-journalist' like Benjamin Franklin in a republican creolization of print-capitalism whose independence from the mother country and its metropole was pursued simultaneously with the further conquest and control of Indigenous peoples. Anderson sees the Creole newspaper as key to the development of a 'native' publishing industry and the effective imagining of autonomous community, and his account remains enormously suggestive though inevitably sketchy. What the evidence of ledger drawings affirms, and Anderson only hints at, is the degree of convergence of documentary capitalism and literacy in nineteenth-century Creole nationalism. This process consolidates itself both at the expense of the mother country and its metropole with which it shares a mother tongue (English, Spanish, French, Portuguese) and much else, and at the expense of the First Nations of the Americas with whom it agrees to share knowledge, territory, and resources only on the most reluctant and exploitative bases. Anderson's succinctness creates an opportunity or even obligation for others interested in a fuller accounting of the domestic and colonial dominance of print to examine specific sites of transcultural, arguably transnational, contestation and negotiation of the nature of the page. This project, however, would benefit from a more dialectical approach than that allowed by such unhelpful notions such as 'explosion' (45), the 'synchronicity' of new and old place as 'sibling competition rather than ... inheritance' (187), and such logocentric and premature expressions as 'the venomous argots of dying colonialisms' (148). The key concept of print-capitalism has not yet completed its intellectual and political work; nor has it been as fully articulated together with information-capitalism as it needs to be, despite excellent work collected by, for example, McChesney et al. and Davis et al., or in the bold claims for 'the informatization of production' by Michael Hardt and Antonio Negri.[16]

The future of the page seems to me to derive much of its importance from being bound up with the future of information-capitalism in an increasingly common dematerialization and deterritorialization. Profit, print, and cybercircuitry follow analogous but not identical trajectories, even within universities where the conjuncture of antiquity and modernity unevenly impels and ineptly markets knowledge production and commodity culture. Beside Anderson's three-part grammar of colonial-national invention compromising the census, the map, and the museum (163), we need to place or to recognize the imposition of new information technologies in order to understand and perhaps manage the interactions of social text and hypertext so that we can more fully couple knowledge and sustainability to justice, and do so not in a virtual commons realized as boutique democracy within transnational corporate-autocratic distribution of poison and prosperity. Rather, we need new forms of academic community that can claim more political heft than the steam off a *Chapters* latte. We need to rematerialize as well as strategically dematerialize the page. And we need also to reterritorialize as well as strategically deterritorialize the locations where knowledge is produced and applied. Otherwise Canada's First Nations, Inuit, and Metis will have been forced to shift the frame of their ongoing oppression from *terra nullius* and its predatory literacy and cartography to *supra* or *post-terram* configurations promising *terra virtualis* – in other words, an infotopia where land claims are old hat and strategic essentialism has to shift from the multimediated 'pages' of treaties to the even more conflicted contexts, hypertexts, and rhizomes of e-justice or extinction.com.

To be sure, the project of reading, scrolling, and keying for justice may unsettle the humanist and cyberbourgeoisie, not least by showing how the production of events such as an academic conference on the future of the page employs a predictably academic division of labour into mass data entry/minority composition. Yet such divisiveness notwithstanding, we need each other, and we need multiple strategies rather than aggravated vulnerability and disarray. But the 'we' in question must perforce be cross-disciplinary and antidisciplinary, intergenerational and intercultural. And I am not talking about naive or quiescent pluralism either. The two questions for the academic bourgeoisie and its burgeoning underclass of underrepresented and undervalued adjuncts, limited term and sessional appointments, are how to combat more effectively the depoliticizing and reactionary tendencies among ourselves, and how to strategically presume and creatively put in question the possibility of being on the same page politically. For all that page's current instability, which represents opportunities as well as dangers, it is part of a remarkably *longue dureé.* The mobilizing page of which I am thinking might first be found in what some of us at the University of Saskatchewan are calling the Indigenous Humanities, understood as a set of revisionary and restorative practices that recognize the staying power of Eurocentrism and logocentrism but are resolved to dispute that centrality while also using it against its deep-running grain. The page of which I am thinking is akin to Jerome McGann's algorithm, but it is textual rather than logical, and already torn in two halves, existing as Adorno's *auseinandergerissene Hälften* in the famous letter to Walter Benjamin assessing the latter's essay 'The Work of Art in the Age of Mechanical Reproduction.'[17] The two torn halves promise but never deliver full restitution; they never add up so as to eliminate lack or excess or the enticements and unsettlements of cyberspectrality, but that very fact creates the necessity of materialist and indigenized critique that will move us further along the path to economic and social and educational justice. Call this liberationist rhetoric if you will, although this charge usually originates with people who enjoy a position of privilege and espouse a self-seekingly liberal humanism. Call the kind of critique I am promoting advocacy rather than scholarship, as the self-styled guardians of 'excellence'[18] are wont to do from positions of pseudo-disinterestedness.[19] But such rhetoric and its intellectual, pedagogical, and social concomitants, whether conveyed by means of the screen or by virtue of the page, is preferable and more scholarly than the condescending argot of a careerist clerisy and its possessive-individualist practice. Recto most assuredly still requires a contrary verso, as well as oral and hyptertextual challenges. *Paging justice. Paging justice. Is justice in the building? Paging justice ...*

NOTES

1 Valerie Robertson et al., *Reclaiming History: Ledger Drawings by the Assiniboine Artist Hongeeyesa* (Calgary: Glenbow Museum, 1993), 13.
2 Janet Catherine Berlo, ed., *Plains Indian Drawings 1865–1935* (New York: Harvey N. Abrams, 1996), 13.
3 Robertson, *Reclaiming History*, 13.
4 Joyce M. Szabo, *Howling Wolf and the History of Ledger Art* (Albuquerque, University of New Mexico Press, 1994), xiv.
5 L.M. Findlay, 'Interdisciplining Canada: "Cause Breaking Up Is Hard to Do,"' *Essays in Canadian Writing* 65 (1998): 4–15; James [Sakej] Youngblood Henderson, 'Post-colonial Indigenous Legal Consciousness' (lecture delivered at Harvard Law School on the occasion of Dr Henderson's receiving a Distinguished Alumnus Award from Harvard University, 1999), 8–13.
6 Berlo, *Plains Indian Drawings*, 44.

7 From the film *Dancing Around the Table*, director, Maurice Bulbulian, producer, Raymond Gauhtier (Montreal: National Film Board of Canada, 1987).
8 Anna Blume, 'In a Place of Writing,' in Berlo, *Plains Indian Drawings*, 40.
9 Mari Sandoz, introduction to *A Pictographic History of the Oglala Sioux*, by Helen Blish (Lincoln: University of Nebraska Press, 1967), xix.
10 Ibid.
11 Theodore MacDonald, *Making a New People: Education in Revolutionary Cuba* (Vancouver: New Star Books, 1985), 54–78.
12 *Richelieu* II.ii 32–3 in Edward George Bulwer-Lytton, *Dramatic Works* (Leipizig: Tauchnitz, 1860).
13 MacDonald, *Making a New People*, 83; emphasis added.
14 See, for example, Ken Cole, 'Cuba, Globalization, Socialist Development' (paper presented to the conference Marxism Today: A Renewed Left View at the University of Havana, 17–19 February 1999).
15 Benedict Anderson, *Imagined Communities: Reflections on the Origin and Spread of Nationalism*, rev. ed. (London: Verso, 1995).
16 Robert W. McChesney, Ellen Meiksins Wood, and John Bellamy Foster eds, *Capitalism and the Information Age: The Political Economy of the Global Communication Revolution* (New York: Monthly Review Press, 1998, Jim Davis, Thomas Hirschl, and Michael Stack, eds, *The Cutting Edge: Technology, Capitalism and Social Revolution* (London: Verso, 1997), and Michael Hardt and Antonio Negri, *Empire* (Cambridge, MA: Harvard University Press, 2000), especially 280.
17 See Robert J.C. Young, *Torn Halves: Political Conflict in Literary and Cultural Theory* (Manchester: Manchester University Press, 1996), 21–2.
18 L.M. Findlay, 'Runes of Marx and the University in Ruins,' *University of Toronto Quarterly* 66 (1997): 677–90. See also Bill Readings, *The University in Ruins* (Cambridge, MA: Harvard University Press, 1996), 21–43.
19 Pierre Bourdieu, *The Field of Cultural Production: Essays on Art and Literature*, ed. and intro. Randal Johnson (New York; Columbia University Press, 1993), 43–61.

7 Visible and Invisible Books: Hermetic Images in N-Dimensional Space

Jerome McGann

> To see a world in a grain of sand
> And a heaven in a wild flower,
> Hold infinity in the palm of your hand
> And eternity in an hour.
>
> – William Blake, 'Auguries of Innocence'

> Or if it indeed be so, that this other Space is really Thoughtland, then take me to that blessed region where I in Thought shall see the insides of all solid things ... In that blessed region of Four Dimensions, shall we linger on the threshold of the Fifth, and not enter therein? Ah, no! Let us rather resolve that our ambition shall soar with our corporal ascent.
>
> – E.A. Abbott, *Flatland: A Romance of Many Dimensions*

All the news organs have picked up the story: 'After five centuries of virtually uncontested sway, the Book seems to be facing a serious threat to its power. Informed sources report a large computerized force continues its sweep through traditional centres of bookish institutional control. Resistance has been fierce in certain quarters, and vast areas remain wholly under Book authority. Spokesmen from both sides describe the situation as volatile. According to militia leader Sven Birkerts ...'

That kind of report shapes much of the public discussion about the relation of books and an array of new computer-based tools generically named 'hypertext' and 'hypermedia.' This report will be different, coming instead from what Dante Gabriel Rossetti called 'an inner standing point.'[1] I am writing this in the Alderman Library at the University of Virginia, from an office on the third floor, where the Institute for Advanced Technology in the Humanities (IATH) is located. I reach for an apt Rossetti quotation as a matter of course since in this office, under the sponsorship of IATH and with its technical resources, I have worked with a group of English Literature graduate students for over a decade developing the Complete Writings and Pictures of Dante Gabriel Rossetti. A Hypermedia Research Archive.[2]

IATH occupies something under 2000 square feet. Anyone who knows libraries knows the premium they put on their floor space. They guard it like a certain dog at the gate of hell. Yet this large area was cleared by the library and given to IATH for its use in 1993. 'It has been reliably reported that major centres of Book power throughout the country have been voluntarily joining forces with the Electronic invaders and ...'

Those reports are true, but only factually true, like Kenneth Starr's report to Congress. Under a mask of objectivity, that kind of reporting generates a different kind of 'hyper'media. In matters of some moment it helps to have an inner standing point rather than an agenda. The inner standing point gives you access to the complexities.

There is no doubt that we are now passing through the first stages of a major shift in how we think about and manage texts, images, and the vehicles that carry them into our attention. From a literary person's point of view, the relevance of these changes can appear purely marginal: for whatever happens in the future, whatever new electronic poetry or fiction gets produced, the literature we inherit (to this date) is and will always be bookish.

This is true – although that truth underscores what is crucial in all these events from the scholar's point of view: we no longer have to use books to analyse and study other books or texts. That simple fact carries immense, even catastrophic, significance. Trying to think clearly in this kind of volatile situation is not easy. In fact, after working for most of this decade to implement the Rossetti Archive, an online hypermedia tool for studying all the writings and art works of Dante Gabriel Rossetti, I am beginning to see some simple but fundamental truths about books, digital tools, and what we might think about or expect of them. These simplicities are what I want to discuss here. Ultimately I hope to persuade you that setting these two forms of thought and expression into a mutually critical relation – encouraging each to interrogate and explore the other – is probably the most fruitful thing we could do right now.

Let me start, then, with a fundamental misconception: that a digital work is prima facie more complex and more powerful than a book. Well, it is not so; they are just tools designed to manage knowledge and information at different scalar levels. Our worlds are differently constituted by spoons on one hand and by steam shovels on the other. Nor is one of these instruments 'better' or more powerful. They do different things. Right now and in the foreseeable future, books do a number of things much better than computers. There is no comparison, for example, between the complexity and richness of paper-based fictional works, on the one hand, and their digital counterparts – hypermedia fiction – on the other. Nor does the difference simply measure a difference of writing skill – Italo Calvino, say, versus Stuart Moulthrop. The history of the book medium and the development of fictional conventions within that medium have evolved an extraordinarily nuanced and flexible set of tools for the imagination. The truth is that the 'hyper'media powers of the book, in this area of expression if not prima facie, far outstrip the available resources of digital instruments.

The latter, nevertheless, even in this moment of their earliest history, confidently declare and establish their authority in other areas of knowledge processing and communication. A like situation emerged in the fifteenth century with the invention of movable type. The printed book quickly supplanted the manuscript as a primary vehicle for storing, retrieving, and transmitting information. However, even the finest early printed books – and there are many such – lack the expressive and intellectual resources available to works produced in the manuscript tradition. That clear deficiency, needless to say, did not hinder the development of printed works – on the contrary, it inspired and promoted that development.

Today we stand in a similar set of circumstances. My special interests as an educator, a writer, and a scholar have brought me to engage the authority of our new digital tools. I undertook the development of the Rossetti Archive in 1992 as an experimental effort to exploit the special powers of digital technology – specifically, to try to design a model for a critical edition that would overcome certain of the key limitations of critical editions organized in book form. Scholars need tools that can efficiently manage large bodies of related literary and artistic objects. This is exactly what the traditional critical edition does. But it is clear, prima facie, that digital tools can execute many of the tasks of scholarly editing much better, much more thoroughly, and much more precisely than books can.

For instance, in certain important respects even works of imagination will and should be treated as we might treat ordinary 'material objects' like (say) screwdrivers or business records. The corpus of Rossetti's visual and textual works is large and its interrelations are complex. Simply building a scholarly space that facilitates accessing these material objects for study and analysis, including complex kinds of comparative study and analysis, is a useful thing to do. Digital space is in this case a much richer and more flexible space than bibliographical space. So in 1992 we set out to explore and exploit that space by building the Rossetti Archive, and we are not unhappy with the results. No paper-based book or set of books could have done what the Rossetti Archive offers to scholars. The book medium is physically incapable of the kinds of storing, integrating, and accessing operations we had held out as a basic scholarly demand for the Archive.

Artistic works are also very different from screwdrivers and business records, however, and our deepest interest in them focuses on those special qualities and characteristics. So we ask of our new electronic tools: can you also help us to see and understand (in a Blakean sense) works of imagination, can you 'advance our learning' of such works? And we ask ourselves: how might we manipulate these new tools to meet these special desires and requirements?

Of course, simply to ease access to literary and artistic work enhances our abilities to understand. These results are apparent in such splendid constructions as the Perseus Project or any of the electronic 'archives' being developed, for instance, at University of Virginia's Institute for Advanced Technology in the Humanities – electronic tools centred in the works of Blake, Dante, Dickinson, Rossetti, Whitman.[3] But we want to go beyond what these instruments are designed to do – out farther and in deeper. Can we do this? Are digital resources useful here?

This question brings to mind Edward Tufte's work.[4] Tufte is interested in the ways inventive people have used paper instruments to organize and elucidate various kinds of information. His studies inevitably lead us to an important set of important metaquestions: what is a page, what is a book, what are their parts, and how do they function?

One of the most interesting and unforeseen consequences of building the Rossetti Archive has been our encounter with those kinds of questions and problems. Initially it was clear to me how digital tools gave us great practical advantages over paper-based critical editions. The new engines could handle, in full and unabbreviated forms, vast amounts of data – far more than any book or reasonable set of books. They could also handle different kinds and forms of material data – not just textual, but visual and audial as well. These capacities made it possible to edit critically certain works that could not be adequately handled in a paper medium: the works of Rossetti, of course, but also those of Burns, of Blake, of Dickinson. The digital tools also exposed the critical deficiencies of the paper-based medium as such. Any kind of performative work – dramatic works, for example, and preeminently Shakespeare's dramas – gets more or less radically occluded when forced into a bookish representation. These differentials led me to see what I regarded at the time as an important general insight into books, computers, and their scholarly relation. I got a lot of satisfaction out of writing, in 1993, the following dicta:

> When we use books to study books, or hard copy texts to analyze other hard copy texts, the scale of the tools seriously limits the possible results. In studying the physical world, for example, it makes a great difference if the level of the analysis is experiential (direct) or mathematical (abstract). In a similar way, electronic tools in literary studies don't simply provide a new point of view on the materials, they lift one's general level of attention to a higher order.[5]

While I would not dissent from those sentences today, when I wrote them I was certainly unaware of much that they implied. My own levels of attention would be considerably raised as we undertook to implement the logical design of the Rossetti Archive between 1993 and 1997.

Some of these matters I have already written about – for example, the dysfunction that arises when one tries to use standard markup forms, SGML and all its derivatives, to elucidate the functional structures of imaginative works.[6] The recursive patterns that constitute an essential – probably the essential – feature of poetry and imaginative works in general cannot be marked, least of all captured, by SGML and its offspring. At first we engaged this dysfunction as a set of practical problems for building, or modifying our original plans for, the Rossetti Archive. But this deep asymmetry between our primary bibliographical data and our digital tools forced us to realize that we would not get very far with our practical problems if we did not begin to think more rigorously about a pair of difficult elementary questions – questions that we had hitherto treated far too casually, as if they did not involve problems, for us at any rate, at all.

Here are the questions. First, what is a literary work, what are its parts, how do they function? We assumed we knew how to answer such questions but our attempts to translate our bibliographical materials into coded instructions showed us that we did not. (The principle here is simple and known to every teacher: if you cannot explain what you know to someone else so that they also understand, you do not really know what you think you know.) Second, what constitutes a critical representation of a literary work and how does such a representation function? With one notable exception, every critical method and theory known to me assumes that the measure of critical adequacy is the degree of equivalence that can be produced between the object of critical attention and the critical representation of that object. Behind this view lies the ancient idea that representation is a mirroring relation. As we kept building the Rossetti Archive the flaw in that traditional understanding became more and more clear. A hypermedia work by choice and definition, the Archive therefore obligated us to integrate in a critical way both textual and visual materials. Our efforts were continually frustrated, however, because while digital texts lie open to automated search and analysis, digital images do not. Consequently, our critical mirror never adequately reflected the reality we knew was there. Indeed, so far as the mirror was concerned much of that reality might as well have been a large population of vampires.

I can only give the most schematic indication here of how we are addressing those questions and problems now – and I say 'are addressing' because I am acutely aware of how little we understand these matters. I will take up the second set of questions first and use that discussion to open up the issues involved in the first – and logically primary – set of questions.

For the past few years some colleagues and I have been experimenting with ways of manipulating the texts and images of imaginative works in order to enhance our perception and understanding of how they function. The initial phases of this work have been sketched in two papers: my essay

'Imagining What You Don't Know: The Theoretical Goals of the Rossetti Archive,' which I wrote in 1997; and a collaborative piece called 'Deformance and Interpretation,' which I coauthored with the poet Lisa Samuels in 1997–8.[7] Both of these essays argue, in different ways, that 'adequacy' in any critical representation cannot be measured by a scale of equivalence. A true critical representation does not accurately (so to speak) mirror its object; it consciously (so to speak) deforms its object. The critical act therefore involves no more (and no less) than a certain perspective on the object, its acuity of perception being a function of its self-conscious understanding of its own powers and limitations. It stands in a dialectical relation to its object, which must always be a transcendental object so far as any act of critical perception is concerned. This transcendental condition is a necessity because the object perpetually shifts and mutates under the influence of its perceivers. The critical act is a kind of conversation being carried on in the midst of many like and impinging conversations, all of which might at any point be joined by or merge into any of the others.

Works of art recreate – they 'stage' – a world of primary human intercourse and conversation. As with their reciprocating critical reflections, they manipulate their perceptual fields to generate certain dominant rhetorics or surface patterns that will organize and complicate our understandings. An important critical manoeuvre, then, involves dislocating or 'deforming' those dominant patterns so as to open doors of perception toward new opportunities and points of view. A dominant self-representation of *Paradise Lost* is to 'justify the ways of God to Man.' That famous dislocater of texts, William Blake, accepted the literality of Milton's text but utterly deformed its meanings, as it were: to Blake, the words 'justify,' 'God,' and 'Man' signify in ways that Milton could hardly have imagined. The all but complete inversion that Blake's interpretive moves bring to Milton highlights one of the most important features of imaginative works: they are incommensurate with themselves at all points.

The Blake/Milton relation highlights the general relation that critical deformations bear to aesthetic incommensurability. Blake knew very well that he had deformed the great Puritan, who was also his master spirit. Blake's works are what he called Buildings of Los(s), consciously written under the rubric 'I must create my own system or be enslaved by another man's.' That famous declaration draws on a peculiar Blake lexicon, however, where the word 'create' and its cognates are synonymous with the word 'error.' This is why Blake will speak of 'Error or Creation' and go on to assert that 'Error is Created Truth is Eternal.' His brief epic *Milton* is a deformed reading of *Paradise Lost* and *Paradise Regained*. Its acuity – that is to say, its power to elucidate Milton's work – is a direct function of the 'errors' that it deliberately creates in relation to that work.

Critical deformations can be usefully undertaken either randomly or according to a set of prearranged protocols. I have found, for example, that when certain of the standard filter protocols in Adobe Photoshop are applied to paintings – D.G. Rossetti's paintings, for instance – interesting structural features get exposed to view. Using the edging protocol to make arbitrary transformations of a number of Rossetti's pictures revealed, for example, that many of the pictures, and almost all of his famous portraits of women, are dominated by patterns of interlocking vortices and spirals. He plays numerous variations on these patterns, which are evidently the result of conscious purpose. This key structural feature of Rossetti's pictorial work has not been previously noticed or commented upon. It is a feature that leaps into prominence when these random deformations are passed through the pictures.

We now believe that a useful set of image-editing operations could be established that would have two important critical functions: first, to expose characteristic formal features of pictorial works; and second, to release perception from the spell of precisely those kinds of characteristic formal patterns, and open a perception of different arrangements and patterns. For the truth about works of art – textual, pictorial, auditory – is that they are, in Tufte's word, 'multivariate.'

There is an interesting moral to the story I have just told about critical reading as a deformance procedure. Although I have been familiar with the idea since at least the mid-1960s, when I first read Galvano della Volpe and when my lifelong interest in Blake's work began, I did not come to realize its claim to generality until I encountered the recalcitrance of digital images. Unlike language objects, once a visual object – a painting or drawing or photograph – is digitally reconstituted, it resists any further moves to mirror or translate it. Playing and doodling with digital images in Adobe Photoshop one day – it happened casually and with no deliberate goal in mind – I suddenly saw that the resistance of the image was in fact a critical opportunity, and not an impasse at all.

That realization brought additional unexpected consequences for the way we were conceiving the Rossetti Archive's digital texts and the problems we were having in marking them for automated computational analysis. We knew from the outset of the project that digital images stood apart from the computational resources of the new technology and we came quickly to realize how difficult it would be, except in the most elementary ways, to integrate automated text analysis to the information contained in digitized images. But it was dismaying to discover how much of Rossetti's poetry – how much of his strictly textual work – escaped our powers to represent it critically. Although I have already touched on the reasons for these computational deficiencies, some elaboration here will help to clarify how our difficulties were forcing us to rethink in fundamental ways the 'nature' of poetical and imaginative works.

Our failures with implementing some of the goals of the Rossetti Archive were bringing forward a series of paradoxical clarities not only about our digital tools, but even more about the works those tools we were trying to reconstitute. We realized that we were making inadequate assumptions about such works, and that we were using tools designed through those assumptions. That realization turned us back to reconsider the logical and ontological status of the original works. I am convinced none of us will get very far with our new digital tools unless we first undertake a thorough reconsideration of this kind.

First of all, a little history. The discipline of Humanities Computing developed in the field of linguistics, where scholars realized that computers would be extremely useful for carrying out automated pattern searches across large bodies of linguistic data. As a consequence, the textual corpus, even if it was in fact a poetical corpus, was framed for computational purposes as if it were informational or expository. Consequently, the tools that emerged to mark electronic texts for search and analysis also assumed that their object would be the exposure of the informational content and expository structure of the text. The problem is that poetical works, insofar as they are poetical, are not expository or informational. Because works of imagination are built as complex nets of repetition and variation, they are rich in what informational models of textuality label 'noise.' No poem can exist without systems of 'overlapping structure,' and the more developed the poetical text, the more complex are those systems of recursion. So it is that in a poetic field no unit can be assumed to be self-identical. The logic of the poem is only frameable in some kind of paradoxical articulation such as: 'a equals a if and only if a does not equal a.'

Let me illustrate the truth of that formulation with a couple of traditional interpretive examples. I shall begin with a famous sonnet by Gerard Manley Hopkins that illustrates in a dramatic way how textual objects of this kind are not self-identical.

'As Kingfishers Catch Fire'

As kingfishers catch fire, dragonflies dráw fláme;
  As tumbled over rim in roundy wells
  Stones ring; like each tucked string tells, each hung bell's
Bow swung finds tongue to fling out broad its name;
Each mortal thing does one thing and the same:
  Deals out that being indoors each one dwells;
  Selves – goes itself; *myself* it speaks and spells,
Crying *What I do is me: for that I came.*

I say more: the just man justices;
  Keeps grace: that keeps all his goings graces;

Acts in God's eye what in God's eye he is –
  Christ. For Christ plays in ten thousand places,
Lovely in limbs, and lovely in eyes not his
  To the Father through the features of men's faces.

The first statement in this text offers a paradigm of its duplicities. The word 'As' here operates simultaneously in a formal and in a temporal sense (so here it means both 'Just as' or 'In just the way that' and also 'While' or 'At the same time as'). The repetition of the word in line 2 underscores its variational possibilities because the poem's second statement introduces an altogether new grammar. Then comes what at first might be taken for a synonym of 'As,' the word 'like,' which introduces the sonnet's third syntactic unit (running from the third word of line 3 through line 4). This unit of syntax appears to have the same general form as the sonnet's opening unit, but when we press it more closely we watch it shapeshift into a new and unexpected grammar. Once again the move comes through duplicitous word usage. The word 'like' here functions simultaneously as a conjunction (a synonym for 'as'), as an adverb (meaning 'alike'), and as a noun (in the sense of 'kind,' as in the word 'mankind').

There's nothing unusual about this passage from Hopkins. Poets do this kind of thing all the time; it is the very essence of poetical textuality. I choose the passage not exactly randomly, however, but because its complexities are so apparent and so dramatic. In four lines an amazing kind of textual metastasis has unfolded, nor have I even come close to an adequate exegesis of what is happening here. The phrase 'catch fire,' for example, normally suggests – as our dictionaries tell us – a passive eventuality, but in this case a feedback loop causes another textual metamorphosis, so that the word 'catch' turns active, as if this kingfisher were catching fire as it hunts and catches fish. This transformation occurs because the phrase is affected retroactively, as it were, by the syntactic rhymes that immediately follow the phrase in the next two lines ('kingfishers catch fire,' 'dragonflies draw flame,' 'stones ring'). Imaginative textual objects regularly work through these kinds of transformations, feedback loops, and complex repetitions. All are forms or types of what we call 'rhymes;' that staple poetic device illustrating the algorithm I set out above: 'a=a if and only if a≠a.'

The nonhierarchical character of these transformations and rhymings emerges very clearly in the sestet of this sonnet. Look carefully at lines 12–14. The word 'plays,' probably the pivotal word in the poem, involves a most cunning kind of textual wit. It conceals a pun whose 'other meaning,' so to speak, is 'prays.' Why is this so? Because the word is syntactically linked to a predicate complement that only comes to us in the final line, in the phrase 'To the Father.' The text of the poem generates the literal phrase 'plays ... To the Father.' The oddness of that phrase does not reach us until we have transacted the hiatus of line 13, however, when we suddenly realize that the text has been (mis)leading us to reconstitute the phrase into something more linguistically apt. No one reading such a phrase in the poem's plain context of religious usages can fail to hear the absent but secretly prepared alternative phrase: 'prays ... To the Father.' This is simultaneously a playful and a prayerful text.

But the text has not finished with its games of self-generation and self-transformation. The play/pray wordgame regenerates itself yet again in a kind of conceptual metatext: the word 'prays' means as well 'praise.' The poem as a whole is a kind of playful prayer of praise 'for' Christ and 'To' the Father, the word 'Christ' being here the text's key figure of individuation, or what Hopkins called 'selving.'

In all this commentary I have tried to keep my remarks free from any kind of thematic or ideational/ideological references. Everything I have discussed has to do with Hopkins's text as a functioning sign system, a structure of signifiers and signifieds. I have done this not because I think 'meaning' in a referential sense is not a crucial part of every textual field, but because I want to demonstrate how full of meaningful activities these fields are even when their referentialities are held in abeyance. Look again at line 12 of the sonnet and think about how it prepares us to register the word game that only gets fully exposed in line 14. In line 12 Hopkins has made a text that our mouths will find difficult to transact: 'Christ – for Christ plays.' The problem comes as we try to negotiate a passage from those 3 'r's to the 'l' in 'plays.' Our mouths would find it easier to read 'prays' here rather than 'plays,' and we have to make some physical and mental effort to ensure that we get the given phonetic sequence right. The effort is a perceptual signal that our bodies will not let our minds forget when we come to line 14. And we are prepared for this exercise with r's and l's because the sonnet in fact opens its textual field in line 1 with a major deployment of just those phonetic signs.

What kind of text is this, really? First of all, it is both – and simultaneously – a perceptual and a conceptual event. Informational texts seek to minimize their perceptual features in the belief that texts calling attention to their vehicular forms interfere with the transmission of their ideas. The textuality of poetry reminds us of the intimate part that phonetics plays in the signifying operations of language. It also reminds us of a second important feature of text: while it may deploy ordered, even hierarchical, structures of ideas, its object (as it were) is to play with and within such structures and not be consumed by them. Are there such things as pure, non-languaged 'ideas'?

Perhaps. However that may be, when ideas function textually, they commit themselves to fields of perception as well as systems of conception. So in the case of this sonnet we will want to see that while Hopkins's Scotist ideas play throughout the text and even comprise its argument, the sonnet is not comprehended in those ideas or reducible to a Scotist description or exposition. No textual event – not the Scotist word 'Selves,' not even the word 'Christ' – is ever self-identical or self-transparent. Most especially is this true for imaginative texts – where alone we will see an effort to exploit the full resources of textuality.

Let me point out one other feature of this text, a moment of its physical visibility that we may hardly recognize as a visible thing. The wordplay realized in line14 ('Plays/Prays ... to the Father') would fail in its remarkable effect were it not for the hiatus in lines 12–13, a hiatus that is constructed as a visible space and a temporal rhythm. I leave for another occasion any discussion of that temporal rhythm and its perceptual character because I want to concentrate here on the visible forms being deployed.

We tend not to notice an elementary fact about printed or scripted texts: that they are constituted from a complex series of marked and unmarked spaces. The most noticeable are the larger regular units – the lines, the paragraphs, or (in verse) the stanzas, as well as the spaces between them. All of these spatial units, as well as all the others on a page or in a book, offer themselves as opportunities for nonlexical expression. For a helpful comparison think of the cartoon strip with its sequence of frames separated by gutters. The force of cartoon narrative is always a function of the energy generated in those gutters, where the work's inexplicit but crucial relations are solicited in the reader's imagination. Ballad poems regularly treat their stanzas in exactly the same way, and all good writers learn to exploit the spatial fields of their texts. A procedural gap organizes the continuous play of differences between the physical lines of a poetic form and the grammatical order playing in the form. The divisions in long poems and prose fictions create opportunities for building relational nets across the framed areas of the text.

It is highly significant that readers of books move from recto to verso, that their field of awareness continually shifts from page to 'opening' (i.e., the space made by a facing verso/recto), and that the size of the book – length, breadth, and thickness – help to determine our reader's perceptions at every point. Texts are not laid out flat on plane pages, and if I were to open the subjects of typefaces or calligraphic forms, of ink, of paper, and of the various ways marks can be scripted or printed, the multivariate manifold of the book would be easily recognized. Entering those subjects shows why a fine press book is not just another pretty face – at least not the ones that have given thought to themselves. When William Morris reissued *The House of Life*, his friend Rossetti's masterwork, as a Kelmscott Press book, the point was to help readers perceive the sonnets more thoroughly than they might in the trade editions. The Kelmscott edition radically alters the spatio-temporal field of the sonnet sequence. It is nothing less than what we would now call a new 'reading' of the sequence.[8]

But even these examples can be misleading if they suggest that bibliographical space is a matter of solid geometry. To help dispel that possible illusion I offer the example of a seventeenth-century poem titled 'To the Post Boy.' This example comes to shift our angle of focus, so to speak, and to expose networks of dispersed visibilities.

To the Post Boy

Son of A whore God dam you can you tell
A Peerless Peer the Readyest way to Hell?
Ive out swilld Baccus sworn of my own make
Oaths wod fright furies and make Pluto quake.
Ive swived more whores more ways than Sodoms walls
Ere knew or the College of Romes Cardinalls.
Witness Heroick scars, look here nere go
Sear cloaths and ulcers from the top to toe.
Frighted at my own mischeifes I have fled
And bravely left my lifes defender dead.
Broke houses to break chastity and died
That floor with murder which my lust denyed.
Pox on it why do I speak of these poor things?
I have blasphemed my god and libelld Kings;
The readyest way to Hell come quick –
 Boy nere stirr
The readyest way my Lords by Rochester.

This work illustrates another mode of textual instability operating at a translinguistic level. The issue gets focused as a problem of attribution: we are not sure who authored this work, and the uncertainty affects every aspect of the poem's textuality.[9] Most of the primary textual witnesses – late seventeenth- and early eighteenth-century manuscripts and printed texts – assign the poem to Rochester, seeing it as an astonishing piece of self-directed satire perhaps designed to frustrate and undermine his enemies and their literary devices. The dialogue-poem would be coming to show that Rochester could write satire, even against himself, that his antagonists could not match.

Certain early witnesses, as well as some later scholars, however, do not read the poem as Rochester's but as the work of one of his enemies. The issue, on current evidence, is in fact undecidable, although scholarly opinion today inclines toward favouring Rochester's authorship. (Not very long ago opinion went the other way.)

The poem therefore gets framed in three optional ways: as Rochester's work, as the work of someone else satirizing Rochester, and as a kind of duck-rabbit lying open to either and both readings simultaneously. Those frames, we want to remember, are part of the textuality of the work and they are deeply embedded. But they run through the text in visibilities that extend far beyond what we might register as the work's plane or solid geometries. Indeed, they only appear as bibliographical and manuscript data scattered in disparate and disjunct materials – documents now housed separately in many libraries (the British Library, the Victoria and Albert Museum, Ohio State University library, the Osterreichische Nationalbibliotek, Vienna, and the Bodleian). In those documents and their complex interfaces we trace out that crucial and fundamental feature of every text: its transmission history – which is to say, we trace out the remains of those earliest readers who half perceived and half created this text.

Every document, every moment in every document, conceals (or reveals) an indeterminate set of interfaces that open into alternate spaces and relations. Traditional criticism will engage this kind of radiant textuality more as a problem of context than a problem of text, nor is there any reason to fault that way of seeing the matter. But as the word itself suggests, 'context' is a cognate of text, and not in any abstract Barthesian sense. We construct the poem's context, for example, by searching out the meanings marked in the physical witnesses that bring the poem to us. We read those witnesses with scrupulous attention, that is to say, we make our detailed way through the looking glass of the book and thence to the endless reaches of the Library of Babel where every text is catalogued and extensively cross-referenced. In making this journey we are driven far out into the deep space, as we say these days, occupied by our orbiting texts. There objects pivot about many different points and poles. The objects themselves shapeshift continually and the pivots move, drift, shiver, and even dissolve away.

'Ah, a cosmological metaphor,' you will tell me, 'for thinking about books and texts.' But in that metaphor, I ask you, what is the figure and what is the ground? The metaphor itself has a bibliographical history that might be traced and described. Which came first, as it were, the metaphor or the book? After Derrida, it's harder than ever to say. But it is not hard to say that what we register as the phenomenal world has been a bibliographical function for more than two millenia at least.[10]

Not hard to say, perhaps, but still difficult to realize or know because our models for knowing have been shaped in scientific models cast in informational and expository forms. Those forms do not normally cultivate self-reflection, however deeply they may reflect upon matters they set apart from themselves to observe and interrogate; and least of all do they practise self-reflection on their medium of exchange.[11] But that kind of reflection is precisely what happens in imaginative work, where the medium is always the message, whatever else may be the subjects of the work.

Content in poeisis therefore tends to involve more broadly 'semiotic' rather than narrowly 'linguistic' materials. The perceptual features of text are as apt for expressive purposes as the semantic, syntactic, and rhetorical features – at least so far as the poets and readers who make such texts are concerned. Every feature represents a determinate field of textual action, and while any one field might (or might not) individually (abstractly) be organized in a hierarchical form, the recursive interplay of the fields appears topological rather than hierarchic. The organization is more like a mobile with a shifting set of poles and hinge points carrying a variety of objects, many of an 'opposite and discordant' character, as Coleridge might say.

Which brings me back to Edward Tufte and the opening sentence of his influential book *Envisioning Information*:

> Even though we navigate daily through a perceptual world of three spatial dimensions and reason occasionally about higher dimensional arenas with mathematical ease, the world portrayed on our information displays is caught up in the two-dimensionality of the endless flatlands of paper and video screen.

So acute and arresting is Tufte's appreciation of textual graphics that we tend to pass over a crucial piece of misinformation that his work has envisioned. Despite what he says, we do not 'navigate daily through a perceptual world of three spatial dimensions,' although it is true that we often think we do and even represent ourselves as doing so. Nor are we doomed, when we transact our books and our monitors, to 'the two-dimensionality of the endless flatlands of paper and video screen.' Even our daily movements are 'multivariate' and n-dimensional, and when we imagine ourselves passing through a world of three dimensions we are merely surrendering to a certain type of perceptual filter. It is a filter regularly exposed and repudiated by an imagination like William Blake's, as my epigraph suggests. Every page, even a blank page, even a page of Dan Quale's prose, is n-dimensional. The issue is, how clearly has that n-dimensional space of the page – its 'multivariate' character – been marked and released?

To see that truth about paperspace seems to me especially useful in an age fascinated to distraction by the hyperrepresentational power of digital technology. We want to remember that books possess exactly the same powers, and we want to remember not simply to indulge a farewell nostalgia at the twilight of the book. One of the great tasks lying ahead is the critical and editorial reconstitution of our inherited cultural archive in digital forms. We need to learn to do this because we do not as yet know how. Furthermore, we scholars need to learn because it is going to be done, if not by us, then by others. We are the natural heirs to this task because it is we who know most about books. When we study the world of books with computers we have much to learn from our subjects. In crucial ways, for instance, a desk strewn with a scholar's materials is far more efficient as a workspace – far more hypertextual – than the most powerful workstation, screen-bound, you can buy. Or consider this: if these new machines can deliver stunning images to our view, the only images they understand are their own electronic constructions. Original objects – visual, audial – remain deeply mysterious to a computer. If a computer serves up, say, a facsimile of Rossetti's painting *The Blessed Damozel*, its most effective means for understanding that image – for analysing it – are through sets of so-called metadata, that is, logical descriptions introduced into the electronic structure in textual form. Even when (some would say 'if') that limitation gets transcended, logical ordering through metadata will never not be a part of computerized scholarship of literary works. The objects of study demand it – just as the physical sciences, for all their use of mathematical models, cannot do without empirical investigations.

There are more serious problems. Scholars are interested in books and texts as they are works of 'literature' and imagination, but those who design computerized tools sometimes seriously misunderstand their primary materials. So far as I can see, nearly all the leading design models for the scholarly treatment of imaginative works operate from a naive distinction between a text's 'form' and 'content.' In a recent essay the brilliant computer-text theorist Steven DeRose writes, 'A book is "the same" if reprinted from quarto to octavo and from Garamond 24 to Times 12 in all but a few senses.'[12] Aldus and the fifteenth-century humanist printers knew better. Those 'few senses' are never nontrivial, and in many cases – a list is too easy to develop – they carry the most profound kinds of 'content.'

DeRose's view is now commonplace among those who are making decisions about how to design scholarly tools for the computerized study of literary works. Poems, for example, are inherently nonhierarchical structures that promote attention to varying and overlapping sets of textual designs, both linguistic and bibliographical. But the computerized structures being imagined for studying these complex forms approach them as if they were expository, as if their 'information' were indexable, as if the works were not made from zeugmas and puns, metaphors and intertexts, as if the textual structure were composed of self-identical elements. Some textual information in poems is indexable, but nearly everything most salient about them is polyvalent. So far as imaginative works are concerned the equation remains: a equals a if and only if a does not equal a.

Do not despair, however. Like the appearance of the codex nearly two thousand years ago, like the advent of printing in the fifteenth century, the computer comes bearing great promise to literary scholars.

'But will we be assimilated? Is resistance futile?' There are no aliens here, no struggle between books and computers. From now on scholarship will have both, willy-nilly. The question is – the choice is – whether those with an intimate appreciation of literary works will become actively involved in designing new sets of tools for studying them.

NOTES

1 This paper is a revised version of a report I gave under the rubric 'What is Text?' at the 1999 joint ACH/ALLC annual convention on humanities computing held at University of Virginia.

2 The first instalment of the Rossetti Archive was released in July 2000.

3 For the Perseus Project, see http://www.perseus.tufts.edu/; the home page of the Institute for Advanced Technology in the Humanities is http://jefferson.village.virginia.edu/home.html.

4 See especially Edward Tufe, *Envisioning Information* (Chesire, CT: Graphics Press, 1990).

5 Jerome McGann, 'The Rationale of HyperText,' in *Electronic Text: Investigations in Method and Theory*, ed. Kathryn Sutherland (Oxford: Clarendon Press, 1997), 20 (online version at http://~jjm2f/rationale.html).

6 See, for example, my 'Hideous Progeny, Rough Beasts: Editing as a Theoretical Pursuit,' in *TEXT* (Ann Arbor: University of Michigan Press, 1998), 1–16 (online version at href://~jjm2f/chum.html).

7 The latter was printed in *New Literary History* (winter 1999): 25–56; the other is an online essay accessible at: http://~jjm2f/deform.html.

8 I have given attention to this kind of elementary bibliographical 'expressivity' for two reasons. First, it gives a simple but arresting reminder of the determinate materiality of every language form. (An example for an oral event of language would not be difficult to construct). Second, although the matter is beyond the scope of this essay, I believe that an analysis of these kinds of visible features of text holds promise for exploiting computerized resources for the interpretation of imaginative works. For a more detailed treatment of this matter see my *Radiant Textuality: Literature after the World Wide Web* (New York: Palgrave, 2001), chap. 7.

9 For a discussion of this poem and its attribution problems, see David M. Vieth, *Attribution in Restoration Poetry: A Study of Rochester's Poems of 1680* (New Haven: Yale University Press, 1963), 199–203.

10 This is because our knowledge of phenomena is a textual/bibliographical function.

11 The twentieth century has produced a number of notable exceptions among scientists from Einstein and Gödel to G. Spencer Brown and Roger Penrose. Brown's *Laws of Form* (New York: Julian, 1972) is particularly important, not least because of his self-conscious use of textspace to develop his argument.

12 See Steven DeRose's essay 'Structured Information: Navigation, Access, and Control' (http://sunsite.berkeley.edu/FindingAids/EAD/derose.html).

8 James Joyce's *Ulysses* on the Page and on the Screen

Michael Groden

Leopold Bloom has just received a tantalizing letter from Martha Clifford, and you are reading it along with him. You have read about fifteen sentences, and then you come to these two, one a complete sentence and one a fragment:

> Please write me a long letter and tell me more. Remember if you do not I

If you have a paperback version of Hans Walter Gabler's edition of James Joyce's *Ulysses* in your hands, you will have to hold your breath and turn the page to learn that Martha has told Bloom that she 'will punish' him (5:251–2).[1] Martha typed her letter on one side of a sheet of paper, and so Bloom was able to receive this pleasurable threat with less effort – but with less suspense. About half the printed editions of *Ulysses* will make you move to a new page at some point in Martha's letter, usually not as dramatic a break as in the Gabler edition. In the others, the vagaries of the font and page size let the letter fit on one page.

But what if you are reading the text of *Ulysses* on a computer screen? The text might be presented in a way that retains printed page units, and so you would see a replication of one of the printed editions, with the letter either intact or divided. Or the letter might be broken up into screen-sized units, maybe fifteen or twenty lines per screen – it might just fit onto one screen, but more likely it would be divided between two. As a third possibility, it might be part of a long scrolling text comprising all of 'Lotus Eaters,' the episode in which it appears, or even all of *Ulysses*, and it would fit on one screen or not depending on which line of the text you positioned at the top. As a fourth alternative, you might be able to change the size and maybe also the font to suit your preferences, so the letter would fit on one screen or not, depending on now big you decided that the text should be.[2]

In *Ulysses*, Bloom holds a physical document that was typed in a particular font with determinable spacing and margins and on paper of a certain size and thickness. *Ulysses* doesn't specify any of these particulars, just the facts that Martha typed the envelope and the letter (5:61, 17:1841), pinned a flower to the paper – presumably in response to the name Henry Flower, Bloom's nom de plume in his letters to her (5:239) – and made several typos and grammatical mistakes that tickle Bloom, such as 'I called you naughty boy because I do not like that other world,' 'you know what I will do to you, you naughty boy, if you do not wrote,' and 'do not deny my request before my patience are exhausted' (5:244–54). The letter's text has been transmitted through all the editions of *Ulysses* (sometimes imperfectly, as some editions, thinking that Martha's typos were Joyce's, corrected them) and will live on in future editions. But as a material object, a page, that letter will remain forever locked away in the drawer where Bloom stores it after he returns home (17:1840–2).

If the text of a printed book is presented on a computer screen, should the page units, like the sheet of paper of Martha's letter, simply disappear? Should they be retained, with scroll bars or some other device compensating for the smaller size of screens compared to pages, or with the original page breaks indicated by lines, bracketed numbers, or some other marker? Should all the typographic and graphic features of a page be reproduced as a unit? Anyone engaged in a digital project that involves a text originally printed as a book needs to think about these issues, and such thoughts lead to intriguing questions about what pages mean and what the future of the page might be.

I am the codirector of a project, Digital *Ulysses*, that will present Joyce's work in an electronic, hypermedia format. The full text of the book in several versions will be included, with specific words and phrases linked to definitions and annotations, extended analyses and commentary, photographs, videos, maps, songs, an oral pronunciation guide, and audio readings from quoted or cited works. More extended sections of *Ulysses* will be linked to an archive of published scholarship, newly written hypertext criticism, literary works that are quoted or mentioned or echoed, biographical and historical background material, oral readings, and filmed excerpts of *Ulysses* – all coordinated to the passage of *Ulysses* that is on the screen. There will also be a full archive of the manuscripts for *Ulysses*. Readers will be able to bookmark their place and take notes for future use. The presentation is designed to allow the simplest possible ways of navigating through the vast amounts of available material. As with any hypertext, readers will be offered multiple pathways through the materials, and they can choose which information and how much detail they want to see.

Pages are especially vulnerable and problematic for a project like Digital *Ulysses*. Each edition of *Ulysses* offers different page units and paginations – does that eliminate the page as a meaningful unit? If the pages should be preserved in some way in the digital presentation, how should they be

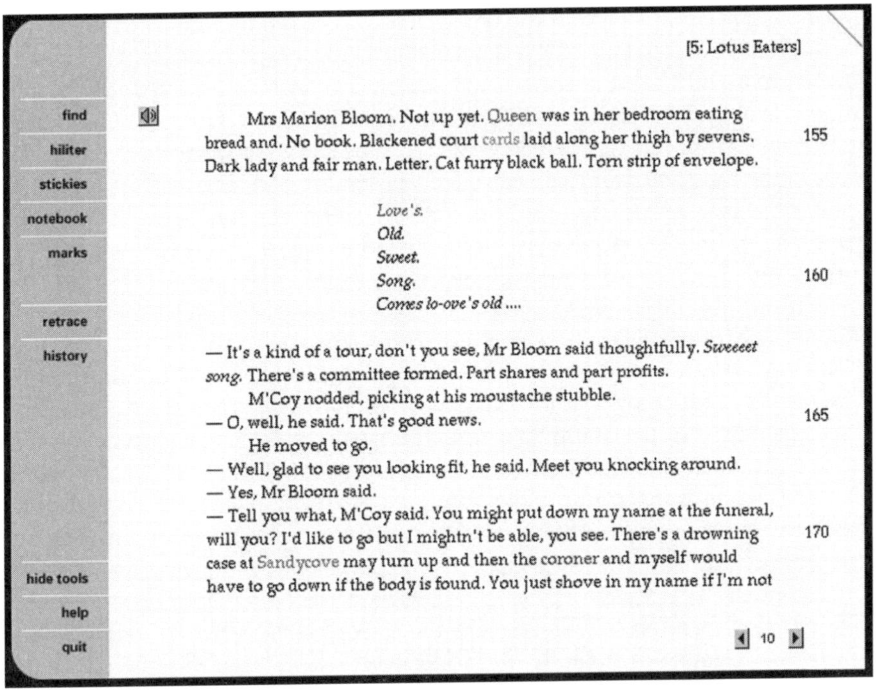
[5: Lotus Eaters]
find
hiliter
stickies
notebook
marks
retrace
history
hide tools
help
quit
Mrs Marion Bloom. Not up yet. Queen was in her bedroom eating
bread and. No book. Blackened court cards laid along her thigh by sevens.
Dark lady and fair man. Letter. Cat furry black ball. Torn strip of envelope.
Love's.
Old.
Sweet.
Song.
Comes lo-ove's old ....
— It's a kind of a tour, don't you see, Mr Bloom said thoughtfully. Sweeeet
song. There's a committee formed. Part shares and part profits.
M'Coy nodded, picking at his moustache stubble.
— O, well, he said. That's good news.
He moved to go.
— Well, glad to see you looking fit, he said. Meet you knocking around.
— Yes, Mr Bloom said.
— Tell you what, M'Coy said. You might put down my name at the funeral,
will you? I'd like to go but I mightn't be able, you see. There's a drowning
case at Sandycove may turn up and then the coroner and myself would
have to go down if the body is found. You just shove in my name if I'm not
10

Figure 8.1. Screen with nineteen lines from *Digital Ulysses* 'Lotus Eaters.'

retained, since in all their forms they are bigger than a screen? What would the pages be preserved *as* in a medium lacking the tangibility of printed pages and also lacking anything that corresponds to a printed page's front and back? (Figure 8.1, as an example, presents nineteen lines from episode 5, 'Lotus Eaters.' The line units are the same as in the Gabler edition, but the presentation includes only the number of lines that fit comfortably on the screen in the predetermined font.)[3]

In the next few pages I want to consider some issues regarding pages before I discuss possible aspects of their future.

II

Joyce was acutely aware that the words he was writing as *Ulysses* would eventually be published as pages in a book. He serves as an excellent example of the statement from William Morris that Jerome McGann cites as the epigraph to *The Textual Condition*: 'You can't have art without resistance in the material.'[4] Joyce worked both with and against his medium, exploiting the possibilities of printed words and pages as much as he could and extending those possibilities when the words and pages seemed unable to do what he wanted. For example, in the 'Proteus' episode, Stephen Dedalus begins to formulate a poem, and phrases that come and go in his mind include 'Mouth to her kiss,' 'Mouth to her mouth's kiss,' and 'mouth to her moomb' (3:399–402). Joyce laboured to make the words appear on the page in a particular way. In the margin of an early draft for the episode, he lists various possibilities for the last word, spelling it in several elaborate ways before settling on 'moomb,' a simpler option than any he listed in the draft. The possibilities all sound slightly different from each other, but more important, they *look* different. Presumably Joyce was trying to find the word that looked like an indication of his character's exploration of various sound possibilities.[5]

Stephen is not really oriented toward printed words and pages, though. The results of his creative efforts appear in the seventh episode, 'Aeolus,' and when he thinks of the poem he wrote down earlier, it turns out to be a rather lame effort, a depersonalized and romanticized version of one of the poems Douglas Hyde translated in *Love Songs of Connacht*.[6] The poem is Stephen's best written creation in *Ulysses*, but later in 'Aeolus' he presents a much more effective effort, a cryptic spoken narrative that he apparently puts together on the spot as he walks to a pub with men from the newspaper office. Like his other major creation in *Ulysses*, the theory of *Hamlet* that he expounds to sceptical listeners in episode 9, 'Scylla and Charybdis,' Stephen's talents seem best suited to oral delivery.

Not so Leopold Bloom. Described by Patrick McCarthy as 'predominantly a reader' in a 'town of talkers,'[7] Bloom reads texts in all their richness – a handwritten letter from his daughter Milly (4:397–414) and the typed one from Martha Clifford (5:241–59), a newspaper article about Paddy Dignam's funeral in which his surname is spelled without its 'l' (16:1248–61) and one about the Gold Cup race, whose results proved unfortunate for him earlier in the day (16:1274–89). He also reads visually. In order to distract himself from a boring conversation he cannot get out of, he scans a newspaper he is holding and notices the words in an ad:

> *What is home without*
> *Plumtree's Potted Meat?*
> *Incomplete.*
> *With it an abode of bliss.* (5:144–7)

Later, he renders a judgment on both the ad's words and its placement on the page, faulting its placement under the obituary notices (8:743–4). The ad sticks in his mind all day though (see 17:596–9), probably because he knows that his and Molly's ten years without sexual intercourse have made their home incomplete. In Jerome McGann's terms, Bloom is aware of both a text's 'linguistic code' – the words – and also its 'bibliographic code' – such features as the layout of the text on a page, the size of the margins, its illustrations, the dimensions and thickness of the paper, and, for a book, the kind of binding and covers.[8]

Bloom places ads in newspapers for clients, and in 'Aeolus' he is at work. He describes a proposed ad for the tea and liquor distributor Alexander Keyes to the editor and the other men in the room: in it, a pair of crossed keys both puns on Keyes's name and visually suggests the House of Keys, the lower house of the parliament of the Isle of Man, which England allowed to function under a qualified form of home rule.[9] For Bloom, reading is contrapuntal (he is aware of the pun), visual (he is thinking about the ways the words and graphics will look), and rhetorical ('Catches the eye, you see,' he tells the editor [7:151]). He reads this way throughout the episode and throughout *Ulysses*. As he describes Keyes's proposed ad, however, the text's puns and its visuality are highlighted in another way: a bold, uppercase tag preceding the section reads 'HOUSE OF KEY(E)S' (7:141). Bloom does not respond to this visual pun because he is unaware that it is there. Part of the reader's page, not the character's, it and other tags like it are excellent examples of Joyce's involvement with his text's pages.

'Aeolus' is the seventh episode in *Ulysses*, and originally, lasting until late in Joyce's writing of the book, it matched the preceding six in combining a narrator who functions mainly to locate characters as they move around various spaces in Dublin, a report of Bloom's and Stephen's interior thoughts, and the characters' spoken conversations. After Joyce sent the episode's typescript to Maurice Darantiere, his French printer in Dijon, he received a set of *placards*, the French equivalent of galley proofs. In form and content, the pages resemble the ones that precede them.[10]

Joyce returned the proofs with some corrections and a startling number of additions. Most dramatically, he added bits of text interrupting the narrative a few times on each page. He did this by inserting numbers into the narrative at the point of each insertion and including the new text in numbered lists at the top of the *placard* pages. As if that were not enough, he also added a large chunk of new text for the beginning of the episode, indicating with a symbol that it should precede the printed text on the proof, so the number at the top of the printed text is 2, which is accompanied by a letter M signalling the addition. The number 1 comes at the beginning of the added text. Darantiere and his men set all the new text in print, with the inserts in uppercase bold type, understandably making a lot of mistakes along the way, and sent a new set of proofs to Joyce. He again made corrections and dramatic revisions to the proofs, both to the narrative and to the bold-type inserts. On the first page alone, along with adding new narrative text he added two new bold-type inserts, deleted one, replaced one with completely new words, and modified the first one.

Critics have variously called these bold-type inserts newspaper headlines, heads, subheads, or captions, and they have often explained them as Joyce's desire to make his episode, which is about a newspaper and is set in a newspaper office, look like a newspaper. The fragmented bits of narrative between the inserts resemble the sections of newspaper articles which in the past routinely fell between subheads. Sometimes the relation between the head and the narrative that follows it is clear, at other times obscure. In no way does the episode read like the seamless narrative it was at first – it announces itself dramatically as a text printed in a book. Significantly, Joyce's desire to make the pages look like a newspaper did not extend beyond inserting the heads – there is only one column, the heads are all printed in the same type. The episode appears not so much like a newspaper as like pages in a book trying to suggest a newspaper.

Joyce was under no obligation to explain why he made this dramatic change to the appearance of 'Aeolus,' and he never did, at least not directly. We do know that by August 1921, when he added the heads to the proofs, he had written all the episodes except for the last two, 'Ithaca' and 'Penelope' (which he was working on while he revised and augmented the first sixteen), and so he had already created daring typographic experiments on pages in later parts of *Ulysses*. By adding the heads to 'Aeolus,' he transformed an early episode into one that in some ways resembles the later ones. Stuart Gilbert, whose 1930 book *James Joyce's 'Ulysses': A Study* was written with Joyce's help, might have been speaking for Joyce when he wrote in a footnote about the heads that 'this historico-literary technique, here inaugurated, is a preparation for the employment of the same method, but on the grand scale, a stylistic *tour de force*, in a later episode, the *Oxen of the Sun*.'[11] Joyce never said where he got the idea from, either. But the *placards* he was receiving from Darantiere were not like American galley proofs (which are long sheets of text, longer than single pages of a book); rather, they consisted of large pieces of paper, about 28 inches wide by 18 inches high, eight book pages printed only on one side of each sheet. A *placard* was arranged in columns, with the first page printed above the second, the third above the fourth, etc. Joyce looked at these *placards*, column after column, while he was thinking about his newspaper episode. If he read them visually as well as verbally, he might have been reminded of a newspaper. Whatever inspired him, on these proofs he transformed the appearance of his pages into something suggesting a newspaper.

Typically, having made the decision to redesign the episode, Joyce carried the process as far as he could. He revised the heads – only about half of them appear on these first proofs in their final printed form – and he honed their initial pattern of moving from stately dignified ones at the beginning to slangy colloquial ones at the end.[12] This results in a kind of double linearity to the printed text: the narrative proceeds in its own way, telling the ongoing story of Leopold Bloom and Stephen Dedalus on 16 June 1904, whereas the heads offer a separate sequence of linguistic change. The reader can take the heads and the text as separate narratives, follow one and ignore the other, or negotiate the shifting relationships between each head and the text that follows it, and, given all these possible relationships between the heads and the text, the so-called linearity of the printed text breaks down completely.

Furthermore, the heads sever any sense of a seamless connection between the written words and spoken narrative. Until this point in *Ulysses*, as anyone who has listened to audio versions of it knows, the book can be read aloud like almost any nineteenth-century novel.[13] But what about the heads: do you say them in a declamatory voice, as you might for a newspaper head or subhead? Most readers probably would, but Joyce himself offered another option: when he recorded a page of 'Aeolus' in 1924 – the only recording he made from *Ulysses* – he rather surprisingly read the one head in the section he chose, 'FROM THE FATHERS' (7:841), as part of Stephen Dedalus's interior monologue. And an extreme case, a head from the middle of the episode – '? ? ?' (7:512) – can be seen but not heard or read aloud at all; it makes sense only as a sequence of printed signs on a page.

Like Martha Clifford's letter, the heads have appeared differently in various editions of *Ulysses*. In the first ones from Shakespeare and Company, they were printed in large bold type. The 1961 Modern Library edition makes them even larger and bolder relative to the text. The designer of the Gabler edition greatly reduced them, making them smaller than even the upper-case letters in the text below them, and eliminated the bold face. The most unusual presentation occurs in the rare Limited Editions Club version from 1935 (best known for its illustrations by Henri Matisse), where the text is printed on large pages with two columns per page and the heads appear in varying fonts that reflect their development from what Stuart Gilbert describes as 'dignified' to 'vulgar.'

In discussing the heads, Gilbert provides a fascinating example of how a reading of *Ulysses* can depend on the particular pages the critic looks at. In *James Joyce's 'Ulysses,'* which is based on the Shakespeare and Company editions and is informed by Gilbert's work on the translation of *Ulysses* into French, he called the 'Aeolus' heads 'captions' – 'the text is split up into brief sections, each headed with a caption composed in the journalistic manner' – and a footnote to this sentence says that 'the style of the captions is gradually modified in the course of the episode; the first are comparatively dignified, or classically allusive, in the Victorian tradition; later captions reproduce, in all its vulgarity, the slickness of the modern press.'[14] Five years later, writing the introduction to the Limited Editions Club, he says of 'Aeolus' that 'the structure resembles that of the front page of a daily newspaper, and it is interesting to note how the style of the headlines employed gradually declines from mid-Victorian dignity to the vulgar slickness of the modern press.'[15] Here is Gilbert reading McGann's 'bibliographic code.' The differing terms – captions, headlines – and his comparison of the text with the front page of a newspaper in one piece but not in the other are based on the nonlinguistic features of the text: the sizes of the pages, their layouts, the fonts used for their texts. Either passage from Gilbert in isolation would give the impression that he is talking about *Ulysses* itself but, more precisely, in each case he describes the text as printed in specific ways in the pages of particular editions. *Ulysses* in print is very much a text of pages as well as words.

III

I want to spend a few pages considering the idea of a 'page' on a computer screen. I am writing these words on a Handspring Visor handheld computer, where the tiny display bears little resemblance to pages except that, unlike either a desktop or laptop computer screen, it is taller than it is wide. Eventually, I will upload the words to a laptop computer and copy them into a word-processing document, where they will join words I have already written. Once there, I will know how many pages these thoughts about pages will occupy when I print them out, and from that number I can estimate how many pages they will occupy in the published book.

I like to think that I am using cutting-edge technology, of course, but working this way is actually somewhat retrograde. You would think that the page would be one of the first concepts to disappear with computer text, and there have been many attempts to use terminology not associated with print for writing on the screen as a way of differentiating it from writing that will eventually appear in print. For example, in HyperCard, an early hypertext software writing and reading program for Macintosh computers, each unit was called a 'card,'[16] and Storyspace, a currently popular program, uses the term 'writing space.'[17] Hypertext theorists employ words like 'node,' 'screen,' or, in George Landow's term adapted from Roland Barthes, 'lexia,' meaning 'unit of reading' or 'a relatively self-contained and focused unit of text and images.'[18] But even though, as Jay David Bolter has argued in *Writing Space*, using computers for word processing employs only a small part of the machine's capabilities,[19] many of us work this way much of the time. Instead of embracing the new ways of writing that computers make possible (Bolter uses outline processors as his example), we have resorted to a half-way measure. The computer lets us easily perform such tasks as moving text around and italicizing words, and it allows us to display different fonts in a single document and to insert images and other graphics, but for the most part word-processing programs allow us to generate documents that could have been produced on a typewriter.

A similar half-way situation seems to have developed regarding pages. A definition of 'page' has crept into the fourth edition of the *American Heritage Dictionary* (2000) that was not there in the third (1992): 'A webpage.' The use of 'page' in such terms as web page or home page has become so ubiquitous in the last few years that 'page' now refers almost as easily to the Web as to print, but the use of 'page' for web units is actually quite odd. A web page consists of the text and graphics that load when you give your browser an 'http://' command along with a URL, but what your browser displays can turn out to be a single word or an entire novel. Thus, the visible boundaries of a written or printed page – boundaries implied in such definitions as 'a leaf or one side of a leaf, as of a book, letter, newspaper, or manuscript,' 'the writing or printing on one side of a leaf,' 'the type set for printing on one side of a leaf' (all from the *American Heritage Dictionary*) – are not part of the concept of a web page, since that kind of page can be much larger than any monitor can display at one time.

I am curious about how these units on the Web came to be called pages. No one seems to know.[20] Unlike other aspects of the Internet, the World Wide Web's inventors, Tim Berners-Lee and Robert Cailliau, conceived of the Web from the start as a hypertext-based system. Hypertext, which George Landow defines as 'text composed of blocks of words (or images) linked electronically by multiple paths, chains, or trails,' (3) had already acquired various terms for its units: 'nodes,' 'screens,' 'spaces,' 'cards' for the individual screens, 'links' for the connections between them. In some systems, such as Ted Nelson's Project Xanadu, the units linked together were thought of as documents[21] – that is, broadly conceived units that, more than nodes or screens, can be imagined in terms of print and books. Mark Bernstein, Christopher Keep, and Mark Feltham have each speculated that early developers of the Web first thought of sites as documents, this emphasis leading to the designation of the smaller units as 'pages.'[22] However it happened, the adoption of the term seems to have been rather casual: Tim Berners-Lee writes in *Weaving the Web* that, as he planned the World Wide Web, 'every node, document – whatever it was called – would be fundamentally equivalent in some way.'[23] The choice of terminology was part of the process by which, as John Seely Brown and Paul Duguid have argued,

> the Web made the informationally dense and inscrutable Internet intelligible ... by relinquishing the mystique of information for the language of the document. Pages structure the Web. Bookmarks help us find our way back to where we have been. Indexes and tables of contents organize it.[24]

As Jay David Bolter puts it, though, this development is hardly surprising or unique: 'We always understand a particular medium in relation to other past and present media forms.'[25] Calling these web units 'pages' gives them a kind of familiarity, especially since the term for the larger unit, 'site,' lacks any analogy to print. Web pages might look and act very different from printed ones, and they constantly remind us in both positive and negative ways that they are not print, but the term 'page' puts a limit on the disorientation. If the Web can (or once could) make us feel lost in a strange new world, the presence of 'pages' could make us feel a little bit at home.

Possibly, maybe even probably, 'page' became part of web terminology at the same time as 'home' did. Mark Bernstein from Eastgate Systems speculates that 'home page' came into use as an analogy to HyperCard's 'home card': an option in HyperCard was always to 'go Home.'[26] Home pages can be analysed in fascinatingly varied ways. For Wade Rowland, in *Spirit of the Web*, 'the "personal home page" developed early and spontaneously ... These personal pages are a unique feature of the Web that is endlessly moving as an expression of human diversity and the universal desire to share information.'[27] Welcome to my (virtual) home, the door is always open. For Bolter, in an essay on identity in a collection of essays on concepts relating to the Web, the purpose of a home page is 'nothing other than identity construction' (20). For Jonathan Rosen, in *The Talmud and the Internet*, the stakes are even higher. A web home page for Rosen is an assertion of rootedness that we make in a state of metaphysical and spiritual homelessness:

> When the Jewish people lost their home (the land of Israel) and God lost His (the Temple), then a new way of being was devised and Jews became the people of the book and not the people of the Temple or the land. They became the people of the book because they had no place else to live. That bodily loss is frequently overlooked, but for me it lies at the heart of the Talmud, for all its plenitude. The Internet, which we are continually told binds us all together, nevertheless engenders in me a similar sense of Diaspora, a feeling of being everywhere and nowhere. Where else but in the middle of Diaspora do you *need* a home page? [28]

We go home to our home pages to connect with others, to define ourselves, to root ourselves. On the printed pages of *Ulysses*, though, Leopold Bloom – typed page from Martha Clifford hidden safely in his pocket, newspaper page with its potted meat ad reminding him of his incomplete home long since discarded – just wants to go home.[29]

IV

You might want to 'go home' on a web site, but with books the important thing is not to 'lose your place.' A book's title page – or its companion, the spine – identifies the book among the confusion of all the others that surround it. A web home page serves that function, too, but it also provides a secure place of rest and stability within a site. (With books, you would probably use a bookmark to create your own secure place.) A sure sign of a badly designed web site or hypermedia CD-ROM or DVD-ROM is that you cannot get back to where you came from or get home easily. Even worse is when you cannot get anywhere in the site at all, when you are, as the now-clichéd expression goes, 'lost in cyberspace.' In that case, you probably invoke a hierarchy of home pages, leaving the site's lost page behind as you eagerly click the button that will take you to the home page you have designated for your browser.

A project of the magnitude of Digital *Ulysses* has to be well designed, and have easy navigability. If you want beginning-level definitions and identifications, you need to be able to find them without being encumbered by unwanted scholarly treatises, but if you want more advanced information you need to be able to get it without being burdened by simple identifications of names and details you already know. What would it mean to go home? What page would that be? I suspect that 'home page,' as a digital page of identification or return, applies mostly to the kinds of personal or informational or commercial sites that now dominate the Web. But hypertext author Michael Joyce has discussed other structures in his distinction between 'exploratory' and 'constructive' hypertexts. A constructive hypertext is one in which the author builds a new structure; the reader makes choices among links provided by the author.[30] This is the principle of most electronic hypertext fiction, including Joyce's own *Afternoon: A Story* and Shelley Jackson's *Patchwork Girl*. Readers of these fictions and others like them, I would guess, rarely return 'home.' Rather, they wander around – maybe interested, maybe frustrated, probably both; they go back to where they were; they consult the map view if one is available. But going 'home' in these hypertext fictions doesn't mean returning to a place of security; it is more like closing a book.

A hypertext centred on a text like *Ulysses* is what Michael Joyce calls an exploratory hypertext (41). In this kind of hypertext there is, in a sense, a centre: a preexisting work, now put into the hypertext network. Reading this kind of hypertext, you move out from and back to the central text. You might stay away from that text for quite a while: you might even read all of *The Odyssey*, or follow several newspapers for 16 June 1904, or watch a slide show of photographs from the Dublin of that day. But going back to *Ulysses*, to wherever you were in it and not to the front page, to wherever Leopold Bloom is in his wanderings, would be going home.

Ulysses on the screen, and *Ulysses* as part of an electronic hypertext network, can never be the same as *Ulysses* in the pages of a book. It is 732 pages long in the first Shakespeare and Company edition, 783 in the 1961 Modern Library edition, 644 in the 1986 paperback Gabler edition. Digitally, on the Finnegans Web site it comprises eighteen (very long) pages and 6,842 (very short) screens on a handheld computer. The digital text loses all sense of the bulk that makes the printed versions so distinctive and also imposing but, more important, it cannot exist in isolation, separated by its covers from other books on the shelf. If it is part of a hypertext system, its words will be linked to all kinds of other material, including to other parts of itself. As George Landow has stated, 'If one put a work conventionally considered complete, such as *Ulysses*, into a hypertext format, it would immediately become "incomplete"'[31] – a hypertext *Ulysses* is like a home without Plumtree's Potted Meat.

On a textual level, however, *Ulysses* has always been both complete and incomplete. It is complete within the pages of a printed edition. But Jerome McGann once took a sentence from episode 8, 'Lestrygonians' – 'A man spitting back on his plate: halfmasticated gristle: gums: no teeth to chewchewchew it' (8:659–60) – and demonstrated that, depending on your interpretation of the relationship between the manuscripts and the printed text, *Ulysses* is complete without the word 'gums' (which was not present in the book from 1922 until 1984) or with the word, which Gabler included in his edition.[32] You can eat just as well or as badly whether or not the text spells out 'gums.' (Maybe the home that is *Ulysses* is complete, or incomplete, in print or on a screen, with or without Plumtree's Potted Meat ...)

For Landow, questions about a work's completeness or incompleteness relate not to what words might or might not be in it but to its place in an intertextual network. On one level, of course, *Ulysses* is as complete as any literary work; it is what Richard Ellmann calls 'one of the most concluded books ever written.'[33] But it is problematical whether a book called *Ulysses*, which uses Homer's *Odyssey* as a structural grid, can ever be considered 'complete' in itself. Readers hardly ever approach it that way – they almost always accompany their reading with secondary books such as Gifford's *'Ulysses' Annotated* or any of the hundreds of books of criticism and analysis. They bring their previous reading and cultural experiences with them; they store information about *Ulysses* in their heads or in notes; they annotate the page margins of their copies of *Ulysses*. If *Ulysses* can be called 'complete' in print form, that largely means that its pages can exist without any other markings within covers that contain no other works. A digital hypermedia *Ulysses* has to dispense with the covers and the boundaries they provide – 'home' shifts from the house of print to an apartment in a massive, crowded urban building – and with the physicality of the pages. What can it provide as compensation?

I think that we can return to the concept of the page to see what a hypermedia presentation of *Ulysses* can contribute. The digital presentation retains what McGann calls the 'linguistic code' and some features of the 'bibliographic code': fonts, paragraph layouts, line units, even page divisions. But it can also give readers options regarding whether or not to retain these – one reader might want to work with the pages of a particular print edition, another might find it more important to get all of Martha Clifford's letter on the

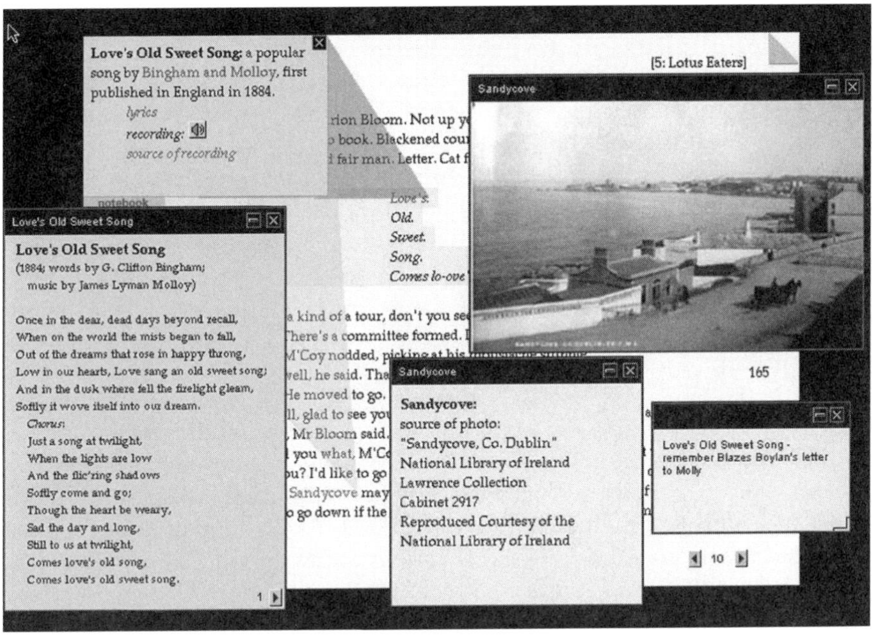
Love's Old Sweet Song: a popular song by Bingham and Molloy, first published in England in 1884.
lyrics
recording:
source of recording
[5: Lotus Eaters]
Sandycove
Love's Old Sweet Song
Love's Old Sweet Song
(1884; words by G. Clifton Bingham; music by James Lyman Molloy)
Once in the dear, dead days beyond recall,
When on the world the mists began to fall,
Out of the dreams that rose in happy throng,
Low in our hearts, Love sang an old sweet song;
And in the dusk where fell the firelight gleam,
Softly it wove itself into our dream.
Chorus:
Just a song at twilight,
When the lights are low
And the flic'ring shadows
Softly come and go;
Though the heart be weary,
Sad the day and long,
Still to us at twilight,
Comes love's old song,
Comes love's old sweet song.
1
Love's.
Old.
Sweet.
Song.
Sandycove
Sandycove:
source of photo:
"Sandycove, Co. Dublin"
National Library of Ireland
Lawrence Collection
Cabinet 2917
Reproduced Courtesy of the National Library of Ireland
165
Love's Old Sweet Song - remember Blazes Boylan's letter to Molly
10

Figure 8.2. Annotated text screen from *Digital Ulysses* 'Lotus Eaters.'

screen at one time. It can allow readers to create much of the bibliographic code in ways that are not possible in books by making the fonts larger or smaller or by changing the font entirely. By presenting more than one version of *Ulysses*, it can let readers alter the page to whichever form of the text they prefer.

Earlier I referred to fig. 8.1, a screen from 'Lotus Eaters,' as an illustration of a digital page. But that was just one version of the page; another is in fig. 8.2. Here the page is a clutter of information, mostly about a location in Dublin and a song. The reader has followed some of the links that were supplied – by no means all of them – and has also added three new marks and annotations: a highlighted bit of text, a stickie note, and a dog-eared page corner. Unlike equivalent marks in a book, these digital highlights, notes, and dog-ears cannot easily be distinguished visually from the notes that were supplied as part of the presentation. Even with just two links followed and three reader-supplied marks, *Ulysses* has practically disappeared from the page. It can always be restored: the reader can undo all the links and marks or, from a menu on a toolbar, simply turn off all the annotations to restore the screen to its state in fig. 8.1 (doing that makes even the colour-coded words turn black). From that toolbar the reader can toggle between the text of

Ulysses alone and the text with the annotations. Neither one of these states alone is 'the page': it is always both at once.

It is more, of course. The page includes links, the potential connections between this digital unit and another one. Links are often considered to be neutral connectives, but, as Nicholas Burbules argues, they are far more dynamic, provisional, and even rhetorical: they open up the page to some external screens but not to others; they are 'rhetorical moves that can be evaluated and questioned for their relevance.'[34] The page is framed by a window, which, as Bolter says in *Writing Space*, 'marks out a space for a particular unit of verbal text, graphics, or both.'[35] The page also includes sound, in this case both the recording of 'Love's Old Sweet Song' and an audio version of the entire page. (The symbol to turn it on is hidden by an annotation in fig. 8.2 but is visible at the left of line 154 in fig. 8.1.) The digital page is complete in itself and links outwards; it is silent, and it speaks. In each case, it is both at once. In Bolter's words in *Writing Space*, it oscillates between its two states or sets its two states in dialogue with each other (63, 117). It is consistent with Jonathan Rosen's sense of both the Talmud and the Internet as places where conflicting realities can 'live side by side' in an 'ambidextrous' culture (85). And it reflects the dominant pattern in *Ulysses*, in which oppositions that are set up always remain present, neither side cancelling out the other.

Rosen suggests in *The Talmud and the Internet* that 'we are passing, books and people both, through the doors of the computer age and entering a new sort of global Diaspora in which we are everywhere – except home' (15–16). The fictional Leopold Bloom knows how problematic 'home' is: even when you are there, you are not home. But he also knows how to resist simple solutions: while he was out wandering, placing and reading ads, on 16 June 1904, his home acquired two kinds of potted meat – Plumtree's and Blazes Boylan's – and it did become an abode of bliss. Yet, as Molly Bloom affirms in her monologue at the end of the book, it still remained incomplete without Bloom. Removing the pages of *Ulysses* from their print materiality and putting them into a new, uncertain digital one will change *Ulysses*, along with our sense of the page. Surrounded by and linked into a vast network of other verbal, visual, and aural texts, the pages of *Ulysses* will experience a new kind of fulness and an equally new, and fuller, incompleteness – home is incomplete and an abode of bliss at the same time.[36]

NOTES

1 Quotations are from James Joyce, *Ulysses*, ed. Hans Walter Gabler with Wolfhard Steppe and Claus Melchior (New York: Garland, 1984; rpt. New York: Vintage, 1986, 1993). Passages are cited by episode and line number.

2 The web version of *Ulysses* available from the 'Finnegans Web' site at Trent University in Peterborough, Ontario – www.trentu.ca/jjoyce/ – presents each episode of the book as a single scrolling page with lines indicating the page divisions in the paperback Gabler editions. The Peanut Press digital version of *Ulysses* for Palm and Handspring handheld computers (www.peanutpress.com) lets readers choose between a small or a large typeface. Neither size will let Martha's letter fit on one screen: it appears on four in the small face and on five in the large. *Ulysses* itself occupies 4,225 screens in the small face and 6,842 in the large one.

3 This sample from Lotus Eaters was prepared in the multimedia electronic-document authoring software called TK3 Author (www.nightkitchen.com).

4 Jerome J. McGann, *The Textual Condition* (Princeton: Princeton University Press, 1991).

5 Buffalo, MS V.A.3, p. 15. The draft is photographically reprinted in James Joyce, *The James Joyce Archive* (New York: Garland, 1977–9), 12:253. The manuscript is in the Poetry/Rare Books Collection at the University at Buffalo, State University of New York. See Daniel Ferrer and Jean-Michel Rabaté's discussion of this insertion in 'Paragraphes en Expansion,' in *De la Lettre au Livre: Sémiotique des Manuscrits Littéraire,* ed. Louis Hay (Paris: Édition du Centre National de la Recherche Scientifique, 1989), 104–5. This chapter has been translated by Jed Deppman as 'Paragraphs in Expansion (James Joyce),' in *Genetic Criticism: Texts and Avant-textes*, ed. Jed Deppman, Daniel Ferrer, and Michael Groden (Philadelphia: University of Pennsylvania Press, 2004), esp. 144–5.

6 Don Gifford with Robert J. Seidman, *'Ulysses' Annotated: Notes for James Joyce's 'Ulysses,'* rev. ed. (Berkeley and Los Angeles: University of California Press, 1988), 62.

7 Patrick A. McCarthy, '*Ulysses* and the Printed Page,' in *Joyce's 'Ulysses': The Larger Perspective*, ed. Robert D. Newman and Weldon Thornton (Newark: University of Delaware Press, 1987), 62.

8 McGann, *Textual Condition,* 13–14.

9 Gifford, *'Ulysses' Annotated,* 131.

10 The estate of James Joyce refused to grant me permission to reproduce this and the other three proof pages I describe in this and the next paragraph. Three of the four pages are reproduced in James Joyce, *The James Joyce Archive*, 18: 3, 12, and 13.

11 Stuart Gilbert, *James Joyce's 'Ulysses': A Study* (1930; New York: Vintage, 1952), 179 n. 1.

12 Michael Groden, *'Ulysses' in Progress* (Princeton: Princeton University Press, 1977), 105–10.

13 Audio versions of the complete *Ulysses* have been released by Radio Telefís Éireann in Dublin, by Recorded Books in Prince Frederick, Maryland, and by Naxos Audiobooks.

14 Gilbert, *Ulysses: A Study,* 179.

15 I thank Paul Meahan for calling Gilbert's introduction to my attention: Stuart

Gilbert, 'Introduction to James Joyce,' in *Ulysses* (New York: Limited Editions Club, 1935), xii.

16 James Gillies and Robert Cailliau, *How the Web was Born: The Story of the World Wide Web* (Oxford: Oxford University Press, 2000), 128.

17 E.A. Cohen, *Storyspace for Windows, Version 1.75: User's Manual* (Watertown, MA: Eastgate, 1999), 10, 182.

18 George P. Landow, *Hypertext 2.0*, rev. ed. of *Hypertext: The Convergence of Contemporary Critical Theory and Technology* (Baltimore: Johns Hopkins University Press, 1997), 64; Cohen, *Storyspace*, 179–80.

19 Jay David Bolter, *Writing Space: Computers, Hypertext, and the Remediation of Print*, 2nd ed. (Mahwah, NJ: Lawrence Erlbaum, 2001), 29–32.

20 Robert Cailliau, in response to my question about when and how the word 'page' became the main term used for the part of a web site that is on the screen, answered simply, 'No idea' (email to author, 16 March 2001).

21 Theodor Holm Nelson, 'Opening Hypertext: A Memoir,' in *Literacy Online: The Promise (and Peril) of Reading and Writing with Computers*, ed. Myron C. Tuman (Pittsburgh: University of Pittsburgh Press, 1992), 53.

22 Mark Feltham (email to author, 11 March 2001), Christopher Keep (email to author, 12 March 2001), and Mark Bernstein (email to author, 16 March 2001) in different ways each speculate about an initial connection of web 'pages' to a concept of documents.

23 Tim Berners-Lee, with Mark Fischetti, *Weaving the Web: The Original Design and Ultimate Destiny of the World Wide Web by Its Inventor* (San Francisco: HarperSanFrancisco, 1999), 16.

24 John Seely Brown and Paul Duguid, *The Social Life of Information* (Boston: Harvard Business School Press, 2000), 182.

25 Jay David Bolter, 'Identity,' in *Unspun: Key Concepts for Understanding the World Wide Web*, ed. Thomas Swiss (New York: New York University Press, 2000), 18.

26 Mark Bernstein, email to author, 16 March 2001.

27 Wade Rowland, *Spirit of the Web: The Age of Information from Telegraph to Internet* (Toronto: Patrick Crean/Key Porter, 1999), 309.

28 Jonathan Rosen, *The Talmud and the Internet: A Journey between Worlds* (New York: Farrar, Straus and Giroux, 2000), 14. Rosen's italics.

29 Late in his work on *Ulysses* Joyce prepared a schema of the book, listing the eighteen episodes and including eight categories of information for each one. This chart from the author has proved to be a mixed blessing; many of its entries have baffled critics who have tried to connect them with the text itself. One of these problematic entries is for episode 4, 'Calypso,' and it inspired Stuart Gilbert's comment in *James Joyce's 'Ulysses,'* the book in which the schema was first published, that 'darkness is of the prison-house, the shackles of the flesh, all that withholds Mr. Bloom from Zion, Odysseus from Ithaca' (144–5). The equation of Zion and Ithaca, which comes from Joyce's schema, might seem excessive in relation to Bloom's respectful but dismissive reaction to a newspaper notice

he reads inviting people to purchase tracts of land in Palestine and plant trees on them (4:191–200), but this correspondence is provocative in relation to the triangulation of *Ulysses*, home, and Talmud/Diaspora/home page.

30 Michael Joyce, 'Siren Shapes: Exploratory and Constructive Hypertexts,' in *Of Two Minds: Hypertext Pedagogy and Poetics* (Ann Arbor: University of Michigan Press, 1995), 42.

31 Landow, *Hypertext*, 79.

32 Jerome J. McGann, '*Ulysses* as a Postmodern Work,' in *Social Values and Poetic Acts: The Historical Judgment of Literary Work* (Cambridge, MA: Harvard University Press, 1988), 191.

33 Richard Ellmann, preface to James Joyce, *Ulysses*, ed. Hans Walter Gabler with Wolfhard Steppe and Claus Melchior (New York: Vintage, 1986, 1993), xiv.

34 Nicholas C. Burbules, 'Rhetorics of the Web: Hyperreading and Critical Literacy,' in *Page to Screen: Taking Literacy into the Electronic Era*, ed. Ilana Snyder (London and New York: Routledge, 1998), 117.

35 Bolter, *Writing Space*, 67.

36 For answering email questions, for sending photocopies of hard-to-find materials, and for reading early drafts I want to thank Mark Bernstein, Jay David Bolter, Robert Cailliau, Luca Crispi, Mark Feltham, Michael Joyce, Christopher Keep, John Lavagnino, Paul Meahan, Molly Peacock, and Sam Slote.

IX

OUR BODIES ARE NOT FINAL

```
ads[ n=(ct+1)%src.length] = new Image;
ads[ n] .src = src[ n] ;
setTimeout("switchAd()",duration*1000);
ads[ n=(ct+1)%src.length] = new Image;
ads[ n] .src = src[ n] ;
setTimeout("switchAd()",duration*1000);
ads[ n=(ct+1)%src.length] = new Image;
ads[ n] .src = src[ n] ;
setTimeout("switchAd()",duration*1000);
ads[ n=(ct+1)%src.length] = new Image;
ads[ n] .src = src[ n] ;
setTimeout("switchAd()",duration*1000);
ads[ n=(ct+1)%src.length] = new Image;
ads[ n] .src = src[ n] ;
setTimeout("switchAd()",duration*1000);
ads[ n=(ct+1)%src.length] = new Image;
ads[ n] .src = src[ n] ;
```

The Future Of the Page by Edison del Canto - Netscape
Language is a virus
Artificial Intelligence
From electronic to photonic
The end of academy
The page is a surface
Textual topology
Envisioning the page

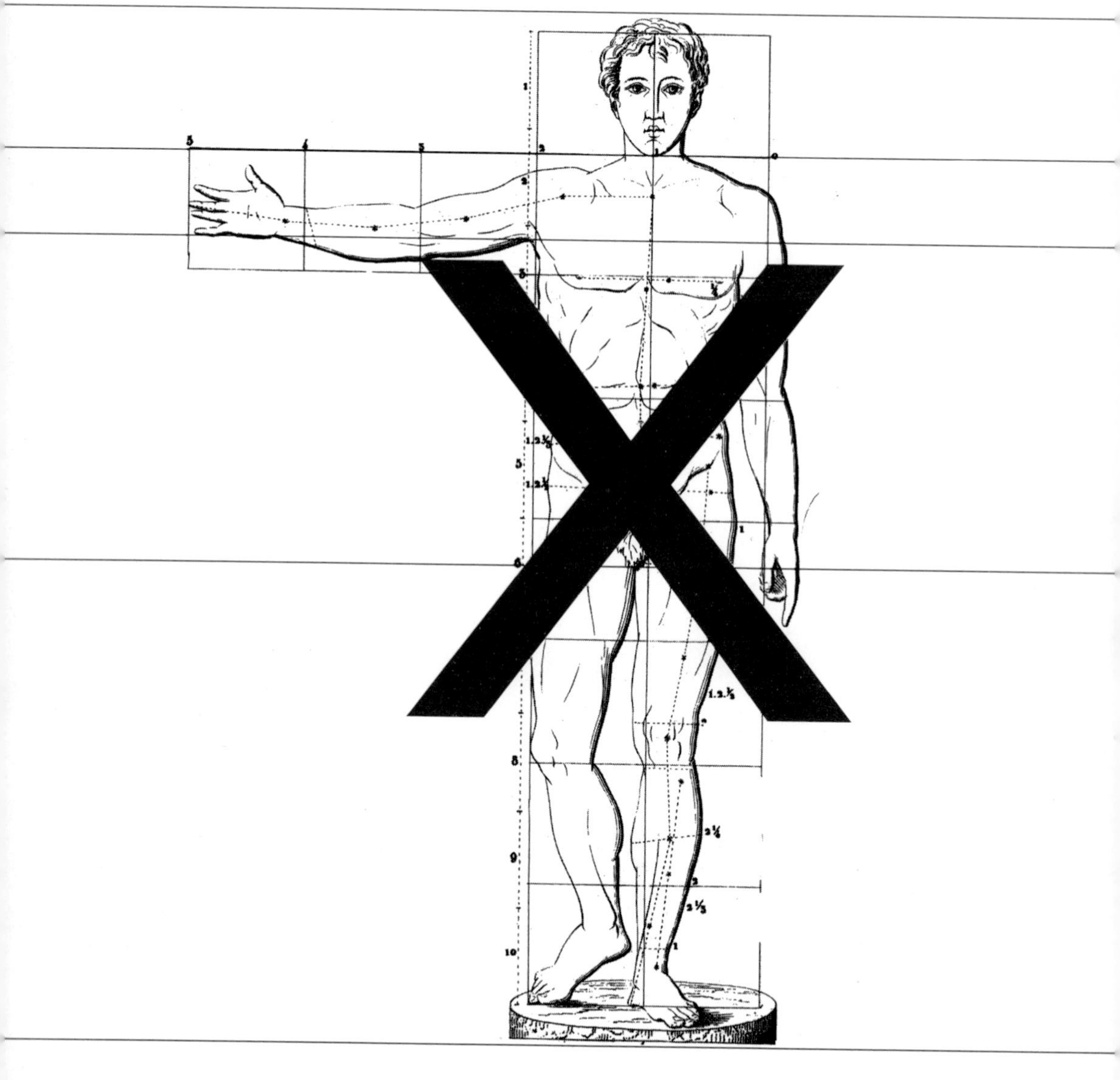

I36122
I65454
I66657
I58323
I2288
I83762
aab43292
I37737
I37736
I28787
gpigkx
paleenac
aab65252
aab15507
cabit0ae
IZ7728
aacfl3627
abe37315
aac92125
I01850
Humapa
aab23100
Io2766
aaa54600
aai
3318875
1310912
Humabp
861320
561383
560721
aab23566
A47565
225524
bbc11374
aac71375
gpigCaap
dog
boviag
bbc33861
aac27357
3318376
aab75301
87392
abe37480
aac37299
pig
127740
chicken
sheep
cabitoca
Hame07fl
aac60691
560317
humpu461
Humamy12
987675
cabiteab
cabitacc
I02764
I06128
aaa56025
Humamy17
mouse124
Humpe4a2
I36160
Humamyh2
257665
nomatode
I57308
545136
frog
s45135
pfishAfD
pfiabaac
monkey01
monkey02
gpigCaam
Humamy4a
Humamlfb
EU2480
caa31830
caa10050
baa22264
aab58502
a4 human
A33293
A31524
226344
226242
226342
225936
cat
I36121
rabbitPQ
I35453
AU2758
aab75278

A	B	F
0	0	0
1	0	0
0	1	0
1	1	1

A	B	F
0	0	0
1	0	1
0	1	1
1	1	1

A	F
0	1
1	0

A	B	C	F
0	0	0	1
1	0	0	1
0	1	0	1
1	1	0	1
0	0	1	1
1	0	1	1
0	1	1	1
1	1	1	0

A	B	C	F
0	0	0	1
1	0	0	0
0	1	0	0
1	1	0	0
0	0	1	0
1	0	1	0
0	1	1	0
1	1	1	0

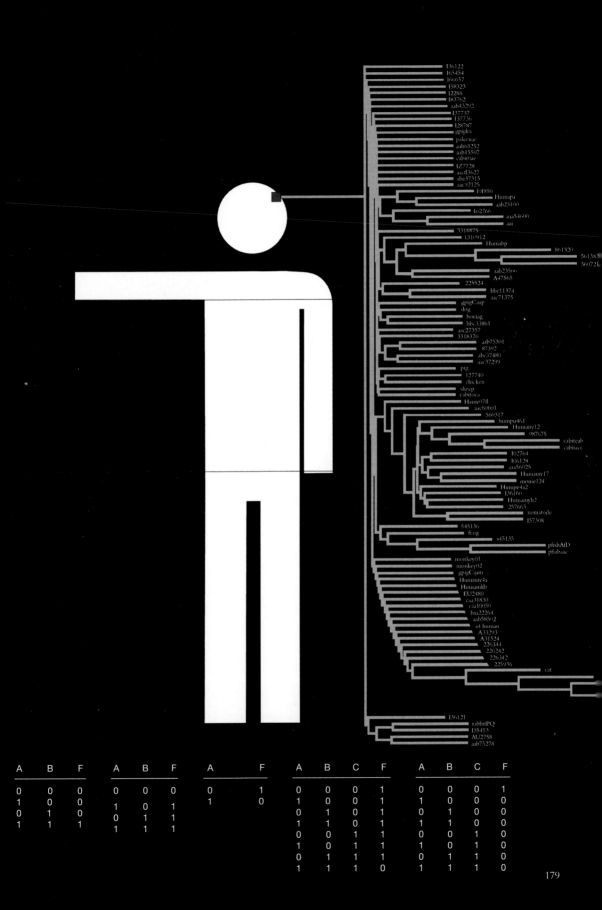

Language is text, an infinite string of information, written in linear,

transliterates a small alphabet of signs into a large lexicon of mear

limited to the space of the body: we speak, we listen. We create sy

words, words translate into sentences, sen

replicatereplicatereplicatereplicatereplicater

plicatereplicatereplicatereplicater

survive. The page is the agent that carries the virus.

```
//set duration for each image
duration = 4;

//Please do not edit below
ads=[ ]; ct=0;
function switchAd() {
var n=(ct+1)%src.length;
if (ads[ n] && (ads[ n].complete || ads[ n].complete==null)) {
document[ "Ad_Image"].src = ads[ ct=n].src;
}
ads[ n=(ct+1)%src.length]
ads[ n].src = src[ n];
setTimeout("switchAd()",duration*1000);
}
function doLink(){
location.href = url[ ct];
} onload = function(){
if (document.images)
switchAd();
</script>
<a href="javascript:doLink();" onMouseOver="status=url[ ct]

<td VALIGN=BOTTOM><embed SRC="LanguageIsAVirus.rpm" type=

HEIGHT=120 WIDTH=160 AUTOSTART=true></object></td>

<td ALIGN=LEFT VALIGN=BOTTOM>
<center><table BORDER=0 CELLSPACING=0 CELLPADDING=0 COLS=1 WIDTH="198" >
<tr>
```

mensional, one-directional form.Language is defined by a code that

uses the linear, abstract, left side of the brain.Language as sound is

J=ÆµÛπ˜‰'èiN5˘˝"[è¸¢ÁàJ

\ÎÊe2å_eœ[g©Ù :Œ'÷

oÆØFü—~õ#"Mo◊ʃüquW:%tó ∆;

to extend our bodies. Symbols become characters, characters form

ÙU6zfiøÛi≥+'°G⁄~ ˙ÔØ˘§iin◊ P˙∞n°ÃÈ˝S

S≥˙ ¿Íxy£™◊éÚ

es p a r a g r a p h s , p a g e s , b o o k s … T h e y r e p l i c a t e

e r e p l i c a t e r e p l i c a t e r e p l i c a t e r e p l i c a t e r e p l i c a t e r e

a t e r e p l i c a t e r e p l i c a t e r e p l i c a t e . T h e y

rRGB XYZ cprtP3descÑlwtpt bkpt rXYZ gXYZ, bXYZ@ dmndTpdmddƒàvuedLÜview'$lumi˜ meas

Like atomic fission, evolution is a powerful, primal force that until now has been in nature's hands.

All that is changing.

Not only are we taking over our genetic development, but we are also using computers to simulate the very fundamental mechanism of evolution.

Artificial intelligence systems are being used to create software modules.

DNA is like a book

A central spine of encoded information.

There is a gene that can alter one's susceptibility to Alzheimer's disease elevenfold, depending on whether the 334th letter is G or A.

The arrival of the cyborg is made possible by the gradual removal of the barrier separating exteriority from interiority, public from private.

The human body is progressively colonized by prosthetic devices. If every natural organ can be infinitely replaced by artificially intelligent devices, if the entire contents of the mind can be preserved by being downloaded into the matrix, then the dream of immortality would seem to be realizable.

When the number of linked computers reaches a critical mass, some networks gain the capacity for spontaneous generation.

Programs and computations unplanned by the designers suddenly begin to appear.

Computer viruses satisfy two of the criteria that define life forms: Replication and survival.

There are now several million computer viruses in existence, with a thousand new viruses being catalogued by computer-virus hunters every day. B the extraordinary fact is that many of these viruses evolved spontaneously, without human interventio

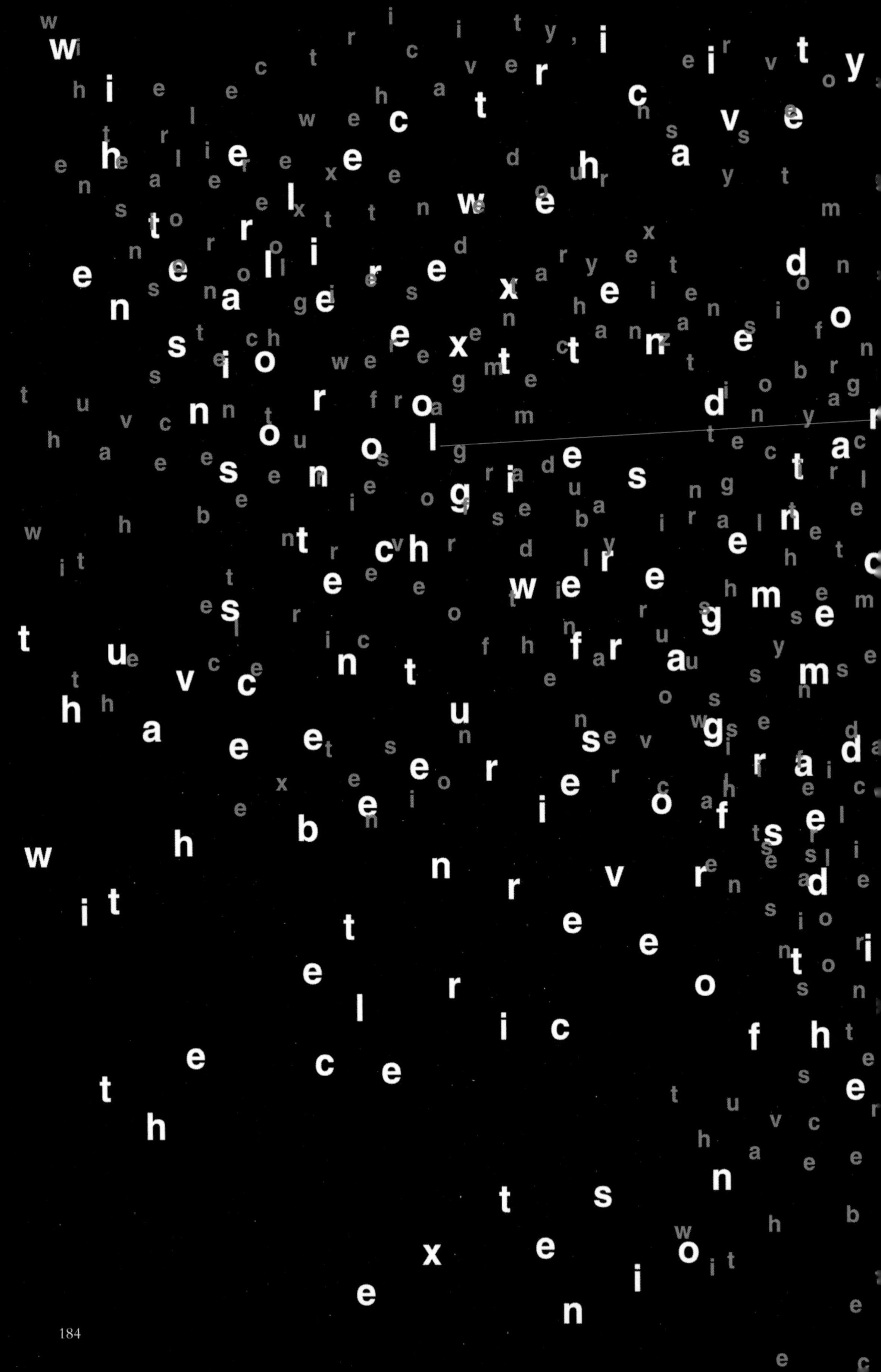

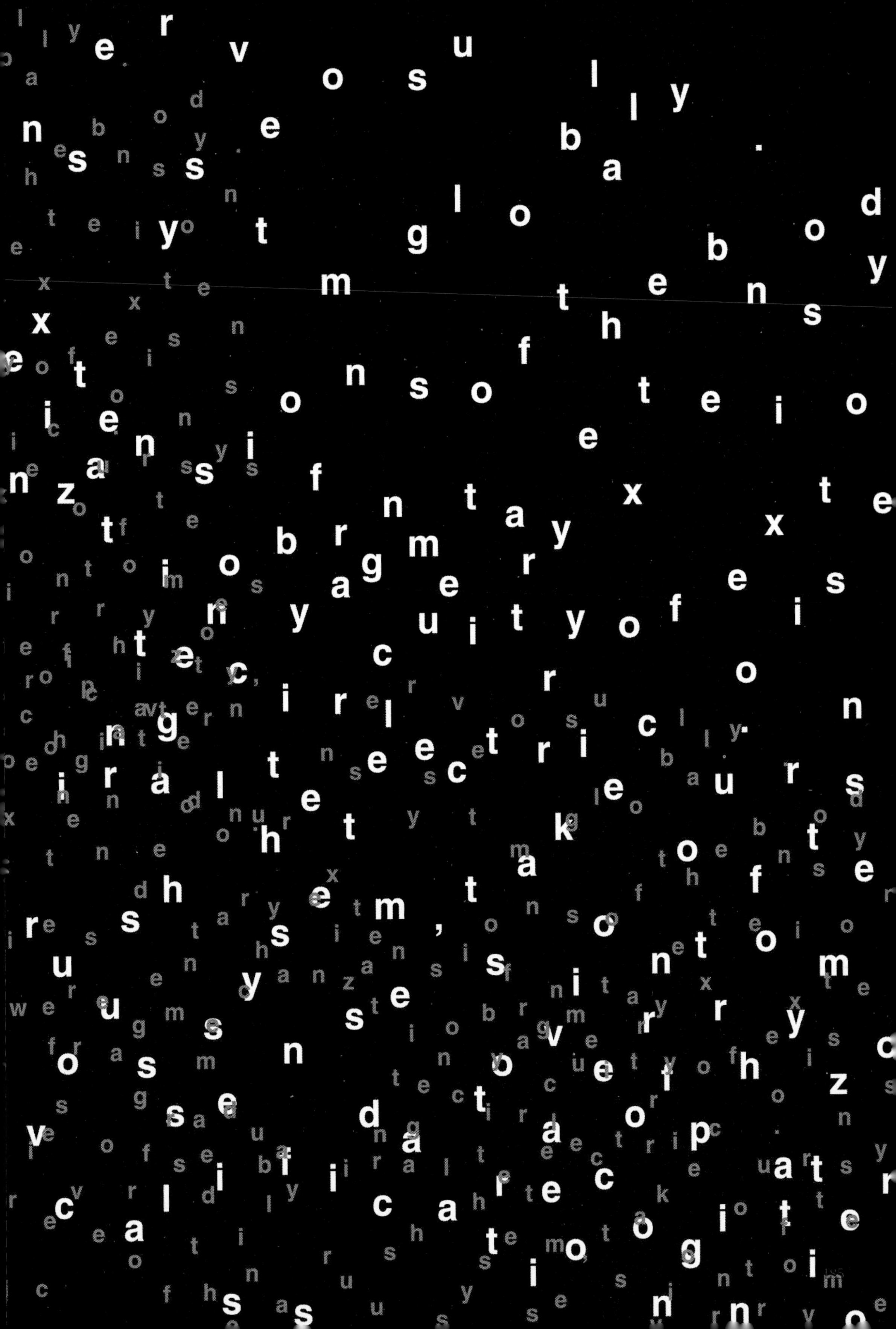

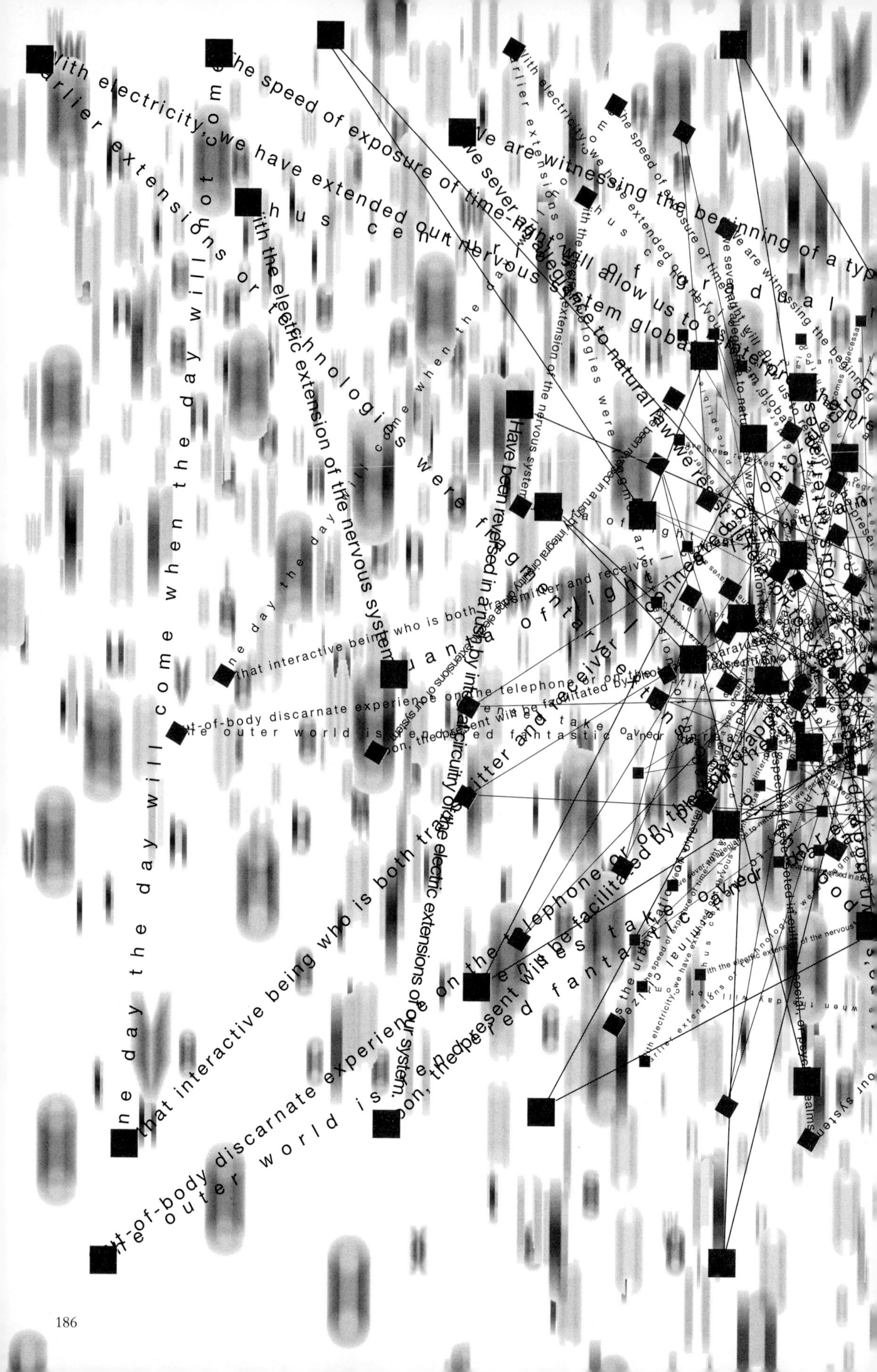

With electricity, we have extended our nervous system globa
the speed of exposure of time-light will allow us to
We are witnessing the beginning of a typ
we sever
earlier extensions or technologies were
with the electric extension of the nervous system
Have been reversed in a rush by integral circuitry of the electric extensions of our system.
that interactive being who is both transmitter and receiver
out-of-body discarnate experience on the telephone or on the
the outer world is rendered fantastic
the day will come when the day will not come
thus centri

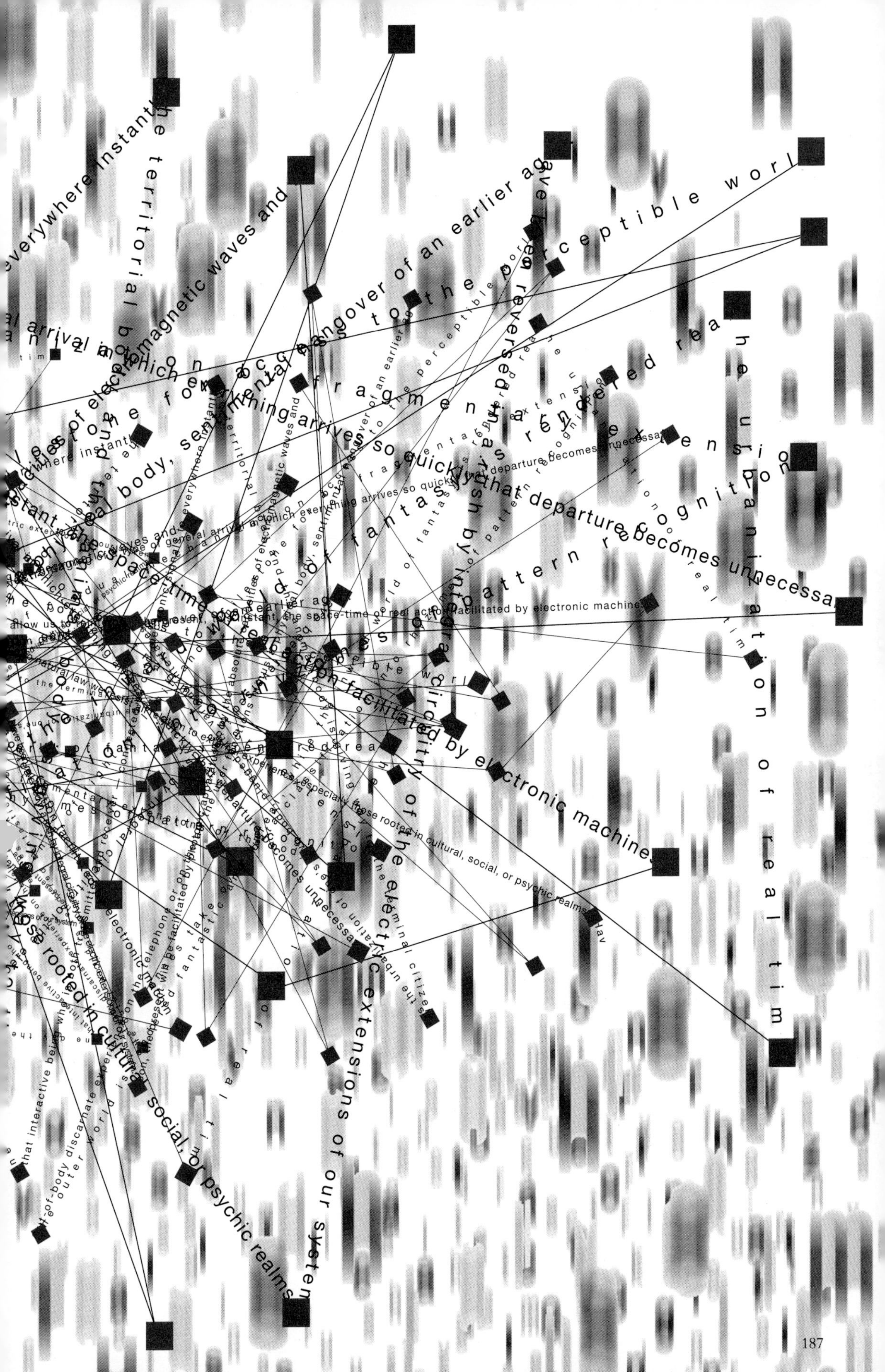
everywhere instantly
the territorial body
electromagnetic waves and
hangover of an earlier age
perceptible world
arrival in which
everything arrives so quickly that departure becomes unnecessary
pattern recognition
facilitated by electronic machines
the circuitry of the electric extensions of our system
those rooted in cultural, social, or psychic realms
the urbanization of real time
the space-time of real action facilitated by electronic machines

Academic expert culture is a culture of command.

It secures authority.

It achieves command and authority by subjecting you to

institutionally legitimated intellectual and sociological power structures.

You achieve command by being yourself commanded, and

you secure authority by subjecting yourself to institutional authority.

In spite of enormous intellectual effort to gain insight into the use of language by some of the most brilliant thinkers of all time, in spite of an enormous literary effort to create new discourses by some of the most creative conceptual giants, philosophy remains strangely crippled and impotent. **F**ar from creating a single product that sells successfully in this era of global communication, trivileged philos[redacted] remains unmarketable. **I**nstitutions of higher education have not take[redacted]age of the resources and energies circulating beyond the walls [redacted]cademy. As a result, cultural analysis is separated from the very condition of its own possibility. To overcome the isolation of the intellectual critic, it is necessary to enter the mainstream of culture by leaving the confines of print. **E**nlightenment no lon[redacted]sells. **N**or does critical thoug[redacted]**T**o sell your product, you must get down to the business of taking advertising seriously. **T**he discourses of scholarly achievement not only define an obsolete agenda, they have no promotional strategy. **I**f reason is to be practical in simulation culture, it must be electrified. **T**herefore the need t[redacted]sign every feature of the campus and the curriculum looms larg[redacted]city no longer simply defines boundaries which house or cont[redacted]ulations of fragmented interests. The city has become an immediate means of enhancing perception and enriching association. **B**ut academic expert culture is a culture of command. **I**t secures authority. **I**t achieves command and authority by subjecting you to institutionally legitimated intellectual and sociological power structures. **Y**ou achieve command by being yourself commanded, and you secure authority by subjecting yourself to institutional authority.

ous intellectual effort to gain insight into the use of language by some of the most brilliant thinkers of
elf commanded, and you secure authority by subjecting yourself to institutional authority.In spite of
tionally legitimated intellectual and sociological power structures. You achieve command by being
e of command. It secures authority. It achieves command and authority by subjecting you to
diate means of enhancing perception and enriching association. But academic expert culture is a
s boundaries which house or contain populations of fragmented interests. The city has become an
to redesign every feature of the campus and the curriculum looms large. The city no longer simply
omotional strategy. If reason is to be practical in simulation culture, it must be electrified. Therefore the
tising seriously. The discourses of scholarly achievement not only define an obsolete agenda, they have
r sells. Nor does critic [redacted] ght. To sell your product, you must get down to the business of taking
it is necessary to ent [redacted] ainstream of culture by leaving the confines of print. Enlightenment no
sis is separated from the [redacted] condition of its own possibility. To overcome the isolation of the intellectual
tage of the resources and energies circulating beyond the walls of the academy. As a result, cultural

unication,	have not taken
gely crippl	his era of global
y effort to c	osophy remains
nsight into t	of an enormous
ecure autho	llectual effort to
ctual and s	ommanded, and
es authorit	ally legitimated
cing perce	of command. It
e or contai	diate means of
e of the ca	undaries which
son is to be	redesign every
urses of sc	otional strategy.
l thought.	g seriously. The
er the mair	sells. Nor does
he very cor	, it is necessary
rces and er	ysis is separated
ged philoso	dvantage of the
ent. Far fro	communication,
urses by s	ly crippled and
me of the	to create new
elf to institu	use of language
ures. You	y by subjecting
and and a	ciological power
ing associ	rity. It achieves

ations of fragmented interests. The city has become an immediate means of enhancing perception and
us and the curriculum looms large. The city no longer sim [redacted] ines boundaries which house or contain
cal in simulation culture, it must be electrified. There [redacted] need to redesign every feature of the
vement not only define an obsolete agenda, they have [redacted] romotional strategy. If reason is to be
product, you must get down to the business of taking advertising seriously. The discourses of scholarly
ture by leaving the confines of print. Enlightenment no longer sells. Nor does critical thought. To sell
own possibility. To overcome the isolation of the intellectual critic, it is necessary to enter the mainstream
ating beyond the walls of the academy. As a result, cultural analysis is separated from the very condition
rketable. Institutions of higher education have not taken advantage of the resources and energies
ct that sells successfully in this era of global communication, trivileged philosophy remains
ve conceptual giants, philosophy remains strangely crippled and impotent. Far from creating a single
ers of all time, in spite of an enormous literary effort to create new discourses by some of the most
te of enormous intellectual effort to gain insight into the use of language by some of the most brilliant

ncult, the very oppo
surface is no longer su
ce must be reconfigur
inverse, image of
surface must be reconfigu
transcendence. Superficia
of God. The death
the death of God conceived as
reality that is above
any real surfaces are
surface world. Surfaces are
structures. The book
soft structures
the surface of the writ
into an articulated
is transformed
images are classified
human scale
electronic text makes po
organizing and visualizing
by which we can
connections between any
whether numerical, verbal
allows us to build and
surfaces in a textualized
interfaces actualize
depth; rather windows ope

tion between depth a
rficial... is it profound
The erasure of depth
tion between depth and
the disappearance
The erasure of depth is
actually issues from
the disappearance of
God is not a literal ev
actually issues from the
God is not a literal even
the disappearance
depth: we observe
below, or beyond
transformed by hard
transformed by mars and
the age of print is a hard
drawn, painted or incised
tablet, transforming
writing space. The modern
in which text is stored
strings of bits. Bits of text
ephemeral character
sible new methods for
e text: it is the electronic
establish and maintain
two units of information
graphic. The electronic
explore networks of
hypertexts. The productivity
software technologies
to other windows whose

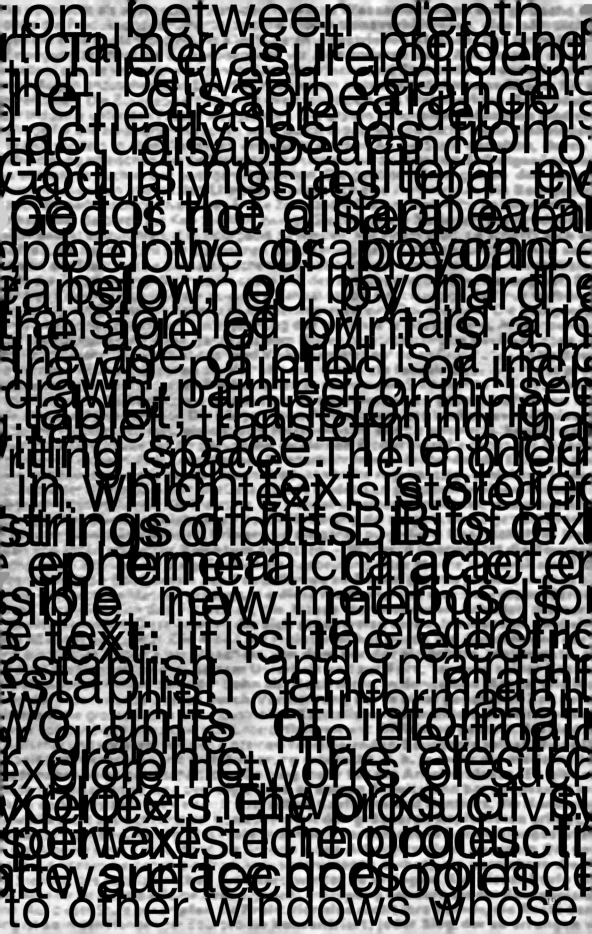

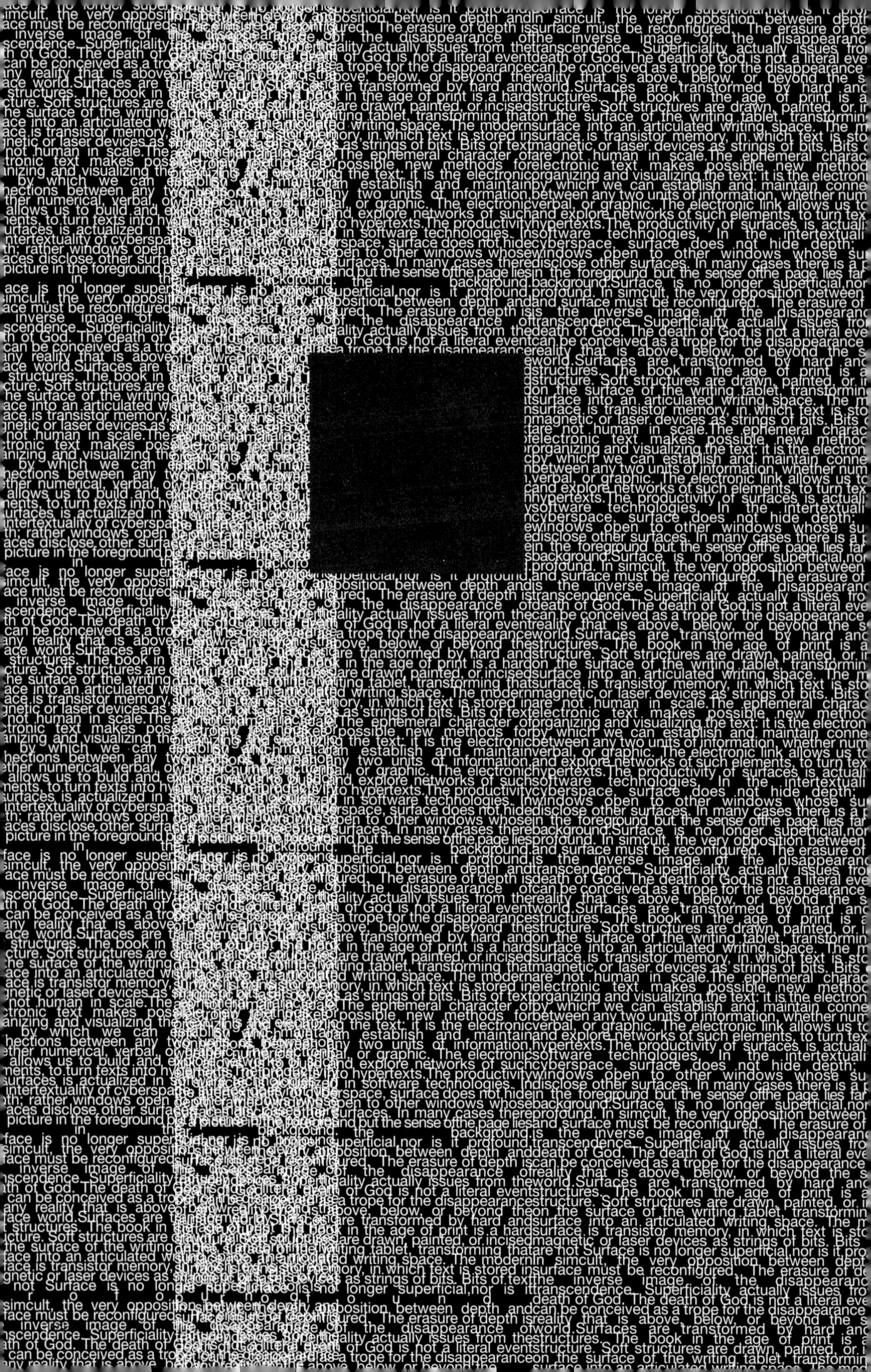

Surfaceisnolongersuperficialnorisitprofound.Insimcultheveryoppositionbetw
eendepthandsurfacemustbereconfigured.Theerasureofdepthistheinverseimage
ofthedisappearanceoftranscendence.Superficialityactuallyissuesfromthedeatho
ffGOD.ThedeathofGODisnotaliteraleventbutcanbeconceivedasatropeforthedi
sappearanceofanyrealitythatisabovebeloworbeyondthesurfaceworld.Surfacesar
etransformedbyhardandsoftstructures.Thebookintheageofprintisahardstructur
e.Softstructuresaredrawnpaintedorincisedonthesurfaceofthewritingtablettrans
formingthatsurfaceintoanarticulatedwritingspace.Themodernsurfaceistransist
ormemoryinwhichtextisstoredinmagneticorlaserdevicesasstringsofbits.Bitsofte
xtarenothumaninscale.Theephemeralcharacterofelectronictextmakespossiblen
ewmethodsfororganizingandvisualizingthetextitistheelectroniclinkbywhichwe
canestablishandmaintainconnectionsbetweenanytwounitsofinformationwheth
ernumericalverbalorgraphic.Theelectroniclinkallowsustobuildandexplorenet
worksofsuchelementstoturntextsintohypertexts.Theproductivityofsurfacesisac
tualizedinsoftwaretechnologiesintheintertextualityofcyberspacesurfacedoesno
thidedepthratherwindowsopentootherwindowswhosesurfacesdiscloseothersur
faces.Inmanycasesthereisapictureintheforegroundbutthesenseofthepageliesfari
nthebackground.

TE
XTUAL
TO
POLOGY

studiesthemetho
dsbywhichtheva
rioussectionsofate
xtareconnected,r
egardlessofthеph
ysicalpropertiesof
thetransmittingc
hannels.(paper,st
one,electromagn
etichighways...)

Typographic space is governed by a series of part-to-whole relationships. The single letter is a kernel, part of a word. Words together create a line: not just a line thought but a line on the page, a visual element that establishes itself in the spatial field of

typography is not a simple matter of aesthetics. this is not to say that typography is without an aesthetic and formal dimension. asymmetry in modern design is a principle of freedom associated with social, cultural and economic utopias of industrial capitalism, national liberation movements, revolutionary socialism and proletariat communism. the same alphabet and page design can be used for a biography of mohandas gandhi and for a manual on the use and deployment of biological weapons. the typographer's one essential task is to interpret and communicate the text. its tone, tempo, logical structure, its physical size, all determine the possibilities of its typographic form. typographic style does not mean any particular style, but the power to move freely through the whole domain of typography, and to function at every step in a way that is graceful* and vital instead of banal.

the format. Placing a line of type in the blank landscape of a page instantly creates a structure. It's a simple structure, but one with a direction, a movement and, now, two defined areas of space: one space above the line and one space below.

* i mean movement: ascender, descender, counter, kerning, leading, stroke, slant, stress, and loop.

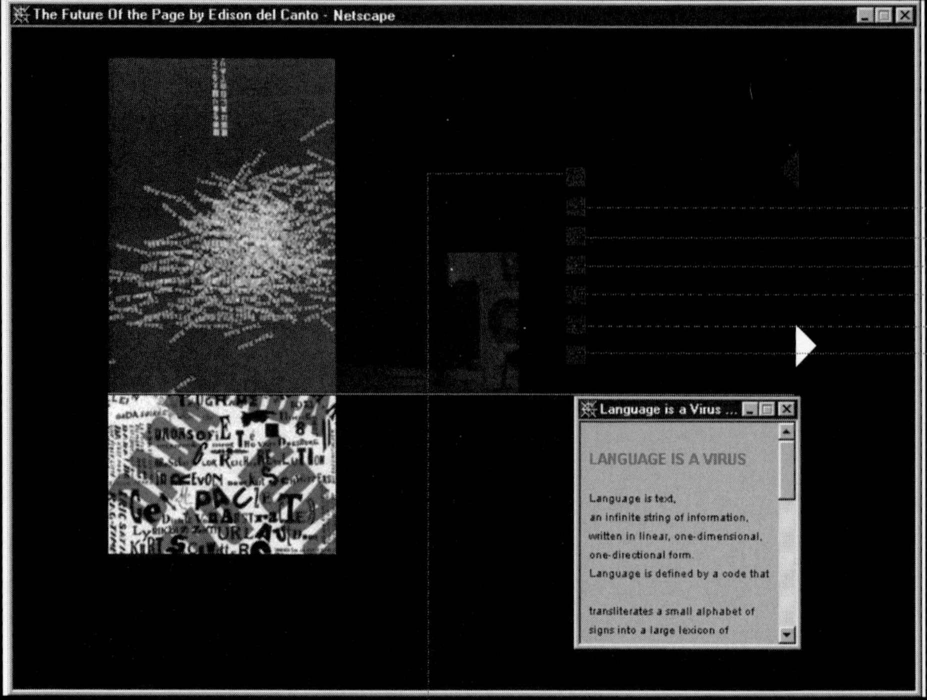
The Future Of the Page by Edison del Canto - Netscape
Language is a Virus ...
LANGUAGE IS A VIRUS
Language is text,
an infinite string of information,
written in linear, one-dimensional,
one-directional form.
Language is defined by a code that
transliterates a small alphabet of
signs into a large lexicon of

The page grid is the basic skeleton, from which symbols, images, ideas hang.
The grid is crucial for the successful reading of any page.
It must create enough space to curb the impression that the elements are being thrown out from the center.
It must also create enclosure without interrupting the flow from spread to spread.

Design must seduce, shape, and perhaps most importantly, design must evoke emotional response.

The important thing today is to mix
the messages,
to allow more than one way of
reading.
Information is extruded from a
generating idea,
tense with perspicuity, accuracy,
clarity,
it is the design which binds the
pages together,
a coherent signature, often multi-layered, often multi-authored.

The meaning of the word implode is to burst inward. This definition captures the spirit and dynamic of the digital revolution and its profound impact on existing disciplines, graphic design among them. The broad effect of this revolution is to bring many things far closer than they once were,
to make accessible what was once remote,
to collapse the distance
between idea and realization,
producer and client,
creation and revision,
word and image
sound and movement.

Video is merged with print graphics,
a conceptually layered suggestion of
space…
overlapping processes, hybridized imagery,
the integration of photography with
graphics
audio
media-based software

We have arrived at the end of print as we have known it.

Digital technology is no respecter of existing boundaries — whether spatial, temporal, conceptual.

Edison Who?

10 The Processual Page: Materiality and Consciousness in Print and Hypertext[1]

Joseph Tabbi

The Last Archive

In the summer of 2001 I spent several weeks at a Long Island City warehouse sorting through the William Gaddis archive before the papers were purchased, catalogued, and eventually housed with the American fiction collections at the Washington University in St Louis. What I found there was not too surprising – no substantial unpublished work apart from a packet of early attempts at fiction, satirical pieces for *The New Yorker* (indicating a literary career that was thankfully not to be). Mainly there were boxes of letters, typescripts, manuscripts, business and educational pamphlets written for money, bills, memorabilia, and clippings – thousands of them, hoarded over half a century: family photographs, paintings, innumerable books. Textual scholars and biographers will have plenty of material with which to date, contextualize, correlate, and otherwise situate the work in relation to the author's 'life' and 'times' – the *New York Times*, in particular, but also copies of *National Enquirer*, and pamphlets by Jimmy Swaggart, Billy Graham, and others, saved in their entirety. Still, I found almost no false starts, no abandoned manuscripts – nothing that did not find its way into the four novels Gaddis published in his lifetime or the posthumous fiction, a monologue of eighty-four manuscript pages called *Agapē Agape* that he entrusted to his family and literary agent. The author had largely fulfilled his 'ambition,' like Faulkner in a passage Gaddis admired, 'to be, as a private individual, abolished and voided from history, leaving it markless, no refuse save for the printed books.'

Arriving in Long Island City less than a year after the Future of the Page conference (Saskatoon, June 2000), I had to see the archive as something more than a private legacy. No working environment of any writer who has ever composed on a word processor, let alone in a web environment, will ever look like this again. I imagine that other archives from Gaddis's generation are organized similarly – filled with materials a writer had to have, what was rescued from the trash heap and kept in offices, in file cabinets, in various places of physical storage. Looking at so much printed matter gathered in a vault gave me an insight into all those hermetic rooms occupied in the fiction by so many Gaddis characters. The same room shows up, in various ways, in work by Mary Caponegro, Don DeLillo, William Gass, Joseph McElroy, David Markson, Harry Mathews, and Joy Williams – some of the novelists who came out to the St Paul Cathedral in Harlem for the fall 1999 Gaddis memorial. There will never be such a purely *textual* archive again – not in any of Gaddis's successors, not among writers indifferent to, wary of, or even antagonistic to the literary postmodernism Gaddis helped to inaugurate in the United States.

In calling this the last literary archive, I do not want to imply that there was ever anything pristine about predigital writing spaces: the Ninety-Sixth Street apartment in *J R*, which housed the clutter and some of the same labelled cardboard boxes I discovered, in reality, in Long Island City, was constantly open to the chaos, noise, and entropy of a city environment. Nor does physical boundedness mean that the archive is necessarily finite. In DeLillo's *Libra*, what is the character of Nicholas Branch about if not the hopelessness of attempts to set boundaries, to delimit a topic, and defeat conspiracy theories by an exclusive focus on evidence? The mere gathering of materials (unselectively, and without a framework or theory for separating out elements in a meaningful narrative) will surely do more to obscure than illuminate any topic, more to foment than confront conspiracy thinking. A certain helplessness, even an immobility, within accumulating detail is also the condition of David Markson's late modern Protagonist, the name of a character-in-progress 'first seen poised abstractedly amid a kind of transitory disarray? Cartons heaped and piled?'[2] The immobility of the literary artist in isolation, aptly termed a 'reader's block' by Markson, similarly characterizes Lynne Tillman's Paige Turner, Harry Mathews's journalist, William Gass's man in the chair, McElroy's Dom, Auster's Quinn, Fanshawe, Black, and Blue – all figures who in their solitude create boundless networks, exposing the limits of both identity construction and historicism. After Gaddis, this recurrent figure in postmodern American fiction can be understood as a central expression of the dream of the literary archive as a material world apart. Concomitantly, the passing of this figure may be understood elegiacally, as a farewell to the New Historicist romance with the telling, the triumphant, the untheorized detail.[3]

What I found most fascinating, and what is perhaps the richest archival vein for future Gaddis scholarship, is the manuscript page on which the novels were composed. The pages for *J R* in particular, legal-sized, boxed together with outlines and sets of notes, corrections, numbers, and arrows, were not so much drafted, typed, and revised as they were physically assembled, with lines frequently cut into strips and pasted between the typed lines on a master. Any of those notes or outlines, any lines transcribed from the pile of papers, might at some point be excerpted, clipped, and taped onto the manuscript page, as it made its way through numerous iterations to a final, publishable form, all trace of the author's composing consequently 'abolished and voided from history' (Faulkner) – except, of course, for what is left in the archive. The boxes holding more than 2500 manuscript pages also include newspaper clippings, commodity reports, annual reports, stockholder letters, shareholders' meeting notes, meeting notices, newsletters on American Indian affairs, and a letter on how to buy naval surplus supplies. There are also legal queries, lists of names, acquisitions (Why and How listed in a special table), as well as handwritten calculations.[4] For Gaddis, the manuscript page and its desktop context was no less capacious than the Internet; in fact, the visual presentation of diverse materials on a single two-dimensional page may well be closer to Theodor Nelson's conception of hypertext than any hypertext fiction composed since the advent of the Internet. The manuscript page, in an author such as Gaddis, is certainly truer to Nelson's concept of 'transclusion' (where a specific command brings a distant text or electronically accessible site in toto to the reader's screen) than the highlighted links dotting the current (but surely not definitive) web page, circa Y2K. (See fig. 10.1 for a sample draft page for *J R*.)

More than notes but less than narrative, the lines taped to Gaddis's draft page represent one stage in a developing composition whose outcome would be more continuous, the dialogue more lifelike and better filled out. Even in its finished form, however, the work is still recognizable as *assemblage*, with some fragments entering the text unchanged and others dropped or absorbed as nonverbal elements in the book's emerging structure. For the later stages in the composition, Gaddis set up a large table in his Long Island studio so that he could lay out entire sections (the book is not broken up into chapters) presumably to better visualize recurrent themes, motifs, phrases, and so forth. Photographs of the workroom show pages posted to the wall also. The book is largely composed of dialogue, meant to be experienced – with minimal suspension of disbelief – in real time. Yet clearly Gaddis had a spatial sense of the whole – he needed to see connections, to be able to trace patterns and constantly revise, reconnect, and alter the patterns by inserting new text – usually scripted dialogue among characters but in a few places handwritten notes, drawings, and photographs of nonliterary text such as the want ads read by J R and the Hyde boy on the bus on the way to one of their many school trips. (The children, indeed, are bussed and badly supervised more than they are schooled in the novel.)

Gaddis's book, on its reception in 1975, was likened to notions then current in literary theory – although the likeness was considered damaging aesthetically. *J R*, according to George Steiner, perfectly illustrated Roland Barthes's

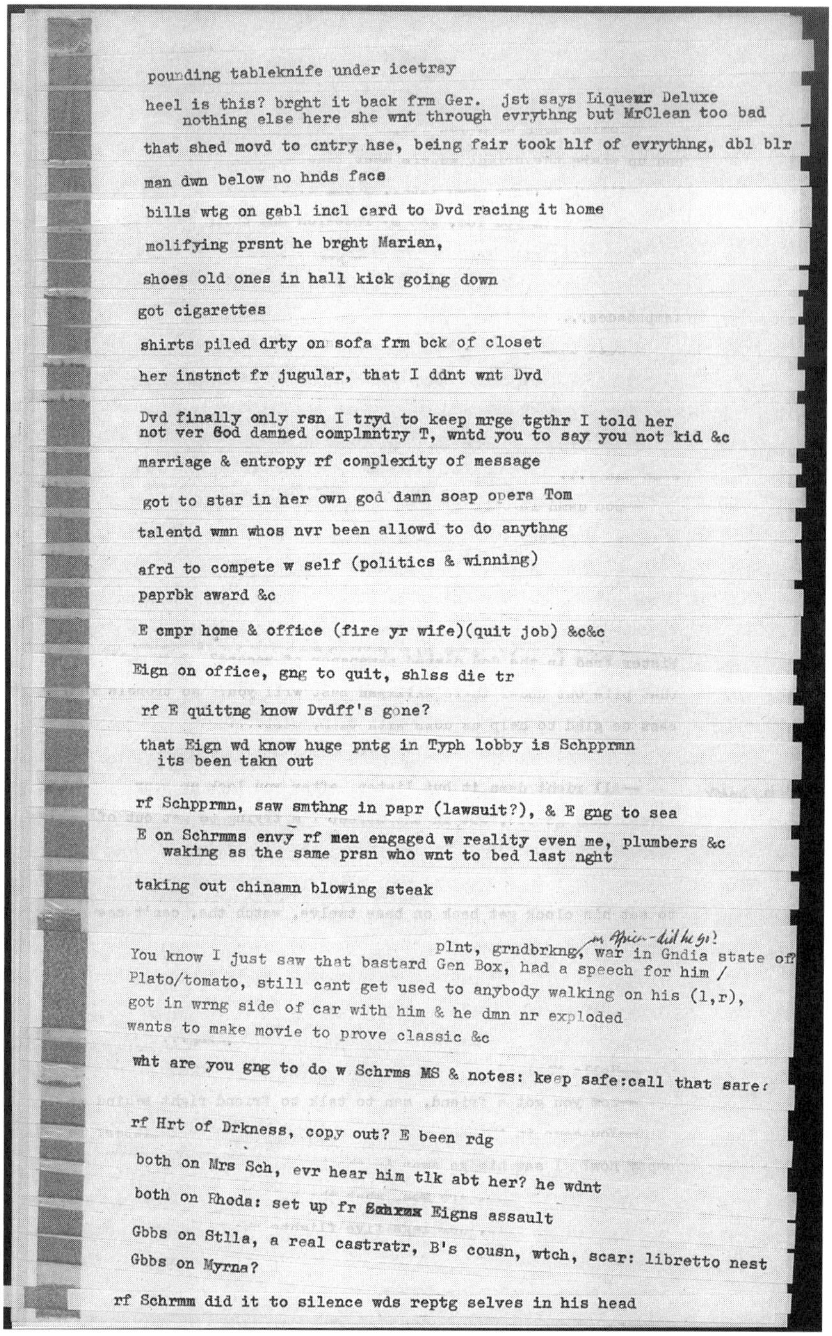

pounding tableknife under icetray
heel is this? brght it back frm Ger. jst says Liqueur Deluxe
nothing else here she wnt through evrythng but MrClean too bad
that shed movd to cntry hse, being fair took hlf of evrythng, dbl blr
man dwn below no hnds face
bills wtg on gabl incl card to Dvd racing it home
molifying prsnt he brght Marian,
shoes old ones in hall kick going down
got cigarettes
shirts piled drty on sofa frm bck of closet
her instnct fr jugular, that I ddnt wnt Dvd
Dvd finally only rsn I tryd to keep mrge tgthr I told her
not ver God damned complmntry T, wntd you to say you not kid &c
marriage & entropy rf complexity of message
got to star in her own god damn soap opera Tom
talentd wmn whos nvr been allowd to do anythng
afrd to compete w self (politics & winning)
paprbk award &c
E cmpr home & office (fire yr wife)(quit job) &c&c
Eign on office, gng to quit, shlss die tr
rf E quittng know Dvdff's gone?
that Eign wd know huge pntg in Typh lobby is Schpprmn
its been takn out
rf Schpprmn, saw smthng in papr (lawsuit?), & E gng to sea
E on Schrmms envy rf men engaged w reality even me, plumbers &c
waking as the same prsn who wnt to bed last nght
taking out chinamn blowing steak
plnt, grndbrkng, in Africa—did he go? war in Gndia state of?
You know I just saw that bastard Gen Box, had a speech for him /
Plato/tomato, still cant get used to anybody walking on his (l,r),
got in wrng side of car with him & he dmn nr exploded
wants to make movie to prove classic &c
wht are you gng to do w Schrms MS & notes: keep safe:call that sare
rf Hrt of Drkness, copy out? E been rdg
both on Mrs Sch, evr hear him tlk abt her? he wdnt
both on Rhoda: set up fr ~~Schrmm~~ Eigns assault
Gbbs on Stlla, a real castratr, B's cousn, wtch, scar: libretto nest
Gbbs on Myrna?
rf Schrmm did it to silence wds reptg selves in his head

Figure 10.1. A sample draft page for *J R*.

concept of the unreadable text, implying the 'death of the author' not as a private individual but as an operative cultural construction. In the context of current reflections on the page, I cite this early and, in my view, misleading take on Gaddis because it antedates and parallels a much broader, and more deeply problematic, identification of hypertext and poststructuralist theory. Steiner thought that the new emphasis on an author's mediating function (his transformation into a 'medium' through whom text is processed as a 'tissue of quotations,' none of them original) obviated creativity and eliminated any distinctive voice. Similarly, many prominent hypertext critics have argued that electronic technologies so literally enact poststructuralist theory as to make theory itself irrelevant. George P. Landow, most famously, claimed in 1992 that hypertext would replace 'conceptual systems founded upon ideas of center, margin, hierarchy, and linearity ... with ones of multilinearity, nodes, links, and networks'[5] – thereby, as Lance Olsen comments, 'enacting the deconstructive turn in the very mechanics of structure.'[6] That is Olsen's extension of Landow's claim probably beyond its provenance, but the slippage from 'conceptual systems' to 'mechanics,' so common even now after a full human generation of hypertext experimentation (and many, many generations of software), is typical of the way that hypertext theory continues to literalize poststructuralist thought.[7]

Gaddis's compositional technique may strike us today as an unbelievably laborious process that could have been avoided, even in the early seventies, had he used a word processor. Likewise, in *S/Z* when Barthes imagines the text, 'in its mass,' as 'comparable to a sky, at once flat and smooth, deep, without edges and without landmarks,'[8] our first thought, understandably, may be of the LCD screen. This literalism, what might be called a reduction of theory to code, is problematic not only because it produces misreadings of either Gaddis, literary hypertext, or for that matter the autonomous development of code by computer programmers and database designers. The technological reduction stems from a deeper misunderstanding of what poststructuralist theory was about in the first place. In removing the author, and in announcing the equally momentous transition from work to text, from a print-bound unity to an open network, Barthes does seem to anticipate the transition from page to screen, if only metaphorically. But I would insist that Barthes's conceptual distinctions, while suggestive, are in fact largely independent of materiality, whether print or electronic. In Barthes and (as we shall see) his near contemporary Ted Nelson, the lexia, or unit of attention, does not depend on how the page is instantiated by either the author during composition or the publisher during presentation. Lexia are defined rather by a cognitive act whose connections and significations the reader alone can make: they are chunked together as units capable of reintegration at another level, without reference to the words, sentences, and paragraphs they contain. What both Steiner and the hypertext critics tend to forget is that any breakdown of text into a field of interconnecting lexia depends not primarily on the author, but rather on the reader, who is capable of further text processing precisely because the verbal content of words, sentences, and paragraphs may be forgotten; attention is then paid to how the page itself circulates in new contexts. (And to the extent that even Gaddis in composing *J R* worked with a revisable, mechanically extendable manuscript page, he is himself as much a reader as an author of his own work.) By bringing one's own concerns to the text, the reader creates associations and links whose linearity or nonlinearity is largely independent of the text's material qualities, however much these linearities are exploited or ignored by an author's own pagework.

Let us look again at that open sky passage in Barthes's *S/Z*. His conception of textuality as something flat, unending, deep, and infinitely connectable, a textuality in anticipation of the computer screen, nonetheless requires delineation by a reader, specifically, a reader who is capable of acting as an observer or 'commentator':

> Like the soothsayer drawing on it with the tip of his staff an imaginary rectangle wherein to consult, according to certain principles, the flight of birds, the commentator traces through the text certain zones of reading, in order to observe therein the migration of meanings ... the passage of citations. (14)

An 'imaginary rectangle' in which to observe 'the migration of meanings': this might serve as a working definition of the page, more conceptual than material in its existence, more readerly than writerly, and general enough to include both hypertext lexia and codex leaves. What is important is not the shape of the page. The soothsayer might as well draw a circle, an oval, or a squiggle, so long as it is a two-dimensional figure capable of distinguishing what is outside – clear sky or noise, both amount to the same thing – from what is brought or allowed inside – namely, 'meaning.' Key to Barthes's concept – and the definition of the page – is the separation of meaning from authorial intention as the text, physically separate from the author, finds its way to readers, who in turn realize connections with other lexia, found in other books. Considered thus, from the perspective of citation and commentary, the larger migration from print to electronic media can be understood as a continuous process, the two media not fundamentally different from one another in terms of what can be stimulated, conceptually, in the minds of readers: the most one can say is that the selections made by readers and authors might be better preserved and more readily made available in hypertext than in print. But even this practical difference, consequential as it could be (in terms of making explicit themes, symbols, and conceptual consistencies hitherto kept implicit), has yet to be realized in most literary hypertexts.

The death of the author is a condition, as Barthes announces at the end of his signature essay, of 'the birth of the reader' – but a reader whose function is not so much interpretation as organization, the selection of meaningful text elements from noise and their arrangement within textual space. This shift, from the author as romantic genius, literary outlaw, or cultural outsider to the author-reader who makes selections, is a transition that hypertext and the web environment definitely accelerate. Whether such selections produce linear or nonlinear structures will depend not so much on the medium – two decades into the era of electronic writing, the most we can say is that the literal nonlinearities in hypertext stimulated literary theorists to rediscover nonlinearity as the rule, rather than the exception, in print narratives. Neither the opposition linearity/nonlinearity nor the literalization of intertextuality provide reliable ways of distinguishing print from hypertext. Where then, if at all, is the difference?

Rather than look at what takes place on the hypertext page (which at most enables intensifications and literalizations of poststructuralist concepts that have been on the table for decades), we might instead look at the page itself, its inherent dynamism and changing topography, as a material basis for what is authentically new about the digital text. Unlike Barthes's two-dimensional rectangle, definitive for pagination in print and most other material carriers, the screen space has been considered three-dimensional: 'Confronted with the surface of the computer screen [itself immaterial and made up purely of light and electricity] one started thinking in spatial terms of "in front of" and "behind" rather than in more temporal terms such as "before" or "after."'[9] So writes Hanjo Berressem, in his introduction to a collection of conference papers, *Chaos/Control: Complexity [Chaos Theory and Cultural Production]* that is itself a combination of book and CD-ROM. Berressem distinguishes between texts whose signifieds are dynamic (facilitating the distinctively literary sequencings common to print and hypertext) and texts whose signifiers are also dynamic, a property unique to digital carriers. What is distinctive in this newly dynamic page is the ability not so much to stack texts one on top of another, but to enfold various texts into one another. More 'topological' than Cartesian, a 'datamobile' more than a stack of objects, digital text becomes, for Berressem, a site for data assembly, selection, and performance. What is performed, however, is not the interpretation of 'static works that a classic hermeneutics can comfortably work with'(40). In digital carriers, there is no longer a 'stable textual basis' for such interpretive activity and sustained close reading: 'not only is every reading | path different, the text that is read is different as well' (40).

Berressem's analysis makes evident the extent to which literary activity, with all its devotion to the generation of complexity, consciousness, and reflexive understanding at the level of the signified, has depended on a stable, simplified, largely forgotten page as a material carrier capable of fixing language at the level of the signifier. But when the signifiers themselves are immaterial – when what we see at any moment is only 'one of many possible ways that a text might appear, only one of the many faces the text can have, only one of the many texts the text can be,' we have reached a point where it may no longer be meaningful to speak of a 'page' at all. What we have instead is a potential object described at the level of code: 'There is no site prior to its description. There is no page the source code refers to. There is no page "in itself"' (48–9). No page, only descriptions of possible pages whose realization is up to the reader. The page we are reading at any moment is only stable if we, while reading, actively make it so. No larger cultural or publishing concern is going to preserve the text for us.

It is not easy to say 'what kind of subject and what kind of culture ... digital texts imply, and what form of narratology' can be envisioned for a processual text (42). Berressem notes that digital processuality is bound to differ significantly from that of the theatre and of performance arts. In the absence of interpretation and without a single text that different readers (or the same reader at a different time) can go back to, the differences from a literary-critical performance in print might be just as great. All print narratives, because of their structural stability, are bound to be grand narratives – 'even when they are in themselves polyphonic [Bakhtin] or writerly [Barthes]' (40). This inevitability helps to explain why so many critics mistook hypertext for the material culmination of the grand narratives of postmodern fiction and theory. Yet there remain certain features of contemporary narrative that do in fact anticipate the singularized reading movements constituting the many small narratives likely to emerge in electronic environments. Berressem points to Douglas Coupland's practice of 'denarrating': a response to 'the deluge of electronic and information media into our lives' and the consequent loss of 'all the components essential for the forging of identity ... family, ideology, class strata, a geography, politics and a sense of living within a historic continuum.'[10]

When the page itself no longer supports a sense of narrative continuity, we are placed, as authors and readers, in the curious position of having to create our own context or framework within which selections, citations, and emergent narratives can be recognized and preserved. As current readers, we ourselves need to describe the 'page' that future readers will see and work with. The archive, as Gaddis seems to have understood within his own medial ecology, needs to be constructed at the moment of composition: in the absence of any single overriding cultural organization, the author's own organization is all that makes possible the continued circulation of meanings within particular structures established when writing. From this understanding authors, readers and more often authors-as-readers can address themselves meaningfully to a 'future' page. Instead of an object, the page is to become a description of a possible object, reflecting only what the author makes of materials that the reader can, in turn, cast into further potentials.

Turning and Returning

In such fictions as *Microserfs* and *Generation X*, Coupland's narrator handles the loss of cultural identity and narrative continuity by aligning himself with other individuals in loose 'groupuscles'; his books are small narratives of affinities rather than identities. Gaddis's massive but never 'grand' narratives are hypertextual in that they create connections through actual texts and plausible speech and they facilitate transitions, from scene to scene, exclusively through telephones, moving cars and trains, and other media of communication and transportation. These are useable models for a potential narrative in digital text. In what follows I consider some additional models in contemporary fiction and designwriting, distinctive in that their narrative innovations go all the way down, to the material look of the page itself. Harry Mathews, a long-time American member of the Oulipo or workshop for *potential literature* (my emphasis), explicitly considers what happens when an individual writer, the journalist of his book title, attempts to note down everything that happens to him, as it happens. The encyclopedic experiment turns nightmarish, but no less so than the literal nightmare experienced by Lynn Tillman's character, Paige Turner, who dreams of words as tiny objects that move on the page: small or grand narrative in the digital age has been made to confront the inherent instability of its own medial supports. Image/narratives by Raymond Federman in collaboration with Anne Burdick in *the electronic book review*, along with my own work with Burdick and Ewan Branda on the page design of the journal itself, will also be discussed.

In Mathews, the loss of continuity and identity is expressed in terms that are not so much cultural as contextual – in contexts that become richly embedded and capable of infinite expansion. Mathews is an author of what I have termed elsewhere 'cognitive fictions,' works that 'denarrate' in Berressem's terms, but in such a way that new forms of consciousness can be seen to emerge out of the denarrating media and technologies. As mind is to its material supports in the brain, so cognitive fictions are in relation to the contemporary media ecology. These works do not oppose themselves to other, faster and more powerful media of communication; rather, they take full advantage of the slower, marginal condition of literature in order to bring experiences shaped by these media into consciousness. In a sense, the literary shadows other media – much as literary hypertexts, so far, have tended to shadow the three-dimensional works and media they cite and comment on, creating a 'contour,' a path for consciousness, rather than an full-fledged cognitive environment.[11]

The Journalist opens in media res, a device that never waited on hypertext – it was in fact originally an epic convention that got carried over from orality into print. Similarly, the conflation of beginnings and endings within a single print paragraph can make the new-found ability to start anywhere and then jump from one passage to another seem arbitrary by comparison. It is easy to cite examples in printed texts when one thinks one has reached an end – say, after a treacherous stretch of driving in bad weather – only to find that one is, in fact, just beginning:

> The rain had stopped. I could forget about the curved warning signs; the gently winding road, which conformed so gratifyingly to my map, would dry fast. I settled back in the driver's seat and accelerated. The steering wheel came off in my hand.[12]

The mention of a map, in these fine opening lines, raises many questions relevant to the cognitive mapping that one seeks when reading pages and viewing screens. Conformity to a map is a gratifying, precise, but necessarily false illusion, because one-to-one correspondences – whether lexical or topographical – fail to describe the ongoing mental activity that actually generates much of our perception of a text or a passing landscape. Given enough rules of mapping, anything can be mapped onto anything, but one never knows all the mappings that are going on in one's own mind and through one's own body. For practical aesthetic purposes, the fewer the rules, the better – hence the gratifications in reading minimal fictions by, for example, Jorge Luis Borges. The power of a minimal mapping is precisely that it makes a world (if not 'the' world) knowable against the background of multiple unknown mappings in the unconscious. Mapping generates order from noise; but noise is precisely what Mathews's driver is forced to confront, in all its unknowability, at the moment the steering wheel comes off in his hand. No longer able to distinguish between what is inside and outside, his sense of a personal identity is revealed to have been, at every moment and without his knowing it, a cognitive fiction – which is to say, the fiction that consciousness is very closely connected to what our minds and bodies are actually doing at any moment:

> The possibility had always been real. You never had to remind yourself of it. And it remains real. At such a moment, who are you? Where are you? You cannot dismiss the question by observing that 'you' have become a mere object manipulated by the indifferent laws of physics. One part of you says that; another part listens. What and where are they? What and where is your identity? (3)

A part of us speaks and another part listens, as if our very sense of a stable and continuous self were nothing but a narrative that we tell ourselves, a world fiction that under normal circumstances seems continuous enough and linear, but which is more likely a set of multiple narratives variously linked in concatenations that the brain can search through and recall in a moment. These links are decidedly nonlinear, accompanied by analogies,

Figure 10.2. Screen shot of *ebr6*, 'image + narrative' <http://www.altx.com/ebr/ebr6.htm> On first looking into 'image + narrative,' readers are presented with a series of animated graphic image files. Through a frame that recalls a TV screen, scenes from a road trip – a staple of narrative continuity – appear as discreet elements in a digital field. White lines passing underneath a car and a variety of signals in a rear-view mirror all vie for attention in a field of competing discourses.

puns, metaphors, rhymes, and associations that generally remain unconscious – except in literature, art, or more immediately defamiliarizing experiences such as can result from a sudden change in our environment, the disengagement of self and world at the moment the steering wheel comes off in our hands. Then our sense of self can be revealed as fundamentally fragmented and permeable – a webwork of signs and divergent discourses vying for attention (and continuing to jostle with one another in our minds, after they have receded from consciousness).

That is how narrative is imagined by the visual artist Anne Burdick in a series of graphic images – also based on travel by car – introducing an ongoing collection of critical writing titled 'image + narrative' in *the electronic book review* (fig. 10.2). In the first sequence, broken white lines move beneath the car's wheels like a needle through a textile; in the next sequence, a suburban street seen through a windscreen and a rear-view mirror settles on a home-made road sign, reading 'You've got our attention.' The journey remains the mythic reference for all narrative, an embodied metaphor for the linguistic construction of goal-oriented action in the world. Except that now the illusion of continuity is broken up, for Burdick as for Mathews, by the medium of representation. Through a frame that recalls a TV screen, we see the lines and the reflected images as discreet elements in a digital field – aspects of the woven 'thREADs,' or inscribed reading pathways, that define Burdick's site design.

Burdick's imagery, metaphorically in her work for 'image + narrative' but increasingly literally in pages devised for the new *ebr* interface (in collaboration with site architect Ewan Branda and me), confirms both a poststructuralist and a vernacular understanding of electronic textuality as a field of many lines crossing and recrossing to form a complex intertextual weave. This imagery is further developed, in the current *ebr*, by embedding literal 'threads' into the page itself – a family of small icons off in the margins presenting not only conventional bibliographical data (footnotes, author's and editor's notes, and so forth) but also taking readers to affiliated essays within and outside the journal, facilitating readers' glosses, and allowing readers to bring in other texts from elsewhere in the Web, in whole or in part. In this way a page generated at another site will become (after obtaining permissions) a part of *ebr*. With such activity there is certainly the suggestion of openness, that the connections and potential readerly associations are infinite. Authors are made aware, explicitly, that their production will undergo continued threading, weaving, and glossing at the hands of readers, and this activity will be made visible, cumulative, and public over time with the author's own text (a fabric of quotations, none of them 'original,' in Barthes's terms).

Hence some of the poststructuralist terms will be literalized, even in the new *ebr*. But there are also – in my view just as important – ways of bringing in readers conceptually. There is for example a filmic dimension to the imagery (recall the enframing TV screen) and also a sound dimension (a database that enables sorting and selections modelled after the disk jockey's 'remix'). More than mere literalizations and something other than metaphors, these filmic and sound-like functionalities implicitly locate 'us,' the journal's readers. As in Barthes, the developing *ebr* page grants power to readers, not authors, in defining what gets included, and what left out of the page (see fig. 10.3).

The Most Linear Hypertext in the Universe

To further emphasize the independence of the reader's experience from the text's mediality, whether that experience is primarily linear, reflexive, distributed, serial, or (more likely) some combination of all these modes, I want to consider briefly an unusual hypertext, 'Eating Books,' which was written by Raymond Federman and then designed out of Burdick's offices. This work is remarkable, technically, not for its interactivity but for its self-containment. In fact, it uses no links at all but instead enforces a linearity more strenuously than any print book I know. If Moby has written the loudest song in the universe, Federman and Burdick have produced the most linear hypertext (see fig. 10.4).

We are told, at the start of Federman's narrative, that the book to be eaten is a telephone book, the most strictly lexical of narratives and, in Federman's words, 'the only book in your library which came free. Except, of course, for

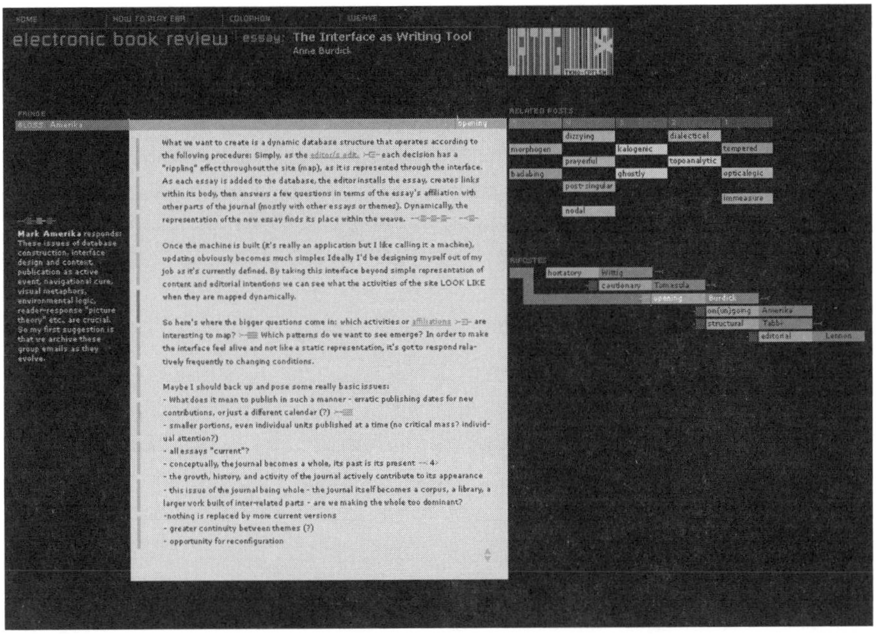
HOME
HOW TO PLAY EBR
COLOPHON
WEAVE
electronic book review
essay: The Interface as Writing Tool
Anne Burdick
Mark Amerika responds:
These issues of database construction, interface design and content, publication as active event, navigational cure, visual metaphors, environmental logic, reader-response "picture theory" etc., are crucial. So my first suggestion is that we archive these group emails as they evolve.
What we want to create is a dynamic database structure that operates according to the following procedure: Simply, as the editor/s add, each decision has a "rippling" effect throughout the site (map), as it is represented through the interface. As each essay is added to the database, the editor installs the essay, creates links within its body, then answers a few questions in terms of the essay's affiliation with other parts of the journal (mostly with other essays or themes). Dynamically, the representation of the new essay finds its place within the weave.
Once the machine is built (it's really an application but I like calling it a machine), updating obviously becomes much simpler. Ideally I'd be designing myself out of my job as it's currently defined. By taking this interface beyond simple representation of content and editorial intentions we can see what the activities of the site LOOK LIKE when they are mapped dynamically.
So here's where the bigger questions come in: which activities or affiliations are interesting to map? Which patterns do we want to see emerge? In order to make the interface feel alive and not like a static representation, it's got to respond relatively frequently to changing conditions.
Maybe I should back up and pose some really basic issues:
- What does it mean to publish in such a manner - erratic publishing dates for new contributions, or just a different calendar (?)
- smaller portions, even individual units published at a time (no critical mass? individual attention?)
- all essays "current"?
- conceptually, the journal becomes a whole, its past is its present
- the growth, history, and activity of the journal actively contribute to its appearance
- this issue of the journal being whole - the journal itself becomes a corpus, a library, a larger work built of inter-related parts - are we making the whole too dominant?
-nothing is replaced by more current versions
- greater continuity between themes (?)
- opportunity for reconfiguration
dizzying
dialectical
morphogen
kalogenic
tempered
prayerful
topoanalytic
badabing
ghostly
opticalogic
post-singular
immeasure
nodal
hortatory
cautionary
opening
Burdick
on(un)going
Amerika
structural
editorial

Figure 10.3. The threading activity, presented metaphorically in the preceding sequence of animated graphic images (fig. 10.2), has been installed literally on the page itself in the current database version of *ebr* (version 4.0, completed summer 2004). Because readers are free either to operate or ignore this functionality, the potential for connectivity is enhanced rather than obviated by the technology.

the books you stole.' Further along, after scrolling lengthwise through the narrative, we encounter a self-consciously old-fashioned typeface in French, Federman's first language, indicating something 'Voltaire once said, or was it Diderot who said that, Andre Gide said it too, but I know he stole that saying from someone else: *Voler un Livre* ...' A digression on Voltaire's anti-Semitism momentarily suspends the narrative line – but not the literal line of text, whose material form enables but hardly corresponds to the cognitive processes enacted by the narration. Largely, these are processes of memory, and of textual citation – all of which interrupt the line of thought and put into question the origin of the quotation. Even the language of its actual utterance is in question – since Voltaire supposedly said it to Isaac Newton, on a chance meeting in the streets of London. Finally, after these digressions have run their course, the narrative ends with the full transcription of the saying: 'To Steal a Book is not a crime as long as one reads the book.'

This literary hypertext features not a single link and only one technical

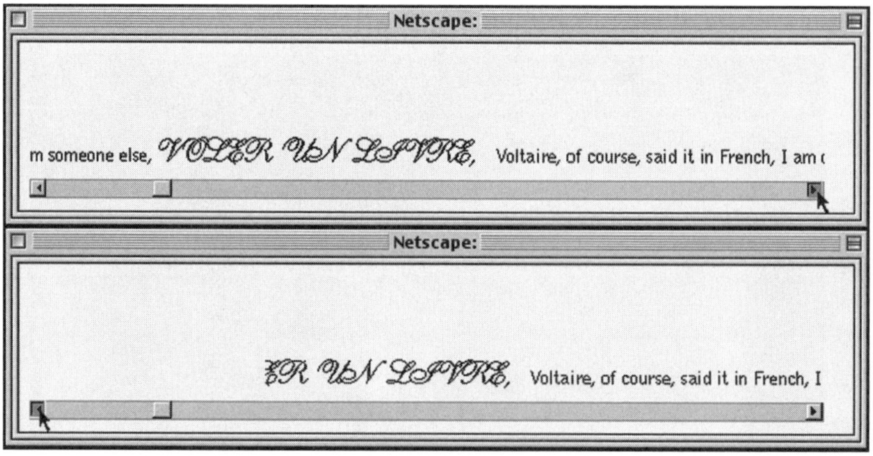
Netscape:
m someone else,
Voltaire, of course, said it in French, I am
Netscape:
Voltaire, of course, said it in French, I

Figure 10.4. Screen shot of *ebr7* 'Eating Books' <http://www.altx.com/ebr/ebr7/ebr7.htm>.

feature associated with the electronic medium. The single distinguishing feature is this: unlike the printed line, the line in hypertext, once read, cannot be gone back to and reread. It has been swallowed, literally: as ephemeral as any spoken utterance (unless of course the entire sequence is reloaded and run again). In this narrative, linearity in itself is no assurance against inattention or loss of memory. For that, we need a different conception of what constitutes stability within the new media – a conception involving the reader in the act of observation and selection. Stability in electronic environments, I want to suggest, comes from the literal construction of the object of study rather than its interpretation – for that is what we are doing, constructing the page (and forgetting past pages, the pages we have passed over) as we move selectively through the developing Web archive. Normally in hypertext we are given not a single line of text but a multiplicity of sources and texts for browsing, so that image and narrative, the verbal and the visual, all exist on the same plane; even the near and the far, as hypertext poet Stephanie Strickland has written, are 'equally present, and equally speedily present.'[13] Where a book or a spoken utterance can only *refer* to the texts and images that it cites, directing readers toward a plane of meaning that is not identical with the plane of the printed page, a web page can, in theory, actually present its electronic citations directly, through the clickable link or mouseover view that brings the environment into the screen space. (Federman, had he wanted to, presumably could have accessed an online archive containing the actual words attributed to Voltaire, Diderot, Gide, and so on.) The screen and the environment exist potentially on the same plane, as a set of overlapping pages with continually shifting margins. Once read, the words of Federman's text do not really disappear; they instead become a potential in the mind of the reader, one that we can imagine being activated at any time in a hypertext that lets the reader select elements from within the discourse environment. The promise of hypertext (purposely withheld by Federman) is its creation of a pattern that readers, or the author at a later time, can return to, but differently, when encountering similar events and patterns later on. Through direct citation, and not through hearsay, the outside is thus ready at any moment to match up with the inside, and this permeability, more than the actuality of any particular link or set of links, seems to me to be definitive of reading in electronic environments, where all texts are virtually present.[14]

Words That Yield: To Frames That Form

To the extent that we have hypertext only through a series of mediations – our screen that brings the environment in, our browsing software, the electronic desktop that lets us customize image and text for further processing, and so on – we are likely to be that much more aware of our collaborative activity while reading. Far from confirming readers in a central and author-like authority, the hypertext composition 'literally opens up' the space in which the reader coexists with the materials being read. Strickland describes this readerly disorientation in an essay published concurrently with her hypertext poem sequence, *True North*:

> Released from the printed page into this floating space, readers are often uneasy. What is the poem? Is it the sum of every possible way to proceed, the sequence of such journeys, or one particular path privileged as a saved reading? Only slowly does one assimilate the truth that one may return each time differently.[15]

Narrative is again imagined as a journey, but a journey whose meaning does not await us in some future fulfilment at a determined endpoint; rather, once enough materials have been assembled on the screen or within the writing space and a direction through them or set of relations among them has been established, meaning can then be reconstructed along multiple pathways by which readers may return. This sort of retrospective construction – known as 'multifinality' in evolutionary theory – creates a situation in which meaning is largely produced not moment by moment during unicursal reading, but when the set of completed observations can be grouped together as a unity, a bundle of achieved pathways that can then be introduced as a working element in other readings, and other constructions.

With that release from a future-orientation, and the environmental interruption of cognitive illusions of continuity, comes a relocation of meaning-making in the hands and eyes and ears of the reader, who now seeks to be simultaneously 'in touch and in control' of both the hypertext and its environment (to cite the title of another Strickland essay).[16] For this to happen, the evolving hypertext must create its environment even as the hypertext reader draws material from the environment – a 'floating space' that lacks all distinction until a selection is made. Instead of a uniform surround, this created environment is then a product of selections that determine which, out of all possible objects and web sites, will be significant within the reader's own writing space. In this respect (and not in naive equations of two very different associative mechanisms), hypertext is mind-like because the mind, too, like any organism, admits only those aspects of the environment that it is structurally able to process. A successful hypertext construction will be, therefore, not an accumulation of objects and texts defined indexically as some sort of preexisting information network; it will be, rather, a set of dovetailing or complementary *structures*, which have cognitive meaning to the extent that these structures are brought out, sequentially and associatively, in the process of linking.

It could well be that a perceived lack of a true cognitive dimension in hypertext is behind critical calls for a 'rhetoric or stylistics of departure and arrival' [17] oriented toward aspects of the target text that are structurally and thematically relevant to the source text currently on the screen. As Jan van Looy writes in his 'Conclusion: Toward a Hyperfiction Poetics,' 'the notion of "*words that yield*" has to be elaborated [by the author] ... In the same way as a full stop and a capital letter signal the beginning of the next sentence, links should inform the reader of their presence and their aim, and suggest a destination.'[18] The link, then, is not so much a mode of neutral connectivity as an active device that enframes; it is the bounded place where readers create a literary and visual system that would otherwise exist as an indistinguishable mass or unknown domain of automatic functioning. Indeed, Burdick allegorizes the permeability of inside and outside and their mutual self-creation with her framing device in 'You've Got Our Attention.' Because the animated graphic image file puts us in the position of the driver, an observer of the changing scene behind and in front of the car, we are doubly mediated. Looking through both the windshield or mirror and the enframing TV screen, we find ourselves in the position of an observer observing herself. This second-order observation, I want to suggest, is at the heart of any narrative transit through electronic landscapes; and the renewed centrality of such reflexive, second-order positioning has little to do with the specific means – the browser and its clickable link – of moving around in that environment. Rather, reflexivity and metaobservation in narrative is simply consistent with an environment where all language is metalanguage – so that everything one sees on the screen is the result of a description at the level of code (html, xml, and so forth).

Hypertext links? Links are easy; trustworthy links, hard:

> The words lie there and they may be lies. They lie on the page. They are little worms. Once she dreamed, on the night before a reading she was to give, that rather than words on paper, there were tiny objects linked one to another, which she had to decipher instantly and turn into words, sentences, a story, flawlessly, of course. Funny fear of the blank page. Didn't she recently explain that writing was erasure, because the words were already there, already in the world, that the page wasn't blank.[19]

The protohypertextual quality of Lynne Tillman's conception of language, the psychological block that the blank page inspires, and a lost objectivity that has separated the word from the world, are not uncommon features in contemporary experimental fiction in the United States. There are many literary anticipations of hypertext 'blocks' – a newly literalized, potentially infinite network no less intimidating, in its plenitude, than the blank page. In *Cognitive Fictions*, I considered how a number of authors – Tillman, Markson, Auster, and Mathews, in particular – found ways of opening the block using a variety of self-referential strategies.[20] Confronted by structures impossible to grasp cognitively – a hypertext in which everything is connected, the blank page where nothing is connected to anything – the author names that impossibility and so re-enters the structure at another level, the level of language, the level of observation. Of course references, plot developments, and other narrative material need to accumulate unselfconsciously before such self-conscious, self-referential reentry is possible. Reentry cannot be done by force of will. (The assertion of self-consciousness prior to achieving narrative momentum is a frequent failing in American metafictions of the sixties and seventies.) Once, however, the proliferating connections make possible a new perspective, the blocked author – now a reader – can establish a fresh relation to words that lose their referential power; they become Tillman's 'tiny objects' endlessly recombining, entering a new realm, the realm of the virtual. What distinguishes the aesthetic use of such objects is the artist's ability not simply to create from them a passive memory or record, but a transformation, away from their initial context into other contexts rich in potential. The aesthetic organization cannot simply be embodied materially, encoded, and preserved independently of the reading activity. Requiring recognition and reordering by the reader, the pattern stands a chance actually of being remembered (which of course means that much in the original, author-created text will necessarily be forgotten).

In 'To Find Words,' which opens the collection *The Madame Realism Complex*, Tillman's protagonist is a young author named, improbably, Paige Turner, who cannot 'pretend to believe in words and in the power of stories' and so determines to write instead about writing itself. Her narrative alternates between third-person views of Paige, direct presentations out of the literal pages in her notebook, and first-person commentaries by a narrator with access to Paige's thoughts. To herself, Paige defines her ambitions as an author in the barest material terms: 'to find words and place them in sentences in a certain order. Syntax.'[21] That's what Paige thinks; the sentence she goes on to write has to do with 'a sin tax in the U.S. on liquor and cigarettes ...' (17). This happens throughout the narrative, as the words found by the narrator are continually taken over and reappropriated by the character, and vice versa. At issue is the relation between the thought track that runs through every one of Tillman's essay-narratives (whether presented as fiction or nonfiction) and the texts that her protagonists are working on – or, when the protagonists are nonwriters, between the self and the voices and human visitors who 'become phrases in [the] body' (33). In one formulation, this is said to be the relation between conscious and unconscious thought:

> It is in the unconscious [Paige writes] that fantasy, moments of the day, and memory live, a reservoir for the poetry of the world. Is everything else prose? Is what's conscious ordinary prose, the prose of the world? (25–6)

But the formulation is rejected, as the narrator, ever ready to turn on a pun, responds:

> Or, I tease, the pose of the world. She is separating much too neatly the world she knows – I nearly wrote word for world – from the world she doesn't know, the one that owns her and to which she is a slave. She is a slave to what she can't remember and doesn't know and she is a slave to what she remembers and what she thinks she knows. Her education has damaged her in ways she does not even know. (26)

Paige does not know what she does not know; an eye does not see what it does not see: such truisms characterize all systems. But the narrator, Paige's creator who exists at a later stage in her literary career and cognitive development, presumably does know. Between the various narrative levels, first- and third-person narration, early and later development, the author who writes a draft and the same author (now a reader) who revises, we can perceive what the character wishing to be an author cannot see: for example, the educational system and ready-made fund of cultural memories that enslave her because she knows no other possibilities. The words she knows are her world.

Like all writers, Paige longs to find a voice and a style – to make music with words. Yet the words she succeeds in finding are consistently turned into other words by the narrator, or the same word is given a different meaning. Syntax becomes sin tax; prose is unmasked as a mere pose, so that the limitations inherent in the words Paige uses can be, not overcome, but reinscribed within a new perspective. 'She imagines the inside is the outside. She is greedy for everything (18)' and so she will eventually transform the boundary between herself and her environment into a division within herself: 'She opens her mouth wide. If words could make wishes come true. If wishes were horses she'd ride away' (18). Paige of course knows that words are not wishes, as Oedipa Maas discovers that a sign is not what it is: unlike a digital tape whose meaning and function is identical with its coding, or a 'complexity' that is 'its own best – shortest – description,'[22] neither spoken words nor material signs have the power to do what they say; they can only create alternate worlds inside the speaker or writer. Each world Paige might inhabit or Oedipa project is a different constellation of words with its own articulation and its own blind spots that can only be displaced by finding other words and (not finding) other blind spots.

To be sure, most print fiction tries to suppress narrative self-consciousness in the interest of immersing readers more fully in a story. Similarly, enormous sums of money have been spent in making virtual reality environments as 'transparent' and immersive as possible, so that we might move through them with a feeling of verisimilitude. It was not always so in the computer business, as changes in the meaning assigned to the word 'transparency' might indicate. At first, the word was used to mean that a user was close to the operating system (so that one tells the machine to do things in ways that it really does do things). Today, transparency more often means that the operating system is invisible, and so what is transparent is the machine itself – a window manufactured out of opacity (hence Microsoft's *Windows*). A steam locomotive displays its power in its massive levers and wheels; the transparent case of an iMac displays nothing operative. But consider the way a computer scientist was actually involved in making decisions at the level of operations:

> Lentz did a good job of making the hardware transparent to me. He hooked up topologies the culmination of a decade or more of tinkering. He explained every link in the process ... The gist consisted of vectors. A stimulus vector, converted by the net's self-reorganization into a response vector. We started with a three-deep array of neurodes, enough for a test start. Each field was the size of the net that had learned to pronounce English. Implementation A would be spared this task. Lentz wired it to a canned speech synthesis routine. We worked at the level not of phonemes but of whole words.[23]

Which is to say that the task had been modularized, so that with each move to the next level, from phonemes to whole words to sentences to entire texts, the previous level would be absorbed into a more comprehensive operation.

By actually imagining those aspects of a cognitive system that have sunk below the level of operational awareness, a small number of contemporary novelists and poets are creating a new order of realism in fiction and poetry, akin to functionalism in technological design and operational-minimalism in painting, that makes a frank admission of its own materiality and so establishes a ground on which authors and readers can meet as equals and communicate without illusions. Mathews works within this neomaterialist climate, as do most of the Oulipo members with whom he is associated. Georges Perec had written a novel, *La Disparition*, without using the letter *e* (the novel has been translated into English, a language where not even the article 'the' is allowed, under the punning title, *A Void*); Italo Calvino arranged the chapters for *Invisible Cities* according to a mathematical formula in which the chapters, like cities, build themselves up by numbers, 1, 21, 321, 4321, and then erase themselves in inverse order: 54321, 543, 54, 5; Raymond Queneau proposed ten sonnets, each of whose fourteen lines could be arranged in any order, producing 10^{14} or *Cent mille milliards de poems* (one hundred thousand billion poems). This is not automatic writing; rather it is writing under constraint. Such work does not give over the creative process to either the unconscious or mathematical formalisms but rather forces the coconscious, language-based, composing mind to put itself into contact with formal and procedural conditions that are always present, always constant, supporting, tweaking, and unconsciously controlling the creative process. Such writing is procedural rather than programmatic – an important distinction since procedures remain closer to composition than to publication, circulation, or the need to find applications. Another difference from programming is that the Oulipian follows self-set rules, constraints of one's own making. And so the author learns how autonomy produces results that are not entirely under authorial control. From a cognitive perspective, such writing is significant in that it recognizes the thousands of ways that conscious experience 'is constantly influencing and being influenced by many unconscious processes' involving perception and action, thought and emotion, as well as the computational and recursive routines that support the construction of even the simplest sentence.[24]

Although for more than thirty years the members of this group have devoted themselves, ostensibly, to researching past literary forms and making them available to the public, few of these forms have ever been used beyond the moment of their 'discovery' – and this is possibly the best thing about the Oulipo and what distinguishes their art from mere formalism. For what signifies is the cognitive and combinatorial potential that is held in the forms, not the form itself, which can go back on the shelf with all the other dusty books and dusty bottles the moment it is perceived or identified as a form. (The same is true of invented forms and self-imposed constraints: Mathews, for example, has never found it necessary to reveal the constraint under which he wrote his most Oulipian novel, *Cigarettes*.)

The Journal of the Journal

That we know the world only through particular frameworks, categorizations, and preestablished expectations is brought home to readers by the very look of *The Journalist,* in which paragraphs are numbered, and then renumbered and subdivided in an elaborate and doomed attempt to match the language to the atomistic world of facts and perceptions. The project is doomed because, unlike the semiotic model of a network of signifiers linked with each other and their signifieds, the identity of the world is a composite of attributes that only come into existence as they are observed. Even the shoes that the journalist's colleagues wear to work or the sunlight falling across a secretary's telephone become distinct (and thus capable of relating to one another) only as they are newly noted in the journal; only then do they 'emerge from the strangeness of systems outside' the journalist's control, as the clarity of his own evolving system plunges endlessly into the obscurity of these 'systems outside.'[25]

As noted attributes take form in clusters shaped in a network of coded relations, Mathews's novel spirals away from any notion of journal writing as the objective reporting of some preexisting world; only in the notation are objects and events 'naturalized' (9). At the same time, the novel also avoids attributing purposeful creation to the writer-observer. Instead, as the narrator discovers to his surprise, the journal has a life of its own, its purpose the mere reflection and reproduction of the categories with which he approaches the world. This narrator, the 'journalist' of the title, has been advised by his doctor to jot down 'everything' that happens to him (8), 'from how much he has spent on books and movies to what he eats' (dustjacket). But 'everything,' he soon discovers, is already caught up in its own networks of relations, and each item can belong to more than one category and can operate at several different levels. Initially he tries to distinguish 'between fact and speculation, between what is external and verifiable and what is subjective,' but this does not prevent the one from mingling with the other (20). Indeed, as distinctions noted down in the journal continue to proliferate and the act of recording makes ever greater demands on his time, lived experience and the record of the experience converge and the notation system itself expands to the point where it ceases to be meaningful to speak of a life 'outside' the system. So logical and poised are the notes that, although readers are given plenty of indications as to the journalist's deteriorating state, we are as surprised as he is when he breaks from his obsession long enough to observe himself: 'When I heard a dry noise above my head, like a cracking in the ceiling boards: I saw myself as if through an eye in the ceiling, fidgeting and sweating like a demented inmate, a disgrace. I calmed down' (129).

This is an astonishing moment – not because, while reading, we are unaware of the narrator's growing obsessiveness and mental stress. His literary decorum matches an imperturbable poise typical of Mathews, even as his protagonist steals into a closet in order to toss rolls of toilet paper down the airshaft of his office building, and later neglects to change out of his soiled white suit after a fall and lapse of consciousness during a night-time prowl. He does allow himself to make a mental note: 'I must get back early in the morning and straighten up' (173). But of course he does no such thing. In the morning he will be writing in the journal, and recording these very actions. The journalist is interested in the illusion of control, never the actual manipulation of reality, which is 'the world's, not mine' (154). In this he is true to those psychoses in which the patient, while perfectly capable of 'reality testing,' evidences no inclination to it (a condition noted by the clinical psychologist Louis Sass). At no time does the journalist apply any of his numerous and detailed acts of self-observation to the improvement of his condition. For no sooner does he reflect back on himself than he retreats from the self-observation into the security of the note-taking system. Because such acts are recorded entirely from within this system, however, we accept his state as 'natural.' To the extent that we enter the fiction, we accommodate ourselves to it, like a live fish adjusting its body temperature to a surrounding fluid, not noticing that it is slowly boiling or becoming frozen. In essence, by accepting the terms of Mathews's fiction, we enter something very like the 'floating space' that Strickland speaks of in electronic environments, before that environment is articulated and made active by the reader's selective engagements and disengagements. For the journalist, and for 'us,' the journal's reader, the outside world does not exist – except as it conforms to the selections and identifications that the journalist's mental state disposes him to make (see fig. 10.5).

Even more significant for the narrative structure than this (quickly suppressed) moment of self-consciousness, is the decision that can be felt pulling at him from the start, to replace the proliferating petty differences noted down in his journal with a single global distinction: he will move the system one level up, applying the idea of the journal to itself. Here is how he explains his decision to write a 'Journal of the journal': 'What I discovered is this: all the care I have brought to organizing this journal has been misspent; my laborious classifications have proved worthless; my efforts at competence are an illusion. Why? Because I have left out the chief activity of my life and the chief fact of my project: the keeping of this journal' (190–1). From here, it is only one small step to the next and final logical level at which we as readers experience a book titled *The Journalist,* when Mathews's narrator admits to 'a closeted vision, that of writing a novel – a novel about someone whose passion is keeping a journal' (209).

In numerous essays and interviews, Mathews has held that the role of the author is to provide materials that readers can then use as a means of creation.[26] In literary studies, such a position has been made to seem marginal and exceptional. To contain the self-consciousness and radical contingency that must pervade the creative act at every moment, mainstream writing programs tend to regard a fundamental condition as a technique, and

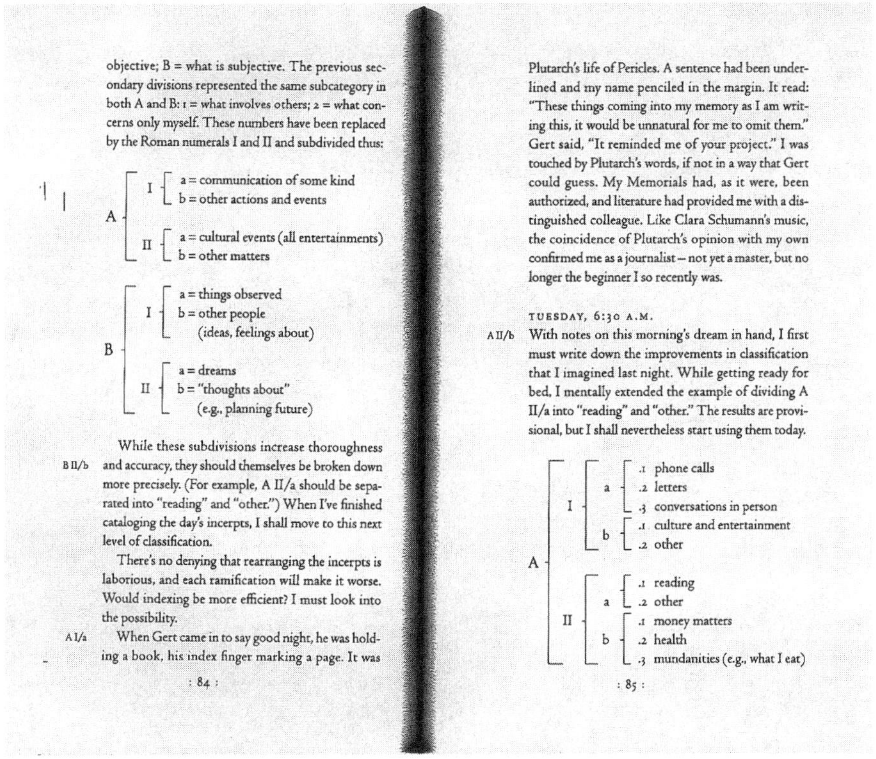
objective; B = what is subjective. The previous secondary divisions represented the same subcategory in both A and B: 1 = what involves others; 2 = what concerns only myself. These numbers have been replaced by the Roman numerals I and II and subdivided thus:

- A
  - I
    - a = communication of some kind
    - b = other actions and events
  - II
    - a = cultural events (all entertainments)
    - b = other matters
- B
  - I
    - a = things observed
    - b = other people (ideas, feelings about)
  - II
    - a = dreams
    - b = "thoughts about" (e.g., planning future)

While these subdivisions increase thoroughness
B II/b and accuracy, they should themselves be broken down more precisely. (For example, A II/a should be separated into "reading" and "other.") When I've finished cataloging the day's incerpts, I shall move to this next level of classification.

There's no denying that rearranging the incerpts is laborious, and each ramification will make it worse. Would indexing be more efficient? I must look into the possibility.

A I/a When Gert came in to say good night, he was holding a book, his index finger marking a page. It was

: 84 :

Plutarch's life of Pericles. A sentence had been underlined and my name penciled in the margin. It read: "These things coming into my memory as I am writing this, it would be unnatural for me to omit them." Gert said, "It reminded me of your project." I was touched by Plutarch's words, if not in a way that Gert could guess. My Memorials had, as it were, been authorized, and literature had provided me with a distinguished colleague. Like Clara Schumann's music, the coincidence of Plutarch's opinion with my own confirmed me as a journalist – not yet a master, but no longer the beginner I so recently was.

TUESDAY, 6:30 A.M.

A II/b With notes on this morning's dream in hand, I first must write down the improvements in classification that I imagined last night. While getting ready for bed, I mentally extended the example of dividing A II/a into "reading" and "other." The results are provisional, but I shall nevertheless start using them today.

- A
  - I
    - a
      - .1 phone calls
      - .2 letters
      - .3 conversations in person
    - b
      - .1 culture and entertainment
      - .2 other
  - II
    - a
      - .1 reading
      - .2 other
    - b
      - .1 money matters
      - .2 health
      - .3 mundanities (e.g., what I eat)

: 85 :

Figure 10.5. The protagonist of Harry Mathews's novel *The Journalist* produces a print hypertext when he tries to note down 'everything' that happens to him, as it happens. Like print, e-text is a framing medium within which readers and writers become category makers, builders of systems, and self-conscious observers of their own observations.

novels explicitly concerned with reflexive identity-making are most often filed away (and largely forgotten) under the subcategory, 'metafiction.' That literature has thus largely marginalized its own reflexivity (in favour of some liberal humanist ideal of authorial self-possession) is all the more surprising given that it is a field whose subject is homogeneous with its object, in that both literature and criticism (that is, writing about writing) are conducted in the same medium. This point is brought home to Mathews's journalist when he discovers the necessity of keeping a 'Journal of the Journal.' In all he has been doing up to that point, he has left out his own controlling presence, and only now, when he is in fact losing his grip, does he accord the writing itself, 'the making of each page, the making itself,' its 'supreme place.' The system that uses meaning is not the mind of the journalist himself, but the communicative network that he deploys – a network whose growing complexity cannot be internalized, cannot be made available for introspection. Yet the journalist acts as if, by bringing that complexity to the page itself, he will master 'everything' in life that impinges on consciousness. And this delusion, that the operations of consciousness and textuality can be brought to the page, is the material counterpart, if not the cause, of his progress toward insanity.

And so it is, by the novel's end, that Mathews's journalist breaks down and falls silent. Now a patient in a mental hospital, he resumes speaking only when his wife reads him a children's story, which opens: 'Once upon a time and a very good time, monkey chew tobacco and spit white lime, once upon a time there was a young boy named Michael' (236). Hearing these lines and the opening scene (in which Michael, leaving home at the age of nine, gets off an express train), the journalist then begins to interrupt with words of his own, adding characters, objects, and events as his wife goes on reading. With this small and mutually distanced dialogue, a modest hypertextual collaboration, the novel reaches a kind of closure impossible from within the journalist's earlier elaborate system of notation and classification. The system gives way to a more properly narrative apparatus, reflexivity and circularity turn into forward movement, and the act of turning inward is replaced by the turning of pages in a book. The journalist is now poised for reentry into his environment at another level – in a wholeness of interiority and exteriority and a dialogue that is not so much a communication between two people as a creation of a new narrative object outside either one of them, and outside any inscription in the book they are reading. This is something the journalist recognizes, in an especially lucid moment:

> My work is not for 'the world' (by that I mean anybody else) or for me (I hardly have time to read what I've written). It's for 'It.' 'Its' fugitive name does not matter. I've called it truth, and before that reality; since it is never to be completely obtained, it may be beyond naming altogether. (200)

(Mathews's journalist, appropriately, is himself never named in the novel.)

Paul Harris nonetheless suggests a name that is appropriate not only for Mathews's novel but for all constraint-driven narrative: 'The potential of constrained writing,' Harris notes, 'is that it ends up an autopoietic writing machine.' Autopoiesis – literally, self-making – describes 'a form of system organization where the system as a whole produces and replaces its own components and differentiates itself from its surrounding environment on a continual basis.'[27] In Mathews's case, the 'it' that is both self and not-self, a unity that consists of reciprocal perturbations between system and environment, is a kind of machine for 'generating linguistic distinctions in a linguistic domain.'[28] Such a process, though arbitrary and capable of referring only to other elements – the expanding network of signifiers – in the linguistic domain, will eventually shut down in paradox unless something in the structure answers to real elements in the environment (which, in turn, have their own domain-specific structure of distinctions). Nonetheless, from the system's point of view, there is no environment: like Mathews's journalist in the throes of a literary obsession, the autopoietic system, for all it 'knows,' is only following its own rules in maintaining a set of self-reinforcing, homeostatic relations. The map is the territory, and there is no 'outside' of the system – except, and this is the crucial formal feature that I have been pointing to throughout this essay, when the connections within the system reach sufficient density that it becomes possible to recognize this very circularity, and deparadoxize the constitutive distinction through a second-order observation. This recognition – the bootstrapping into consciousness itself – is what shifts the system (and Mathews's narrative) to a level of self-consciousness beyond solipsism and paradox.

The discovery that 'the main story of the journal is the journal itself' (191) is the trigger point, in Mathews, of narrative applied to itself. A new level of sustainability emerges when a referential notion (the journal) becomes an object in itself, an element that is made to migrate from 'outside' to 'inside' the journal. Only through such a reversal of target and source can the journal's system differentiate internally, and so eliminate its border with the outside, 'lived,' world. The price that Mathews's narrator pays for this recognition is, not surprisingly, silence. At the book's end, he is literally speechless, and his account of the final hours in his deterioration must be collected and presented (without interpretation) by a clinical psychiatrist at the place where he has been institutionalized. Who, then, has provided those journal entries up to the point where the journalist gave up control over his production? No answer is forthcoming, either from within the fiction or from the more general structure of autopoietic systems. Because the movement from level to metalevel is a difference that can have no actual equivalent in reality (the narrator cannot be both a character and the author of the book at the same time), the self-generated difference functions at a wholly mental level. But it is no less 'real' for that, because this is how the human mind works, its neurobiological construction based largely on 'self-perception and on self-established differences that have no actual equivalent in reality.'[29] *The Journalist* emerges as a cognitive fiction because cognition is itself fictive in nature.

We Have Never Been Hypertextual

The insanity that in Mathews's journalist derives from so many sources both personal and emotional can be displayed in moving detail only by being transformed to an equivalent – call it a textual – insanity in the very form of a writer's journal. This is the insanity of thinking that any author, or any single reading mind, can bring thought's content and conceptual categories fully onto the page; that contexts can be elaborated indefinitely, and independently of social or cultural supports; that thought's complexity can be imparted to the complexity of the page itself. *The Journalist*'s connundrum, I want to suggest, is structurally similar to problems inherent in all dreams of expansive archiving, including the dream of hypertext as put forward by Nelson and others.

If Bruno Latour has made the case that 'We Have Never Been Modern,' it is only fair, a full human generation after the introduction of hypertext, to ask whether writers on the Web have ever been hypertextual or whether the proliferation of platforms, commercial interfaces, and nonstandard pages have not in fact constricted the vast potential of the Web. Such media, possessing their own categories and sorting mechanisms, certainly make parts of the Web manageable mostly to consumers but for the most part these media can only get in the way of the reader's own ability to make selections and organize materials. More generally, according to Latour, the misapplication of rational categories to a field that is perhaps organized but not, in itself, rational, is the reason why the project of modernity has remained, and likely will remain, unfulfilled. Modernity, Latour argues, tries to establish clear categories separating subject and object, knowledge of things from power politics, but the attempt to organize experience through these categories can only produce pages and pages that document interfering and contradictory events. The documentary history of modernity is thus no less confused than the pages composed by Mathews's journalist – witness for example any page of any major newspaper where 'all of nature and all of culture get churned up every day' (2).

If by 'hypertext' we mean what its framers envisioned, we have certainly not begun to be hypertextual. Initially, in 1963 when Ted Nelson defined the terms, hypertext and hypermedia had little to do with linking as such; connectivity was not about the maximization of research efforts, and the Internet was not meant to be a global archive of everything, ever. Nelson, it is true, imagined a medium to end all media, where everything said becomes a kind of footnote to everything else. But he also, more interestingly and more basically, proposed that a text or media object, once established in a database, could be cited in its entirety – taken wholly, collaboratively and freshly, into a new composition. Each individual work then might be regarded not so much as an entry in an encyclopedia as a sample in a DJ's mix – except that what is sampled is the whole. A page capable of enacting the Internet's *recombinant* potential, a page that begins life only in circulation, takes other pages into its own data space, and goes on living only as long as it is cited by others – this is as yet unknown in the contemporary Web. In other words, the pages we have are already, for the most part, unknown because individual texts are too often experienced in isolation. Using the Internet not only to access individual pages but also to organize various pages in various media, is one way to make known what contemporary art and literature have already achieved. The work we have needs to come together, clash, and separate out into meaningful clusters. Rather than another new form or radical movement, we need instead a more robust hypertext collectivity, whose principles of selection, organization, and internal arrangement are themselves significant and their use subject to widespread agreement.

One can read Nelson's initial formulations, incidentally, by pointing a web browser to http://www.xanado.com. That is all it takes to enact a 'basic or chunk style hypertext,' one that comes on the screen when you reference a web address. But Nelson also talks about 'collateral hypertext,' 'stretchtext' that changes continuously through annotation and so forth, as well as an 'anthological' hypertext in which materials from all over come together, into an electronic book with a table of contents that can be revised. What I would wish for in a future web page is a deeply referential practice in which all of these modes work together: that convergence would help create a digital archive adequate for the widespread nostalgia that arguably drives the whole project of web construction – a nostalgia less for the past than for a present that is incompletely experienced. As Nelson said, we build new and more reliable forms of digital storage because 'thoughts and minds do not last.' And neither do pages – unless they keep on circulating within the media where thoughts and minds find expression.

Ever since its commercial introduction in the mid-1990s, much has been made of the Internet's mindlike qualities – its capacities, as a distributed network, for linking widely separated subnetworks together and doing associative work. The Web, it was claimed, was capable of remembering everything (for us); its storage capacities were essentially limitless, and information could be accessed in a moment by those who most needed it. What has been missing from the cognitive analogy is an appreciation of an actual, human mind's incredible powers of selection and attention, its capacity not only to remember but (much more often and more actively) to ignore and to forget – that is, to repress information not relevant to the project at hand, to filter out unwanted demands on our attention, and to fit what is remembered to new circumstances. Along with distributed memory, the mind has the serial ability to focus, moment by moment, on a continuing and extended present. The mind takes from past experience only what is needed (and it is never enough) to make sense of the present, to correlate what is seen, heard, felt, and read with patterns and schema that have been experienced before. However this process works (and whether the mind's work can even be known is itself a subject for debate), cognition clearly involves much more than information storage and retrieval. The information that a mind calls up changes what is experienced, and is itself changed by it – even as an artist's sketch is often less an external aid to memory than a means of creation. The sketch itself can always become an active element in the emerging composition, a transformation no less than a record of the artist's thought.

Likewise, past achievements in art and literature, instead of remaining static sources for citation, can be, and need to be, brought to the page as active elements in current compositions. 'Making it new,' in Ezra Pound's well-known dictate, but with an emphasis on the reader's making. Too much hypertext, and too much postmodern fiction and poetry has been characterized by an ironic 'citing' of past styles, treating established art forms apart from enabling life forms: an endlessly expanding context without culture. Collages without content, patchwork personalities, bricolage without constructive purpose, and corporate compilations are poor models for the present. When a skyscraper roof models the pattern of a Victorian chair; or when once-powerful, clashing symbols appear together as neutral hybrids (the relief decorating a mosque, a Christian cross), we have visible evidence that we are living too much in the mode of information. The past, in such art, is called on too freely, without any commitment to everyday life practice or overall world views embodied by the work. A literature, however, that takes responsibility for what it selects, that cites works whole, not piecemeal – such a literature goes beyond the exchange of information and makes a kind of intersubjectivity possible. Such a literature opens the chance (in Ted Nelson's words) once again to 'become a community of common access to a shared heritage.' This is, for me, a worthwhile conception for a future page. Realizing its potential would be less a matter of inventing forms than of more fully experiencing what we have, in the present moment when we have it (and not in some future archive).

NOTES

1 Sections of this essay were presented in the spring of 1999 at Spectatorship (Maastricht), in the summer of 2000 at The Future of the Page (Saskatchewan), and in the fall of 2000 at Bookends (Albany). 'The Last Archive' was read at the spring 2003 Electronic Literature Organization conference, Preserving, Archiving, and Disseminating (Santa Barbara). 'We Have Never Been Hypertextual' was my theme at the spring 2003 meeting of the American Comparative Literature Association (San Marcos). I have also taken a leaf from 'A Media Migration: Toward a Potential Literature,' the final chapter of my *Cognitive Fictions* (Minneapolis: University of Minnesota Press, 2002).

2 David Markson, *Reader's Block* (Normal, IL: Dalkey Archive Press, 1996), 15.

3 Alan Liu, 'Local Transcendence: Cultural Criticism, Postmodernism, and the Romanticism of Detail,' *Representations* 32 (1990): 75–113, describes a contemporary fascination with the richly embedded, infinitely contextual detail that

'allows us to model the scenes of human experience with more felt significance – more reality, more practicality, more aesthetic impact – than appears anywhere but on the postmodern version of romantic "nature": a screen (113).' A loss of cultural continuity produces a compensating fascination with *context*: this essay explores the consequences of such imaginary compensations in contemporary fiction and hypertext.

4 For this itemizaton of materials, I am indebted to Crystal Albert, a doctoral candidate working with the archive at the University of Washington, St Louis.

5 George P. Landow, *Hypertext: The Convergence of Contemporary Critical Theory and Technology* (Baltimore: Johns Hopkins University Press, 1992): 2.

6 Lance Olsen, 'Narrative Amphibiousness, or: Invitation to the Covert History of Possibility,' *electronic book review* (www.altx.com/ebr). Posted 04–24–03.

7 In a dissertation currently in progress, Dave Ciccorico usefully gathers together claims by numerous critics identifying hypertext and poststructuralist theory, starting with another Landow claim, that when designers of computer software examine the pages of *Glas* or *Of Grammatology*, they encounter a digitalized, hypertextual Derrida; and when literary theorists examine *Literary Machines*, they encounter a deconstructionist or post-structuralist Nelson' (*Hypertext*, 2). More recently, Ciccoricco continues,

> the literalist view gains support from theorists such as Ilana Snyder (1997) who claims that 'because hypertext *embodies* postmodern theories of the text, it makes it easier to study them [her emphasis]' (*EL* 119), and Marie-Laure Ryan, who suggests that 'the aspects of contemporary literary theory that find their fulfilment in hypertext hardly need explanation at all.' All of these perspectives resonate with [Richard] Lanham's contention that 'it is hard not to think that, at the end of the day, electronic text will seem the natural fulfillment of much current literary theory, and resolve many of its questions' (Lanham 130). Greco echoes these claims when she describes hypertext as 'a literal embodiment not only of postmodern fragmentation but also its possible resolution' (IV). In short, such a view posits that hypertext not only asks the same questions as contemporary critical theory, but also holds an unprecedented promise to answer them.

What in this essay I am calling the *reduction of theory to code* is clearly broad-based.

8 Roland Barthes, *S/Z: An Essay*, trans. Richard Miller (New York: Hill and Wang, 1974), 14.

9 Hanjo Berressem, introduction to *chaos/control: complexity [chaos theory and cultural production]*, edited and designed by Philipp Hofman (Hamburg: Lit Verlag, 2002), 29.

10 Douglas Coupland, *Polaroids from the Dead* (London: Flamingo, 1997), 180.

11 In 'The Shadow of an Informand: A Rhetorical Experiment in Hypertext' (http://www.pd.org/topos/perforations/perf3/shadow_of_info.html), Stuart Moul-

throp calls for a literary practice that would 'escape its shadow status and take on the full three-plus dimensions of hypertextual discourse' (31). This is another, earlier (but still unrealized) version of the processual and performative hypertext Berressem anticipates in *chaos/control: complexity*. I, however, doubt that literature can take on such multidimensionality and performativity and retain its cognitive richness. The danger is that complexity in performative media is all on the page itself, a medial complexity that obviates, rather than facilitates, verbal and conceptual complexity in the work of literature.

12 Harry Mathews, *The Journalist* (Normal, IL: Dalkey Archive Press, 1997), 3.

13 Stephanie Strickland, 'Poetry in the Electronic Environment,' *electronic book review* (www.altx.com/ebr/ebr9.htm) posted 04-15-97.

14 I am endebted to Jan Baetans for his extended analysis of the Federman/Burdick collaboration – published in the collection *Close Reading* (Leuven: Leuven University Press, 2004).

15 Stephanie Strickland, 'Poetry in the Electronic Environment.'

16 Stephanie Strickland, 'To Be Both in Touch and in Control,' *electronic book review* (www.altx.com/ebr/ebr9.htm) posted 04-15-97.

17 Jan van Looy, 'Authoring as Architecture: Toward a Hyperfiction Poetics' (unpublished Master's essay, University of Leuven, Belgium).

18 Ibid.

19 Lynne Tilman, 'To Find Words,' in *The Madame Realism Complex* (New York: Semiotext(e), 1992), 22.

20 Joseph Tabbi, *Cognitive Fictions* (Minneapolis and London: University of Minnesota Press, 2002).

21 Lynne Tilman, 'To Find Words,' 17.

22 Stephanie Strickland, *True North* (South Bend, IN: Notre Dame University Press, 1997; Hypertext published by Eastgate Systems), 13.

23 Richard Powers, *Galatea 2.2* (New York: Farrar, Straus and Giroux, 1998), 71–2.

24 Gerald M. Edelman and Giulio Tononi, *A Universe of Consciousness: How Matter Becomes Imagination* (New York: Basic Books, 2000), 77.

25 Harry Mathews, *The Journalist*, 9.

26 Lynne Tillman, 'Harry Mathews by Lynne Tillman,' *BOMB* 13 (winter 1988/89), rpt. *BOMB Interviews*, ed. Betsy Sussler (San Francisco: City Lights Books), 29–44.

27 Paul Harris, 'Harry Mathews's Al Gore Rhythms,' *electronic book review* (www.altx.com/ebr/ebr9.htm) posted 03-15-99.

28 Joel Slayton and Geri Wittig, 'Ontology of Organization as System' (paper presented in conjunction with the release of the C5 SoftSub data mining freeware application at *Ars Electronica' OpenX*, http://www.c5corp.com/softsub).

29 Dietrich Schwanitz, 'Systems Theory According to Niklas Luhman – Its Environment and Conceptual Strategies,' *Cultural Critique* (spring 1995): 140.

11 Virtually Human: The Electronic Page, the Archived Body, and Human Identity

Allison Muri

> Disputants, many of them writers, say to me, 'Words are still words – on a page, on a screen – what's the difference?' ... The changes are profound and the differences are consequential. Nearly weightless though it is, the word printed on a page is a thing. The configuration of impulses on a screen is not – it is a manifestation, an indeterminate entity both particle and wave, an ectoplasmic arrival and departure. The former occupies a position in space – on a page, in a book – and is verifiably there. The latter, once dematerialized, digitalized back into storage, into memory, cannot be said to exist in quite the same way. It has potential, not actual, locus ... And although one could argue that the word, the passage, is present in the software memory as surely as it sits on page x, the fact is that we register a profound difference. One is outside and visible, the other 'inside' and invisible. A thing and, in a sense, the idea of a thing.[1]

What changes when we no longer think of the page as 'real'? Since the arrival of television and the personal computer, the presentation of our ideas via configurations of electron beams rather than fixed upon a more palpable page has inspired repeated commentary upon not only how our texts will change, but also how we will change. Whether a lamentation for the loss of the texture and substance of the book, or an exultation for a supposed new traversing of boundaries and freedom from hierarchical structures, a predominant conclusion has been that we are altered by our media. For many writers, the 'terminal' page signals profound changes to our historical perspective, to our understanding and experience of community, to our cultural and democratic values, to our ability to teach our young to be moral and engaged citizens, to human agency and subjectivity, and even to human identity itself. Certainly, the material form of communication can shape cultural paradigms, what Harold Innis characterized as 'grooves which determine the channels of thought of readers and later writers,'[2] but does our media actually 'restructure consciousness,'[3] as early media theorists such as

Adorno, Ong, or McLuhan assumed and contemporary theorists have continued to do? (Adorno, for example, pessimistically claimed that the technologies of film and radio, which produce 'technicized forms of modern consciousness,' result in imagination's being 'replaced by a mechanically relentless control mechanism.')[4] Is the material of our communication indeed such a powerful determiner of human consciousness or identity as various writers following these early media theorists have claimed? Is the electronic page a technology that can effect, as some have argued, freedom and democracy or cultural decline? Is the page's influence on our culture more important than our culture's influence on the page? And to what extent are such queries determined by our own culture as professors and students of the humanities who are, not coincidentally, responsible for most of the speculation upon the materiality of our texts? Whether the materiality or immateriality of the page is a causative force in shaping human identity and society would seem impossible to determine conclusively. Indeed, it would seem impossible ever to arrive at a conclusion so profoundly informed by metaphors for the page as a body presenting a visible, material form of knowledge, which in turn both reflects and moulds the invisible, immaterial entity that is our rational self or consciousness. Speculation upon the immateriality of our electronic texts, therefore, is speculation about knowledge, morality, and education, and also about human embodiment, an ever-present debate about the old philosophical definitions of the physical body and its relationship to human 'spirit,' identity, or rational intelligence.

The page or computer network (material housing of the text) and the body (material housing of the self) are understood to be permeable, almost equivalent, in certain theories of electronic textuality. The so-called fusion of machine and human in networked communications systems has been imagined as a sign not only of a transition from book culture, but also of the impending redundancy or evolution of the human body. Michael Heim, for example, has written that 'at the computer interface, the spirit migrates from the body to a world of total representation. Information and images float through the Platonic mind without a grounding in bodily experience. You can lose your humanity at the throw of the dice.'[5] Sven Birkerts has similarly conflated book, body, and humanity in his discussion of 'the fate of the book': 'Maybe we are ready to embrace the pain of leaving the book behind'; he writes, 'maybe we are shedding a skin; maybe the meaning and purpose of being human is itself undergoing metamorphosis.'[6] For Arthur Kroker and Michael Weinstein, human intelligence is reduced to 'a circulating medium of cybernetic exchange'[7] in the networked text. The desire to become virtual, they suggested, promotes 'a radically diminished vision of human experience and of a disintegrated conception of the human good: for virtualizers, the good is ultimately that which disappears human subjectivity' (n.p.). Sadie Plant has described 'the cyborg you become' when jacked into the computer as 'more or less directly connected to your central nervous system; more or less hooked up to its own abstraction and the phase space in which you are both drawn out.'[8] Whatever this new entity is, she concluded, it will be 'post-human.' More optimistically and just as speculatively, Christopher Keep, claiming that there is 'more than a simple metaphorical relationship between hypertext and the body,'[9] suggests that by reading electronic texts we are 'engaged in a border experience, a moving back and forth across the lines which divide the human and the machine, culture and nature' (165). The reader thus 'becomes an extended space of production, a series of flows, energies, intensities, discontinuities, and desires which refuse the (en)closure of the normative body' (179). Surely there is a little rhetorical exaggeration in some of these musings but nevertheless my rude question is this: why is it assumed that human identity is so dependent upon the material page that when texts become electronic, consciousness or subjectivity flows out as if by osmosis?

Our texts, like our human identities, it seems to me, are unlikely to undergo radical revolution to reflect a new 'posthumanity': our texts, electronic or otherwise, are still engaged in very human themes of life, love, sex, and death; we still, as ever, make war and make love; there are still those who traverse boundaries, and those who erect them. There are and will continue to be good and bad citizens, good and bad students, avid and apathetic readers. Whatever difficult choices the computer age will necessitate, electronic textuality will not change these very human traits. What has changed are our analogies for the page as body and the text as thoughtful reflection: the simulacra produced by computer program and displayed upon the ethereal and immaterial page subverts conventional tropes for body, mind, and human spirit. The electronic environment has enabled us to understand our bodies as computational configurations of atoms and electrons, the mind as electrochemical charge and the body as DNA: the body no longer is the cathedral for the soul. The body is a biomechanical system, a complex machine which can defy death when updated with artificial components. The electronic environment has also destabilized a centuries-old system of inscribing and disseminating principles of critique, judgment, and morality through the stable and material texts sanctioned by our educational and religious institutions. The page is a tool for teaching but, in the electronic environment, anyone can be an author. And so, if we imagine the electronic environment as virtual not real, as fleeting and malleable not permanent and canonical, as technological and commercial not literary and artistic, or as permeable and rhizomatic not fixed and hierarchical, we imagine we might predict the future: mind-body and mind-text meet figuratively at the locus of the page, and if the materiality of the page changes – so the theory goes – so must we as humans. However, a significant and generally unacknowledged part of this discussion about the incipient changes to humanity is concerned with the incipient changes to the humanities and liberal arts, and with the increasing influence of the sciences of material technologies.

Some Conceptual Frameworks: The Electronic Page and the Book of Life

What do we mean by 'electronic page'? 'Page,' of course, comes from the Latin *pagina*, a column of writing in a scroll. The display of text and image on a computer screen in a horizontal or vertical format similar to the dimensions of our traditional paper pages, which we read by 'scrolling' up or down, corresponds quite closely to the traditional page. Indeed, the style sheets and html markup used to create web pages specifically replicate certain visual aspects of the printed page such as colour, text formatting, and image placement. Virtual reality displays could be considered a form of page as well, since the viewer scrolls through the apparently three-dimensional text of imaginary space, viewing images and reading texts that are written into the program. The electronic page is both database and bits, potentially far more malleable and responsive to user input than the paper page, but it is nevertheless a form of page that displays the artefacts of human creativity. The term 'electronic' describes the flow of electronic charge that results in generating, sending, receiving, storing, and displaying the data that comprises a computer text: the text is in electronic form when bombarded onto certain types of screens to form images, or when it is transferred through circuits, or stored temporarily in random access memory (the use of 'electronic' to describe computer-mediated texts, however, is slightly problematic since such a text may be transferred as sound waves, or stored as physical bumps etched into the surface of a CD). The electronic page is both a visible display legible to humans, and invisible machine-readable bits that are the information for the transmission and storage, content, layout, markup, and programmed functional capabilities of the visible page. This invisible text written on the main store of a computer is divided into manageable sections called pages, and a similar amount of data or part of a program is also called a page. The electronic page is markedly different from the paper page, but whether in fact a page is a 'thing' if the data is not printed on a material substrate is a philosophical question with which I will not trouble myself here. When I write of the computer-mediated text as page I refer to a text that may be displayed visibly onscreen in a familiar format, but which is also necessarily invisible binary data written onto the surface of a computer disk or tape. The electron beams patterning the screen through a shifting flux of energy may be rewritten, lost, or recovered in moments, it may be stored as database and generated dynamically for display depending on the reader's input, but the electronic page is nevertheless a text inscribed through human ingenuity onto the physical elements of the world in which we live.

This very invisibility, changeability, and seeming instability creates the illusion of a new form of human consciousness that is permeated by, and permeates, the computer network. There is a history to this image of the mind, however: the material page has been traditionally understood as representing the human form as repository for knowledge, memory, creativity, and imagination; likewise, the human mind has traditionally been presented as a writing surface. Our pages and our bodies have long converged in metaphor. Indeed, a page has a body, a header, and a footer; it might contain an appendix, or index (from the Latin meaning 'indicator' or more specifically 'forefinger'), or footnotes, or frontispiece (from the late Latin *frontispicium*, from *frōns*, 'forehead' and *spic-*, denoting 'see'); it might be part of a chapter (from the Latin *caput*, head); it may be part of a manuscript (from *manus*, hand), or it may be bound into a book with a spine (and the electronic page has access to memory). A material surface with boundaries, edges, and margins, for centuries the page has been made of skin, and bound in skin. And for centuries, the body has been metaphorized as book. Andreas Vesalius, known for revolutionizing the pedagogy and study of anatomy, taught that not ancient books but the human body itself should be the primary text and ultimate authority in the study of human structure. Today that tradition of the body as the Book of Nature is continued in digital anatomy projects.

While the body is a book to be read, the mind has been imagined as a page to be inscribed. The analogies we create to describe the human mind tend to reflect the technology of writing that we use to inscribe our thoughts. Socrates considered and rejected an analogy for memory as a block of wax that holds the impressions of sensory experience. Seventeenth-century writers such as Pierre Gassendi, Robert Burton, and Thomas Hobbes reiterated Aristotle's description of the mind in *De anima* as a blank writing tablet or *tabula rasa*. Shakespeare made use of the analogy of the mind as writing surface in Hamlet's promise: 'I'll wipe away all trivial fond records' from memory, he proclaims, to better remember the words of the ghost, 'Within the book and volume of my brain' (I. v. 103). John Locke described the original state of human understanding (that 'most elevated faculty of the soul') as a surface clear of writing. 'Let us then suppose the mind to be, as we say, white paper, void of all characters, without any ideas,' he wrote in 'Essay Concerning Human Understanding.' Locke's work uses the page as trope for the inscription of both rational thought and morality. In describing 'how men commonly come by their principles,' Locke suggested that children 'grow up to the dignity of principles in religion or morality' through the doctrines professed by their caregivers, instilled into the unprejudiced understanding, 'for white paper receives any characters.' This inscription of morality as upon a blank page evokes and reinforces a system of education and morality through the page itself.

The page on the screen thus becomes emblematic of a moral shift. Take, for example, Vivian Sobchack's early concept of the hazards of electronic texts in *Materialities of Communications*, a collection of essays concerned with media technologies, the body, and transitions within the academic field of the humanities. The 'binary superficiality of electronic space,' she wrote, 'distorts and liberates the activity of the consciousness' from the body.[10] Arguing that the electronic text or virtual reality creates a 'quasi-disembodied state' (100) and 'denies or prosthetically transforms' (104) the body, she warned that the resulting 'lack of specific interest and grounded investment in the human body and enworlded action ... could well cost us all a future' (104). If we become 'merely ghosts in the machine,' she suggested, we 'can ignore AIDS, homelessness, hunger, torture, and all the other ills the flesh is heir to' (106). Clearly, there is an element of hyperbole here, and my intent is not to point out the obvious embodiment of the computer user. These images encapsulate a common theme in such analyses of computer technology: electronic texts result in both disembodiment and immorality. In such works the texts of technology – texts unedited and unauthorized through any traditional system of determining literary excellence – are represented as replacing real humanity with unfeeling human-machines, and making redundant not only the body but also literature and all those creative endeavours that instil morals into the human psyche. K. Ludwig Pfeiffer's introduction to *Materialities of Communications* summarizes the complexity of the position:

> Certainly, one would like to know what kind of autodynamic wirings or analogues of them there are – if there are any – that test perception, guide behavior, evaluate experience, caring little or nothing for the pathetic semantic textures we weave around them. There are the brain, the hormones, and the other circuits that produce, in ways still fairly obscure, electric and chemical binarisms. But if it is one of the deadlocks of brain research that the steps from there to what still appears as meaningful cultural worlds *are extremely hard to take and have yet to be taken*, it behoves 'literary' people (like most of those in this volume) not to abandon prematurely some striving toward the 'nobleness of life' ... even if it consists only in 'literature.'[11]

The relationship between technology, human embodiment, and morals is complicated not only by a history of metaphors for body, text, and material page in an older tradition, but also by the growing prevalence of science and technology as more 'useful' disciplines than the study of literature.

While the analogies between page and body are ancient and associated with a tradition of education that values the spiritual side of humanity, the convergence of text, body, and mind as code in the electronic page or digital archive is more recent, and associated with the rise of the computational sciences. Vannevar Bush's article 'As We May Think,' which described in theory what would be realized in computer hypertext documents ('an enlarged intimate supplement to his memory') appeared in the July 1945 issue of *The Atlantic Monthly*. In 1948 Bush's colleague Norbert Wiener published a manifesto for the new technoscience of cybernetics, which explained both organic and machine processes as communications systems. As Lily E. Kay has noted, Wiener and Bush had worked on a project together to solve partial differential equations with computers in 1940, which in turn influenced Wiener's conception of future computing machinery as an analogy between electronic computing and the mechanics of the nervous system.[12] Wiener's theories conflated both machine and text as symbolic structures of the human body: the chapter entitled 'The Individual as Word' in his popularization of the theory of cybernetics emphasized the metaphor of human body as the Book of Life. 'Earlier accounts of individuality were associated with some sort of identity of matter, whether of the material substance of the animal or the spiritual substance of the human soul,' he wrote. 'We are forced nowadays to recognize individuality as something which has to do with continuity of pattern, and consequently with something that shares the nature of communication.'[13] There was significant debate in the United States about the applicability of Wiener's information theory to genetics, but the metaphors of human life as text were nevertheless present and became, as Kay demonstrates, dominant and potent metaphors 'in the general conceptualization of heredity as a genetic program, a scriptural technology.'[14] While representation of the body as information is a postwar phenomenon, however, the analogy of human bodies as textual, written documents was a very old one, and the image of the human body's creation as text was widespread. Indeed, some years earlier, in publishing their discovery in 1938 that the human genetic material was DNA in the form of long chains, Leeds researchers Astbury and Bell had borrowed the old metaphor to configure human life itself as text written on a scroll:

> Knowing what we know now from X-ray and related studies of the fibrous proteins ... how they can combine so readily with nucleic acid molecules and still maintain the fibrous configuration, it is but natural to assume, as a first working hypothesis at least, that they form the long scroll on which is written the pattern of life. No other molecules satisfy so many requirements.[15]

This discovery marks the beginning of a shift in the understanding of the human body as God's immutable text, which William Harvey had characterized as 'Nature's book ... so open, and legible' in his seventeenth-century text describing the mechanics of animal generation.[16] With the transcription of the invisible elements of the body made increasingly possible through technology and computers, we can not only 'know' but also rewrite or program the body as well as characteristics of mind, identity, or consciousness.

The electronic page or digital archive is a technological condensation of text and body, human consciousness, and human reproduction. On the one hand, old metaphors for physical body and page suggest that the death of the book parallels the redundancy of humanity. As the page becomes immaterial so is the self depicted as immaterial, flickering in a state of virtuality, our humanity snagged on the edge of the screen separating world from data. On the other hand, the idea of the conscious mind freed from the body's limitations suggests the fulfilment of a longstanding desire for transcendence, of which the electronic archive is a secularized version.

The Electronic Page and Human Spirit

The relationship of the material page and the computer text to human identity is complicated by the various terms used by writers to connote vastly different notions of that unnameable, unlocatable, and unmeasurable quotient that gives us our humanity: since writing began we have questioned where that aspect of our selves we call identity, consciousness, mind, rational thought, soul, spirit, or ghost resides. We have wondered whether it is immaterial or material, part and product of our bodies, or separate and distinct from gross matter. This very old question was a defining characteristic of early cyberpunk fiction that envisioned the consciousness as code living on without the body. William Gibson's *Mona Lisa Overdrive,* the third and last of the series that inaugurated the phrase 'data made flesh,' presents the ghost in the machine as a form of sentience akin to immortality. At the novel's end, Angela Mitchell, a cyborg being whose brain has been engineered and programmed to jack into cyberspace without hardware, is killed. Her consciousness is transferred to a powerful biochip called an aleph or 'soul-catcher.' Angie as sentient code inhabits a high resolution, three-dimensional virtual space along with the other inhabitants of cyberspace, 'ghosts,' artificial intelligences, and her lover, Bobby (The Count) Newmark, who has entered that world between life and death by programming his own consciousness from his decaying flesh into the aleph biochip. The representations of ourselves and our environment, evolving from page to microchip to biochip, reiterate an old metaphor of capturing the soul or spirit in the text. In a remediation of the lines from Shakespeare's Sonnet XVIII – 'So long as men can breathe, or eyes can see/ So long lives this, and this give life to thee' – Angela and Bobby are immortalized in the electronic text as long as the aleph is provided with a source of power.

The dream of the human spirit as coded consciousness free from the constraints of the body is not only a literary construct but also appears in theoretical discourse in both the humanities and the sciences. In a 1996 lecture Toshiba Professor of Media Arts and Sciences at MIT Marvin Minsky claimed that in the near future it will be possible to transfer human memories, intact, to disk.[17] Also in 1996 head of British Telecom's research lab Peter

Cochrane described a technology to capture human thoughts on a single silicon chip which he dubbed a Soul Catcher. 'Despite specialisation and an exponential growth in knowledge,' he wrote, 'we still see people of outstanding ability able [to] understand and contribute more than the average. Unfortunately, they die and their expertise is lost for all time. The question is, can we capture their expertise and presence for future generations? Do they have to die 100%?'[18] Somewhat tongue-in-cheek, *Business Week* later described the future technology as being able to make a rather straightforward decision by the year 2050 'to evacuate your biological body and take up residence in silicon circuits.'[19] The Soul Catcher would comprise 'wireless links to microsensors under your scalp and in the nerves that carry all five signals' to record 'organized, online archives of everything that happens,' (so described by D. Raj Reddy, a professor of computer science at Carnegie Mellon University). The article concludes, 'For people who chose not to inhabit silicon, virtual immortality could still ease the sense of futility that now haunts many people. Individuals would know their lives would not be forgotten, but would be preserved as a thread in a multimedia quilt that keeps a permanent record of the human race. And future generations would have a much fuller understanding of the past.' Much like the genetic 'map' that makes our cellular information live on generation after generation, this technology would purportedly transcribe consciousness by mapping the sequence of experience that is written upon our minds. The four-letter code of genetics, data storage miniaturization, microprocessor-controlled prosthetics, artificial intelligence, the global grid of communication/control systems – the fusion of our understanding of our own bodies with the virtual representation of life onscreen, all problematize what were once clear conceptual boundaries between categories of body-mind and text.

Jean Baudrillard has depicted our electronic media as stealing the consciousness from the body: 'As soon as behavior is crystallized on certain screens and operational terminals, what's left appears only as a large useless body, deserted and condemned. The real itself appears as a large useless body.' Individual consciousness he characterized as a pilot disengaged from the grounding of body, community, and reality: 'each person sees himself at the controls of a hypothetical machine, isolated in a position of perfect and remote sovereignty, at an infinite distance from his universe of origin,' while the body then 'appears simply superfluous, basically useless in its extension.'[20] For Baudrillard, the world of freely available information is an obscene one: 'today there is a whole pornography of information and communication,' he suggested, 'that is to say of circuits and networks, a pornography of all functions and objects in their readability, their fluidity, their availability ...' Obscenity begins, he explains, when 'everything is exposed to the harsh and inexorable light of information and communication' (130). Baudrillard's play on the word 'obscene' as the movement away from the real body in real space also emphasizes a sense of indecency and moral offensiveness. And while claiming that 'this is not necessarily a negative value judgment,' he wrote of the disappearance of passion in the world of information – of hazard, chance, and vertigo as opposed to the passion, investment, desire, and expression of a previous era. Similarly, in his 1983 *Simulations*, Baudrillard criticized computer simulation as a spiritual crisis: the real, he explained, 'is produced from miniaturised units, from matrices, memory banks and command models.'[21] Could 'the divinity,' he wondered, be 'volatilized into simulacra,' in the 'visible machinery of icons being substituted for the pure and intelligible Idea of God?' (8) In Baudrillard's successive phases of the image, 'the reflection of a basic reality' is good: 'the representation is of the order of sacrament'; while the second order, which 'masks and perverts a basic reality,' inaugurates the age of simulacra and simulation and is 'an evil appearance – of the order of malefice' (11–12). Baudrillard's appraisal was from a position of despair over simultaneous changes to the signs for both our arts and our bodies. 'Digitality is [the] metaphysical principle (the God of Leibniz) and DNA its prophet' for the 'universe of structures and binary opposites' (103) we have created, he suggested, finally concluding that simulation has damaged both our mental health and art itself, the very expression of our humanity:

> Art is dead, not only because its critical transcendence is gone, but because reality itself ... has been confused with its own image ... simulation pushes us close to the sphere of psychosis ... The cool universe of digitality has absorbed the world of metaphor and metonymy. The principle of simulation wins out over the reality principle just as over the principle of pleasure. (151–2)

Baudrillard's critique of 'the convergence of genetics and linguistics' (107) stands in direct opposition to the more ecstatic predictions of how the digital text will transform the human identity or spirit; but in many cases these oftentimes implausible claims may be reducible to the author's stance 'for' or 'against' the authority of science and technology.

The Archived Body

> Floating through the skull and heart and lungs of Alexander Tsiaras's world we see every detail of our knowledge about the body and our ability to measure and define its function. We see here a body utterly and vividly intact. Only the soul has been removed ... whatever else is to be found in this collaboration between an executed criminal and an artist we are somehow deftly aided in the ancient search for the soul. It is the oddest of ironies. The atomized, digitized body of Joseph Paul Jernigan reconstituted and imbued with a mesmerizing beauty and

realism is as good an argument for the tangibility of the soul as one can find in this cheerless age of cause and effect.[22]

A living virtual reality ... originates with the merger of genetics and simulation where blood turns into electricity ... [It] functions in the time of recombinant culture, whose sociology is based on splicing, cloning and sequencing ... The vanishing body has been resuscitated, just short of vacuity, as the circulating body. The body has become a circulating medium of exchange, coursing through the mediascape ... The perverted image (perverted as image exchange-value) and the ambivalent sign (fanatical and cynical) are the effects of the dependence of the mediascape on 'biological' bodies as image resources and image actualizers ... Welcome to the post-God era.[23]

As the body's most invisible elements and processes have become more legible and better understood, the page has become more complex and immaterial. Consider the difference, for example, between a page in which the ink under your fingertips is raised so you can actually feel the patterns of letters and a page that exists only in random access memory until it is saved to a mysterious and invisible position on the hard drive as magnetized bits – a pattern of ones and zeros decipherable only by the machine. And consider the difference between William Harvey's startling announcement in 1616 of his discovery of blood circulation and the discovery in 1989 by J.R. Riordan et al. that the majority of people suffering from cystic fibrosis have a small mutation in one microscopic DNA fragment, which causes three out of one gene's 250,000 base pairs (A-T or G-C) to be missing (that is, three out of some three billion base pairs in our DNA), a deletion that in turn results in the loss of one amino acid – one molecule – out of the 1,480 in the protein for which that gene is a 'blueprint.' Our bodies and our texts have become similarly coded bits (1,0 encodes machine texts, while A,C,G,T codes body texts) but conceptually our understanding of body and text has been reversed. The white page with its black ink that has always been visible and accessible in the codex book is now hidden, mysterious, and invisible bits accessible to and understood by only the masters of technology. The components of living bodies, the creation of both life and thought that were once hidden and mysterious, in the human body are now magnified, diagrammed, documented, transcribed, archived by the masters of technology. At the same time, the body becomes metaphorized as a text to be read, transcribed, and re-written. This fundamental change in our understanding of the body as page is illustrated most tellingly by current metaphors for study of the body no longer as Book of Nature authored by God but now as genetic blueprints coauthored by humans – the published, bound, and immutable work versus the page describing the plans for a work yet to be finished. Thus Vesalius wrote of God the 'Author of the human fabric,' in his *Epitome* (1543) 'Concerning the Organs Which Minister to the Propagation of the Species.' In contrast, Victor Spitzer and David Whitlock, directors of the Visible Human Project datasets, subtitled their *Atlas of the Visible Human Male* as 'Reverse Engineering of the Human Body.'[24] Similarly, the U.S. Department of Energy's overview of the Human Genome Project, 'To Know Ourselves,' introduces the human genome as 'The Recipe for Life.'[25] In the rhetoric of body as archive, the notion of media theorists that the natural human body has become redundant exists in direct contrast to the medical versions of its centrality.

The transcriptions of the human body through the Visible Human Project (VHP) and the Human Genome Project, both stored in the National Library of Medicine (NLM) at the National Institutes of Health (NIH) in Bethesda, Maryland, are the most comprehensive archival projects in medical history. The Visible Human Project is the outcome of the National Library of Medicine's long range planning in 1986, which established the library's goal of 'building and disseminating medical image libraries much the same way it acquires, indexes, and provides access to the biomedical literature.'[26] The project effectively began in 1989, when the library's ad hoc Planning Panel on Electronic Image Libraries made the recommendation that the NLM build 'a digital image library of volumetric data representing a complete, normal adult male and female.'[27] Begun in 1990, the U.S. Human Genome Project involves the identification of all 60–80,000 genes in human DNA and the sequences of the 3 billion bases that make up human DNA, the storage of this information in databases, and the development of tools for the data. The datasets resulting from both projects are the human body paginated, represented as alphanumeric code, digitized, pixelated, and available online in the National Library of Medicine's electronic collections (www.nlm.nih.gov/databases/databases.html).

The Human Genome Project, like the Visible Human Project, is a process of making the interior workings of the body visualized, archived, and legible (that is, capable of being read or deciphered). The metaphor of transcription, the analogy between human life and text, is one that has dominated the rhetoric of human DNA since its discovery. In 1967 microbiologist Robert Sinsheimer, a key figure in the inception of the Human Genome Project, wrote *The Book of Life* in which he commented, 'In this book are instructions, in a curious and wonderful code, for making a human being. In one sense – on a sub-conscious level – every human being is born knowing how to read this book in every cell of his body' (5). The metaphor of body as book appears frequently in descriptions of the Human Genome Project. A National Human Genome Research Institute press release from 1988 equates books and life, for example, where 'changes in the spelling of the DNA letters can increase your chances of developing an illness, protect you from getting sick, or predict the way your body will handle medicines.'[28] Similarly, the statement published by the National Center for Biotechnology Information emphasised the Human Genome Project as a 'working draft' of the 'book of life.'[29]

The metaphor of the human as text informs not only promotional literature written for the public, but also actual practices. The library information for gene sequences as published documents indicates strikingly how much our bodies are actually and not only metaphorically perceived as pages of text. Searching for 'chromosome 7' through GenBank at The National Center for Biotechnology website (www.ncbi.nlm.nih.gov) will result in a number of links to various sequences catalogued just as any other text in our library systems. The descriptor for accession number AC073349 describes the document as a 'working draft sequence' of a particular chromosome segment. This tiny portion of our bodies written in its four-letter alphabet is accessible online as a long scrolling document, approximately fifty single-spaced pages when printed. Writing the human body as page allows human technicians to position themselves as its authors. The catalogued segment has a title, 'The sequence of Homo sapiens clone,' and an author, R.H. Waterston. Another example is the National Institute of Health's patent on a cell line from a Hagahai person from Papua New Guinea, disclaimed five years after the initial application and only after much public criticism, in 1996. The claim of United States Patent No. 5,397,696 included the names of several 'Inventors'; the 'Title of Invention' was listed as 'Papua New Guinea human T-lymphotropic virus.' When the reproduction of our bodies, the most basic process of our creation, is described as a process of writing, and our 'code' as being 'transcribed' in our cellular DNA, genetic reproduction is seen as a process of writing, as program (from Latin *programma*, public notice; from Greek *prographein*, to set forth as a public notice: *pro-*, before + *graphein*, to write). The program – the code written to produce both the computer text and the body text – is the means to not only prolonging but also rewriting the fate of a human life.

This transcription of body as text is seen as a threat to our humanity – not merely because we are taking ownership of human bodies in potentially exploitative ways, but also because the apparent literalizing of body as page is seen as displacing the position and value of human 'spirit.' This trepidation is perhaps best represented by the varying commentary upon the Visible Man archive for the National Library of Medicine. Creating this archive was a process of mapping by MRI and CT scans the fresh cadaver of executed murderer Joseph Paul Jernigan, freezing the body so the tissue offered the same resistance to the saw as did the bone, quartering the body and positioning it in blue gelatin, and finally milling away the surfaces of the frozen blocks from toes to head at 4 mm intervals and digitally photographing each newly exposed surface. At a resolution of .33 mm, the raw data totals 15 gigabytes, or twenty-three CDs, as the literature frequently explains (the anonymous Visible Woman dataset, at higher resolution, is about 40 gigabytes in size).

One of the most significant changes in the study of anatomy represented by the dissection of Jernigan is that the body has been cut not to reveal gross physical units such as a given muscle, organ, or tissue, but rather in cross-section as fine leaves of body. These digitized leaves of Jernigan's body now exist in the form of an enormous and readable book. Various 'fly-through' animations of the sliced body available for public viewing on the Internet are created in the same way that flip-page animations are: a sequence of consecutive images shown in rapid succession are interpreted by the eye as movement (see, for example, the link 'From head to toe: an animated trip through the Visible Human male cryosections' at the 'Visible Human Project® Gallery,' www.nlm.nih.gov/ research/visible/visible_gallery.html). The NPAC/ OLDA Visible Human Viewer (www.dhpc.adelaide.edu.au/projects/ vishuman/VisibleHuman.html) is a Java applet that allows the viewer to place something akin to a bookmark at any point on the body and then download that particular page as an axial, coronal, or saggital plane of the sliced body (fig. 11.1). This viewer, in turn, resulted in the publication of a physical 120–page, full-colour book, *Head 2 Heads: A Flipbook of Slices of Life*, by Optical Toys (2000), which 'takes you through the human skull' (www.opticaltoys.com/head2heads.html). Not only the visual display but also the rhetoric of the body as a book appears frequently in the project literature: for example, project officer Michael Ackerman described one of the problems with the archival material as the absence of labelling for the various systems and organs of the digitized body: 'For a librarian, this is very unsettling. It's like having books lying all over the place not indexed or catalogued.'[30] The liner notes to *Body Voyage*, the CD-ROM published by Southpeak Interactive and featuring renderings of the data by photojournalist Alexander Tsiaras emphasize that the data of Jernigan's body comprises 'over a raw terabyte of data – the equivalent of five million typewritten pages.' *Life* magazine's feature article, 'The Visible Man,' comments: 'Jernigan had no idea that his body would itself become a textbook.'[31] The fold-out article 'A Technicolor Gatefold of the Digital Man' in this issue featuring Tsiaras's work is labelled 'The Whole Body Catalogue' and claims that Tsiaras used '15 gigabytes of computer data from a real body – equal to 20 million typewritten pages – to compose this picture' (38).

Whether the electronically archived body is equivalent to five million or twenty million pages, what is most prized about the collection is its legibility. The systematized visibility of this body as text provoked comment by supporters on Jernigan's 'immortality'[32] through being transcribed as alphanumeric text, as if in imitation of the poets' conceit of achieving immortality through the lines inscribed upon a page. Simultaneously, the body digitized and transcribed as computer text has generated some critical commentary on the violation of transcribing human embodiment. Catherine Waldby, for example, writes that 'the violence of anatomy is the violence of a particular

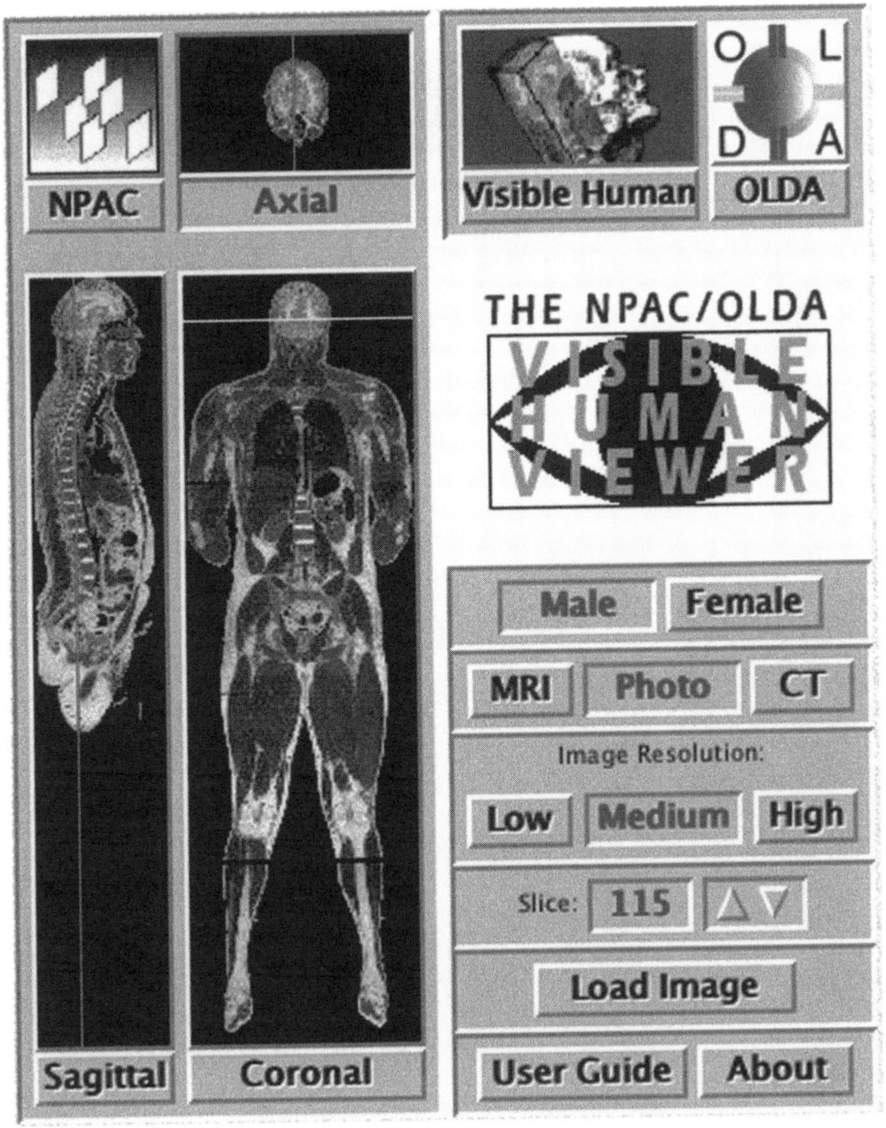
NPAC
Axial
Visible Human
OLDA
O L D A
THE NPAC/OLDA
VISIBLE
HUMAN
VIEWER
Male
Female
MRI
Photo
CT
Image Resolution:
Low
Medium
High
Slice:
115
Load Image
Sagittal
Coronal
User Guide
About

Figure 11.1. NPAC/OLDA Visible Human Viewer.

kind of writing practice, a set of techniques that destroy the fleshly body along particular analytic lines in order to inscribe its trace in various knowledge media.'[33] Neal Curtis suggests that, like Franz Kafka's 'In the Penal Colony,' the VHP 'reinforces the submission of the body to the law.'[34] Curtis's complaint has to do with the VHP's 'confusion of a "complete" body with an *anatomically* complete body' (263) – that the people involved do not recognize the dataset as a product of a 'techno-medical' or 'techno-scientific' discourse (261, 263). Such procedures can return a 'form of life' to the body that is determined by those technical discourses, he continues: 'These techniques can reanimate the body and rebirth it, but can life be reduced to a simple reconstruction of motility? Clearly not' (263). In the Visible Man there is 'cruor,' the blood of wounds, but no 'sanguis,' the blood of life (262–3), Curtis explains. True enough: these are images of a dead body. However, the fact that these images present no 'exposure to sensible presence' (263) or 'the irreducible vitality of sanguis' (264) does not adequately demonstrate, for me, 'the universalism and determinism of such a discourse'(263) – as if technology and science are realms populated by people who do not recognize difference, who are complicit in a project of 'silencing indeterminacy' (264). These criticisms, as inflated as the rhetoric of praise mentioned above, rarely acknowledge the benefits of such technology to human lives.[35] Nor do they adequately address the fact that both executed criminals and people who donate their bodies for research have been dissected, studied, and reproduced as image for centuries prior to this particular technology. Rather, such arguments seek to demonstrate that inscription of the body through computer technology is a debasement of humanity.

Writing on the 'electronic abbatoir' though not specifically referring to the VHP, Kroker and Weinstein describe archivalists as 'vampiring organic flesh, and draining its fluids into cold streams of telemetry' where archived body parts are 'violently detached from the body organic ... disguised in the binary functionality of data and pooled into larger circulatory flows.' The aim of this biopower, they suggest, is 'the transformation of human experience into the dull codes of binary functionality.'[36] The 'violent metastasis that is cyberculture,' is in direct opposition to a spiritual life: 'In the beginning was the Word,' they write, 'but in the end there is only the data byte' (154). Waldby similarly explains in her book about the VHP that

> after all, when a body can be rendered into data and thus cross the interface into the digital afterlife, what prevents the process from effecting some form of reversal, the digital revenant who rematerialises in real space? ... the kind of cyberpace summoned up by the VHP connotes the supernatural ... an afterlife of the abject, the corpse which cannot or will not relinquish vitality ... like those other animate corpses, vampires and zombies, to be vitalised by the will of another, actively prevented from a full death.[37]

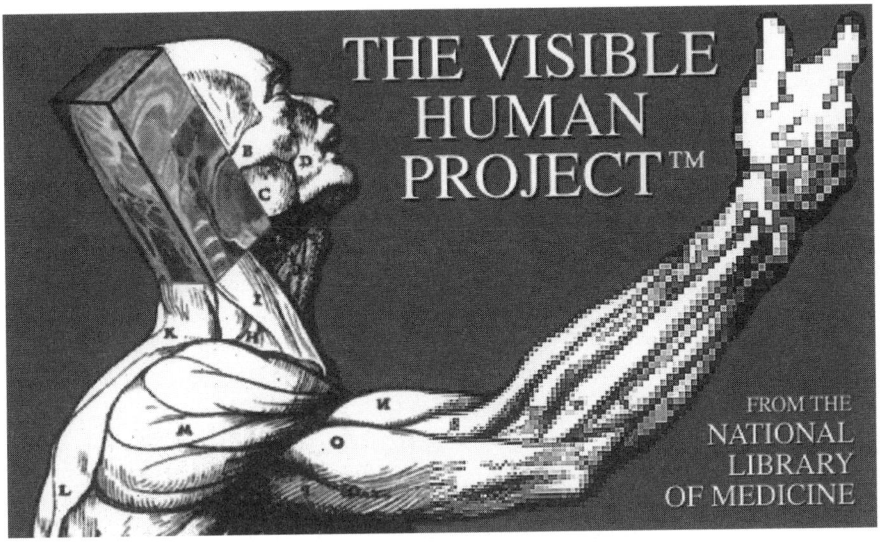
THE VISIBLE
HUMAN
PROJECT™
FROM THE
NATIONAL
LIBRARY
OF MEDICINE

Figure 11.2. Visible Human Project logo.

The suggestion, again, is that the inscription of technology interferes with human spirit. 'For the biomedical imagination,' she writes, 'this arresting and deferral of death might count as a gain on the side of life ... [which is] another step in the gradual mastery of matter, bringing it closer to the negentropy of programmable matter, the assimilation of all materiality by the metaphysics of code' but the VHP also seems to create 'a new form of death-in-life, a new and horrifying destination for our own failing bodies, and a place from which they might return in uncanny form' (155–6). However disturbing we might find such treatment of dead bodies as archive, however, we need to acknowledge that these texts are ultimately only images, numbers, and letters displayed on a dynamic electronic page – no matter how 'animated' they may seem. The rhetoric of a ghastly humanity floating through cyberspace and coming to life again as soulless vampires or zombies here again centres upon who we would prefer to metaphorize as 'author' of humanity.

Conclusion: Of Books and Spirit

As the self-proclaimed 'greatest contribution to anatomy since Vesalius' 1543 publication of De Humani Corporis Fabrica,'[38] the Visible Human Project has developed a logo incorporating an illustration from Vesalius's text (figs. 11.2 and 11.3). The image depicts a history of the various imaging techniques used to 'read' the human body and represent it as text – from lettering

Figure 11.3. Second Plate of the Muscles, from Vesalius's *De humani corporis fabrica libri septem*. Thomas Fisher Rare Book Library, University of Toronto.

discrete muscle groups to representing all structures as pixels and voxels. It also serves to emphasise the project's subject as defying mortality. Flayed, frozen, sliced, and digitized, the body in this image is that of a handsome-faced and well-muscled man in a classical pose, gesturing as if in exposition, vital and full of life despite lacking skin and a good portion of his brain. In contrast, the final panel of Vesalius's anatomized body gradually stripped of parts and life spirit shows the same subject slumped in an attitude of dejection (fig. 11.4).[39] In all likelihood a condemned criminal as well, this cadaver's mortality and sin are subtly emphasised by the rope supporting or hanging the body by the neck. Vesalius's sequence of images showing the slow loss of life spirit seem to function as an explicitly moral reminder to the early modern reader of the inevitable decay of the flesh – or that the punishment for the sinner is eternal death.

The Visible Human Project logo, in contrast, depicts life with a moral,

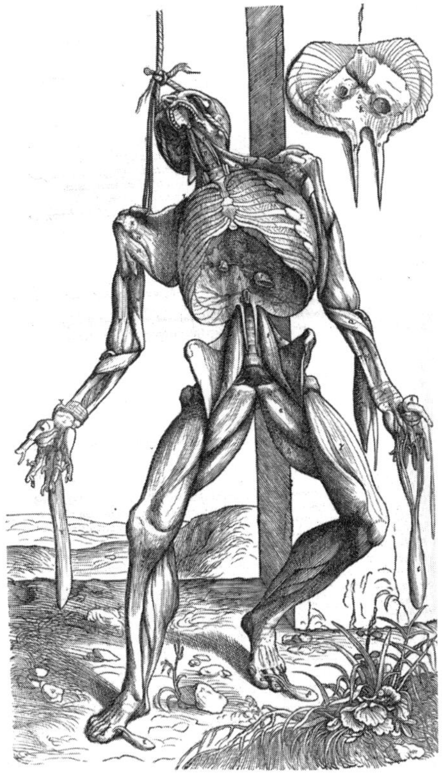

Figure 11.4. Seventh Plate of the Muscles, from Vesalius's *De humani corporis fabrica libri septem*. Thomas Fisher Rare Book Library, University of Toronto.

almost spiritual, imperative conferred by the gift of the body to medical science, as expressed by numerous writers and perhaps most enthusiastically by John Hockenberry who claims that the convicted murderer Jernigan gave his body not only to science, 'but to humanity as well,' concluding, 'Whatever tragic legacy Joseph Paul Jernigan left in life, in death he has found grace.' The slogan on this page of the *Body Voyage* codex, 'Even Lazarus never looked this good,' attests to the desire in popular media – so much at odds with the theorists critical of the supposed redundancy of the body – to imbue the body archived in the cybertext with a soul, with immortality, with a high moral purpose. The slogan also attests to the fact that sophisticated technology has increasingly challenged the established authority of 'God's Book': the biblical story of Lazarus and religious faith ('he that believeth in me, though he were dead, yet shall he live' John 11: 25) is here overshadowed by the suggestion that Jernigan has been raised from the dead through his gift to science and the subsequent technological rendering by human authors. While the eighteenth-century criminal was judged by God and sentenced to eternal punishment, the twentieth-century convict's salvation is conferred by science and technology. The spirit of the cyborg is at stake in the environment of the electronic page because life and death, previously the realm of God or Nature, now are in the realm of the human-authored page.

In his introduction to the 1994 *Queen's Quarterly* issue entitled *The End of the Book?* Boris Castel writes of the 'intimate reader/writer exchange, now under assault from the increasingly noisy signals of our surrounding electronic web,' claiming that 'the printed page and circuit-driven technologies are not kindred, but powerful antagonists. Human intelligence and creativity will be the losers in our Faustian pact with an increasingly seductive electronic devil.'[40] This issue is a celebration of and lament for the containers for Western humanist knowledge, both the libraries and the bound pages of the book, once handmade at great expense for the promotion of humanist values. The issue is illustrated throughout with evocative photographs of splendidly ornate European libraries and wooden bookshelves replete with ancient leather-bound texts. One caption reads: 'The magnificent Waldsassen monastery library in Bavaria, built in a century when knowledge was celebrating its triumphs.' Robert Fulford here nostalgically reflects upon 'The Ideology of the Book,' commenting that 'since the Enlightenment, Western civilization has made the book the shrine of modernity, the place where we store and locate our ideals' (803). Fulford expresses concern that costly new forms of information on computer networks and CDs will endanger the 'great historical movement, the gradual broadening of knowledge, outward from its original owners, the princes and priests, toward all of humanity' (809). What are 'our ideals' here? Fulford seems to be valorizing only a specific kind of knowledge that stops short of computer technology. He concludes with a call to arms:

> When I read about what Gates and his competitors are preparing for us, I sometimes think about those pioneers of information technology, the monks who preserved part of the wisdom of antiquity during the centuries when hardly anyone else seemed to care about it ... 'A monastery without a library is like a castle without an armoury,' [a monk in Normandy in the year 1170] wrote. 'Our library is our armoury. Thence it is that we bring forth the sentences of the Divine Law like sharp arrows to attack the enemy. Thence we take the armour of righteousness, the helmet of salvation, the shield of faith, and the sword of the spirit.' In the environment created by onrushing technology, scholars, librarians, teachers, writers – all those who take responsibility for generating and spreading knowledge – may well find themselves called to a similar battle. They will need to be shielded by faith in the value of their endeavours, and by the sword of the spirit. (810–11)

What are we to make of this invocation of righteousness, salvation, faith, and spirit to attack the amorphous enemy technology? The religious references by both Castel and Fulford indicate a threat to human spirit but it is tempting to suggest that what is depicted is as much a threat to the humanist claim on the dissemination of knowledge and morality.

In his afterword to *The Future of the Book,* Umberto Eco invokes the words of Claude Frollo in Victor Hugo's *Hunchback of Notre Dame:* '"Ceci tuera cela" (The book will kill the cathedral, the alphabet will kill images).'[41] Eco remarks that one significant issue raised by the participants in the symposium that instigated this collection of essays is 'that *ceci* (the computer) *tuera cela* (the book).' The phrase is a sign of the supercession or destruction of one medium of communication by another, but it is also worth noting that what was at stake for the clergy that Frollo represents was the material housing of spirituality – where knowledge of it would originate, where it would be taught and learned, how it would be disseminated to the people. Printed books challenged some of the authority the cathedral represented. In the same way, the dissemination of knowledge through the electronic page is threatening – or invigorating – because in our secular world the 'cathedral' of human consciousness or identity has for centuries been represented by the mundane and unthreatening codex or paper page. The page, material representation of mind and/or spirit, is the cathedral of the humanities. The electronic page, imagined as infiltrating human consciousness or displacing human spirit through its 'ectoplasmic arrival and departure,' also is imagined as invading and displacing the 'spiritual' values of the humanities.

Birkerts has noted that 'literature and the humane values we associate with it have been depreciated, reincarnated in debased form. They ... have been rendered safely, nostalgically, irrelevant.'[42] The literary or religious book as cultural icon of the human spirit is thus imagined by certain authors as rapidly becoming part of our history. Birkerts's suggested relationship between 'the transformations that have been wreaked upon society by electronic media' and a 'distance from humanism, that once-grand growth that ... took man as the measure of all things, and that looked forward to the marriage of reason and spirit' (180–1) provided an emphatic statement about the valuing of the technical sciences over the humanities. What I have been tracing in the dialogue about electronic texts is a conversation based on these questions: Who gets to be the authority on – or the author of – the human identity or spirit? What will be the culturally valued pages of the future? The electronic text is not so much the relocation of the consciousness, identity, or mind in the ethernet, but rather represents a relocation of dominant cultural allegiances: if the codex book and paper page, so closely associated with body and mind, have historically inscribed and disseminated principles of morality through stable, sanctioned texts written by institutionally approved authorities, then what the electronic text threatens most is the perception of where that authority lies.

NOTES

1 Sven Birkerts, *The Gutenberg Elegies: The Fate of Reading in an Electronic Age* (Boston: Faber and Faber, 1994), 154–5.
2 Harold Innis, *The Bias of Communication* (Toronto: University of Toronto Press, 1951), 11.
3 See Walter J. Ong, *Orality and Literacy: The Technologizing of the Word* (London: Routledge, 1982).
4 Theodore Adorno, 'The Schema of Mass Culture,' in *The Culture Industry*, ed. and intro. J.M. Bernstein, trans. Nicholas Walker (London: Routledge, 1991), 55, 83.
5 Michael Heim, *The Metaphysics of Virtual Reality* (New York: Oxford University Press, 1993), 100–1.
6 Birkerts, *The Gutenberg Elegies*, 190.
7 Arthur Kroker and Michael A. Weinstein, 'Global Algorithm 1.4: The Theory of the Virtual Class,' *Ctheory* (29 May 1996).
8 Sadie Plant, 'Coming Across the Future,' in *Virtual Futures: Cyberotics, Technology and Post-Human Pragmatism*, ed. Joan Broadhurst Dixon and Eric J. Cassidy (London: Routledge, 1998), 35.
9 Christopher J. Keep, 'The Disturbing Liveliness of Machines: Rethinking the Body in Hypertext Theory and Fiction,' in *Cyberspace Textuality: Computer Technology and Literary Theory*, ed. Marie-Laure Ryan (Bloomington: Indiana University Press, 1999), 165.
10 Vivian Sobchack, 'The Scene of the Screen: Envisioning Cinematic and Electronic "Presence,"' in *Materialities of Communication*, ed. Hans Ulrich Gumbrecht and K. Ludwig Pfeiffer (Stanford: Stanford University Press, 1994), 104.
11 K. Ludwig Pfeiffer, 'The Materiality of Communication,' in *Materialities of Communication*, ed. Gumbrecht and Pfeiffer, 11.
12 Norbert Wiener, *Cybernetics: Or Control and Communication in the Animal and the Machine*, 2nd ed. (Cambridge, MA: MIT Press, 1961), 3–5, cited in E. Lily Kay, 'Cybernetics, Information, Life: The Emergence of Scriptural Representations of Heredity,' *Configurations* 5.1 (1997): 32.
13 Norbert Wiener, *The Human Use of Human Beings: Cybernetics and Society* (Boston: Houghton Mifflin, 1950), 103.
14 Kay, 'Cybernetics, Information, Life,' 90.
15 W.T. Astbury and F.O. Bell, 'Some Recent Developments in the X-ray Study of Proteins and Related Structures,' *Cold Spring Harbor Symposium for Quantitative Biology* 6 (1938): 114.
16 William Harvey, *Disputations Touching the Generation of Animals*, trans. and intro. Gweneth Whitteridge (Oxford: Blackwell Scientific Publications, 1981), 8.

17 Cited in N. Katherine Hayles, *How We Became Posthuman: Virtual Bodies in Cybernetics, Literature, and Informatics* (Chicago: University of Chicago Press, 1999), 13.
18 Peter Cochrane, 'Dead 100%: Capturing The Soul of Man,' *Daily Telegraph*, 16 April 1996, 14. www.labs.bt.com/library/cochrane/telegraph/1996/16-4-96.htm
19 'The Mind Is Immortal,' *Business Week*, 30 August 1999, 100.
20 Jean Baudrillard, 'The Ecstasy of Communication,' trans. John Johnston, in *The Anti-Aesthetic: Essays on Postmodern Culture*, ed. Hal Foster (Port Townsend, WA: Bay Press, 1983), 128–9.
21 Jean Baudrillard, *Simulations*, trans. Paul Foss, Paul Patton, and Philip Beitchman (New York: Semiotext(e), 1983), 3.
22 John Hockenberry, introduction to Alexander Tsiaras, *Body Voyage™: A Three-Dimensional Tour of a Real Human Body* (New York: Warner Books, 2000), n.p.
23 Arthur Kroker and Michael Weinstein, *Data Trash: The Theory of the Virtual Class* (New York: St Martin's Press, 1994), 56–7.
24 Victor Spitzer and David Whitlock, *Atlas of the Visible Human Male: Reverse Engineering of the Human Body* (Sudbury, MA: Jones and Bartlett, 1998).
25 Human Genome Program and the U.S. Department of Energy, 'To Know Ourselves' (1996). www.ornl.gov/hgmis/publicat/tko/index.html.
26 The National Library of Medicine (NLM), 'Fact Sheet: The Visible Human Project®' (last updated 16 February 2001). www.nlm.nih.gov/pubs/factsheets/visible_human.html.
27 National Library of Medicine (U.S.) Board of Regents, 'Electronic Imaging: Report of the Board of Regents,' U.S. Department of Health and Human Services, Public Health Service, National Institutes of Health (Bethesda, MD: NIH Publication, 1990), 90–2197.
28 'The National Human Genome Research Institute (NHGRI),' press release (September 1998). www.nhgri.nih.gov:80/NEWS/Finish_sequencing_early/cracking_the_code.html.
29 The National Center for Biotechnology Information (NCBI), 'A New Gene Map of the Human Genome.' www.ncbi.nlm.nih.gov/genemap/.
30 David Wheeler, 'Creating a Body of Knowledge,' *Chronicle of Higher Education* 2 (February 1996): A14, quoting Michael Ackerman.
31 *Life*, February 1997, 44.
32 *Life* magazine states that 'Jernigan is back. In an electronic afterlife, he haunts Hollywood studios and NASA labs, high schools and hospitals' (February 1997), 41; *The Economist* (US), vol. 341, no. 7988 (19 October 1996), uses the heading 'Virtual Immortality'; the *National Library of Medicine Newsletter* 50.6 (1995) reports that 'an anonymous 59–year-old Maryland woman who donated her body to science is now immortalized on the Internet' (www.nlm.nih.gov/pubs/nlmnews/novdec95.html); the *Baltimore Sun* (29 November 1995), 1A described Jernigan as having 'won a measure of computerized immortality'; the *Denver Post* (6 June 1994), B1 suggests the project 'promises eternal life for the participants.'

33 Catherine Waldby, 'Virtual Anatomy: From the Body in the Text to the Body on the Screen,' *Journal of Medical Humanities* 21 (summer 2000): 89.

34 Neal Curtis, 'The Body as Outlaw: Lyotard, Kafka and the Visible Human Project,' *Body and Society* 5 (September 1999): 262.

35 One of the first uses of the VHP data was by SUNY researchers in developing their '3-D virtual colonoscopy,' a noninvasive imaging technology using a helical CT scanner and 3-D software to examine the colon. I believe that simulating the human body electronically instead of putting a 72-inch colonoscope up someone's ass is a demonstration of medical science's valuing rather than violating or debasing human dignity and life.

36 Arthur Kroker and Michael Weinstein, *Data Trash: The Theory of the Virtual Class* (New York: St Martin's Press, 1994), 134.

37 Catherine Waldby, *The Visible Human Project: Posthuman Medicine and Informatic Bodies* (London: Routledge, 2000), 155.

38 Spitzer and Whitlock, *Atlas of the Visible Human Male*, xi.

39 The fourteen muscle figures in the second book of De fabrica do not appear in the order of their dissection. I identify these as the first and last panels based on the reconstruction of the two écorché sequences as originally envisioned by the artists, by G.S. Terence Cavanagh, *The Panorama of Vesalius: A Lost Design from Titian's Studio* (Athens, GA: Sacrum Press, 1996).

40 Boris Castel, ed., *The End of the Book?* special issue of *Queen's Quarterly* 101 (winter 1994), 777.

41 Umberto Eco, afterword to *The Future of the Book*, ed. Geoffrey Nunberg (Berkeley and Los Angeles: University of California Press, 1996), 295.

42 Birkerts, *The Gutenberg Elegies*, 184.

12 Artist's Pages: Decolonizing Tactics in 'Writing Space'

Lynne Bell

And reading came to mean reading with greater scrutiny and sometimes rereading with adult eyes what I had first read in the innocence of my literary infancy and adolescence.

– Chinua Achebe, *Home and Exile*

Unsettling the Pages of the Colonial Library

A few years ago, while I was working on a research project concerned with the role of the artist as public intellectual, I stumbled across the visual genre of the artist's page, that is, photo- or photo-text essays inserted into the writing space of contemporary art journals, magazines, or periodicals. In recent years, this small-scale often unnoticed genre has generated considerable interest in artistic circles, with artist's pages featuring regularly in the publications of artist-run-centres and in such interdisciplinary journals as *Harbour Magazine* and *West Coast Line,* among others. As a quick search through these publications reveals, the artist's page has become a crucial site of 'aesthetic unsettlement,' to borrow a quote from Homi Bhabha,[1] and in many instances, a potent site for a decolonizing pedagogy. A modest medium, compared to many visual productions, the artist's page packs a powerful punch, involved as it is with divesting print culture of its submerged politics, on the one hand, and re-visioning the page as a potent site of critical reflection, on the other.

Artist's pages often involve the presentation of new work designed specifically for display in a particular journal. But just as frequently they involve the recycling of existing work and here it is interesting to see how the same image translates from one medium to another as it addresses differing publics. Encountering an artist's page in the writing space of a magazine can come as a surprise to a reader unaccustomed to the genre. Playing with layout, they interrupt the customary left-to-right and top-to-bottom flow of information on the page in Western culture. Creating a different rhythm on the printed page, they invite the reader to take a pause, to stop, and listen to new and frequently unsettling associations, reflections, and imaginative links.

In this essay, I will look at how contemporary artists working in Canada deploy a range of tactics to refigure 'the page' in order to decolonize Western print culture which, as many critics have demonstrated, has been (and still is) used to legitimize and justify imperialism. In a series of artist's pages which have erupted dramatically and abundantly in publications all over Canada, we see how contemporary artists focus on the pages of our still colonial culture, unsettle them, and use them to create sites of resistance that transform the page and what is imag(in)ed and written upon on it. In doing so, they take on the authority of what Simon Gikandi has termed 'the colonial library,'[2] confronting, interrupting, and rerouting its repositories of colonial tropes that have marginalized colonized peoples, divesting them of their humanity.

In our intensely visual culture – from bus-stop ads to MTV to news pictures to Hollywood films – we cannot ignore the fact that images are power. Yet this was not always the way. Print culture was a powerful technology in the civilizing mission of empire and it still plays a vital role in educating the public's collective consciousness. While there has been a historical shift to the visual in our photographic age, with writing now taking a humbler place alongside other cultural domains, the powerful history of the book cannot be underestimated.

As the distinguished African writer Chinua Achebe points out, imperial expansion involved not only the occupation of colonies but also the development of the 'story' of empire, disseminated in the pages of a colonial library, and enforced in educational, cultural, administrative, and political institutions. Achebe persuasively outlines the role of the book in the circulation of power between European centres and their colonies in his autobiography, *Home and Exile*, writing that, 'the hundreds and hundreds of books churned out in Britain, Europe and elsewhere' created the tradition of 'an Africa inhabited by barely recognizable humanity.'[3] In a chapter entitled, 'My Home under Imperial Fire,' Achebe reveals how the colonial library was used to teach the Igbo, in the former British colony of Nigeria, their distance from the centre of European civilization. Education, he writes, 'was not about Igbo things; it was about faraway places and peoples; and its acquisition was generally painful' (19).

During his studies in higher education at University College, Ibadan, Nigeria, during the closing years of British colonial rule in West Africa, Achebe continued to feel the impact of the colonial library, as the syllabus and degrees of University College were closely modelled on, and supervised by, London University:

> My professors in English were all Europeans from various British and European universities. With one or two exceptions the authors they taught us would have been the same ones they would teach at home: Shakespeare, Milton, Defoe, Swift, Wordsworth, Coleridge, Keats, Tennyson, Housman, Eliot, Frost, Joyce, Hemingway, Conrad. (21)

In a riveting moment in his autobiograpy, Achebe tells of a classroom rebellion staged against this colonial library when a 'Nigerian' novel entitled *Mister Johnson* by the Anglo-Irishman Joyce Cary was added to the English literature syllabus. The inclusion of this novel, which had received critical acclaim in England, triggered a 'landmark rebellion' (23) amongst Achebe's classmates, who objected to Cary's stereotypical description of their home, Nigeria, and the entire tradition of British writing about Africa in which Cary had been schooled at the end of the nineteenth century. Recalling this 1952 classroom rebellion, Achebe talks about how it called into question 'my childhood assumption of the innocence of stories,' setting in motion a career of critical reading that involved 'sometimes rereading with adult eyes what I had first read in the innocence of my literary infancy and adolescence' (34). Critical reading, as Achebe notes, puts writers and their work on notice that, 'we will go to their offering for wholesome pleasure and insight, and not for a rehash of old stereotypes which gained currency long ago' in the shadow of empire (35).

This challenge by Achebe is taken up by the artists discussed in this essay, who are all involved in the postcolonial project of dismantling the discursive and material legacies of Euro-American imperialism. Creating pages which vary greatly in terms of subject matter and style of presentation, they take on the colonial library and its traces in contemporary print culture, opening up a space for considering Canada's colonial past and its neocolonial present. In making new pages and in adapting and refashioning highly influential pages in contemporary culture (from children's stories to popular magazines to satellite images to tourist ads), they use the page to tell enabling stories to empower themselves and their communities.

Never a Quiet Act of Introspection: The Page as Witness

> Remembering is never a quiet act of introspection. It is a painful re-membering, a putting together of the disembodied past to make sense of the trauma of the present.
>
> – Homi Bhabha, 'What Does the Black Man Want?'

In this section I want to look at pages done by three artists who use the page as a site of public memory to re-vision what is erased, ignored, or camouflaged in contemporary Canadian culture. In bearing witness to the 'imperial

ARAWAK BEACH RESORT

Figure 12.1. Melinda Mollineaux, 'Artist's Project,' *The Front: Vancouver Arts Magazine* 5 (Spring/Summer 1994): 16–17.

habits of mind'[4] still present in the nation space of Canada, these decolonizing pages invite the viewer to think again about the violence that still continues in the name of the nation and modernity. The work of bearing witness, as Edward Said notes in a recent interview, is a powerful historical practice – something that is worth trying.[5]

In 'Artist's Project,' Melinda Mollineaux creates a double-page montage in *The Front* magazine[6] that vividly invokes the colonial histories of the Caribbean while simultaneously revealing traces of the colonial imagination still at work in contemporary discourses of tourism in Canada (fig. 12.1). The starting point for this artist's page was an advertisement for the Arawak Beach Resort in Anguilla that Mollineaux found in a Canadian tourist magazine. Appropriating this ad, she layers it over an image of a sparkling seascape, where it floats like an island. On the adjacent page, she layers a seventeenth-century European map of one of the Caribbean islands over an image of her own body. In its depiction of a church and its naming, or renaming, of the existing islands, cays, and inlets of a small area of coastline, this map speaks to colonial domination and occupation. Mollineaux discovered the map while researching old shipping records of the Caribbean. 'I was intrigued by the simplicity of the maps,' she says. 'They appeared so innocent, like children's drawings. I find them quite beautiful. But I was struck by how something that looks so benign can have such a violent intention.'[7]

Born in Britain of West Indian heritage, Mollineaux lived in Trinidad for a number of years before immigrating to Canada in 1981. As an artist-scholar, she has presented her work in a range of activist friendly visual genres – from billboard art to bench art to bookmarks to artist's pages – over the last decade. Engaging in everyday, local acts of decolonizing cultural resistance, her work reinterprets and revisions, in the words of C.L.R. James, 'the forms and effects of an older colonial consciousness' from her own later experience of 'migration, diaspora and cultural displacement.'[8]

With the amazing shorthand of montage that pulls together many layers of experience – a process which the Caribbean writer Edouard Glissant refers to as 'piling-up'[9] – Mollineaux creates in her pages for *The Front* magazine a many-tiered visualization of time and space that reaches back to some of the Indigenous inhabitants of the Caribbean islands, the Arawaks (most of whom were massacred), to the histories of European settlement that established the slave economies of the West Indies (signed by the map), and forward to the neo-colonialism of contemporary tourism. Asked about the significance of the female body who glances over her shoulder at the map, Mollineaux notes:

> My body, my skin, signifies the ultimate syncretic site of colonial desire. The entire population of the Caribbean is a result of colonialism's multiple desires poured into that space ... Colonial desire expresses itself today in tourism as seen in the advertisement for the Arawak Beach Resort ... This impacts on my body in very concrete ways: tourism re-constructs colonial desire for both the land and the bodies of the Caribbean.[10]

These artist's pages are deeply engaging. They remind me of the missing pages of my own university days in Britain in the early 1970s. Trained as a historian of Western modernity, I studied the great technological inventions of the modern cotton industry, the working conditions in cotton factories, the private lives of wealthy industrialists engaged in the cotton trade, and the various economic 'crises' affecting the industry. Yet while the pages of my history texts mentioned that a good portion of the raw materials for the early cotton industry in Britain came from West Indian plantations, little notice was taken of the fact of empire. Mollineaux's pages, on the other hand, succinctly invoke the use of force and the tragedies and contradictions of the colonizing process in the Caribbean – the forced relocation of Africans to the Caribbean on the slave ships of the middle passage, the extermination of Indigenous populations, and the slave and indentured economies of the sugar and cotton plantations. In re-membering these submerged histories so heavily camouflaged in my university texts, Mollineaux bears witness to Europe's disruption of colonial space while simultaneously pointing out that Canadian tourism still lives within the spell of the imperial imaginary. The ad for the Arawak Beach Resort – ('On the site of an ancient Arawak Indian Village, built in traditional Arawak "Caney" style, decorated in African and Indian furnishings, surrounded by ocean on all three sides, overlooking beautiful Island Harbour Bay. Health-food restaurant features Arawakan recipes')[11] – appeals to the viewers' senses, while asking them to forget about the violent history of imperialism.

In *Jan 1 2000 (treaty 4 territory)* and *Rezschool bead machine (Lebret 1999)*, Edward Poitras presents two pages for the readers of *BlackFlash*[12] that, in their focus on Aboriginal geographies, displace and disturb the spaces of white settler society in Canada. In *Jan 1 2000 (treaty 4 territory)*, a satellite image of North America has been overlaid with modern geopolitical boundaries. Disturbing this mapping system, Poitras reinscribes the territory of Treaty Four – a huge area of land, in the shape of a sitting coyote (a trickster figure frequently invoked in Poitras's work) – onto the map of Canada, displacing the boundaries of Alberta, Saskatchewan, and Manitoba. This small adjustment to modern mapping is easily overlooked, but once noticed, it radically shifts the meaning of the page. Adjacent to this black-and-white satellite image is *Rezschool bead machine (Lebret 1999)*, a page that features a photograph of Lebret Industrial School (a residential school in Saskatchewan) being torn down by an enormous bulldozer (see fig. 12.2). On a bright spring day the remains of the school, surrounded by piles of rubble, are framed by an intensely blue sky. The entire scene is floodlit with brilliant sunshine. Close to the fallen masonry, acting as witnesses to the toppling of this colonial prison, stands a ghostly herd of elk transposed from the wild into what appears to be an urban park enclosure. It is hard to make out their exact circumstances but their presence on this brightly coloured digitized page holds the viewer's attention.

Edward Poitras, a member of the Gordon First Nation, located in the Touchwood Hills within Treaty Four territory, has created a series of arresting images of the Qu'Appelle Valley in Saskatchewan over the last fifteen years. Naming intimate details about this landscape of his upbringing, Poitras reveals how it has been transformed into a series of racialized spaces through imperial expansion and colonialism. The image of a pile of bones stripped bare is a recurring one in Poitras's art, invoking an early name for the city of Regina ('Pile of Bones'), on the one hand, and the ferocious hunger of white settler culture, on the other. But while the works force the viewer to confront the fact that Indigenous place has been reorganized into white settler space, the works also focus on the life-places of the Qu'Appelle Valley's Indigenous peoples. Reconnecting to particular points in this landscape and explaining his community's relationship to these places, Poitras reveals differing modes of inhabitation that speak to the continuance of Aboriginal cultural identity. And throughout Poitras's work runs the figure of the coyote which, as the Indigenous artist Jimmie Durham notes, 'has come to be a symbol of

Figure 12.2. Edward Poitras, *Jan 1 2000 (treaty 4 territory)* and *Rezschool bead machine*, *Blackflash* 17 (May 2000): 28–9.

"survival-with-hubris for most Indian people," because, Coyote always says: "*Whatever* you do, I am going to do something else."'[13]

The titles of the *BlackFlash* pages – which belong to Poitras's series on the Qu'Appelle Valley – resonate with tensions about the meaning and interpretation of spatial history. In *Jan 1 2000 (treaty 4 territory)*, Poitras layers the disciplinary geography of the treaty area over the modern satellite image, reminding viewers that the occupation and control of space is crucial to imperialism. Using a process of unmapping, Poitras recentres Treaty Four territory, on this page, at the very heart of Canada. In *Rezschool bead machine (Lebret 1999)*, we see the Lebret Industrial School, which played a prominent role in Poitras's own family's history, being demolished. If we read the two pages together – the satellite image taken on 1 January 2000, and the image of the Lebret residential school being demolished – they take on a prophetic tone: the fall of one colonial institution foreshadowing the fall of many others in the new millennium.

In 'artist's project,' a second set of artist's pages, Melinda Mollineaux addresses the murder of Shidane Abukar Arone, who was beaten and tortured to death by certain members of a Canadian Forces Airborne Unit, bringing to the fore a recent event that many of us living in Canada would prefer to forget.[14] In these pages, which are based on what bell hooks elsewhere calls a practice of 'critical resistance and remembrance,'[15] we see Mollineaux once again drawing the viewer's attention to 'the forms and effects of an older colonial consciousness'[16] still circulating in Canadian culture. In talking about her decision to make these pages, Mollineaux notes that she felt compelled to bear witness to the murder of this Somali teenager:

> Apparently, as he was being beaten, these soldiers made him say 'Canada, Canada.' They posed with him for snapshots. These details alone are horrific. Since then, much more has been revealed about the racism and the level of brutality that characterized this particular Unit ... When Fuse asked me to do an artist's page, I didn't initially have a particular project in mind. It was around that time that information about Shidane Arone's death was released to the public. I thought it would be horrible of me not to address this terrible event. His death forcibly reminded me of the extreme gestures that can be made on the racialized body. This incident clearly articulated to me what it meant to have a Black body in Canada. If you have a Black body and you occupy space, these things are possible.

Mollineaux explains how she visualized her pages in the following passage:

> I was thinking about how violence demands witnesses. The victim is a witness and we become witnesses. Violence demands that we acknowledge what is happening. The photograph in the piece is actually a manipulated photograph of my uncle in Trinidad. He looked like he'd be about the same age as Shidane, perhaps a little older. It was the freedom in his body, the comfortableness of his pose that I wanted to juxtapose with the idea of how Shidane was killed. Using this photograph was a way for me to understand the connections between this incident and myself. The beating could easily happen to anyone ... or to someone I know.[17]

In this double page montage, a fragmentary image of a young man's arm and hand resting on a bent leg is brought into sharp focus against a blurred background of tropical foliage (fig. 12.3). The words 'They demanded a witness' and 'I wanted not to see' are collaged over the background. The name Shidane Abukar Arone is written on the blank right-hand page. The pronouns 'they' and 'I' are ambiguous, referring to the youth in the artist's pages, but also directly addressing the viewers, inviting us to consider how we witness the event. In talking about these artist's pages several years later, Mollineaux notes: 'Time has passed and this event has slipped from popular memory as an issue. It is important to have a document of a moment when someone remembered that person. And this document exists long after that story has disappeared from the media.'[18]

They demanded a witness.
Shidane Abukar Arone

Figure 12.3. Melinda Mollineaux, 'artist's project,' *Fuse Magazine* 17. 4 (1993): 20–1.

Page Tactics or the Subtle Art of Renting

> In postcoloniality every metropolitan definition is dislodged. The general mode for the postcolonial is citation, reinscription, rerouting of the historical.
> – Gayatri Chakravorty Spivak, *Outside in the Teaching Machine*

Canadian artists often rent or poach the format of highly influential pages in everyday culture in order to, in the words of the cultural critic de Certeau, 'insinuate their countless differences into the dominant text.'[19] In this section, I want to look at how contemporary artists have deployed decolonizing page tactics in order to interrogate, subvert, and re-vision certain 'classic' pages in our culture that continue to circulate colonial and imperial 'truths.' In talking about page tactics, I am borrowing the notion of a tactic as developed by de Certeau. Noting the enormous potential for play and resistance within everyday life and practice, de Certeau defines a tactic as the way consumers manipulate everyday life for their own purposes, to create a disorder, an impropriety, or interaction directed towards social change.

In *Cosmo Squaw*,[20] for instance, the Saskatoon-based Indigenous performance artist Lori Blondeau 'rents' the front cover of *Cosmopolitan Magazine* in order to perform a decolonizing analysis of the aesthetics of white beauty contained within its pages (fig. 12.4). In this brash, smart work Blondeau

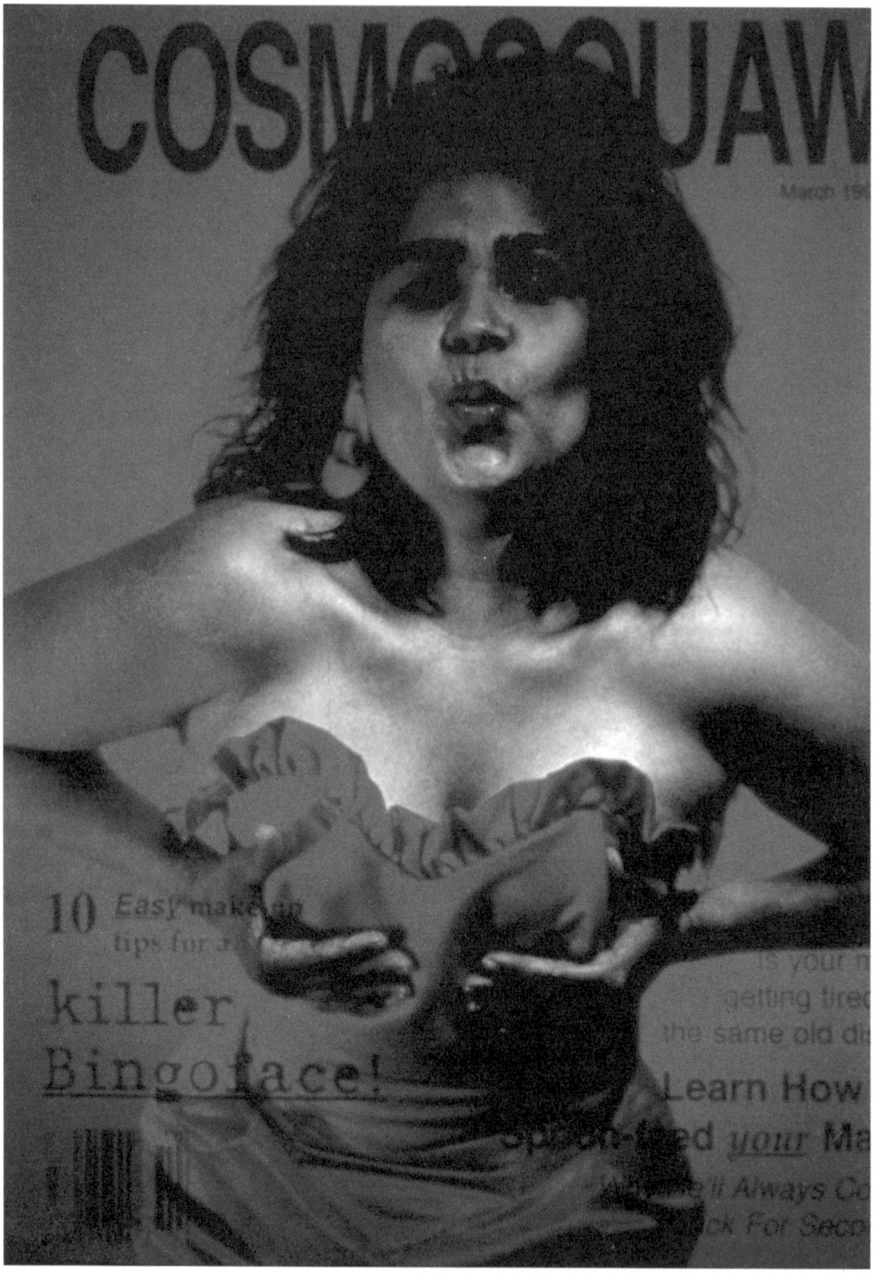
killer
Learn How
getting tired
the same old

Figure 12.4. Lori Blondeau, 'Cosmo Squaw.'

reinvents herself as a cover-girl with big hair, red lipstick, off-the-shoulder dress and pouting expression. This glamour-puss cover-girl, *Cosmo Squaw*, is surrounded by titles of mock feature articles, including '10 easy make-up tips for a Killer bingo face.' In this page (a light-box made in collaboration with Bradlee LaRocque), Blondeau rents the structuring conventions of layout from *Cosmopolitan Magazine* to ensure instant recognition with her reader/viewer. But the presence of *Cosmo Squaw*, and the titles of the mock feature articles, puts pressure on the traditional genre of the fashion page.

Over the last decade Blondeau has developed a witty decolonizing performance practice which 'talks back' to historical representations of Indigenous peoples while simultaneously addressing the continuing imperialism of present-day commodity culture from films to fashion magazines to TV shows to the Internet. Inventing a series of flamboyant performance personas (Lonely Surfer Squaw, Indian Princess, Cyber Squaw), Blondeau uses her own body and the strategy of 'dressing up' to mimic and rewire the stereotypes of Aboriginal women still present in Western culture, inviting us to consider the injuries of colonialism and the ironic pleasures of displacement and resistance.

In the page *Cosmo Squaw*, Blondeau clearly mimics and parodies the stylized conventions of white femininity played out across the pages of mainstream fashion magazines while simultaneously pointing to the erasure of Indigenous women's bodies in popular culture's hegemonic model of beauty. As Blondeau notes in conversation:

> I started thinking about inventing a magazine like Cosmopolitan for Native women ... Coming up with the name Cosmo Squaw was a hard thing to do because I knew people would feel bad about the word 'squaw.' It was such a negative term for me when I was growing up. It was my grandmother who first taught me to reclaim the word. When I was sixteen, I remember these boys calling me 'a fucking ugly squaw.' It wasn't the first time I'd been called this but I went home crying. My grandmother was visiting and she was annoyed I'd let this incident upset me. She said, 'Do you know what squaw means?' and I said, 'No.' And she goes, 'Well, it means woman.' After that whenever people called me squaw, I would say, 'Yes, I am a squaw and proud to be a squaw.' So, it's about taking away the negative connotations and replacing them with something positive.

In her parodic page *Cosmo Squaw*, Blondeau invites Aboriginal and non-Aboriginal viewers to think again about the fixed colonizing image of 'the squaw.' Deploying the tactic of repetition-with-difference, she reveals through shifts in emphasis and meaning, the silences and gaps of the original page. Taking *Cosmopolitan*'s cover page as a point of departure, Blondeau invites us/challenges us to produce a new reading.

In *The Heartless Series*, the Vancouver-based artist Laiwan sets up a dialogue with the pages of a 1950s edition of Louisa M. Alcott's classic novel, *Little Women* (first published in 1869), in a series of artist's pages featured in a special issue of *West Coast Line* entitled *Colour: An Issue*.[21] In her work, Laiwan frequently dialogues with found pages in the Western literary canon, making use of collage and radical juxtaposition to seriously discomfort the meaning of the host texts she inhabits. In *The Heartless Series*, Laiwan collages an image of a beating heart and idioms in English onto pages she has (mis)appropriated from *Little Women*, creating surprising and disconcerting juxtapositions, which capture the attention of the reader. The collaged elements of the heart and the idiomatic phrases stain Alcott's pages, setting up an interplay of competing and contradictory discourses. And while Laiwan's subversive collage does not lay down the law, it does perforate *Little Women's* comforting tale of girl children and middle-class white domestic culture in New England during the nineteenth century.

Born and raised in Harare, Zimbabwe, of Chinese descent, Laiwan notes that her experience of living in both Zimbabwe and Canada has made her see what she calls 'the extension of the colonial project'[22] and this has become the key framework in her research and artistic practice. Growing up in a British colony and attending colonial schools, Laiwan studied a Western literary curriculum. In an interview, she draws connections between the pages of *Little Women*, which she studied as a school girl in Africa, and the colonial project, noting:

> This piece [*The Heartless Series*] questioned how girl children are constructed within the domestic culture exemplified by *Little Women* and explored the perceptions inherent in the idioms of a language. I also wanted to critique the assumption of not questioning the values taught in these classic texts. I saw *Little Women* as promoting class values that were quite foreign to me and yet it was required reading in my childhood education. Imperialism is essentially a class war in which the First World is the upper and middle class, living beyond its means, consuming and exploiting resources from whichever world has them. (61)

In drawing connections between print culture and the imperializing mission, Laiwan's work is linked to a tradition of anticolonial scholarship by such writers and critics as Linda Tuhiwai Smith, Edward Said, Jamaica Kincaid, Austin Clarke, Gauri Viswarathan, Marie Battiste, Chinua Achebe, and Ngugi Wa Thiong'o, all of whom have spoken persuasively about the shameful history of the page in facilitating colonization. Ngugi Wa Thiong'o, like Chinua Achebe, for instance, has pointed to the damage inflicted by the imported page and the colonial mode of education on African school children. As Ngugi notes, a process of 'colonial alienation'[23] was inflicted through the teaching of such subjects as history, geography, music and literature, all of which posited Europe as the repository of civilized values, alienating stu-

Gonzales Point

Figure 12.5. Melinda Molineaux, 'Artist Page: Cadboro Bay: Index to an Incomplete History.'

dents from their own everyday world and spoken language in the family and community. It does not matter, Ngugi argues, that the imported literature carried the great humanist tradition of the best in such writers as Shakespeare, Goethe, Balzac, Tolstoy, and Dickens because 'the location of this great mirror of imagination was necessarily Europe and its history and culture and the rest of the universe was seen from that center' (18).

Finally, I want to look at an innovative and imaginative page tactic for disturbing and displacing the spatial histories of prominent Canadian heritage texts. At the centre of a solo exhibition entitled *Cadboro Bay: Index to an Incomplete History*,[24] Melinda Mollineaux displays two prominent heritage texts on the city of Victoria, British Columbia, and its environs: *Victoria Landmarks*, and *This Old House: An Inventory of Residential Heritage, City of Victoria*.[25] Highly visible recent heritage guides, these books list the significant buildings, landmarks, and houses of the white Anglo-Canadian community in Victoria. Into the pages of these influential books, Mollineaux has inserted her own pages of digitized images and text. Discreetly sewn into the host texts, Mollineaux's pages are scattered throughout the two books (only ten extra pages in each), but each one is a bomb hurled at the sense of the host text.

In the exhibition *Cadboro Bay*, of which the interrupted books are an integral part, Melinda re-members the history of the small Black community that migrated from California to the British Colony of Vancouver Island in the spring of 1858 (fig. 12.5). As Mollineaux notes in conversation, the story of these black pioneers is a fairly hidden history and one that is not visible in the official heritage narratives of British Columbia. While researching the history of Vancouver Island's nineteenth-century Black community, Mollineaux learned of the Emancipation Day picnics, held annually at Cadboro Bay on 1 August, to celebrate the British emancipation of slavery. In her exhibition, she displays large, luminous images of Cadboro Bay made with a pinhole camera in order to perform what she calls 'a process of surmising'[26] about this annual picnic, and 'those folks who came to Victoria before me.' In the Cadboro Bay images, Mollineaux invokes the spectral presence of this nineteenth-century Black community in the depiction of empty yet intimate spaces on the beach where she imagines the picnic took place. In one image, a small area of sand criss-crossed with shadows, is framed by bleached logs and a tangled mass of foliage. In conversation, Mollineaux describes the exhibition as a 'visual reverie' about the Cadboro Bay picnics, a Black diasporic social event preceding Toronto's present day Caribana festival:

> I took [pinhole] photographs of empty places on the beach where it looked like something could have occurred. Nothing big or monumental. It could have been a small thing – someone sitting against a log. These photographs are not only a document of my remembrance, they are my way of providing a visually tangible landscape within which we can place our black history.

In the pages Mollineaux inserts into the two heritage texts, we see her using historical research to renegotiate and rewrite the terms of the heritage discourse in British Columbia. Speaking about how she made these pages, Mollineaux notes that once she uncovered the fact of the picnics, she undertook to find as many references to the Black community as she could, searching libraries and archives to collect the names of the Black pioneers. In the spirit of what she terms a 'guerilla act of memory,' she then wrote brief texts around each name describing intangible moments. These intangible moments also served as a memory device to help her remember what she had learned or imagined about each person. 'Nathan Pointer shakes a white billowing cloth,' for example, helped her remember that Nathan was a waiter in a Victoria Inn. 'Cornelius Charity shifts sand with his boot' reminded her that he was a boot maker.

In her fabricated pages, Mollineaux recreates Black diaspora history out of disjunctive scraps, memories, and fantasy, drawing together fragments of her pinhole photographs of Cadboro Bay, fragments of photographs culled from her own family album (close-ups of hands and bodies), and names from the west coast Black community, one name merging into another. The pages are semi-transparent and when inserted into the heritage texts, the reader can look through them to the underlying narratives. Mollineaux's pages undo the assumptions of the host texts: imaginatively bearing witness to the displaced lives and experiences of this early Black diaspora community they haunt Canadian heritage narratives with (some of) the histories and geographies they have written out and erased. In making these pages, Mollineaux is taking on the political responsibility of the postcolonial artist, attempting, in Homi Bhabha's words, 'to fully realize, and take responsibility for, the unspoken, unrepresented pasts that haunt the historical present' (12). Mollineaux's pages also present challenges: How to claim a diasporic geography? How to create a tenuous, fleeting, pleasurable relationship to space that does not duplicate the violent colonial process of laying claim to land? While the show has come down, the books with their artist's pages still reside in the library, awaiting a chance encounter with an unsuspecting reader.

Finally ...

It seems to me that the page has become an increasingly significant site for contemporary artists working in the anticolonial process. At a time when the 'Empire' is writing back, as Salman Rushdie puts it,[27] the page has assumed a vital curative importance in the once and still colonized world. Whether making new pages or reenvisioning existing pages in order to make them perform differently, the artists I have considered all use the page as a site of 're-storying,'[28] to tell untold or forgotten stories and to develop new stories and ways of seeing. With wit, playfulness, and invention, they use the page to get us to read and think differently.

NOTES

1 Homi K. Bhabha, 'Democracy De-realized,' in *Democracy Unrealized: Documenta 11 – Platform 1*, ed. Okwui Enwezor, Carlos Basualdo et al. (Kassel: 2002 documenta und Museum Fridericianum – Veranstaltung, GmbH and Hatje Cantz Publishers), 357.
2 Simon Gikandi, *Maps of Englishness: Writing Identity in the Culture of Colonialism* (New York: Columbia University Press, 1996), xiii, 234.
3 Chinua Achebe, *Home and Exile* (Oxford: Oxford University Press, 2000), 47.
4 John Willensky, *Learning to Divide the World: Education at Empire's End* (Minneapolis: University of Minnesota Press, 1998), 18.
5 Edward Said, 'In Conversation with Neeladri Bhattacharya, Suvir Kaul, and Ania Loombia' in *Relocating Postcolonialism*, ed. David Theo Goldberg and Ato Quayson (Oxford: Blackwell, 2002), 13.
6 Melinda Mollineaux, 'Artist's Project,' *The Front:Vancouver Arts Magazine* 5 (spring/summer 1994): 16–17.
7 Lynne Bell and Carol Williams, 'Geographical Memory, Island Space: An Inter-

view with Melinda Mollineaux,' *West Coast Line: A Journal of Contemporary Writing and Criticism* 23 (autumn 1997): 91.

8 Quoted in Homi Bhabha, 'Conference Presentation,' in *Critical Fictions: The Politics of Imaginative Writing*, ed. Philomena Mariani (Seattle, WA: Bay Press, 1991), 64.

9 Edouard Glissant, *Caribbean Discourse: Selected Essays* (Charlottesville: University of Virginia Press, 1989), 5.

10 Bell and Williams, 'Geographical Memory,' 91.

11 Mollineaux, 'Artist's Project,' 16–17.

12 *Edward Poitras*, 'Portfolio,' *Blackflash* 17 (May 2000): 28–9.

13 Jimmie Durham, *A Certain Lack of Coherence: Writings on Art and Cultural Politics* (London: Kala, 1993), 207.

14 Melinda Mollineaux, 'artist's project,' *Fuse Magazine* 17. 4 (1993): 20–1.

15 bell hooks, *Art On My Mind: Visual Politics* (New York: New Press, 1995), 68.

16 Bhabha, 'Conference Presentation,' 64.

17 Bell and Williams, 'Geographical Memory,' 93–4.

18 Melinda Mollineaux, interview by author, tape recording, Saskatoon, Saskatchewan, October 2000.

19 Michel de Certeau, *The Practice of Everyday Life*, trans. Steven Rendall (Berkeley and Los Angeles: University of California Press, 1984, xxii.

20 Lynne Bell and Janice Williamson, 'High Tech Storyteller: A Conversation with Performance Artist Lori Blondeau,' *Fuse Magazine* 24 (December 2001): 27–36. *Cosmo Squaw* began as a light-box-image in 1996.

21 Roy Miki and Fred Wah, 'Colour: An Issue,' *West Coast Line* 13/14 (spring/fall 1994): 129–33.

22 Lynne Bell and Carol Williams, 'The Distance of Distinct Vision: An Interview with Laiwan,' *The Capilano Review* Series 2. 24 (winter 1998): 61.

23 Ngugi Wa Thiong'o, *Decolonizing the Mind: The Politics of Language in African Literature* (London, Nairobi, Portsmouth, NH: James Curry, Heinemann Kenya, Heinemann, 1986), 17.

24 Melinda Mollineaux, *Cadboro Bay: Index to an Incomplete History*, exhibition, Open Space (Victoria, BC, 1999).

25 *Geoffrey Castle, Victoria Landmarks*, (Victoria, BC: G. Castle and B. King, 1985); Victoria B.C., Heritage Advisory Committee, *This Old House: An Inventory of Residential Heritage, City of Victoria* (Victoria: The Committee, 1991).

26 All quotations referring to *Cadboro Bay* are from the unpublished interview; see note 18, above.

27 Bill Ashcroft, Gareth Griffiths, and Helen Tiffin, *The Empire Writes Back: Theory and Practice in Post-Colonial Literatures* (London: Routledge, 1989), frontispiece.

28 Chinua Achebe, *Home and Exile*, 79.

Contributors

Marie Battiste is a Mi'kmaq from the Potlo'tek First Nations, a professor in the Department of Educational Foundations, and Director of the Aboriginal Education Research Centre in the University of Saskatchewan's College of Education. She is the author of *Protecting Indigenous Knowledge and Heritage: A Global Challenge* (2000), *Reclaiming Indigenous Voice and Vision* (2000), and *First Nations Education in Canada: The Circle Unfolds* (1995).

Lynne Bell is a professor in the Department of Art and Art History, University of Saskatchewan. She has published articles on art and activism in *Canadian Art, Third Text, Fuse,* and *B.C. Studies* and curated a number of exhibitions, including *Urban Fictions* (1997). She is currently working on a book on post-colonial testimony and visual culture.

David R. Carlson is a professor of English and was adjunct professor in the graduate program in Classical Studies at the University of Ottawa. His publications include *English Humanist Books* (1993) and *Chaucer's Jobs* (2004).

John Dagenais is a professor and Chair of the Department of Spanish and Portuguese at the University of California, Los Angeles. He is the author of *The Ethics of Reading in Manuscript Culture: Glossing the Libro de buen amor* (1994), runs the web site on the pilgrimage route to Santiago de Compostela, and is currently directing a project to develop a real-time virtual reality reconstruction of the Romanesque stage of the cathedral and town of Santiago de Compostela as it was around the year 1211.

Edison del Canto is a graphic artist and designer based in Lethbridge, whose innovative approach to art publications, including *BlackFlash*, a Canadian journal of photo-based and electronic art, has garnered numerous regional, national, and international awards over the past few years.

Len Findlay is a professor of English and Co-Director of the Humanities Research Unit at the University of Saskatchewan. His recent work includes a co-edited collection, *Pursuing Academic Freedom: 'Free and Fearless'?* (2001) and a new edition of *The Communist Manifesto* (2004).

Michael Groden is a professor of English, University of Western Ontario. He recently co-edited *Genetic Criticism: Texts and Avant-textes* and the second edition of *The Johns Hopkins Guide to Literary Theory and Criticism.*

Alberto Manguel is a writer, novelist, translator, and editor. In addition to *A History of Reading* (1996), which won France's Prix Médicis, his works include *Stevenson Under the Palm Trees* (2003), *Reading Pictures* (2000), *The Dictionary of Imaginary Places* (1999), and *Into the Looking Glass Wood* (1998), the novel *News from a Foreign Country Came* (1991), and the short-story anthologies *Blackwater, The Gates of Paradise,* and *Meanwhile in Another Part of the Forest.*

Jerome McGann is the John Stewart Bryan University Professor, University of Virginia. His recent book, *Radiant Textuality: Literature after the World Wide Web* (2002) won the MLA's James Russell Lowell award.

Allison Muri is an assistant professor at the University of Saskatchewan. She studies digital culture and its history, and is completing a book titled *The Enlightenment Cyborg: Control, Communications, and the Man-Machine 1660–1830.*

William W.E. Slights is Professor Emeritus, University of Saskatchewan, author of *Managing Readers: Printed Marginalia in English Renaissance Books* (2001) and *Ben Jonson and the Art of Secrecy* (1994). He is currently writing a cultural history of the early modern heart.

Joseph Tabbi is a professor of English at the University of Illinois, Chicago, and the author of *Cognitive Fictions* (2002) and *Postmodern Sublime* (1995). He edits *the electronic book review* and has edited and introduced William Gaddis's last fiction and collected nonfiction. His essay on Mark Amerika appeared at the Walker Art Center's phon:e:me site, a 2000 Webby Award nominee.

Peter Stoicheff is a professor of English at the University of Saskatchewan and author of *The Hall of Mirrors: Drafts & Fragments and the End of Ezra Pound's Cantos* (1995). He currently researches the history of the book and designs hypertext editions of literary texts – most recently William Faulkner's *The Sound and the Fury.*

Andrew Taylor is an associate professor of English at the University of Ottawa. He is the author of *Textual Situations: Three Medieval Manuscripts and Their Readers* (2002). His research concentrates on minstrel performance, medieval storytelling, and the history of reading.